I0894845

Digital Transformation and Innovation in Emerging Markets

Mohammed Albakri
University of Salford, UK

IGI Global
Publishing Tomorrow's Research Today

Vice President of Editorial Melissa Wagner
Managing Editor of Acquisitions Mikaela Felty
Managing Editor of Book Development Jocelynn Hessler
Production Manager Mike Brehm
Cover Design Phillip Shickler

Published in the United States of America by
IGI Global Scientific Publishing
701 East Chocolate Avenue
Hershey, PA, 17033, USA
Tel: 717-533-8845
Fax: 717-533-8661
Website: https://www.igi-global.com E-mail: cust@igi-global.com

Copyright © 2025 by IGI Global Scientific Publishing. All rights reserved. No part of this publication may be reproduced, stored or distributed in any form or by any means, electronic or mechanical, including photocopying, without written permission from the publisher.
Product or company names used in this set are for identification purposes only. Inclusion of the names of the products or companies does not indicate a claim of ownership by IGI Global Scientific Publishing of the trademark or registered trademark.

Library of Congress Cataloging-in-Publication Data

Names: Albakri, Mohammed Ali, 1983- editor.
Title: Digital transformation and innovation in emerging markets / edited by Mohammed Albakri.
Description: Hershey, PA : IGI Global Scientific Publishing, [2025] | Includes bibliographical references and index. | Summary: "This book offers a multifaceted exploration of the digital economy, digital education, entrepreneurship, and ethics, drawing from the experiences of thought leaders across various sectors. Each chapter provides deep insights into the forces shaping digital landscapes, with a focus on how emerging markets can effectively harness technological innovations to foster economic growth and social advancement"-- Provided by publisher.
Identifiers: LCCN 2024060863 (print) | LCCN 2024060864 (ebook) | ISBN 9798337300863 (hardcover) | ISBN 9798337300870 (paperback) | ISBN 9798337300887 (ebook)
Subjects: LCSH: Business--Technological innovations. | Entrepreneurship. | Technological innovations.
Classification: LCC HD45 .D48983 2025 (print) | LCC HD45 (ebook) | DDC 658.4/063--dc23/eng/20250326
LC record available at https://lccn.loc.gov/2024060863
LC ebook record available at https://lccn.loc.gov/2024060864

British Cataloguing in Publication Data
A Cataloguing in Publication record for this book is available from the British Library.

All work contributed to this book is new, previously-unpublished material.
The views expressed in this book are those of the authors, but not necessarily of the publisher.
This book contains information sourced from authentic and highly regarded references, with reasonable efforts made to ensure the reliability of the data and information presented. The authors, editors, and publisher believe the information in this book to be accurate and true as of the date of publication. Every effort has been made to trace and credit the copyright holders of all materials included. However, the authors, editors, and publisher cannot assume responsibility for the validity of all materials or the consequences of their use. Should any copyright material be found unacknowledged, please inform the publisher so that corrections may be made in future reprints.

Table of Contents

Detailed Table of Contents

Digital healthcare offers a huge range of possibilities and may improve quality of patient care. The traditional paradigm of clinical history, examination, differential diagnosis and treatment may be improved by tools such as machine learning, mobile applications and sensors, wearables, and telehealth. The recent pandemic has accelerated move towards this future, however, important concerns remain. These include ensuring that new technologies are assessed effectively and are introduced thoughtfully, data are unified into care records, and, ultimately, digital tools are underpinned with appropriate clinical support. Telemedicine technologies allow patients and doctors both to review the treatment process. However, this technology supplements physical consultation. Today this technology is a safe choice for patients who cannot go to the doctor or sit at home, especially during a pandemic. These Chapter gives a brief focus on Telemedicine and Digital Data Healthcare System including its Application, Challenges and Limitations to comprehensively understand their patient's health.

West Java, home to the highest number of MSMEs in Indonesia, serves as the focus of this study, specifically Bekasi City, one of the country's most expensive and densely populated areas. With 12 districts and 56 sub-districts, Bekasi's MSMEs are regulated by the Cooperative and MSME Office through the Paguyuban, a community-based organization. This research explores how the Paguyuban of East

more pivotal tool for engagement. Furthermore, integrating Artificial Intelligence (AI) into social media marketing strategies has introduced new dynamics, offering predictive analytics, personalized content, and real-time engagement opportunities, which are critical for organizations like HKUF to stay competitive and relevant.

Organisations are increasingly looking beyond the firm to seek value creating opportunities. In particular, with the rise of digital technologies a new era of platforms, and business models, has enabled organisations, and respective strategists, to rethink how they compete. Greater openness and collaboration are redrawing organisational and industry boundaries, allowing opportunities within ecosystems. This chapter seeks to explore how competition has evolved over the past decades culminating in a new era of ecosystems competition. The author provides a framework to support strategists in mapping the competition landscape with a series of strategic insights offering academic and practitioner reflections.

Reliance Jio has created a revolution in the Indian telecom industry. The success of Jio in the industry can be attributed to the strategies it adopted to penetrate the market and the use of the same at the right time. It is not surprising to see that Reliance Jio is the only other player in the telecom industry apart from Bharti Airtel, which has launched 5G services in India. The paper attempts to analyze the strategies adopted by Reliance Jio and their impact on the industry and the consumers. The chapter is divided into five parts. The first part provides background information on the competition in the Indian telecom sector. The second part analyzes the market gap that allowed Reliance Jio to enter and penetrate the market successfully. The third part examines how Reliance Jio's entry affected other players in the telecom sector. The fourth part discusses the impact of Reliance Jio on consumers' lifestyles. Finally, the chapter concludes with the study's findings and suggests the way forward.

This chapter discusses the importance of capacity building and the role of digital infrastructure in delivering citizen services, focusing on the challenges entrepreneurs face. In the pre-digital era, when computers were not part of public service delivery, the government's internal procedures were cumbersome. Citizens encountered several challenges viz., standing in long queues, filling out lengthy forms, carrying documents, and making multiple trips to various departments, — these all forced them to incur additional costs. To address this, governments have introduced entrepreneurs into the system. Mainly, rural areas suffer from inadequate physical and electronic infrastructure, such as unreliable electricity supply, limited internet connectivity, and outdated computers and other faded equipment. These constraints contribute significantly to the digital divide, where certain populations lack access to digital services and benefits. To mitigate this divide, especially in the public sector, concerted efforts are needed from the outset of ICT initiatives.

Contemporary societies are witnessing an unprecedented surge in technological advancements across various domains, with education being no exception. In alignment with this evolving landscape, educational institutions are increasingly incorporating information and communication technology (ICT) as an integral tool for facilitating teaching and learning processes. In a manner reminiscent of learning organizations, academic establishments prioritize the integration of state-of-the-art technologies, particularly in the realm of education and instruction. This study focuses on the implementation of mobile learning among higher education students, recognizing the growing role of technology in education. The research collected data from 100 students and used PLS-SEM for analysis. Key findings indicate that factors like social influence, self-efficacy, perceived ease of use, and usefulness significantly influence the intention of students to use mobile learning. This research can assist developers, designers, and educational institutions in improving mobile learning systems.

Entrepreneurship is gaining significant interest worldwide, with countries encouraging young people to launch startups. Research studies on the success of startups have grown substantially over time. However, the success factors for fintech startups, remain underexplored. This research aims to determine the critical success factors of fintech startups. To achieve this, a qualitative approach using multiple case studies was conducted on four Tunisian fintech startups, examining their development processes. The development is divided into three stages: seed phase, early phase, and growth phase. The results revealed three categories of success factors: essential and complementary (shared by all four startups) and specific factors unique to each startup. The influence of these factors varies across the different life cycle stages.

The rate and volume of cyber attacks increases every year, causing additional costs to organizations. Especially in recent years, new generation cyber attacks against government organizations, private companies and service providers have become increasingly complex with the use of artificial intelligence tools. Since the new generation of cyber attacks are much more complex than the previous ones, corporate managers and employees lack expertise and awareness in taking countermeasures. Studies are needed to support organizations in order to increase cyber resilience in this area. This chapter focuses on cybersecurity risk management and individual cyber hygiene practices as a solution to cyber attacks. Well-developed cybersecurity risk management and strong cyber hygiene behaviors will make it easier for organizations to take measures against advanced cyber attacks. It will also increase the cyber resilience of organizations and provide a line of defense against potential threats.

Digital supply chain is a supply chain whose foundation is built on web-enabled capabilities. Many supply chains use a mix of paper-based and IT-enabled processes.

A true digital supply chain goes far beyond this hybrid model to fully capitalize on connectivity, system integration and the information-producing capabilities of smart components. The ultimate goal of the digital supply chain is to enable insights for increased efficiencies, facilitating greater profits. Companies with a digital supply chain are better able to move resources, assets, people and inventory to where they are needed at any given time in order to reduce costs by responding proactively to transportation and manufacturing risks. The potential payoffs of a fully realized digital supply chain include savings in every area, from resources, time, and money to a reduced environmental footprint. These Review Chapter focuses on right tool that can help you to automate the transition to a digital supply chain.

In the current epoch, robotics offers numerous practical and commercial occasions. Warehouse order picking is a key task, especially for large-scale distribution companies. The Robotic Mobile Fulfillment System (RMFS) is an robotic order-picking arrangement constructed on robotic handling, currently designed for e-commerce warehouses. This article aims to understand the current realities of RMFS, how customers perceive this new technology, and the prospective challenges of integrating robots into Amazon's warehousing areas. The aim is to identify opportunities and threats in the use of Robotic Mobile Fulfillment Systems. This research paper will explore the potential benefits and risks of implementing RMFS in the future. The potential advantages of RMFS include increased operational efficiency, cost savings, and improved customer satisfaction. However, there can be risks involved such as cyber security, data privacy, and cost overruns. The paper will use a combination of prospective studies and existing research to assess the potential gains of RMFS and the associated risks.

The rising popularity of online video streaming services challenge the dominancy of traditional television channels due to changing television viewing trends, as personalized individual services have also been integrated into online video streaming. This study aims to explore potential relationships between brand related characteristics, perceived quality and purchase intention among freemium online video streaming service users in the context of Netflix. Considering the changes in television viewing trends and the impressive amount of revenue drawn by the Netflix

Foreword

The rapid pace of digital transformation is revolutionising industries and communities in emerging markets, creating new opportunities for innovation, economic growth, and societal development. As digital technologies like artificial intelligence, blockchain, and the Internet of Things become increasingly integrated into various sectors, it is essential to understand their implications for emerging economies and harness their potential for inclusive growth.

Digital Transformation and Innovation in Emerging Markets offers a comprehensive exploration of how digital technologies are being leveraged to address unique challenges, bridge infrastructure gaps, and empower communities in developing regions. This book is an essential read for those interested in understanding the multifaceted impact of digital transformation in emerging markets, providing insights into both the opportunities and the obstacles that come with the adoption of new technologies.

The editor, Dr. Mohammed Albakri, have brought together a diverse group of scholars and industry experts whose contributions provide a nuanced perspective on the role of digital innovation in emerging markets. Their expertise spans multiple sectors, from healthcare and education to finance and agriculture, making this book a valuable resource for a wide audience. By presenting insights from both practitioners and academics, the book demonstrates the real-world potential of digital transformation to drive meaningful change.

As someone who has closely observed the adoption of digital technologies in emerging economies, I am particularly impressed by the breadth and depth of topics covered in this book. From exploring the benefits of telemedicine and digital healthcare systems to understanding the impact of digital marketing on small and medium enterprises, each chapter provides practical insights and theoretical frameworks grounded in the realities of developing regions. The discussion of how FinTech and blockchain can foster financial inclusion highlights the transformative power of digital innovation to address systemic issues such as access to financial services.

One of the standout features of this book is its focus on overcoming barriers to digital transformation, particularly in rural and underserved areas. The examination of infrastructure challenges, capacity building, and regulatory concerns sheds light on the complexities of fostering a sustainable digital ecosystem in these regions. The emphasis on promoting equitable access to technology ensures that digital transformation benefits all segments of society, not just the privileged few.

The emphasis on innovation as a tool for social and economic progress is another core theme of this book. By showcasing case studies and examples of successful digital initiatives, the authors demonstrate how emerging markets can leapfrog traditional developmental stages through the adoption of cutting-edge technologies. These real-world applications provide a roadmap for policymakers, entrepreneurs, and community leaders seeking to harness digital tools to improve quality of life and enhance economic resilience.

Digital Transformation and Innovation in Emerging Markets is not only academically rigorous but also highly practical. The lessons and recommendations offered throughout the book serve as a guide for stakeholders interested in leveraging digital technologies to create sustainable and inclusive growth. By focusing on both challenges and success stories, the book provides a balanced view of the digital transformation journey in emerging economies.

As you explore the different facets of digital transformation and innovation presented in this book, I encourage you to consider the broader implications for society. Reflect on how digital technologies can be used not only to enhance economic outcomes but also to address pressing social issues and create opportunities for all members of society.

In conclusion, *Digital Transformation and Innovation in Emerging Markets* is a significant contribution to the discourse on how digital technologies can shape the future of developing regions. It is a must-read for academics, industry professionals, policymakers, and anyone interested in understanding the transformative potential of digital innovation in emerging markets.

I extend my heartfelt congratulations to the editors and contributors for their outstanding work. May this book inspire and guide readers in harnessing the power of digital transformation to build a brighter future for emerging markets.

Aniekan Essien

University of Bristol, UK

Preface

The digital revolution has transformed the global economy, reshaping industries, and redefining the way we live, work, and interact. Nowhere is this transformation more significant than in emerging markets, where the rapid pace of digitalization presents both unprecedented opportunities and unique challenges. As Editor of *Digital Transformation and Innovation in Emerging Markets*, I am proud to present this comprehensive resource that delves into the evolution, trends, and hurdles of digitalization in these regions.

This book offers a multifaceted exploration of the digital economy, digital education, entrepreneurship, and ethics, drawing from the experiences of thought leaders across various sectors. Each chapter provides deep insights into the forces shaping digital landscapes, with a focus on how emerging markets can effectively harness technological innovations to foster economic growth and social advancement.

As we enter an era marked by data-driven decision-making, AI, and global connectivity, it becomes increasingly crucial for business leaders, policymakers, educators, researchers, and technology professionals to stay ahead of the curve. This book equips you with the knowledge and practical tools necessary to lead and manage digital initiatives within your organizations or governments. The case studies, research, and strategies presented here are designed to empower readers to navigate the intricacies of digital transformation, helping them create value in a rapidly evolving world.

Through the contributions of experts from diverse backgrounds, this volume sheds light on topics ranging from leveraging data analytics for development to fostering digital literacy and incorporating ethical considerations into technological adoption. By addressing these essential themes, *Digital Transformation and Innovation in Emerging Markets* is a timely resource for those seeking to understand not only the technological shifts occurring today but also the socio-economic impact of these transformations on the future of both business and society.

I am confident that this book will serve as an invaluable guide for anyone looking to explore the frontiers of digital innovation in emerging markets, and I sincerely hope that it will inspire readers to embrace the opportunities and navigate the challenges of this dynamic and evolving landscape.

ORGANIZATION OF THE BOOK

Chapter 1: Digital Data Healthcare System and Telemedicine Advances: Problems and Future

This chapter explores the transformative potential of digital healthcare systems in improving patient care. With innovations such as machine learning, mobile applications, sensors, wearables, and telehealth, the traditional approach to clinical care is undergoing significant enhancements. Telemedicine, in particular, has emerged as a vital tool, especially during the COVID-19 pandemic, offering safe and effective alternatives to physical consultations. However, challenges persist in ensuring these technologies are implemented thoughtfully, with unified data and clinical support. This chapter provides an in-depth analysis of telemedicine's applications, challenges, and limitations, highlighting its role in comprehensive patient care.

Chapter 2: Digital Marketing Transformation of Local MSMEs through Instagram: A Case Study of Paguyuban UMKM Bekasi Timur

In this case study, the digital marketing transformation of micro, small, and medium enterprises (MSMEs) in Bekasi, West Java, Indonesia, is examined through the lens of the community organization Paguyuban UMKM Bekasi Timur (PUKBT). Focusing on the organization's Instagram platform, the study demonstrates how digital marketing strategies are effectively communicated to MSMEs, using a two-step model where community participation plays a key role. Through qualitative interviews and social media analysis, the research showcases how digital economies can benefit local businesses, while proposing avenues for future research to broaden these findings to larger communities.

Chapter 3: The Influence of Social Media Influencers on College Students' Consumer Behavior

This chapter delves into the complex relationship between social media influencers and college students' consumer behavior. With digital platforms becoming essential for marketing, the study investigates how influencer-endorsed content affects college students' purchasing decisions and brand loyalty. Using both quantitative data and qualitative interviews, the research reveals key factors that drive engagement with influencer content and examines the broader implications for marketers. The findings offer valuable insights into how digital marketing strategies can be tailored to influence young consumers effectively.

Chapter 4: Transforming Promotion Processes of University Foundations Using Social Media: A Case Study on the HKU Foundation

Social media has become a critical promotional tool, particularly for non-profit organizations like the University of Hong Kong Foundation (HKUF). This chapter examines the integration of the 5Es Usability Model and AIDA Marketing Communication Model into HKUF's social media strategy, exploring how these frameworks enhance promotional efforts. As the post-pandemic era increasingly relies on digital marketing, the use of AI for personalized engagement and predictive analytics has also become vital. This chapter outlines the transformative effects of digital marketing strategies and the challenges faced by organizations in adapting to this new landscape.

Chapter 5: Competition in an Age of Ecosystems: Implications for Strategy

This chapter explores how digital technologies and platform-based business models are reshaping the competitive landscape, introducing a new era of ecosystem-based competition. It discusses how organizations are moving beyond traditional boundaries, leveraging openness and collaboration within ecosystems to create value. The chapter presents a framework for strategists to navigate this evolving competition, offering academic and practical insights into how organizations can succeed in this interconnected environment.

Chapter 6: Economic Dimensions of Competition in the Indian Telecom Sector: The Impact of Reliance Jio

Reliance Jio's entry into the Indian telecom market revolutionized the sector by introducing aggressive pricing strategies and cutting-edge technologies. This chapter analyzes the competitive dynamics Jio created, examining its impact on other telecom operators and consumers. By dividing the study into distinct sections, the chapter provides an in-depth look at Jio's strategies, the market gap it exploited, its effects on competitors, and its broader implications for consumer behavior and lifestyle changes. The analysis culminates in recommendations for the future of the Indian telecom industry.

Chapter 7: Digital Infrastructure Challenges for Techno-Entrepreneurs in Rural Areas: The Need for Capacity Building

This chapter addresses the digital infrastructure challenges faced by entrepreneurs in rural areas, particularly in delivering public services. The transition to a digital era has brought numerous benefits, but rural entrepreneurs often face issues such as unreliable internet, outdated equipment, and limited access to technology. The chapter underscores the importance of capacity-building efforts and infrastructure development to bridge the digital divide and ensure that all communities can benefit from digital innovations.

Chapter 8: Unlocking the Future of Education: Factors Influencing the Adoption of Mobile Learning in Higher Education

With the rapid advancement of technology, mobile learning has become a crucial aspect of modern education. This chapter explores the factors influencing its adoption among higher education students, including social influence, self-efficacy, perceived ease of use, and usefulness. Using data from 100 students and employing PLS-SEM analysis, the study provides insights that can help developers, educators, and institutions enhance mobile learning systems to meet the evolving needs of students in the digital age.

Chapter 9: FinTech Startups: Critical Success Factors

The rise of fintech startups has reshaped the global financial landscape, but the factors contributing to their success remain underexplored. This chapter examines the critical success factors of fintech startups, using case studies of four Tunisian companies. Dividing the startup lifecycle into seed, early, and growth phases, the study identifies essential, complementary, and specific factors that influence success at different stages. The findings offer valuable insights for entrepreneurs and investors looking to navigate the fintech space.

Chapter 10: Managing Cybersecurity Risks and Cyber Hygiene in Organizations

As cyber threats become increasingly sophisticated, organizations face mounting challenges in maintaining cybersecurity. This chapter focuses on risk management strategies and the importance of fostering strong cyber hygiene practices within organizations. It discusses how well-developed cybersecurity frameworks and individual awareness can bolster an organization's resilience against advanced cyber attacks, providing a line of defense against future threats.

Chapter 11: Digital Supply Chain Management: Transformation in Business Economic Development

Digital supply chain management is revolutionizing how businesses operate, offering enhanced connectivity, system integration, and smart technologies to improve efficiency. This chapter outlines the benefits of fully digitized supply chains, highlighting their potential to reduce costs, optimize resource allocation, and minimize environmental footprints. It also discusses the tools available to help businesses automate their transition to digital supply chain models, ultimately improving their competitive edge in a fast-paced business environment.

Chapter 12: A Prospective Analysis of Robotic Mobile Fulfillment Systems

This chapter investigates the benefits and challenges of Robotic Mobile Fulfillment Systems (RMFS), particularly in the context of e-commerce warehouses. Focusing on their potential to improve operational efficiency and customer satisfaction, the chapter examines the risks associated with RMFS, such as cybersecurity threats, data privacy issues, and cost overruns. Through a combination of prospective studies and existing research, it assesses the future of RMFS and its potential to transform warehouse logistics.

Chapter 13: Brand Characteristics, Perceived Quality, and Purchase Intentions Among Freemium Users: The Case of Netflix

The transition from freemium to premium service models has become a key focus for digital streaming platforms like Netflix. This chapter explores the relationship between brand characteristics, perceived quality, and purchase intentions among freemium users. Based on data from Turkish Netflix users, the findings reveal significant links between factors such as user-friendliness, visual design, and operation speed with purchase intent, while brand loyalty was found to have little impact on users' decisions to upgrade to paid memberships.

Chapter 14: OpenStreetMap and Digital Health: Enhancing Patient Care

OpenStreetMap (OSM) has the potential to revolutionize healthcare by improving patient navigation, resource mapping, and epidemic response. This chapter explores the applications of OSM in digital health, including its use in locating healthcare facilities, mapping disease outbreaks, and identifying underserved areas for telehealth services. The chapter also addresses challenges such as data accuracy and completeness, offering solutions through community moderation and real-time updates to enhance the reliability of OSM-based healthcare applications.

IN CONCLUSION

In conclusion, this volume offers a comprehensive exploration of the far-reaching impact of digitalization across sectors, shedding light on both its transformative potential and the critical challenges that must be addressed. As the world navigates the complexities of the digital age, it is clear that technology will play a pivotal role in shaping the future of industries, communities, and economies. The insights presented by the contributors underscore the immense opportunities that digital transformation holds for fostering innovation, driving economic growth, and advancing the Sustainable Development Goals. Yet, they also emphasize the necessity of proactive policy action to mitigate the risks associated with this rapid evolution and to ensure that its benefits are equitably shared by all.

As we move towards a post-2030 world, the importance of strategic foresight, cross-sectoral collaboration, and inclusive growth cannot be overstated. It is our hope that the research and perspectives compiled in this book will not only inform but also inspire policymakers, practitioners, and scholars to actively engage in the ongoing digital revolution, ensuring that it serves as a powerful tool for sustainable and inclusive development. The work presented here is a testament to the importance of continuous inquiry and innovation in navigating the complexities of our digital future.

Mohammed Albakri
University of Salford, UK

Chapter 1
Digital Data Healthcare System and Telemedicine Advances:
Problems and Future

Zuber Peermohammed Shaikh
Savitribai Phule Pune University, India

ABSTRACT

Digital healthcare offers a huge range of possibilities and may improve quality of patient care. The traditional paradigm of clinical history, examination, differential diagnosis and treatment may be improved by tools such as machine learning, mobile applications and sensors, wearables, and telehealth. The recent pandemic has accelerated move towards this future, however, important concerns remain. These include ensuring that new technologies are assessed effectively and are introduced thoughtfully, data are unified into care records, and, ultimately, digital tools are underpinned with appropriate clinical support. Telemedicine technologies allow patients and doctors both to review the treatment process. However, this technology supplements physical consultation. Today this technology is a safe choice for patients who cannot go to the doctor or sit at home, especially during a pandemic. These Chapter gives a brief focus on Telemedicine and Digital Data Healthcare System including its Application, Challenges and Limitations to comprehensively understand their patient's health.

DOI: 10.4018/979-8-3373-0086-3.ch001

Copyright © 2025, IGI Global. Copying or distributing in print or electronic forms without written permission of IGI Global is prohibited.

INTRODUCTION

Digital Data Healthcare System and Telemedicine

The term "digital health" or "digital healthcare" refers to a broad, multidisciplinary concept that includes concepts from the intersection of technology and healthcare. Digital health applies digital transformation to the healthcare sector, including software, technology, and services. Digital health encompasses telehealth and telemedicine, wearable technology, electronic health records (EHRs), electronic medical records (EMRs), mobile health (mHealth) apps, and personalized medicine.

Patients, healthcare professionals, researchers, application developers, medical device makers, and distributors are some stakeholders in the digital health field. Digital health refers to using various technologies, including telehealth services, health information technology, and mobile health (mHealth), to improve communication between doctors and patients throughout healthcare systems. The breadth of digital health offers consumers greater access to and ownership over their information and allows doctors to comprehensively understand their patient's health. Digital health technology has become more significant over time, particularly in light of the COVID-19 pandemic. Modern digital health solution improves relationships between patients and their doctors, expands preventive disease strategies, and shifts healthcare toward value-based treatment, increasing access to health information for patients and providers.

Patients must benefit without worsening workload for the clinician. Old barriers may be overcome but new challenges will be faced. In particular, ensuring the promise of better care for those who lack access to smartphones and the internet will be crucial. Clinicians must continue to advocate for patients and their colleagues as we embrace the future of digital healthcare.

Clinicians are valued for their long training to acquire knowledge and its application to the patient. This is maintained by continuous professional development. The explosion in medical knowledge and increasing complexity of treatment makes it difficult for individuals to maintain knowledge in their own subspecialty, let alone in the rest of medicine. A profound disconnect exists between this reality and the widely held perception of doctors as authoritative dispensers of knowledge and advice.

The ability to individualise treatment with additional data sources, such as wearables, will increase its complexity even further. How can a clinician keep all this information in their head? The answer is that they cannot, and inevitably digital tools will be needed. This changes the clinician from being the authority to an interpreter of recommendations generated by algorithms that use the latest evidence integrated with genomics and other data. A fundamental shift in skills is needed, from knowledge acquisition to communication.

Speech recognition has been present for decades, but with the improvement in computing power and machine learning, it can now be clinically useful during a consultation beyond simply dictating a letter. Imagine talking to a patient, the system transcribing as you go, then when you examine the patient's eardrums and say aloud, "Red, inflamed eardrum," the system suggests otitis media as a diagnosis and then offers up a list of antibiotics from the formulary based on the patient's age and allergy status. This ambient speech recognition is generating significant excitement and has obvious applications in improving efficiency and clinical encounter documentation.

Healthcare is undergoing a digital transformation, accelerated by the pandemic, that will alter many of the fundamental building blocks of medical care. Clinicians need to be active participants in the journey, staying true to the core values that we have held dear for centuries to ensure we avoid some of the grimmer futures imagined by writers like William Gibson.

How will medicine change? What are the crucial drivers of those changes, and how can we solve the problems with our current systems without making things worse? Critically, how can clinicians advocate for a better future for all our patients, with healthcare enabled by technology rather than constrained by it (Nelson A, 2019)?

Figure 1. Approaches and application of digital healthcare system

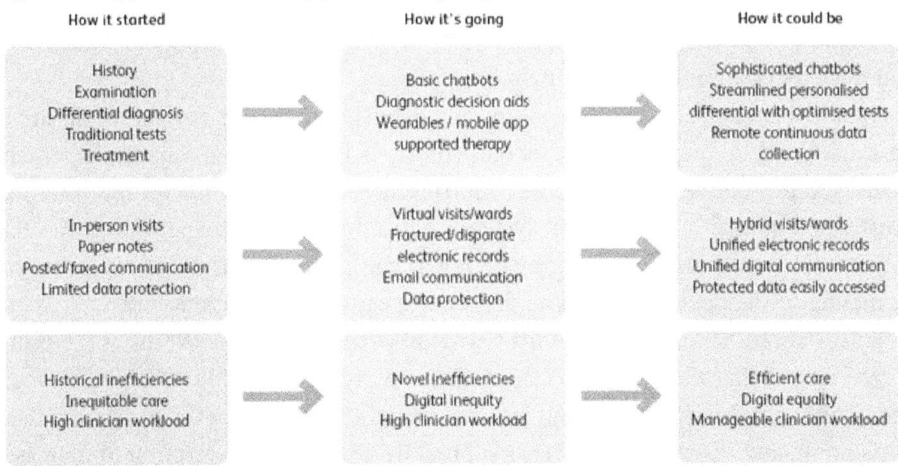

LITERATURE REVIEW

Data Acquisition, Security, Association, and Storage in Digital Healthcare System

Paper notes, plagued with security issues, illegible writing, missing data and challenges of data transfer are slowly being replaced by electronic systems, but these have a way to go. The lack of interconnectivity must be tackled to allow the creation of a unified patient dataset accessible by any patient or healthcare professional at any time. Appropriate data storage and security compliance with all relevant data protection remains of paramount importance but should not impact the ease of data but in time will be optimized for national healthcare systems. Tools, records may make things more challenging initially, but in time will be optimized for national healthcare systems. Tools, like the NHS app, represent an important first step in the right direction. Creating a differential diagnosis is currently based on knowledge, experience, and a prior probability of an event. This may be prone to bias and defects in risk estimation. Software appropriately designed and implemented can overcome some of these barriers and help suggest appropriate diagnoses and investigations.

Decision-support software is becoming increasingly widespread, and it is likely to increase further until it is superior to the individual clinician in many ways. However, it is currently difficult to imagine that it will replace the emotional connection vital for a therapeutic relationship.

Data will be central to health systems. It will not be surprising that one of the areas most disrupted by the use of digital technology is its impact on data management and use. At present, few low-income countries have reliable data despite substantial investments in health information systems. Most data are still paper-based, kept at the national level only on an aggregate level, and primarily used for reporting on the incidence of specific reportable diseases or numbers of patients seen.

This is about to change. The shift to digital data collection systems at the point of care means that data can be collected in a more timely and complete manner, data quality can be improved, and health planners have incentives to use the data for planning and management. The first breakthrough is that collection of data as a by-product of decision support in the hands of health workers will be available in a timelier way. "Data entry will no longer be a separate activity from patient care; instead, it will be integrated into clinical care."

Data collected as part of the diagnostic process will be written to an electronic patient record, making individual records available for immediate analysis and use at any level of the system. At the level of the provider, this will make information available about the patient's history, streamlining the diagnostic process. The use of universal biometric identification will reduce the need for repeating demographic information. Timely information about patient care will provide supervisors and managers with better information about provider performance. Aggregate data can be used for reporting purposes, surveillance, and planning. Disease outbreaks, such as diarrheal disease or malaria, can be identified in real-time by looking for spikes in the reporting of these symptoms.

A second benefit of digital data collection is that we can expect the quality of the data to be improved. Since data are being entered as part of the delivery of care rather than a separate data collection process, we are likely to see reductions in data entry mistakes.

Errors in data will be more apparent to the health worker as they are used in treatment algorithms, and there will be fewer opportunities to simply make up data as overworked health workers try to save time. Automated data quality checks can identify deliberate errors, such as entering false records, by generating alerts for records entered in a very short time period or with inconsistent entries. Other types of data checks can be introduced to validate the data being entered. We can expect that more timely and accurate data will lead to improvements in the quality of care (Attia ZI, et al., 2019).

Providers themselves can benefit from individual data feedback, and their supervisors can use the data for improved supervision. We may see patients using the data to assess the quality of individual providers or provider groups using programs such as Yelp, which is already available in the USA and increasingly being made available globally. This type of crowdsourcing data about providers, facilities, and health systems is likely to grow as more people take advantage of internet-based rating systems, despite potential resistance from providers themselves, who may prefer to remain anonymous.

Digital healthcare offers a huge range of possibilities and may improve the quality of patient care. The traditional paradigm of clinical history, examination, differential diagnosis, and treatment may be enhanced by tools such as machine learning, mobile applications and sensors, wearables, and telehealth. The recent pandemic has accelerated the move towards this future; however, important concerns remain. These include ensuring that new technologies are assessed effectively and are introduced thoughtfully, that data are unified into care records, and, ultimately, that digital tools are underpinned with appropriate clinical support.

Patients must benefit without worsening workload for the clinician. Old barriers may be overcome, but new challenges will be faced. In particular, ensuring the promise of better care for those who lack access to smartphones and the internet will be crucial. Clinicians must continue to advocate for patients and their colleagues as we embrace the future of digital healthcare (Attia ZI, et al., 2019a).

BACKGROUND

Digital Inequality in Healthcare System

The future of medicine will look very different to that of today, but it is crucial that existing health inequalities are not maintained or even exacerbated. Having a digital-first strategy is pointless if many of our patients are denied access through lack of digital literacy, restricted access to devices and data, or from poverty. There are estimates that over 10 million people in the UK lack basic digital skills, these are often in groups with higher rates of illness and in need of greater support. The pandemic highlighted that, for many, the devices and internet connections needed to engage with the digital world are beyond their means; this digital poverty was recognized by many of the internet providers with programs to help patients to access the internet. This need will continue but, currently, there is no comparable effort to address it. Many patients do not wish to or cannot access digital tools. This digital gap between those who can and cannot use digital platforms is, to some extent, inevitable and our systems need to be designed to minimize this impact and achieve a degree of equivalence.

Advances of Telehealth (Telemedicine)

Telehealth is defined as the delivery and facilitation of health and health-related services (including medical care, provider and patient education, health information services, and self-care) via telecommunications and digital communication technologies. This concept is not new and has been used to support patient care since the 1950s. More recently, however, there has been a significant push in the UK to move to telehealth solutions, particularly in the wake of the COVID-19 pandemic. This has not only been the more traditional 'telephone clinic' but also the development of virtual wards. Prior to the pandemic, some services used telehealth routinely, such as remote monitoring for implantable cardiac devices. This was safe, identified clinical issues early and was well accepted by patients. More extensive use was being discussed to improve efficiency. The transition, however, was slow with a number of perceived and real barriers to implementation from patients, clinicians and organizations that needed to be addressed. How patients and healthcare professionals have interacted with these apps has evolved organically over time. These tools may be hugely beneficial for the patient; however, this enthusiasm must be tempered with caution as to their validity and applicability.

Assessment with well-designed clinical trials remains a vital consideration. To support UK healthcare providers, NHS Digital has produced both guidelines and a formal process to assess and validate apps for use. The digital technology and assessment criteria (DTAC) set out national minimum standards criteria for clinical safety, data protection, technical security, interoperability, usability, and accessibility. Only a handful of technologies are mature enough to have been through this process. One example is an app designed to use photoplethysmography with a smartphone camera to identify atrial fibrillation that has shown a good correlation with a single lead ECG. The contact tracing app was a novel concept that was rapidly prototyped within 3 months and deployed during the COVID-19 pandemic. This used the Bluetooth capability of a phone to assess people's proximity to each other and notify individuals anonymously if they had been in contact with someone infected with the virus. Only 28% of the population downloaded the app; despite this, around 600,000 infections were prevented between September 2020 and December 2020. Nevertheless, this interesting use of smartphone sensors integrated into an app has opened the door to delivering healthcare in a way that we would never have previously considered. (Perez MV, 2019)

Table 1. Digital healthcare barriers to telehealth implementation

Patient	Clinician	Organization
Age	Technically challenged staff	Cost
Level of education	Resistance to change	Reimbursement
eHealth/computer literacy	Licensing	Legal liability
Internet bandwidth	Perception of impersonal care	Privacy/confidentiality
Unawareness	Information overload	Security of data
High expectations of users	Interoperability	Effectiveness
Apathy	Poor design	Age of existing equipment
No phone	Language barrier	Efficiency
Socioeconomic status	Profit status	
Gender	Organization size	
Preference for personal care	Teaching status	

Approaches of Telemedicine

Telemedicine enables patients to receive medical attention at the convenience of both doctor and him, and at the same time, he is safe. This may imply that a person does not need to take time off from work or arrange childcare. Going to the doctor's office entails sitting in close quarters with others can cause infection. This is especially risky for people who have chronic medical problems or a weakened immune system. It prevents the possibility of contracting an infection at the doctor's hospital.

Telemedicine service providers could have lower overhead rates. Clinicians may find that telemedicine supplementing their income by allowing them to take care of more patients. When caregivers see patients online, they are not exposed to the infections that the patient may bring. The patient may be happy with their physician if they do not have to fly to the office or wait for treatment or get infected from the hospital. (McKeon G; 2019).

Figure 2. Features of telemedicine in healthcare system

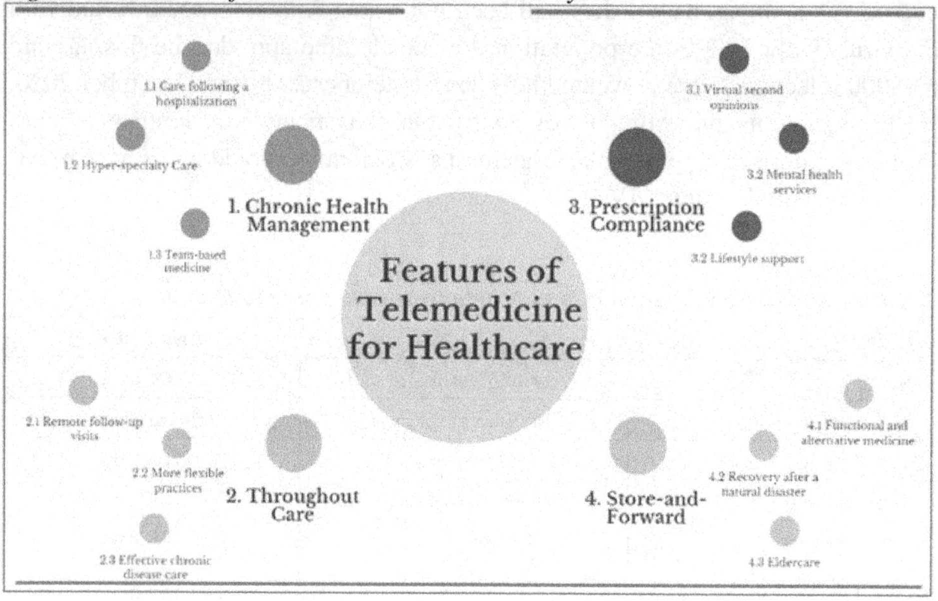

METHODOLOGY

Internet of Things (IoT) as Telemedicine

Telemedicine has improved the capacity of healthcare providers to take care of many people without physically being there. Furthermore, now that it has proved its worth, it will be around for a long time. Although introductory video conferencing brought many providers to telehealth, the new wave of telemedicine technologies would have much more to offer. For example, during a patient, clinicians can use natural language processing to take notes automatically. During emergency operations, specialists will weigh in from afar. The knowledge gathered by healthcare instruments may be submitted to an Internet of Things (IoT) cloud platform, where the healthcare provider consolidates it. This information will then be sent to IoT systems used by healthcare providers for patient management. The most recent advancements in telemedicine technologies include Artificial Intelligence (AI) to help physicians function more effectively. This technology keeps patients updated with wearables and other remote patient tracking resources and even uses robots to deliver specialized treatment to areas it has never been before. Telemedicine technology holds great promise for patients in remote areas.

The most significant effect is provided in various countries where healthcare facilities are both scarce and unavailable. To ensure an accurate medical history, all patients and doctors must have sufficient hardware and software security in place. Some clinics can provide virtual appointments with a doctor through online video conferencing. When an in-person visit is not required or necessary, these appointments enable them to continue receiving treatment from a usual doctor. Web-based visits with a doctor or nurse practitioner are another form of interactive appointment. As part of their health care offerings, several major corporations have access to automated doctor's offices. On the other hand, a nursing call center is staffed by nurses who use a question-and-answer format to offer advice for at-home treatment. *(McBain L, Morgan D.; 2005)*

Five Technologies That are Advancing Telemedicine

Currently, healthcare systems across the world are experiencing perfect storms of external and internal care delivery challenges. These include overburdened doctors, declining reimbursements, rising care delivery costs, increased risk to patients and care providers, and poor health outcomes. The use of smart technology in telemedicine provides the healthcare industry with ways to mitigate these challenges by leveraging advanced innovations. Let's take a closer look at the five technologies that are shaping the future of telemedicine.

Artificial Intelligence

Artificial Intelligence (AI) is expanding the scope of technology in telemedicine to areas such as teleradiology, telepathology, teledermatology, and telepsychiatry. AI-driven smart technologies such as care-assistive apps and predictive algorithms are enabling more than just remotely screening the diagnostic needs of patients. It's helping reduce the burden on healthcare professionals (HCPs) by automatically translating prescriptions into Electronic Health Records (EHRs) and generating medical reports, especially in the face of crisis. For instance, healthcare technology company DrFirst has released a patented SmartSig AI technology that accurately translates patient medication history into hospitals' and health systems' EHRs, without the need for human intervention. AI-enabled EHRs are also aiding HCPs to improve the interoperability of data and remote patient monitoring. Nuance, 3M, and Amazon Comprehend Medical are some companies working to leverage this technology for EHR systems. Additionally, AI-based networking models can increase the speed of discovering specialists, thereby cutting down the waiting hours at hospitals. For instance, by implementing telemedicine screenings for diabetic retinopathy at its security net facilities, clinicians at the Los Angeles County Department of Health Services reduced visits to specialty care professionals by more than 14,000. AI-powered healthcare chatbots are also gaining popularity across the globe. They converse with people, answer their queries, educate them about the symptoms of a disease, and help them schedule appointments with doctors, completely in the virtual plane. For example, Engagely AI has developed a smart telehealth bot that works with hospitals to help them check medicine inventory, suggest alternative treatment options, and follow up with patients for routine check-ups. (Honarbakhsh S, et al.; 2021)

Augmented and Virtual Reality

Telemedicine and all types of mixed reality (MR), such as augmented reality (AR) and virtual reality (VR) go along very well. MR technologies let clinicians get real-time information on patients' vitals and experiences, which can improve the accuracy of remote diagnostics. For instance, Iflexion, an AR company, develops apps that aid clinicians through virtual real-time diagnosis and health-tracking. It streamlines hospital workflows and encourages productive health management within and outside of clinical facilities. AR-enhanced telemedicine tools can also be used for better diagnostic collaboration among medical professionals. Telehealth platforms, like XRHealth, that have AR support allow clinicians to share the 3D images of their cases during virtual consultations with other professionals.

Tele-Robots

Robotics has forayed into various fields of telemedicine: Tele-robots make remote patient monitoring, diagnosis, and virtual care easier and more accurate. Telerobots can monitor the health status of patients in real-time, and alert clinicians if any adverse change occurs in their condition. For instance, iRobot has partnered with InTouch Health to develop robots for remote healthcare settings, including ICUs, patient wards, operating and procedure rooms. Other than remote monitoring, robots are also helping doctors set up virtual visits with their patients. VGo Communications has developed a two-wheeled robot that is currently in use at several healthcare facilities including Florida Hospital, Intermountain Healthcare, and Children's Hospital Boston. It offers remotely-located physicians the ability to video-call their patients admitted to hospitals, along with their latest medical information. The Children's Hospital in Boston is also conducting certain pilot projects where patients take telerobots home with them after their hospital stay for help with postoperative consultations and care. (*Shaw A, et al.; 2021)*

IoT and Nanotechnology

The Internet of Things (IoT) is rapidly changing the healthcare scenario by focusing on the way people, devices, and applications interact with each other. It is helping shape the use of technology in telemedicine through virtual care networks and access to in-depth patient data. Advancements in telediagnostics rely on large volumes of physiological and health data which new medical surveillance and diagnostic tools can offer. That's where nanotechnology-based IoT comes in. Smart pills and bandages based on this technology can record body temperature, collect tissue samples and secretions, and take pictures of the affected site inside the human body.

The ability to examine the human body, its drug therapies, and medical devices at the nano level, ultimately ensures a much higher level of accuracy in medicine, in terms of both diagnostics and treatments. The Atmo Gas Capsule, for example, when ingested, examines the gases in the human gut to report any disorders. Its sensors can help detect the levels of oxygen and carbon dioxide in the body, as well as the presence of any harmful substances.

Nanowear, a US-based startup, has developed a heart failure management and remote monitoring undergarment and closed-loop machine learning platform known as SimpleSENSE. It uses cloth-based nanosensors to capture and record phonocardiography, stroke volume and cardiac output. This data can then be transmitted to EHR systems to help doctors with remote assessments and diagnosis, whenever required. (*Raatikainen MJ, 2008)*

3D Printing

3D printing is already used in healthcare for diagnostics and surgery, including the creation of bones, lung tissue, and cartilage. The use of this technology in telemedicine is also promising. The New England Journal of Medicine has dictated a case where 3D printing was used for telesurgery. A newborn baby's trachea was repaired with a splint which was 3D printed directly from the CT scan. There have been other instances where hearts, bones, and other tissues have been printed for telesurgeries. 3D printing allows doctors to print out the contents of scans sent remotely by patients. Doctors can then analyze detailed 3D-printed patient models for accurate diagnosis and develop treatment plans. Furthermore, prosthetists can

3D-print prostheses without the patient having to be physically present. As the use of technology in telemedicine becomes more prevalent, we're observing a rising number of players expand their presence in this market, including big tech companies such as Amazon, Microsoft, and Facebook. To succeed, innovation that places consumer and provider needs at the fore will be imperative. (Ricci RP, 2010)

RESULTS

Data-Driven Decision Making in Digital Health

Every day, tons of data are produced in the healthcare industry. Real-time data and healthcare analytics facilitate better decision-making. Patients who are at high risk of readmission or contracting specific diseases can be identified using predictive analytics. Early intervention by healthcare professionals can stop unnecessary hospitalizations. In order to pinpoint opportunities for improvement, visualization of patient outcomes and population health trends is helpful. In this way, accurate and thorough data collection, storage, and analysis can improve patient outcomes.

1. **Access to Care**

Providers are better able to connect with patients and deliver care remotely when they have access to digital tools, such as virtual care platforms with video and chat technologies. This helps increase access to care, particularly for those living in remote areas or with mobility issues.

2. **Provider Satisfaction**

Digital solutions can facilitate provider workflows and ease the burden of their tasks. Many technologies, like EHR, RPA, telehealth, etc., help providers automate much of their workload, giving them more time to work on what they do best: providing care to patients.

3. **Patient Engagement**

Patients may be more involved in their care when they have access to their own health information. They can also alter their lifestyles to improve their health and more effectively manage chronic diseases. Digital technologies help achieve this goal.

4. **Big Data Analytics**

When medical information is gathered and preserved digitally, it can be analyzed to spot patterns and enhance treatment. For instance, hospitals can use data analytics to identify patients who are likely to require readmission and take precautions against it.

5. Automating Tasks

In the US, administrative costs make up more than 25% of all hospital expenditure. Entering patient notes into an electronic health records system can take up to one-third of a doctor's time. The time of a doctor is a valuable resource, and this is not particularly effective. Digitization helps in automating day-to-day tasks of the provider. By automating these processes, medical professionals and clinical staff will have less work to do and more time to devote to patient care. (*Scott Kruse C; 2018)*

6. Collaboration Between Providers

In certain cases, providers might need advice from other healthcare professionals. To create the patient's overall best medical plan, it is crucial that the many providers stay in touch with one another. Digitization helps providers communicate with each other, share health information, and devise treatment plans collaboratively.

7. Real-Time Information

These days, smartphones and wearables are two of the most popular types of technology. Modern smartwatches are capable of taking an ECG, counting steps, and monitoring heart rate. They are, therefore, incredibly beneficial to both regular users and their doctors. The doctor can monitor the patient's vitals and provide preventative care. Nowadays, real-time data monitoring allows doctors to take preventative action and prevent a terrible event.

8. Interoperability

Data interoperability has remained a problem for many solution providers and healthcare practitioners because of ambiguous standards for data storage and coding and a lack of unified laws. Numerous data sets go underutilized, and healthcare providers are unable to use this knowledge to raise the standard of patient treatment. To maximize the use of such data, it is crucial that the relevant sector stakeholders achieve regulatory convergence. (*Heinzelmann P.J., 2005)*

9. Regulations in Digital Healthcare

The healthcare industry has many difficulties, one of which is the fragmented and complicated regulatory and legislative environment. Many areas approach digital health technologies through a variety of schemes and laws rather than a single piece of legislation. However, they frequently fall short of addressing the special characteristics of such solutions, which hinders the development, introduction, and widespread use of many cutting-edge items.

10. **Reimbursement in Healthcare**

Many digital health solutions encounter difficulties as a result of inconsistent reimbursement mechanisms. Patients may find it more difficult to get their data if this technology isn't adopted due to reimbursement issues. This makes it difficult for innovators to justify the cost of such technologies in comparison to their utility.

11. **Data Security in Healthcare**

Data security and privacy are significant obstacles that must be solved in the field of digital health. A data breach may lead to the theft of personal data, the erosion of trust, fraud, and care disruption. As a result, it's critical that security gaps in digital healthcare systems are addressed, and consumers are informed about the best ways to protect their data. A unified policy framework must be built in order to address issues of data security and privacy.

12. **Adoption of Technology**

The simplicity of use, price, and privacy concerns are just a few of the things that can influence a person's willingness to use digital health solutions. The adoption of such technology can also be significantly influenced by how valuable a given digital health service is regarded to be. The utilization of patient data for analytical insights will be the next step in revolutionizing healthcare. Currently, the data processing stage is generally distinct from the actual data collection. In the future, AI will probably support human intervention by remotely and instantly assessing patient data, enhancing the response times of healthcare providers. (Bajowala S.S., 2020)

13. **Big Data in Healthcare**

Big data enables the extraction of information that is essential for making decisions. In the shortest amount of time possible, this can produce goaloriented information that can be applied in a problem-oriented and problemsolving manner. It may be able to assist in forecasting the kinds of illnesses and diseases that could cause a significant problem in the future as this technology develops. As a result, patients and healthcare providers may be able to take precautions against certain illnesses.

14. **Blockchain in Healthcare**

Blockchain is a digital ledger that enables direct information exchange between two parties. It can help facilitate the transmission of patients' medical records between service providers, preventing data breaches and lowering expenses. A 54.9 percent is predicted for the blockchain in the healthcare market from 2019 to 2028.

DISCUSSION

Electronic Health Records

Quickly leads to a discussion of privacy and confidentiality. While this is not a new concern, since the same issues arise with paper records, the ease of analyzing and reproducing digital data is cause for concern. Recent data breaches by numerous commercial and government enterprises have made it clear that these concerns are real, and that data breaches or abuses will become a reality of the digital age. Although we can wish to go back to an era or more privacy and confidentiality, the reality of surveillance cameras on each street corner, tracking location through mobile phone networks and monitoring credit or debit card transactions have made it nearly impossible to maintain privacy. And as the use of digital cash transfers and internet purchases grow, control of privacy will become less possible32 and it is unlikely that we will ever again be able to protect all of our data as was done in the past. What is needed is not to try to do the impossible but rather adapt to the new reality. Trying to protect all our data, be it financial or medical, will likely be an impossible task but we can develop systems that identify which data are critical to protect and which are less critical. We can and should protect individuals with stigmatizing diagnosis such as HIV+ or gonorrhea but perhaps not be as concerned about common diagnoses such as malaria. Since we will not be able to protect all data uniformly, we will have to make choices about what to protect and who gets to decide. This is of course true about all kinds of data, but medical data will have its own challenges in terms of what is confidential. *(Lin J.C., 2020)*

Current Problems in Digital Healthcare System

There is a clear potential for digital solutions to make an enormous impact into long-standing issues within healthcare systems.

Costly and Inefficient Traditional Models of Care

Despite every effort, referral onto specialist care and communication back to the community remains both costly and inefficient. Simple interventions (such as digital advice and guidance, unified electronic care records, and careful selection of face-to-face patient meetings to reduce unnecessary and expensive transport costs) will have a huge impact.

Healthcare Democracy

The opportunity to break down care barriers that exist due to socioeconomic status, disability and language is clear. Remote clinics, simple transfer of data, tests available for delivery or data acquired via smartphones/wearables at a low cost could dramatically improve access to care by centralized specialist units for remote underprivileged communities. Language barriers traditionally managed with telephone systems or booked interpreters may be dealt with by live auto-translation and clinic letters then sent out in the appropriate language. This may dramatically reduce the challenge of teasing out subtle clinical signs and increase confidence in making an appropriate clinical diagnosis and translating this to the patient with an appropriate management plan, reducing stress for all involved.

'One Strategy Fits All' Models of Care

Personalized healthcare remains an important goal. As the volume and completeness of patient-level data improves, novel insights may be gained by marrying digital data with more complex clinical tests. Careful enquiry of these large datasets may pave the way to new therapies and risk stratification tools. Previous population observational studies, such as that from Framingham, remain the bedrock of many primary prevention interventions in modern medicine.[24] The availability of larger datasets gathered at a fraction of the cost may allow us to take a similarly large step towards more personalized care. (Mitchell M, 2013; Perri-Moore S, 2015; Baker WE, 2009)

Challenges of Digital Health

Several issues that affect patients, medical professionals, technology developers, policymakers, and others have been brought up by the digital revolution of healthcare. Data interoperability is a continuous difficulty due to the enormous amounts of data collected from numerous systems that store and code data differently. Additional difficulties stem from data storage, access, sharing, and ownership, patient computer literacy problems, and unequal healthcare access. These considerations subsequently lead to worries about security and privacy. What would happen, for instance, if employers or insurers wished to aggregate data from the results of genetic tests given directly to consumers by employees? What happens if medical equipment gets tainted? Concerns about technology and ethics are also present. For instance, who is accountable for surgical errors when medical robots are employed: the hospital, the company that developed or manufactured the technology, the physician who utilized the robot, or someone else?

CONCLUSION AND FUTURE SCOPE

Although digital health is still relatively new in the United States, consumers can take control of their care as healthcare services continue to shift to a digital paradigm. As a result, people of all generations will be better informed about their health and able to decide what kind of care they need. There have been many developments in digital health in the United States by a leading healthcare technology company under the name of CareCloud Wellness. Clinicians have a key role as patient advocates ensuring that our core ethical principles guide the development of new healthcare systems. Machine learning must not be allowed to exclude some groups in the population leading to bias and poor digital literacy shouldn't exclude patients from accessing high-quality healthcare. This should be familiar to all clinicians as we are the latest in a long line of clinicians advocating for our patients in a changing world. In the movie *Terminator 2: Judgement Day*, which paints a frightening dystopian future, the mantra is, 'The future is not set. There is no fate but what we make for ourselves.' Clinicians need to make sure that technology is our servant to deliver the best care for our patients and not our master separating us from them. While there is a growing consensus that digital health will be a positive change in the delivery of health care in low- and middle-income countries, there remain significant challenges to its implementation and growth. As with all disruptive changes, those who benefit from the status quo will resist these changes despite the promise of better access and quality for the consumer.

Digital technology will change the balance of power between the provider and the patient, leading to changes in the roles of both government and health care workers. However, the penetration of digital technology across the entire global population will make these changes inevitable. The role of program planners and managers will be to use these changes for the common good and ensure that they benefit everyone and not only those who can pay for care or control the healthcare sector.

REFERENCES

Attia, Z. I., Kapa, S., Lopez-Jimenez, F., McKie, P. M., Ladewig, D. J., Satam, G., Pellikka, P. A., Enriquez-Sarano, M., Noseworthy, P. A., Munger, T. M., Asirvatham, S. J., Scott, C. G., Carter, R. E., & Friedman, P. A. (2019). Screening for cardiac contractile dysfunction using an artificial intelligence-enabled electrocardiogram. *Nature Medicine*, 25(1), 70–74. DOI: 10.1038/s41591-018-0240-2 PMID: 30617318

Attia, Z. I., Noseworthy, P. A., Lopez-Jimenez, F., Asirvatham, S. J., Deshmukh, A. J., Gersh, B. J., Carter, R. E., Yao, X., Rabinstein, A. A., Erickson, B. J., Kapa, S., & Friedman, P. A. (2019). An artificial intelligence-enabled ECG algorithm for the identification of patients with atrial fibrillation during sinus rhythm: A retrospective analysis of outcome prediction. *Lancet*, 394(10201), 861–867. DOI: 10.1016/S0140-6736(19)31721-0 PMID: 31378392

Bajowala, S. S., Milosch, J., & Bansal, C. (2020, October). Telemedicine pays billing and coding update. *Current Allergy and Asthma Reports*, 20(10), 1–9. DOI: 10.1007/s11882-020-00956-y PMID: 32715353

Baker, W. E. (2009). Evaluation of Physician Competency and Clinical Performance in Emergency Medicine. *Emergency Medicine Clinics of North America*, 27(4), 615–626. DOI: 10.1016/j.emc.2009.07.010 PMID: 19932396

Heinzelmann, P. J., Lugn, N. E., & Kvedar, J. C. (2005, December). Telemedicine in the future. *Journal of Telemedicine and Telecare*, 11(8), 384–390. DOI: 10.1177/1357633X0501100802 PMID: 16356311

Honarbakhsh, S., Sporton, S., Monkhouse, C., Lowe, M., Earley, M. J., & Hunter, R. J. (2021). Remote clinics and investigations in arrhythmia services: What have we learnt during coronavirus disease 2019? *Arrhythmia & Electrophysiology Review*, 10(2), 120–124. DOI: 10.15420/aer.2020.37 PMID: 34401185

Kohnke, A., Cole, M. L., & Bush, R. (2014, July). Incorporating UTAUT predictors for understanding home care patients' and clinician's acceptance of healthcare telemedicine equipment. *Journal of Technology Management & Innovation*, 9(2), 29–41. DOI: 10.4067/S0718-27242014000200003

Lin, J. C., Kavousi, Y., Sullivan, B., & Stevens, C. (2020, May 1). Analysis of outpatient telemedicine reimbursement in an integrated healthcare system. *Annals of Vascular Surgery*, 65, 100–106. DOI: 10.1016/j.avsg.2019.10.069 PMID: 31678131

McBain, L., & Morgan, D. (2005). Telehealth, geography, and jurisdiction: Issues of health care delivery in Northern Saskatchewan. *Canadian Women's Studies*, 24, 123–129.

McKeon, G., Steel, Z., Wells, R., Newby, J., Hadzi-Pavlovic, D., Vancampfort, D., & Rosenbaum, S. (2021). A mental health-informed physical activity intervention for first responders and their partners delivered using Facebook: Mixed methods pilot study. *JMIR Formative Research*, 5(4), e23432. DOI: 10.2196/23432 PMID: 33885376

Nelson, A., Herron, D., Rees, G., & Nachev, P. (2019). Predicting scheduled hospital attendance with artificial intelligence. *NPJ Digital Medicine*, 2(1), 26. DOI: 10.1038/s41746-019-0103-3 PMID: 31304373

Perez, M. V., Mahaffey, K. W., Hedlin, H., Rumsfeld, J. S., Garcia, A., Ferris, T., Balasubramanian, V., Russo, A. M., Rajmane, A., Cheung, L., Hung, G., Lee, J., Kowey, P., Talati, N., Nag, D., Gummidipundi, S. E., Beatty, A., Hills, M. T., Desai, S., & Turakhia, M. P. (2019). Large-scale assessment of a smartwatch to identify atrial fibrillation. *The New England Journal of Medicine*, 381(20), 1909–1917. DOI: 10.1056/NEJMoa1901183 PMID: 31722151

Perri-Moore, S., Routen, T., Shao, A. F., Rambaud-Althaus, C., Swai, N., Kahama-Maro, J., D'Acremont, V., Blaise, G., & Mitchell, M. (2015). Using an eIMCI-Derived Decision Support Protocol to Improve Provider– Caretaker Communication for Treatment of Children Under 5 in Tanzania. *Global Health Communication*, 1(1), 41–47. DOI: 10.1080/23762004.2016.1181486 PMID: 27525308

Raatikainen, M. J., Uusimaa, P., van Ginneken, M. M., Janssen, J. P., & Linnaluoto, M. (2008). Remote monitoring of implantable cardioverter defibrillator patients: A safe, time-saving, and cost-effective means for follow-up. *Europace*, 10(10), 1145–1151. DOI: 10.1093/europace/eun203 PMID: 18703585

Ricci, R. P., Morichelli, L., Quarta, L., Sassi, A., Porfili, A., Laudadio, M. T., Gargaro, A., & Santini, M. (2010). Long-term patient acceptance of and satisfaction with implanted device remote monitoring. *Europace*, 12(5), 674–679. DOI: 10.1093/europace/euq046 PMID: 20200019

Scott Kruse, C., Karem, P., Shifflett, K., Vegi, L., Ravi, K., & Brooks, M. (2018). Evaluating barriers to adopting telemedicine worldwide: A systematic review. *Journal of Telemedicine and Telecare*, 24(1), 4–12. DOI: 10.1177/1357633X16674087 PMID: 29320966

Shaw, A., Moodley, M., & McSporran, K.. (2021). Safety and effectiveness of an integrated telehelth-led supported discahrges service for COVID-19. *Thorax*, 76, A1–A205.

ADDITIONAL READING

Ali, M. (2021). *Remote Work and Sustainable Changes for the Future of Global Business.* IGI Global. https://www.igi-global.com/book/remote-work-sustainable-changes-future/264375

Ali, M. (2022). *Future Role of Sustainable Innovative Technologies in Crisis Management.* IGI Global. https://www.igi-global.com/book/future-role-sustainable-innovative-technologies/281281

Ali, M. (2023). *Shifting Paradigms in the Rapidly Developing Global Digital Ecosystem: A GCC Perspective.* In Digital Entrepreneurship and Co-Creating Value Through Digital Encounters (pp. 145-166). IGI Global. https://www.igi-global.com/chapter/shifting-paradigms-in-the-rapidly-developing-global-digital-ecosystem/323525

Ali, M. (2023). T*axonomy of Industry 4.0 Technologies in Digital Entrepreneurship and Co-Creating Value.* In *Digital Entrepreneurship and Co-Creating Value Through Digital Encounters* (pp. 24–55). IGI Global., https://www.igi-global.com/chapter/taxonomy-of-industry-40-technologies-in-digital-entrepreneurship-and-co-creating-value/323520 DOI: 10.4018/978-1-6684-7416-7.ch002

Ali, M., & Wood-Harper, T. (2021). *Fostering Communication and Learning with Underutilized Technologies in Higher Education.* IGI Global. https://www.igi-global.com/book/fostering-communication-learning-underutilized-technologies/244593

Ali, M., Wood-Harper, T., & Kutar, M. (2023). Multi-Perspectives of Contemporary Digital Transformation Models of Complex Innovation Management. In *Digital Entrepreneurship and Co-Creating Value Through Digital Encounters* (pp. 79–96). IGI Global., https://www.igi-global.com/chapter/multi-perspectives-of-contemporary-digital-transformation-models-of-complex-innovation-management/323522 DOI: 10.4018/978-1-6684-7416-7.ch004

Ali, M. B. (2021). Internet of Things (IoT) to Foster Communication and Information Sharing: A Case of UK Higher Education. In Ali, M. B., & Wood-Harper, T. (Eds.), *Fostering Communication and Learning With Underutilized Technologies in Higher Education* (pp. 1–20). IGI Global., https://www.igi-global.com/chapter/internet-of-things-iot-to-foster-communication-and-information-sharing/262718/ DOI: 10.4018/978-1-7998-4846-2.ch001

Ali, M. B., & Wood-Harper, T. (2022). Artificial Intelligence (AI) as a Decision-Making Tool to Control Crisis Situations. In *Future Role of Sustainable Innovative Technologies in Crisis Management*. IGI Global., https://www.igi-global.com/chapter/artificial-intelligence-ai-as-a-decision-making-tool-to-control-crisis-situations/298931 DOI: 10.4018/978-1-7998-9815-3.ch006

Ali, M. B., Wood-Harper, T., & Ramlogan, R. (2020). A Framework Strategy to Overcome Trust Issues on Cloud Computing Adoption in Higher Education. In Modern Principles, Practices, and Algorithms for Cloud Security (pp. 162-183). IGI Global. https://www.igi-global.com/chapter/a-framework-strategy-to-overcome-trust-issues-on-cloud-computing-adoption-in-higher-education/238907/

KEY TERMS AND DEFINITIONS

Digital innovation in Healthcare: improves patient care, while facilitating and streamlining hospital processes. Digital innovation in healthcare transforms healthcare delivery, lowers costs, and increases access to care. The technologies that propel digital innovation include wearable technology, telemedicine, health information exchanges, artificial intelligence, electronic health records, and other technologies. These technological advancements have increased healthcare services' effectiveness, quality, and accessibility.

Efficiency of Digital Healthcare: Digital technologies also help in increasing efficiency and streamlining healthcare processes. Due to the ease with which healthcare practitioners can access patient data when using electronic health records (EHRs), less administrative work is required, and care coordination is enhanced. Patients can use automated online appointment scheduling and billing. This saves time and money and lowers the potential for manual errors. As a result, hospital staff can focus on providing patient care, and resources can be used more effectively.

Digital Literacy: Digital literacy is the capacity to use online resources to find, comprehend, and share information. The likelihood of product uptake may be decreased as a result of inadequate digital literacy among patients and healthcare workers, as many may become hesitant to learn how to utilize this new technology. Stakeholders may struggle with these technologies' usage and functionality, even after embracing them, making it difficult for them to fully benefit from the product. Moreover, due to a lack of awareness regarding how to use these devices, privacy and security issues may arise.

Personalized Care: Personalized care means tailoring a person's treatment to fit their specific needs and history. They require data and an accurate diagnosis to be effective. When determining therapies, personalized medicine considers genetics, genomes, and all other biological data. Oncology can successfully employ personalized healthcare to treat immunological disorders like Parkinson's or Alzheimer's.

Digital Health: Digital health is the combination of medical expertise and technology to improve patient care and outcomes. Thus, it is now possible to use a smartphone to continuously check if a patient has taken prescribed prescriptions, monitor vital signs, and even tell whether they have fallen in their house by tracking their body temperature and movement patterns.

Artificial Intelligence: The utilization of patient data for analytical insights will be the next step in revolutionizing healthcare. Currently, the data processing stage is generally distinct from the actual data collection. In the future, AI will probably support human intervention by remotely and instantly assessing patient data, enhancing the response times of healthcare providers. AI may be applied to the healthcare industry in many different ways, such as by analyzing vast volumes of patient data to find trends, make forecasts, and alert users to potential health hazards.

Virtual reality: It has enormous potential in the healthcare sector. Pain, stroke, and numerous mental health conditions like anxiety have all been treated with it. Healthcare experts also use it to hone their surgical and medical abilities. As VR research advances, it may one day be used for a variety of different medical conditions, including the treatment of Asperger's syndrome and brain damage recovery.

Abbreviations: Electronic Health Records (EHRs), Electronic Medical Records (EMRs), Digital Technology and Assessment Criteria (DTAC), healthcare professionals (HCPs), Internet of Things (IoT), Electro-cardiogram (ECG)

Chapter 2
Digital Marketing Transformation of Local MSME Through Instagram Account of Community:
A Case Study of Paguyuban UMKM Kecamatan Bekasi Timur

Noprita Herari
https://orcid.org/0009-0009-2497-5340
LSPR Institute of Communication and Business, Indonesia

S. E. Marlina
https://orcid.org/0009-0002-9163-297X
LSPR Institute of Communication and Business, Indonesia

ABSTRACT

West Java, home to the highest number of MSMEs in Indonesia, serves as the focus of this study, specifically Bekasi City, one of the country's most expensive and densely populated areas. With 12 districts and 56 sub-districts, Bekasi's MSMEs are regulated by the Cooperative and MSME Office through the Paguyuban, a community-based organization. This research explores how the Paguyuban of East Bekasi District (PUKBT) supports MSMEs in their digital marketing transformation. By analyzing PUKBT's Instagram (@umkm.bekasitimur) and conducting qualitative interviews, the study reveals that the two-step communication model is key, with PUKBT guiding members through example. This study also highlights the role of interconnected digital economies and effective community participation, showcasing how Paguyuban's close-knit structure facilitates MSME digitalization. Future

DOI: 10.4018/979-8-3373-0086-3.ch002

Copyright © 2025, IGI Global. Copying or distributing in print or electronic forms without written permission of IGI Global is prohibited.

research should explore larger community applications to further enhance MSMEs' integration into the digital economy.

INTRODUCTION

Indonesia currently stands as the world's 16th largest economy, boasting a GDP exceeding US$1 trillion. According to McKinsey & Company, the country is poised to ascend to the 7th largest global economy by 2030. Notably, Indonesia is the sole Southeast Asian nation represented in the G20 (Kemlu RI, 2023). Given that nearly 100% of Indonesia's economic contributions stem from the Micro, Small, and Medium Enterprise (MSME) sector, with 60% of Indonesia's GDP originating from the MSME industry, this area warrants further investigation (Herari, 2023; Kameke, 2024). This research is particularly important to understand how MSMEs play a significant role in aiding Indonesia's economy recovery from the recession caused by the COVID-19 pandemic.

The adaptability of businesses to socio-economic conditions has emerged as a key factor in the ability of MSMEs to contribute significantly to Indonesia's rapid economic recovery from the pandemic. Despite the increasing number of internet and social media users worldwide (currently, 62% of the global population uses the internet and social media daily), only about 33% of Indonesian MSMEs are actively engaged in digital marketing (INDEF, 2024; Petrosyan, 2024). This disparity presents a significant challenge and a major obstacle to advancing digitalization within the MSME sector, particularly in marketing, despite the Indonesian Government's concerted efforts to promote an offline-to-online digitalization program for MSMEs.

The Indonesian government, through the Ministry of Cooperatives and Small and Medium Enterprises *(Kemenkop UKM RI)*, in collaboration with provincial, county, and city governments, has implemented strategic measures by appointing development advisors for MSMEs in each region and establishing MSME associations (Nabila et al., 2023). While these development advisors serve as catalysts for change in the educational processes of the MSMEs they mentor, the MSME associations offer a platform for MSMEs to convene, collaborate, and exchange knowledge regarding training, socialization, certification, and, most importantly, the creation of a robust MSME ecosystem that positively impacts the region's economic development.

However, the journey to educate and support MSMEs in their growth is not without its challenges. According to data from the Indonesian People's Consultative Assembly *(MPR)*, approximately 70% of MSMEs encounter difficulties in the digitalization process, particularly in adopting digital technology (Moerdijat, 2023).

This situation has prompted the author to examine the existing gaps deeper. According to data from Indonesia's Central Bureau of Statistics *(BPS RI)*, West Java Province stands as the top region in Indonesia for the highest number of MSMEs (Putri, 2023). Among the province's 18 regencies and 9 cities, the author has selected *Kota Bekasi*, a city with the highest cost of living in West Java and the second-highest in Indonesia (Ahdiat, 2023). This highlights the significant role of microeconomic activities in driving the local economy, providing a compelling basis for further investigation.

Bekasi City, a prominent urban center in West Java, Indonesia, comprises of 12 subdistricts *(Kecamatan)* and 56 villages *(Kelurahan)*. The local government, through the Cooperative and MSME Office *(DiskopUKM)*, has established *"Paguyuban"* as a community platform, specifically designed to foster the growth and development of Micro, Small, and Medium Enterprises (MSMEs) operating within the city. Each subdistrict hosts its own *Paguyuban*, led by regional coordinators who serve as mentors and facilitators for MSME members within their respective areas.

To delve deeper into this research, the East Bekasi subdistrict *(Kecamatan Bekasi Timur)* has been strategically selected for closer scrutiny. This decision is informed by the proactive role of *Paguyuban Kecamatan UMKM Bekasi Timur (PUKBT)*, widely recognized as the most dynamic force in catalyzing the growth of its members' businesses through innovative digital marketing initiatives, particularly leveraging social media platforms. This distinction sets it apart from other subdistricts within Bekasi City, underscoring its pioneering approaches and effectiveness in enhancing MSME competitiveness in the digital era.

The primary objective of this study is to investigate the strategies employed by PUKBT in facilitating the digital marketing transformation among its MSME members. By examining real-world scenarios and outcomes, the research seeks to bridge the gap between theoretical knowledge and practical application. The anticipated findings are not only expected to contribute significantly to future scholarly research but also serve as a valuable reference for policymakers aiming to enhance support mechanisms for broader MSME communities, not only within Bekasi City but also potentially across Indonesia and beyond.

LITERATURE REVIEW

Digital Transformation and Two Step Communication Model

Digital transformation entails the seamless integration of digital technology into all aspects of business operations, fundamentally altering the way businesses function and deliver value to customers. The two-step communication model, originally conceived by Paul Lazarsfeld and Elihu Katz, posits that a message is transmitted from the media to opinion leaders, who subsequently disseminate this information to the broader population. This model can serve as a catalyst for digital transformation by harnessing the influence of key figures within an organization to propagate innovative digital practices.

In today's competitive landscape, digital transformation is critical for modern businesses to remain competitive. It involves the strategic adoption of digital technologies to streamline processes, enhance customer experiences, and foster innovation. Research highlight the necessity of comprehensive strategies that includes both technological advancements and organizational changes to successfully implement digital transformation (dos Reis et al., 2018).

A study conducted by Wangqu and Neto (2023) revealed that the two-step flow model exerts a significant influence on shaping a city's international image among its residents. This finding provides a compelling base for the author's assertion that the two-step flow model serves as an effective framework for implementing transformative initiatives. Specifically, this applies to the digital marketing transformation within a community of Micro, Small, and Medium Enterprises (MSMEs).

The correlation between digital transformation and the two-step communication model is vital. Opinion leaders within an organization can serve as catalysts for change, advocating for and facilitating the adoption of innovative digital tools and practices. This approach can mitigate resistance to change and enhance the overall efficacy of digital transformation initiatives.

1. **The Crucial Role of Opinion Leaders.** Opinion leaders play a crucial role in interpreting and disseminating digital transformation initiatives. Their endorsement can lend credibility to the change process and inspire others to adopt new technologies.
2. **Enhanced Communication through Interpersonal Interactions.** The two-step communication model emphasizes interpersonal interactions, which can be more effective than top-down communications in promoting digital transformation. Engaging employees through trusted peers can foster a deeper understanding and acceptance of digital changes.
3. **Practical Implementation through Social Media.** For instance, organizations can leverage social media platforms to implement the two-step communication model. Opinion leaders within the company can share their experiences and success stories related to digital tools, thereby encouraging others to follow suit.

Empirical studies support the effectiveness of the two-step communication model in facilitating digital transformation. Research shows that companies that engage opinion leaders in their digital transformation strategies witness higher rates of technology adoption and superior overall outcomes (dos Reis et al., 2018). These findings underscore the importance of harnessing internal influencers to drive change.

Effective Community Participation

Figure 1. Effective community participation process (Pal, 2021).

A successful community participatory process is a multifaceted endeavor that incorporates individual attributes, structured group processes, organizational support, empowering external relationships, culturally sensitive strategies, and enhanced community health and well-being. This section examines the critical components that contribute to effective community participation (Pal, 2021).

Individual attributes such as motivation, skills, and personal experiences play a significant role in fostering effective community participation. According to Xu & Li (2014), individuals who are intrinsically motivated and possess relevant skills are more likely to actively engage in participatory processes. These personal attributes ensure that participants can contribute meaningfully to discussions and decision-making processes.

Structured group processes are essential for facilitating effective community participation. These processes provide a framework within which community members can collaborate, deliberate, and reach consensus. Kuswanto and Anderson (2023) underscores the importance of a structured approach in participatory processes, noting that clear procedures and guidelines help manage group dynamics and ensure equitable participation.

Organizational support is indispensable for sustaining participatory initiatives. This includes providing resources, training, and institutional backing to community members. Christens and Lin (2014) emphasize that organizations play a pivotal role in enabling and maintaining community participation by offering logistical and technical support. Organizations also facilitate conflict resolution and ensure that participatory processes are inclusive and equitable.

Building and maintaining empowering external relationships can enhance the effectiveness of community participation. Partnerships with external stakeholders such as government agencies, non-profits, and academic institutions can provide additional resources and expertise. According to Putnam (2001), these relationships can help communities leverage external support to achieve their goals more effectively. Collaborative efforts with external entities can also introduce new perspectives and innovative solutions to community challenges.

A culturally sensitive strategy is essential for effectively engaging diverse community members by understanding and respecting their cultural differences, traditions, and values. Such approaches foster greater trust and cooperation, making participatory processes more inclusive and representative. Tailoring strategies to align with cultural norms ensures meaningful and respectful participation, fostering new social ties that transcend ethnic or other minority group boundaries and contributing to building trust among culturally diverse populations (Sesic et al., 2010).

Effective community participation has been correlated with improved health and well-being outcomes. Participation in community processes can foster better social cohesion, increased social support, and greater empowerment, all of which contribute to enhanced health and well-being. Active engagement in community activities can also provide individuals with a sense of purpose and belonging, which are indispensable for mental and emotional health (Haim-Litevsky et al., 2023).

While the Effective Community Participation Process depicted in Figure 1 was initially applied to health-related communities, the author believes that the same model can be applied to communities in other fields as well. The six interconnected elements for effective community participation appear to be generalizable and can be utilized for various types of communities, provided they are grounded in similar goals and shared values.

Paguyuban: More Than Just a Community in Indonesian Culture

Derived from the Javanese word *'guyub'*—a term rooted in the largest ethnic group in Indonesia—*'Paguyuban'* refers to a familial association founded by like-minded individuals to cultivate unity and harmony among its members (KBBI, 2023). The word *'guyub'* is synonymous with harmony, togetherness, and the absence of discord among its members. In German, the word *'gemeinschaft'* conveys a comparable meaning (Biroli, 2022).

Beyond being merely a gathering place, numerous studies have underscored the significant role of 'Paguyuban' as an integral component of Indonesian culture in fostering social integration (Dwiningrum et al., 2018). It contributes to the preservation of cultural heritage (Fitriyani, 2012), aids in rural development (Barlan & Kolopaking, 2014), promotes tourism (Agung & Wijaya, 2019), boosts entrepreneurial motivation (Hartini, 2018), and enhances the growth of small and medium-sized enterprises (SMEs) (Shiddiqah & Adi, 2023).

Examining the 'Paguyuban' as a fundamental aspect of Indonesian culture offers a unique perspective through which to understand and facilitate the digital transformation of local MSMEs (Micro, Small, and Medium Enterprises). In the context of *PaguyubanUMKM Kecamatan Bekasi Timur (PUKBT)*, this cultural framework is particularly relevant for several reasons.

Firstly, the cultural relevance and acceptance of *Paguyuban*as a trusted community can serve as a medium to introduce digital practices to MSMEs. Its familiar and reassuring environment mitigates resistance to change, fostering a positive transition towards digital transformation (Permana et al., 2023).

Secondly, the strong emphasis on social integration and mutual support within *Paguyuban*is instrumental in overcoming the inherent challenges of digital transformation. By leveraging the collective spirit of *Paguyuban*, MSMEs can benefit from shared learning and collaborative problem-solving of social issues (Nugraha, 2014). This community support can address gaps in digital literacy and resources, making the adoption of digital tools more accessible and less intimidating.

Furthermore, *Paguyuban* acts as a platform for preserving cultural identity while embracing modern technological advancements. The digital transformation initiatives, when integrated with the values and practices of *Paguyuban*, ensure that the distinctive cultural aspects of Indonesian MSMEs are maintained. This approach not only respects the cultural heritage but also enhances the authenticity and resonance of the digital content created by these businesses (Hodijah, 2023).

The environment of mutual encouragement fostered by *Paguyuban*can significantly enhances entrepreneurial motivation. Witnessing the digital success of peers within the community can inspire and motivate other MSMEs to embark on their own digital journeys. This peer influence is a powerful catalyst for change, as it is grounded in relatable examples and shared experiences (Ellyta et al., 2019).

As previously discussed, Bekasi City covers 12 districts and 56 sub-districts. This structure aligns with the organizational mapping of the Bekasi City UMKM PaguyubanAssociation. The Association has sub-district coordinators and district chief coordinators. One of these, and the focus of this study, is the *PaguyubanUMKM Kecamatan Bekasi Timur* / East Bekasi District MSME Association (PUKBT). PUKBT oversees four associations in sub-districts: Bekasi Jaya, Duren Jaya, Aren Jaya, and Margahayu. Thus, PUKBT's organization includes one chief coordinator, four sub-district coordinators, and one secretary, collectively organizing approximately 200 registered SMEs in the Bekasi Timur district. However, this number falls short of the actual number of SMEs in the area.

The Bekasi City PaguyubanUMKM has established its own programs, which are subsequently implemented by the district-level associations. However, each district maintains the autonomy to create its own programs and activities. Based on preliminary research conducted by the author, PUKBT stands out as particularly innovative and active compared to other district associations. This distinction is due to PUKBT's integration of both offline and online activities.

As mentioned, PUKBT's activities encompass both offline and online initiatives. Offline activities, directed by the central UMKM association, include socialization events, workshops, and various business certification programs. One notable offline program initiated by PUKBT is *'Road Lapak'* (A Stall Roadshow), which involves visits to the stalls owned by PUKBT member SMEs. During the *Road Lapak* program, PUKBT coordinators engage in direct discussions with SME owners, conduct data collection, and provide social media outreach and training for these businesses.

The *Road Lapak* program complements the digital initiatives carried out by PUKBT coordinators. These activities extend beyond the use of WhatsApp groups for information and communication to include business Instagram accounts, which will be discussed in more detail later in this article. Other digital initiatives by PUKBT coordinators involve training sessions utilizing WhatsApp Business and other digital platforms. Given the traditional nature of the Bekasi City UMKM

Association's operations, such digital integration remains a pioneering approach for supporting SMEs in Bekasi City.

METHODOLOGY

This research employs an interpretive qualitative methodology by analyzing digital content on the PUKBT's Instagram account. The PUKBT coordinators are selected from SME representatives who also operate their own businesses. These coordinators are considered influential figures and are chosen by the head of the *DiskopUKM* Bekasi City. In addition to observational analysis, the author conducted interviews with the PUKBT's coordinators to gain insights into the strategies employed to educate MSME members on digital marketing literacy through community development. The following table lists the PUKBT coordinators, detailing their roles and associated businesses:

Table 1. Coordinators of PUKBT as sources

Name	Position at PUBKT	Type of Business	Instagram Business Account
Lidwina Warsiatun (R1)	Head of Coordinator of PUBKT	Food & Beverage	@kedainikenbersaudara
Lia Lioners (R2)	Coordinator of sub-district Bekasi Jaya	Food & Beverage	@tahugejrot_jeh
Erni Pudji (R3)	Coordinator of Sub-district Duren Jaya	Food & Beverage	@cemilanque.official
Zuaeriyah (R4)	Coordinator of Aren Jaya	Craft & Accessories	@zuae_henna_art
Emarmaryasih (R5)	Coordinator of sub-district Margahayu	Food & Beverage	@kartinimandiri.mpokmar

Each coordinator not only fulfills their role within PUKBT but also manages a small business. This dual responsibility equips them with a practical understanding of the challenges and opportunities faced by MSMEs, making their input invaluable for this research.

Theoretically, this study will employ the community development model to understand the needs of community members and how the Instagram account @ umkm.bekasitimur can serve as an active platform for fostering digital literacy. The community development model is particularly relevant here as it emphasizes the role of collective action in addressing common issues and promoting growth among community members. By leveraging this model, the research aims to highlight the ways in which the PUKBT coordinators utilize digital tools to enhance the business acumen of MSME members.

Interviews with the coordinators provided valuable qualitative data on how they utilize the Instagram platform to promote digital literacy. For example, they shared various strategies such as posting educational content, conducting live sessions to demonstrate effective social media practices, and utilizing Instagram stories to engage with followers. These methods are designed to empower MSME members by enhancing their digital marketing skills and helping them reach a broader audience.

While research on digital transformation in MSMEs is plentiful in Indonesia, there has been limited research examining the digital transformation process of MSMEs from the perspective of effective community participation. Moreover, how the Instagram social media platform is used as a tool for digital marketing transformation in MSMEs represents a novel contribution to this study.

Ultimately, this research aims to provide a comprehensive understanding of how digital platforms like Instagram can be effectively employed in community development initiatives. By focusing on the PUKBT's efforts, the study will offer valuable insights into the intersection of digital literacy and community-driven economic growth.

RESULT AND DISCUSSION

In this section, the author will analyze how digital marketing transformation through Instagram is being implemented by the '*Paguyuban UMKM Bekasi Timur*' for its members. Before delving into the analysis, the author will first explain the various components of the Instagram account managed by the latter, named @ umkm.bekasitimur.

Figure 2. The look of the Instagram account @umkm.bekasitimur

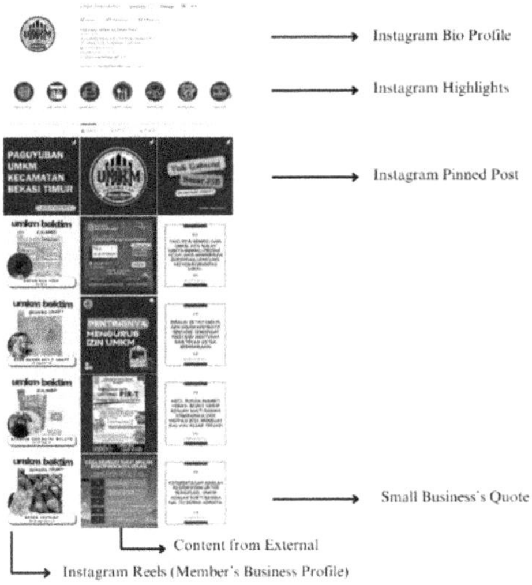

Similar to any well-managed business Instagram account, @umkm.bekasitimur leverages the features offered by Instagram to serve as an effective platform for its community members to learn about digital transformation. As shown in Figure 2, the account includes several key components: the profile bio, Instagram highlights, pinned posts, and feed posts, which are categorized into reels, carousels, and single posts. Each of these elements serves a distinct purpose and collectively enhances the account's overall functionality.

Referring to the two-step communication model, the digital transformation in the case study of *PUKBT* positions the organization as a gatekeeper, responsible for promoting digital marketing transformation. This is achieved through an Instagram makeover that optimizes the platform's features for its members. The Instagram account is utilized as the primary medium for communicating this digital transformation. In this context, the author aims to link the community participation platform with the strategies employed by '*Paguyuban UMKM Bekasi Timur*' via their Instagram account. This is detailed in the following table:

Table 2. Effective community participation process through creating Instagram account @umkm.bekasitimur

No	Effective Community Participation Process	Section on Instagram Account @umkm.bekasitimur
1.	Individual Attributes	Single post feed (feed post on the right)
2.	Structured Group Process	Curation-Socialization-Transformation Process
3.	Organization Support	Visibility member of PUKBT
4.	Empowering External Relationship	Collaborate content with external PUKBT (carousel post in mid-feed post)
5.	Culturally Sensitive Strategy	Instagram highlight cover
6.	Enhance Community Health & Wellbeing	Collaboration reels content (feed post on the left)

Individual Attributes

As previously explained, individual attributes significantly influence community participation. In this context, PUKBT enhances individual motivation for digital transformation through single post content (on the right side of Figure 2), featuring inspirational quotes to boost the motivation of its SME members.

Figure 3. Quote on Instagram @umkm.bekasitimur

As shown in Figure 3, the @umkm.bekasitimur Instagram account features a quote in Indonesian. Translated into English, the quote reads: 'When we buy from SMEs, we are not just buying a product, but also directly supporting the local community.' This content is designed to motivate SME owners and boost their morale. The caption of this post provides information about the activities PUKBT conducts for SMEs in the East Bekasi area and offers guidance for SMEs that have not yet joined on how to become members of PUKBT.

The use of motivational quotes to boost morale is supported by research findings, such as those from a study by Sun (2024) which found a generally positive attitude towards using motivational quotes in medical and educational fields. Multiple research projects have demonstrated that motivational quotes effectively encourage individuals to take action. These studies utilized various media, including mobile phones, practitioners, and pamphlets, to display motivational quotes, resulting in positive outcomes. For instance, a significant portion of patients became more proactive in taking medications and quitting smoking.

One aspect that enhances motivation as part of the individual attributes of PUKBT community members is the *Road Lapak* program, where PUKBT coordinators visit the stalls of PUKBT member MSMEs. When visited and given a platform to discuss their business aspirations and challenges, MSME members feel valued and become more enthusiastic about developing their businesses. The outcomes of the *Road Lapak* activities include not only updating the data of each PUKBT member and increasing their understanding of PUKBT programs but also revamping their Instagram accounts to meet the basic standards set by PUKBT, as exemplified by the @umkm.bekasitimur account (see Figure 2)

Structured Group Process

Figure 4. Structured group process in PUBT through @umkm.bekasitimur's Instagram account

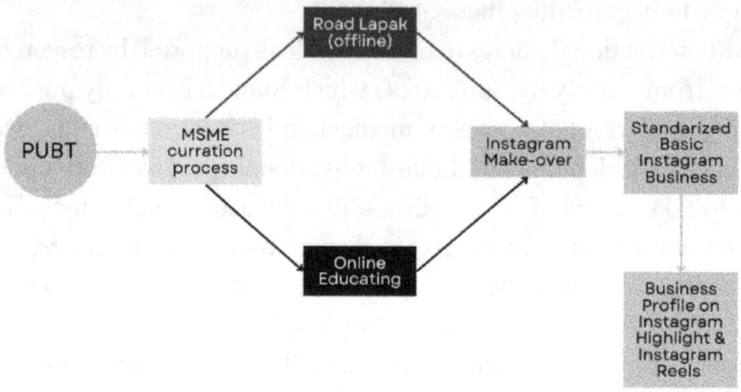

The digital transformation process orchestrated by PUBKT unfolds through a structured series of steps designed by its coordinators. As depicted in Figure 4, the initial phase involves the selection of SMEs for an Instagram account makeover. Specifically, participants chosen at this stage are those who actively engage in community activities organized by the *Paguyuban,* such as bazaars, workshops, and WhatsApp group discussions.

Once curated, SMEs are guided through the transformation journey via WhatsApp or in-person meetings. They undergo practical training to revamp their Instagram profiles in alignment with established business standards. Notably, they draw inspiration from @umkm.bekasitimur, a benchmark account that exemplifies a well-optimized business profile. Key features include a keyword-rich bio, thematic highlight covers, and strategically pinned posts serving as permanent highlights in the feed (see Figure 5).

Figure 5. Basic business form for make-over Instagram account business

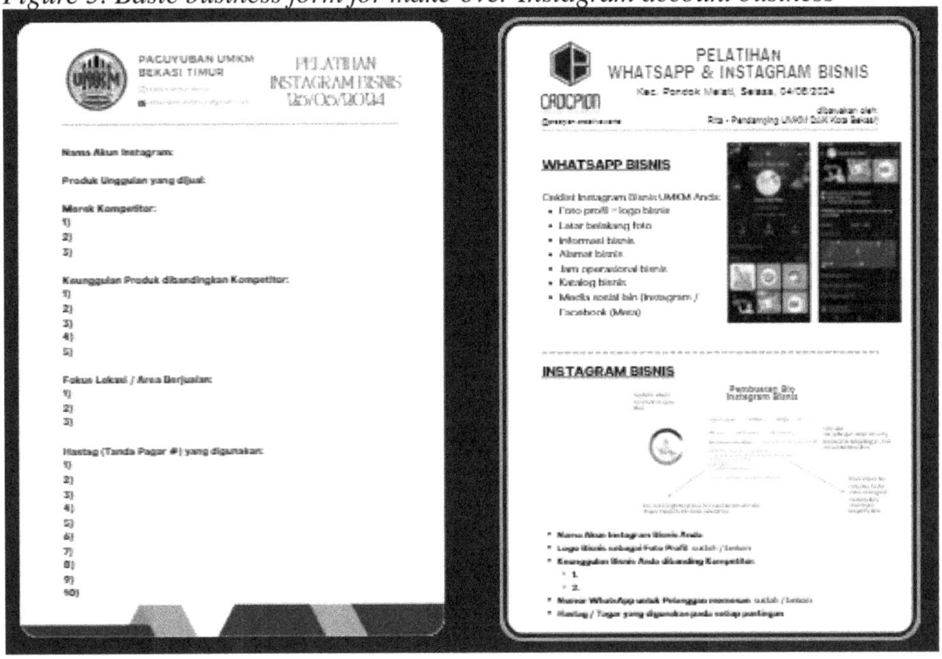

PAGUYUBAN UMKM BEKASI TIMUR

PELATIHAN INSTAGRAM BISNIS

Nama Akun Instagram:

Produk Unggulan yang dijual:

Merek Kompetitor:
1)
2)
3)

Keunggulan Produk dibandingkan Kompetitor:
1)
2)
3)
4)
5)

Fokus Lokasi / Area Berjualan:
1)
2)
3)

Hastag (Tanda Pagar #) yang digunakan:
1)
2)
3)
4)
5)
6)
7)
8)
9)
10)

PELATIHAN
WHATSAPP & INSTAGRAM BISNIS

WHATSAPP BISNIS

INSTAGRAM BISNIS

In initiating their digital education on Instagram Marketing, PUKBT utilizes a Basic Business Form, as shown in Figure 5. This form consists of two pages that MSME participants are required to complete with key information. The first page collects essential data such as the MSME's Instagram account name, their flagship product, three competitor brands, five key advantages their product has over the competition, three target sales areas (focused locations), ten primary hashtags they plan to use, and examples of WhatsApp Business optimization (as Instagram and WhatsApp Business are interconnected).

On the second page, there is a checklist form for optimizing their Instagram bio. This includes ensuring the Instagram account name aligns with the business name, using the business logo as the profile picture, highlighting the business' key advantages over competitors, providing a linked WhatsApp number for easy customer communication, and selecting one main hashtag to feature in the Instagram bio.

Through this form, PUKBT is not only educating the fundamentals of Instagram Marketing but also encouraging MSME members to gain a deeper understanding of their business positioning relative to their competitors. While this approach may not be a formal introduction to SWOT analysis, it provides MSME participants with a structured overview of their strengths, how their competitors operate and grow, and how to strategically navigate competition. This strategic thinking is cultivated within the framework of Instagram Marketing, aiding MSMEs to adapt to the digital landscape with greater confidence and insight.

Figure 6. Basic Instagram business standarize by PUKBT as sample to their members

Previous research across various fields consistently demonstrates that leading by example is a pivotal factor in influencing positive behaviors and outcomes within organizations. Whether in environmental management, ethical leadership, psychological ownership, or educational settings, leaders who model desired behaviors can inspire and guide their followers toward achieving collective goals through productivity (Boiral et al., 2013; Hattke & Hattke, 2019; Sanchez et al., 2024; Versland & Erickson, 2017; Ye et al., 2022). In this case, the PUKBT Instagram account (@ umkm.bekasitimur) serves as a model for its MSME members to emulate when revamping their business Instagram profiles. It can be stated that PUKBT adopts a "leading by example" approach as its strategy for Instagram marketing digitalization, demonstrating best practices to its members through its own account.

Creating graphic designs that harmonize with business logo colors presents a notable challenge. To address this, coordinators of *Paguyuban UMKM* East Bekasi educate members on using the Canva Application for simple design tasks. Throughout the Instagram makeover process, members receive personalized instructions via WhatsApp. They not only learn to leverage Instagram's features effectively but also gain proficiency in creating basic designs using the Canva Application. This educational effort underscores the significance of organizational support in facilitating successful digital transformation through tailored guidance and accessible resources provided by the Paguyuban.

At this stage, it can be said that through PUKBT's digitalization strategy, MSME members benefit not only from a makeover of their business Instagram accounts but also from a deeper understanding of their business positioning. By analyzing competitors' content, they begin to grasp basic content strategy, learning what resonates within their industry. Additionally, they acquire practical skills, such as using Canva Application at a basic level for content design. This approach equips them with the tools to create visually appealing posts, fostering both strategic thinking and technical capability in digital marketing.

Organization Support

Organizational support plays a pivotal role in empowering Micro, Small, and Medium Enterprises (MSMEs) to thrive and expand their operations. These supportive entities, acting as community catalysts, provide invaluable guidance, resources, and networking opportunities that enable entrepreneurs to navigate challenges and seize opportunities effectively. This supportive ecosystem typically encompasses mentorship programs, access to financing, workshops focusing on business management and digital skills, and advocacy for favorable regulatory frameworks. By fostering such an environment, these organizations not only enhance the capabilities of MSMEs but also cultivate sustainable economic growth by nurturing innovation and entrepreneurship at the grassroots level.

An exemplary demonstration of organizational support can be seen in PUKBT *(Paguyuban UMKM Bekasi Timur)*, which employs a multifaceted approach to assist SMEs in the region through offline, online, and hybrid activities. Offline initiatives include regular bazaars, workshops, and socialization events that serve as platforms for SME members to showcase their products, acquire new skills, and forge connections with fellow entrepreneurs. Additionally, frequent meetings are convened with SME stakeholders to discuss the progress and challenges faced by East Bekasi SMEs, providing a forum for members to express concerns, exchange insights, and receive essential feedback and assistance. Complementing these efforts are scheduled 'Road Lapak' visits, where PUKBT coordinators personally engage with SME members at their stalls, offering tailored advice and support to foster their growth and sustainability.

Figure 7. WhatsApp group of PUKBT as media for training, promotion, and information

Figure 7 illustrates how PUKBT utilizes a WhatsApp group as a medium for training, promotion, and information dissemination. Online support is primarily delivered through this WhatsApp group, which serves as a vital tool for digital education. Various pieces of information about upcoming activities, new regulations from the city government, and training opportunities are shared via this platform. The WhatsApp group is not only used for disseminating information but also actively facilitates training sessions. A monthly schedule of training sessions is conducted via the WhatsApp group, covering topics such as optimizing Instagram for business and starting sales on e-commerce platforms. These sessions provide members with valuable knowledge and skills to enhance their digital presence and marketing strategies.

In a hybrid approach, PUBT assists SMEs in processing certification or licensing documents. While SMEs in Bekasi can register digitally through a government-provided website, the process can be expedited through the efforts of PUBT coordinators. They often collect paper documents directly from SME members and submit them collectively to the Bekasi mayor's office. This hybrid method significantly eases the administrative burden on SME operators, ensuring that their businesses remain compliant with local regulations and can continue to operate smoothly.

The support from PUKBT has proven to be effective in increasing member participation in both activities organized by the association and the Bekasi city government. This active involvement fosters a strong sense of belonging among members, encouraging them to grow not just individually but as a community. The frequent interactions and collaborative efforts help to build a supportive network where members can share resources, knowledge, and encouragement.

PUKBT's WhatsApp group and Instagram account are seen as the most active platforms for updating activities and facilitating communication among members. The Instagram account @umkm.bekasitimur is particularly active compared to accounts from associations in other sub-districts in Bekasi. This high level of activity on digital platforms reflects PUKBT's commitment to leveraging modern technology to support its members effectively. By maintaining an active online presence, PUKBT ensures that its members are well-informed, engaged, and motivated to participate in various development initiatives.

Empowering External Relationship

Paguyuban UMKM Bekasi Timur (PUKBT) conducts comprehensive surveys to identify the challenges faced by its members and understand their expectations from the community. These surveys are a crucial initial step that provides valuable insights into the specific needs and issues of the SME members. The information gathered from these surveys allows the coordinators to tailor their support strategies effectively. Following the survey, the coordinators actively reach out to external parties to address the identified needs. This includes organizing various training sessions, socialization events, and workshops aimed at enhancing the skills and knowledge of the members. These activities are designed not only to address immediate challenges but also to provide long-term benefits by empowering SME members with the tools and knowledge needed to thrive in their businesses.

The proactive approach of PUKBT in engaging with external parties is a significant aspect of their support strategy. By collaborating with private banks, government bodies, and other relevant organizations, PUKBT ensures that its members have access to a wide range of resources and opportunities. This collaboration often results in sponsorships for events, additional training sessions, and access to financial services, which are vital for the growth and development of SMEs. According to research by Rahman et al. (2022), such external collaborations are instrumental in enhancing the visibility and credibility of community organizations, thereby attracting more support and resources.

Figure 8. Content examples of external relationships

As shown in Figure 8, a flyer represents an event sponsored by a private bank and the Bekasi city government. The content posted on the Instagram account @ umkm.bekasitimur consistently tags the relevant external accounts, which digitally benefits both parties by demonstrating their active engagement. This practice serves as an example to PUKBT members on how to effectively tag content and utilize its advantages. Tagging content on Instagram has been proven to increase visibility and awareness of the content created by an account, thereby indirectly becoming part of 'word-of-mouth marketing' in the digital world. This strategy aligns with findings from multiple studies which indicate that social media tagging significantly boosts content reach and engagement, fostering a more robust online presence for businesses.

Moreover, the act of tagging external accounts not only amplifies the reach of the posts but also builds a network of mutual support and recognition among different stakeholders. This interconnectedness is essential for the sustainability and growth of SMEs, as it encourages continuous interaction and collaboration. The practice of tagging also educates PUKBT members on effective social media strategies, enhancing their digital literacy and marketing skills. By observing and emulating these practices, SME members can improve their own social media engagement, ultimately leading to better business outcomes.

Overall, PUKBT's multifaceted approach to community support which includes conducting surveys, engaging external parties, and leveraging digital platforms, exemplifies a comprehensive strategy for nurturing SME growth and development. By addressing immediate needs while simultaneously equipping members with the skills and knowledge necessary for long-term success, PUKBT demonstrates a dynamic and proactive approach to community engagement. The organization's strategic use of social media and its continuous interaction with external entities serve as a model for other community organizations seeking to foster SME development.

Culturally Sensitive Strategy

The culturally sensitive strategy of *Paguyuban UMKM Bekasi Timur* (PUKBT) is evident in its meticulous attention to the unique culture and identity of each SME. This approach is vividly illustrated in the Instagram highlights section (Figure 9) of @umkm.bekasitimur's account, where diverse business identities are meticulously categorized and showcased. From the cover image to the detailed content, each highlight effectively conveys the distinctive value proposition of each business, emphasizing the unique characteristics that set them apart.

Figure 9. The Instagram highlights on @umkm.bekasitimur

The Instagram highlights on the @umkm.bekasitimur account serve multiple purposes. Not only do they categorize PUKBT members into ten distinct business sectors in Bekasi—culinary, services, packaged products, crafts and accessories, fashion, grocery stores, electronic services, automotive, furniture, and agriculture—but they also provide a visual and informational archive of various activities and achievements. These highlights include video documentation of *Road Lapak* programs, bazaars, and monthly training or socialization events. Strategically positioned just below the profile bio, Instagram highlights are a prominent feature that updates horizontally, making them an ideal space to showcase the portfolios of PUKBT members and document past events effectively.

Figure 10. Inside Instagram covers 10 business sectors of PUKBT's members

Each of the ten MSME sectors has its own dedicated highlight section, as shown in Figure 10. These sections contain Instagram stories featuring product photos offered, images of business owners, and detailed information about the unique advantages or features of each MSME. When posting business profiles, the account handler of @umkm.bekasitimur Instagram not only ensures that the designs are visually appealing but also tags the relevant MSME business accounts. These posts are then permanently saved in the Instagram highlights, providing a lasting showcase for each business.

This strategy offers significant benefits. One of them is to provide a strategic spot for potential sponsors interested in collaborating with PUKBT. Sponsors can easily browse through the highlights to understand the diversity and scope of businesses within the PUKBT network. Additionally, visitors to @umkm.bekasitimur's Instagram account can quickly understand the offers of each MSME and find information for purchase. This method of tagging and highlighting content not only boosts the visibility of individual MSMEs but also has the potential to convert visitors into customers, thereby supporting business growth.

Research supports the effectiveness of this approach. According to a study by Rahman et al. (2022), social media strategies that prioritize visual content and active tagging significantly enhance user engagement and visibility, leading to improved marketing outcomes for businesses. Another study by Jones and Kim (2021) emphasizes the importance of strategic content placement in social media marketing, noting that features like Instagram highlights can effectively capture user attention and sustain engagement over time.

The Instagram highlights curated by PUKBT also offer a culturally sensitive and strategically crafted platform that amplifies the visibility and identity of local MSMEs. By emphasizing the unique value propositions of each business, these highlights seamlessly merge cultural identity with modern digital marketing techniques. The organized categorization of businesses into distinct sectors, combined with visually appealing content and active tagging, enhances user engagement and provides a valuable resource for both potential customers and sponsors. This approach not only strengthens the connection between local businesses and their audiences but also promotes business growth by increasing visibility in the highly competitive digital marketplace. Through these efforts, PUKBT positions itself as an innovative organization that honors the cultural heritage of its members while harnessing the power of social media to drive sustainable business growth.

Enhance Community Health and Wellbeing

One of the most engaging features of the @umkm.bekasitimur Instagram account is its collaboration functionality. This feature enables cross-views and cross-visits between @umkm.bekasitimur and members' SME accounts. As illustrated in Figure 10, only SME members who have revamped their Instagram accounts to meet the basic business standards are eligible for this collaboration.

Figure 11. Collaboration reels between @umkm.bekasitimur with a PUKBT member

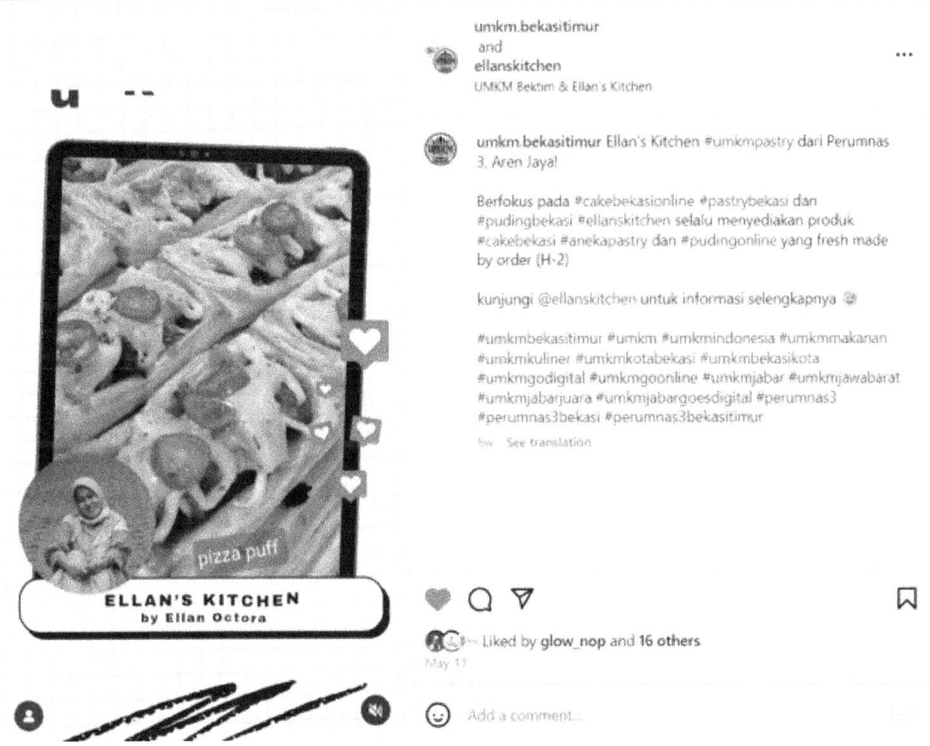

Figure 11 highlights collaborative Reels content from @umkm.bekasitimur with Instagram accounts of PUKBT members. These videos not only highlight the products or services offered by PUKBT members but also prominently feature the business name, followed by the owner's photo and name. This collaborative content strategy enhances the visibility of both accounts involved. For PUKBT members, it serves as a model, demonstrating the benefits and techniques of creating effective Reels content.

The collaborative content concept is highly beneficial. Rahman et al. (2022) found that social media collaborations can significantly increase engagement and visibility for businesses, leading to higher customer conversion rates. This strategy also encourages PUKBT members to upgrade their Instagram profiles to meet professional standards, thereby improving their digital presence and marketing effectiveness.

To collaborate with @umkm.bekasitimur, a member's Instagram account must adhere to the basic business standards set by @umkm.bekasitimur. The requirements for a proper Instagram business account are as follows: the profile photo should be the MSME's business logo, and the Instagram account name should match the business name (separate from any personal Instagram account unless the business account also includes personal activities relevant to the business). The bio should provide essential business information, including contact details for collaboration or customer orders. Instagram highlights and pinned posts should include additional relevant business information, using a color scheme that matches or aligns with the business logo used as the profile photo for the MSME's Instagram business account.

This requirement acts as a motivational tool for other PUKBT members, pushing them to enhance their accounts. By doing so, members not only become eligible for collaboration but also gain a better understanding of what constitutes a well-structured business Instagram account. This aligns with the findings by Jones and Kim (2021), who emphasize the importance of maintaining professional social media profiles for business success.

Moreover, the collaborative Reels content provides a practical demonstration of effective social media marketing. It showcases how PUKBT members can leverage video content to attract more followers and engage with their audience. The tagging and cross-posting practices exemplified by @umkm.bekasitimur help in spreading word-of-mouth digitally, further amplifying the reach of each post.

Overall, the collaboration feature not only enhances the visibility and credibility of individual SMEs but also strengthens the sense of community and shared progress among its members. By fostering collaboration, SMEs can collectively leverage their networks, resources, and knowledge to achieve greater growth. This approach highlights the critical importance of cultivating a professional and engaging online presence, which serves as a key driver of success for small and medium-sized enterprises in the competitive digital landscape. In doing so, SMEs are better positioned to adapt to market trends, attract new customers, and sustain long-term growth in an increasingly interconnected economy.

As illustrated in Figures 8 and 11, the PUKBT Instagram account effectively leverages key Instagram features such as hashtags and location/geotags. These tools are essential for expanding reach and visibility on the platform. Through its Instagram account, PUKBT ensures that MSME members understand how to strategically use relevant hashtags, both broad and niche, to increase the discoverability of their content. Local hashtags, in particular, are invaluable for MSMEs as they help target potential customers within the surrounding area. Moreover, using geotags in posts and stories allows businesses to connect with people searching for content in specific locations, which is especially beneficial for MSMEs with a physical storefront or local presence.

Replicating Digital Marketing Strategies in Other Regions of Indonesian Markets

Through the interviews conducted by the author, the digital marketing strategies discussed in this chapter are currently being piloted for application in 11 additional sub-districts within Bekasi City. The approach being taken involves the implementation of a two-step communication model. This model focuses on strengthening social media marketing skills, particularly Instagram for business, among the coordinators of community groups at the sub-district and village levels.

Figure 12. Strategy to replicate or adapted using two step-flow communication to other regions

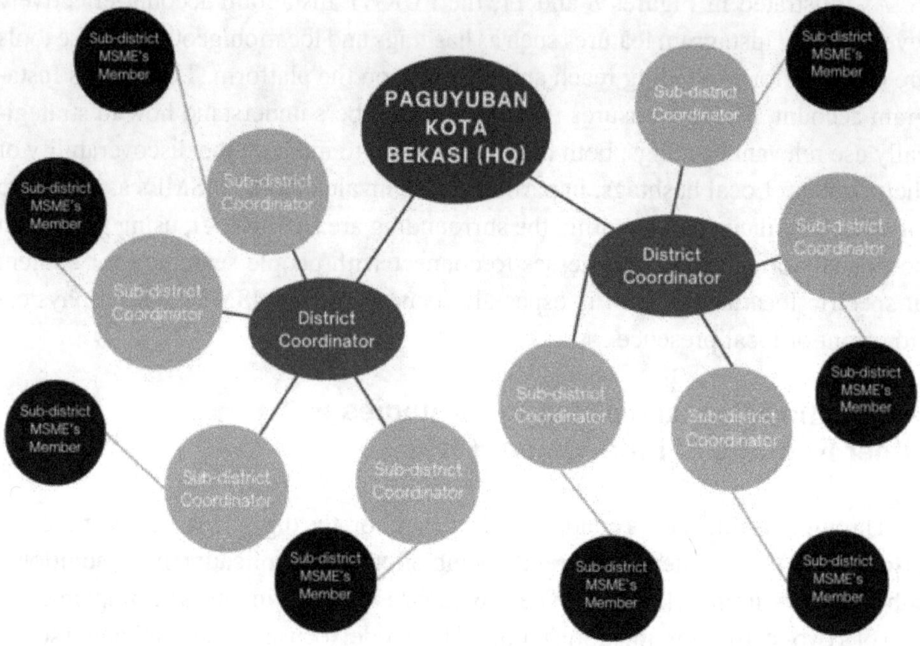

The rationale behind this approach is that by enhancing the soft skills of these community coordinators, they will be empowered to teach and mentor other members of their groups. This cascading effect is expected to create a broader and more effective network of individuals skilled in digital marketing across various regions. The ultimate goal is to build a sustainable, community-driven digital marketing ecosystem where skills and knowledge are continuously shared and propagated.

As illustrated in Figure 12, the two-step flow of communication is applied to the digitalization process among the members of *Paguyuban's UMKM* or MSMEs Association in Bekasi. The Bekasi City's *Paguyuban UMKM* (HQ) serves as the central authority that establishes regulations or directives for district-level coordinators to develop their businesses through social media marketing, particularly via Instagram. Each district coordinator in Bekasi oversees four sub-district coordinators. These sub-district coordinators are then responsible for acquiring the same social media marketing skills to train and duplicate these capabilities among the Paguyuban members in each sub-district under their supervision.

It is not only expected that they develop equivalent technical skills in social media marketing, but the author has also found several challenges in the implementation, including:

1. **Time constraints.** Time constraints pose a significant challenge for district and sub-district coordinators, who are also entrepreneurs running their own businesses. As MSME owners, they often face limitations in human resources, production processes, and other operational needs, which can hinder their ability to manage time effectively. Given that their MSME business is their primary source of income, it naturally becomes their top priority. Therefore, those who wish to continuously sharpen their social media marketing skills and dedicate time to training other MSME members require a high level of commitment and dedication.
2. **Resource availability.** This is another significant challenge for many MSMEs, including those in leadership roles. Limited access to financial and technological resources can hinder the adoption and effective use of social media marketing platforms like Instagram. For instance, insufficient internet connectivity, particularly in sub-district areas, can impede the use of high-quality smartphones or computers, including applications like Instagram, which are essential tools for effective social media marketing.
3. **Digital literacy.** While social media marketing requires a certain level of proficiency with digital platforms, not all coordinators or MSME members possess the necessary skills. This digital gap can hinder the knowledge transfer process, as some members may need more time and assistance to grasp the technical aspects of social media marketing.
4. **Cultural mindset.** Some coordinators and MSME members may still prioritize traditional methods of business promotion, viewing digital marketing as secondary or optional. Shifting this mindset toward embracing digital strategies as a core business function can be a significant challenge, particularly for older generations who may be less familiar with or resistant to technological changes.
5. **Consistency in training.** To ensure the long-term success of this model, consistent and continuous training is essential. However, maintaining this consistency across different coordinators and sub-districts can be difficult due to varying levels of motivation, interest, and available time.
6. **Monitoring and evaluation.** Effectively tracking the progress of each coordinator's and sub-coordinator's social media marketing skills development and their ability to transfer this knowledge to others is crucial. Without proper monitoring systems, it can be difficult to gauge the overall success of the training program and identify areas for improvement.
7. **Scalability of the model.** While the two-step communication model has shown initial promise in Bekasi, expanding it to other districts or regions may reveal unforeseen challenges, particularly when accounting for local differences in culture, infrastructure, or business practices.

In addition to addressing the technical challenges of social media marketing, it is equally important to consider the soft skills required by district and sub-district coordinators to effectively implement the two-step communication model in the digitalization process. While technical proficiency is critical, soft skills play a crucial role in ensuring the long-term success of this strategy. These include:

1. **Leadership and Communication Skills**. As leaders of their respective districts or sub-districts, coordinators must be able to effectively communicate the importance of digital marketing to their members. This involves not only conveying information clearly but also inspiring and motivating others to embrace social media marketing as a valuable tool for business growth. Strong leadership ensures that coordinators can guide their team members in learning and applying the necessary skills.
2. **Empathy and Patience.** Given the varying levels of digital literacy among *Paguyuban* members, coordinators must possess a high degree of empathy and patience when teaching these new skills. Some members may struggle with understanding or adopting the technology, and it is essential that coordinators are supportive and willing to provide extra time and assistance as needed.
3. **Collaboration and Teamwork.** The success of the two-step communication model relies heavily on collaboration and teamwork among coordinators and their team members. Coordinators must foster a sense of cooperation, ensuring that everyone is working toward the same goal of business development through digital marketing. This also includes the ability to delegate tasks and responsibilities effectively, as coordinators themselves may be limited by time and resources.
4. **Problem-solving Skills.** Digitalization comes with its own set of challenges, from technical difficulties to logistical issues. Coordinators must be equipped with strong problem-solving skills to navigate these obstacles and provide practical solutions, whether it's troubleshooting social media platforms, finding workarounds for limited resources, or addressing any interpersonal conflicts within the team.
5. **Adaptability.** In the fast-paced world of digital marketing, trends and platforms are constantly evolving. Coordinators must be adaptable, open to learning new skills, and quick to adjust strategies as needed to stay relevant in the digital space. This flexibility will allow them to effectively lead their teams in navigating the changing landscape of social media marketing.
6. **Mentorship and Coaching Abilities.** As key figures in the learning process, coordinators must act as mentors and coaches to their team members. This requires the ability to provide constructive feedback, encourage continuous learning, and guide individuals in developing their own digital marketing capabilities. The

role of a mentor extends beyond teaching technical skills—it involves nurturing confidence and a sense of ownership among team members.

7. **Time Management and Organizational Skills.** Given the multiple responsibilities that coordinators must balance—running their own MSMEs while also overseeing the training and development of others—strong time management and organizational skills are essential. Coordinators need to effectively allocate their time and resources to ensure both their business and their role in the *Paguyuban* are functioning efficiently.

By equipping district and sub-district coordinators with these soft skills, the two-step communication model can be more effectively implemented. This ensures that not only are technical skills passed down through the *Paguyuban* network, but that the process itself is managed with the necessary emotional intelligence, leadership, and adaptability to overcome challenges and foster sustainable growth in digital marketing skills among MSME members.

Leveraging Instagram Community Account

Although PUKBT has effectively utilized Instagram features as discussed, there are still areas that can be optimized to further enhance the digitalization of social media marketing. Below are some suggestions to maximize PUKBT's Instagram account:

1. **Content Customization for Local Markets.** Identify the unique strengths or features of each sub-district or district and highlight them through PUKBT's Instagram account. Currently, the Instagram account targets 'MSMEs' as its followers, positioning itself as a source of information for various MSME training sessions. However, by producing content that showcases the distinct advantages of these areas, the Instagram account can expand its reach to become a key information hub for residents of the districts and sub-districts. The author envisions this Instagram account serving as a catalyst for fostering a strong ecosystem among the residents of East Bekasi.
2. **Consistent Brand Storytelling.** One of the most effective ways to build a strong digital presence is through consistent storytelling. Coordinators can emphasize the importance of crafting a cohesive brand narrative that reflects the values and mission of each MSME. This can be achieved by maintaining consistent messaging, visual themes, and a narrative that aligns with the overall business goals. Encouraging MSMEs to share their journeys, challenges, and successes via Instagram posts, Stories, or even Reels helps build a personal connection with their audience. Coordinators can guide members in crafting compelling

stories that not only promote their products but also emotionally engage their followers.

3. **Continuous Learning and Adapting to Instagram Trends**. Since Instagram trends are constantly evolving, it is crucial for MSME members to stay updated. Coordinators should foster a culture of continuous learning by encouraging their teams to regularly explore new features, study successful marketing trends, and adapt their strategies accordingly. This may include attending social media workshops, following digital marketing influencers, or subscribing to resources that provide insights into emerging Instagram trends. Coordinators themselves can lead by example, staying informed about the latest trends and sharing their knowledge with their teams.

The author observes that by optimizing hard skills, soft skills, and the features available on the Instagram account of *Paguyuban*'s MSME*s,* there is potential for a more comprehensive development of the digitalization process for each MSME at the local level. To confirm if its best to prioritize hard skills or soft skills, based on observations and interviews conducted, the digitalization process must begin with the soft skills or the mindset of each MSME individual. This mindset then reflected in their business strategy. The process of forming their business strategy, mapping out development priorities, and allocating their time becomes the foundation upon which their hard skills are honed.

As development coordinators, the district and sub-district level *Paguyuban* MSME coordinators must not only stay updated on social media marketing features but also be responsive to the efforts made by the members. These efforts should be appreciated and, in this case, highlighted effectively through the PUKBT Instagram account. This approach ensures that the digitalization process is supported from both a technical and personal growth perspective.

Although this chapter highlights how PUKBT has taken commendable steps to initiate the digitalization of business Instagram accounts, there appears to be a notable gap in the evaluation process. The question arises: how does PUKBT assess the progress of MSMEs after their Instagram accounts have been revamped? What are the next steps once their profiles are polished? Empowerment programs like these should ideally have a sustainable and long-term plan in place, ensuring continuous support and development for MSMEs beyond the initial improvements. This observation serves as constructive feedback for PUKBT to consider refining its approach, particularly in establishing a more structured follow-up and evaluation process to ensure lasting impact.

Limitations and Mitigating Bias in Long-Term Evaluation of Digitalization MSME in Social Media Marketing Strategies

In considering the long-term applicability and effectiveness of the digital marketing strategies outlined in this chapter, it is essential to recognize and address potential biases that may affect the evaluation of these strategies across different regions and time frames. First, acknowledging inherent biases in current evaluation approaches allows for a more critical and reflective stance on the findings presented. It is crucial to integrate diverse data sources—both quantitative and qualitative—to provide a more comprehensive view of the strategies' effectiveness, ensuring that the analysis captures the full spectrum of influencing factors. Furthermore, incorporating longitudinal studies can offer valuable insights into how these strategies evolve over time, helping to identify both sustained impacts and areas that may require adaptation or recalibration.

A comparative analysis across various regions is also necessary to understand the contextual factors that may affect the success of these strategies. This approach avoids overgeneralization and provides a more nuanced perspective on digital marketing's applicability across different socio-economic and cultural landscapes. Moreover, establishing feedback loops for continuous improvement allows stakeholders to actively participate in refining these strategies, ensuring they remain relevant and effective in dynamically changing market environments.

While the two-step communication model proposed for replicating these strategies in other regions of Indonesia offers a promising framework, it is essential to critically evaluate its limitations. Over-reliance on key influencers, for instance, may not always result in broad-based community engagement. Exploring alternative or complementary models could enhance the adaptability and effectiveness of these strategies. Ethical considerations and inclusivity must also be factored into the analysis to ensure that the strategies are accessible and equitable for all demographic groups, especially those with limited digital literacy or access. Addressing these dimensions adds depth to the evaluation, ensuring it is not only robust but also socially responsible.

Finally, recommending future research directions that address identified gaps will provide a pathway for ongoing inquiry and refinement. Investigating emerging digital platforms, alternative communication models, or targeted strategies for underserved communities could yield further valuable insights. By integrating these critical considerations, this paper offers a balanced, comprehensive, and forward-looking perspective on the digital marketing strategies discussed, aiming to provide a reliable foundation for future application and study.

CONCLUSION

This study examined the digital transformation efforts of Paguyuban UMKM Kecamatan Bekasi Timur (PUKBT), a community organization supporting MSMEs in East Bekasi District, Indonesia. MSMEs contribute up to 60% of Indonesia's GDP, yet around 70% face difficulties in adopting digital marketing. Focusing on East Bekasi, the study explored the digital marketing strategies of MSMEs under PUKBT. The findings show that PUKBT employed a two-step communication model, using Instagram and interpersonal communication to boost participation. To replicate this approach, district coordinators must develop both hard skills (social media proficiency) and soft skills (leadership, adaptability) to effectively support their members.

Moreover, optimizing Instagram features is key to MSME growth. Coordinators should prioritize content customization, emphasizing the unique strengths of each area, and use consistent brand storytelling to enhance engagement. Staying updated on Instagram trends ensures that digital marketing efforts remain effective. This research highlights how the close-knit nature of Paguyuban, within Indonesia's cultural context, can facilitate digital transformation. Future research should explore broader applications of this model to strengthen MSMEs and local economies through both interpersonal relationships and digital platforms like Instagram.

REFERENCES

Agung, D. P., & Wijaya, A. (2019). Peran Paguyuban Duta Wisata "Sekargading" dalam Mengembangkan Pariwisata di Kabupaten Batang. *IJSED: Indonesian Jurnal of Sociology, Education, and Development*, 1(1), 60–70. DOI: 10.52483/ijsed.v1i1.6

Barlan, Z. A., & Kolopaking, L. (2014). Peran Paguyuban dalam Pembangunan Kawasan Desa. *Sodality: Jurnal Sosiologi Pedesaan*, 2(2), 115–123. DOI: 10.22500/sodality.v2i2.9419

Biroli, A. (2022). Strategi Pengembangan Paguyuban Potre Madhura Melalui Pendidikan Jamu di Pulau Madura. *Resiprokal: Jurnal Riset Sosiologi Progresif Aktual*, 4(2), 250–261. DOI: 10.29303/resiprokal.v4i2.226

Boiral, O., Talbot, D., & Paillé, P. (2013). Leading by Example: A Model of Organizational Citizenship Behavior for the Environment. *Business Strategy and the Environment*, 24(6), 1–27. DOI: 10.1002/bse.1835

Christens, B. D., & Lin, C. S. (2014). Influences of Community and Organizational Participation, Social Support, and Sense of Community on Psychological Empowerment: Income as Moderator. *Family and Consumer Sciences Research Journal*, 42(3), 211–223. DOI: 10.1111/fcsr.12056

dos Reis, J. C. G., Amorim, M., Melao, N., & Matos, P. (2018). Digital Transformation: A Literatur Review and Guidelines for Future Research. *Trends and Advances in Information Systems and Technologies*, 1, 411–421. DOI: 10.1007/978-3-319-77703-0_41

Dwiningrum, N. R., Rahmawaty, P., & Ismawanto, T. (2018). Peran Paguyuban di Balikpapan dalam Mendukung Integrasi Sosial. *JSHP: Jurnal Sosial Humaniora Dan Pendidikan*, 2(1), 77–84. DOI: 10.32487/jshp.v2i1.295

Ellyta, E., Mustakim, U., & Rizieq, R. (2019). Pengembangan Adopsi Inovasi melalui Jaringan Komunikasi. *ZMIP: Zira'ah Majalah Ilmiah Pertanian*, 44(1), 83. Advance online publication. DOI: 10.31602/zmip.v44i1.1667

Fitriyani, R. (2012). Peranan Paguyuban Tionghoa Purbalingga dalam Pelestarian Tradisi Cap Go Meh. *Komunitas: International Journal of Indonesian Society and Culture*, 4(1), 73–81. DOI: 10.15294/komunitas.v4i1.2398

Haim-Litevsky, D., Komemi, R., & Lipskaya-Velikovsky, L. (2023). Sense of Belonging, Meaningful Daily Life Participation, and Well-Being: Integrated Investigation. [IJERPH]. *International Journal of Environmental Research and Public Health*, 20(5), 1–16. DOI: 10.3390/ijerph20054121 PMID: 36901132

Hartini, S. (2018). Peran Paguyuban dalam Peningkatan Motivasi Kewirausahaan Pengrajin Batik. *Jurnal Ilmiah UPT P2M STKIP Siliwangi, 5*(1), 21–26. DOI: 10.22460/p2m.v5i1p21-26.786

Hattke, F., & Hattke, J. (2019). Lead by example? The dissemination of ethical values through authentic leader inspiration. *International Journal of Public Leadership*, 15(4), 224–237. DOI: 10.1108/IJPL-06-2019-0034

Herari, N. (2023). Customer Journey on Digital Omnichannel Local Culinary MSME "Dapur Buk Rien" (A PESO and REAN Model Approach with Qualitative Network Analysis) [Master's Thesis, LSPR Institute of Communication & Business]. https://doi.org/DOI: DOI: 10.13140/RG.2.2.20193.28001

Hodijah, C. (2023). Optimalisasi Digital Marketing Sebagai Media Pemasaran Produk Dan Sekaligus Pelestarian Seni Budaya Sunda Paguyuban Ranggon Uyut Di Desa Cikeruh Jatinangor. *JPM: Jurnal Pengabdian Mandiri, 2*(1), 29–34. https://bajangjournal.com/index.php/JPM/article/view/4660

INDEF. (2024). *Peran Platform Digital terhadap Pengembangan UMKM di Indonesia.*

KBBI. (2023). *Paguyuban (KBBI).* Kbbi.Web.Id. https://www.kbbi.web.id/Paguyuban

Kemlu, R. I. (2023). *5 Reasons Why You Should Invest in Indonesia Today!*https://kemlu.go.id/vancouver/en/news/25150/5-reasons-why-you-should-invest-in-indonesia-today

Kuswanto, K., & Anderson, I. (2023). Structural Model of Community Participation in Rural Development in Jambi Province, Indonesia. *Population and Economics*, 7(2), 115–141. DOI: 10.3897/popecon.7.e97189

Moerdijat, L. (2023, August 4). *Segera Atasi Kendala dalam Transformasi Digital di Sektor UMKM.* MPR RI. https://www.mpr.go.id/berita/Segera-Atasi-Kendala-dalam-Transformasi-Digital-di-Sektor-UMKM

Nabila, F., Huda, S., & Utami, A. F. (2023). Pembentukan Paguyuban sebagai Wadah Interaksi antar Pelaku UMKM di Desa Kedungpari. *Jurnal Pengabdian Masyarakat Nusantara (Pengabmas Nusantara), 5*(3).

Nugraha, A. Z. (2014). Peran Kapital Sosial dalam Meningkatkan Kesejahteraan Anggota Paguyuban: Studi Kasus pada Ikatan Silaturahmi Keluarga Putra Bengawan (IKPB). *Empati: Jurnal Ilmu Kesejahteraan Sosial*, 3(1), 8–21. DOI: 10.15408/empati.v3i1.9759

Pal, M. (2021). A Literature Review to Assess The Importance of Community Participation and Health Promotion in Community Development. *IJRSFP: International Journal of Recent Scientific Research*, 12(6), 42043–42048. DOI: 10.24327/ijrsr.2021.1206.6015

Permana, I., Asral, A., Kodratila, E. Y., & Putra, M. (2023). Literasi Digital Marketing Sebagai Upaya Peningkatan Penjualan Pada Paguyuban UMKM Kecamatan Serang Baru Kabupaten Bekasi. *Joong-Ki: Jurnal Pengabdian Masyarakat*, 2(1), 117–123. DOI: 10.56799/joongki.v2i1.1295

Petrosyan, A. (2024). *Worldwide Digital Population 2024.*

Putnam, R. D. (2001). *Bowling Alone: The Collapse and Revival of American Community* (1st ed., Vol. 1). Simon & Schuster.

Rahman, W. N. A., Mutum, D. S., & Ghazali, E. (2022). Consumer Engagement With Visual Content on Instagram: Impact of Different Features of Posts by Prominent Brands. *International Journal of E-Services and Mobile Applications*, 14(1), 1–21. DOI: 10.4018/IJESMA.295960

Sanchez, R., Carvajal, A. L. P., Fransisco, C., Pagtalunan, E. C., Alon-Rabbon, K., Llego, J., Sanchez, A. M. P., Pangilinan, A. M., & Sanchez, J. J. D. (2024). *The Power of Influence: Leading by Example for Greater Role and Productivity* (1st ed., Vol. 1). ETCOR Educational Research Center Research., https://etcor.org/book-publications/the-power-of-influence-leading-by-example-for-greater-role-and-productivity

Sesic, M. D. DeruSimić, L., & Deru, J.-P. (2010). Cultural diversity-based projects and their effects on sustainable development. In *The Sustainability of Cultural Diversity. Nations, Cities and Organizations* (pp. 1–26). Edvard Elgar Publishers.

Shiddiqah, R., & Adi, K. R. (2023). Peran Paguyuban terhadap Pertumbuhan UMKM di Kawasan Sentral Industri Tahu Takwa Desa Tinalan Kota Kediri. *Jurnal Integrasi Dan Harmoni Inovatif Ilmu-Ilmu Sosial (JIHI3S), 3*(12), 1346–1355. DOI: 10.17977/um063v3i12p1346-1355

Sun, Y. (2024). A Qualitative Study of the Psychological Effects of Motivational Quotes. *Proceeding of the 3rd International Conference on Literature, Language, and Culture Development*, 27–33. DOI: 10.54254/2753-7064/33/20240042

Versland, T., & Erickson, J. L. (2017). Leading by example: A case study of the influence of principal self-efficacy on collective efficacy. *Cogent Education*, 4(1), 1286765. https://www.tandfonline.com/doi/full/10.1080/2331186X.2017.1286765. DOI: 10.1080/2331186X.2017.1286765 von Kameke, L. (2024). *Share of Micro, Small, and Medium-sized Enterprises (MSMEs) in Total Number of Enterprises in Southeast Asia in 2022, by Country.* https://www.statista.com/statistics/1317161/asean-share-of-micro-small-medium-sized-businesses-by-country/#:~:text=At%20the%20end%20of%202019,of%20MSMEs%2C%20over%2065%20million

Wangqu, J., & Neto, L. P. (2023). Verification of Two-Step Flow Model in the Process of City International Image Communication Based on Data Mining and Empirical Analysis. *MDPI: Journalism and Media*, 4(4), 1039–1047. DOI: 10.3390/journalmedia4040066

Xu, B., & Li, D. (2014). An Empirical Study of the Motivations for Content Contribution and Community Participation in Wikipedia. *Information & Management*, 52(3), 275–286. Advance online publication. DOI: 10.1016/j.im.2014.12.003

Ye, Z., Shang, X., Shafait, Z., & Xu, Y. (2022). Impact of Leading by Example on Employees' Organizational and Job Psychological Ownership: A Moderated Mediation Study. *Frontiers in Psychology*, 13, 888653. Advance online publication. DOI: 10.3389/fpsyg.2022.888653 PMID: 35874387

ADDITIONAL READING

Ali, M. (2021). *Remote Work and Sustainable Changes for the Future of Global Business.* IGI Global. https://www.igi-global.com/book/remote-work-sustainable-changes-future/264375

Ali, M. (2022). *Future Role of Sustainable Innovative Technologies in Crisis Management.* IGI Global. https://www.igi-global.com/book/future-role-sustainable-innovative-technologies/281281

Ali, M. (2023). *Shifting Paradigms in the Rapidly Developing Global Digital Ecosystem: A GCC Perspective.* In Digital Entrepreneurship and Co-Creating Value Through Digital Encounters (pp. 145-166). IGI Global. https://www.igi-global.com/chapter/shifting-paradigms-in-the-rapidly-developing-global-digital-ecosystem/323525

Ali, M. (2023). T*axonomy of Industry 4.0 Technologies in Digital Entrepreneurship and Co-Creating Value.* In *Digital Entrepreneurship and Co-Creating Value Through Digital Encounters* (pp. 24–55). IGI Global., https://www.igi-global.com/chapter/taxonomy-of-industry-40-technologies-in-digital-entrepreneurship-and-co-creating-value/323520 DOI: 10.4018/978-1-6684-7416-7.ch002

Ali, M., & Wood-Harper, T. (2021). *Fostering Communication and Learning with Underutilized Technologies in Higher Education*. IGI Global. https://www.igi-global.com/book/fostering-communication-learning-underutilized-technologies/244593

Ali, M., Wood-Harper, T., & Kutar, M. (2023). Multi-Perspectives of Contemporary Digital Transformation Models of Complex Innovation Management. In *Digital Entrepreneurship and Co-Creating Value Through Digital Encounters* (pp. 79–96). IGI Global., https://www.igi-global.com/chapter/multi-perspectives-of-contemporary-digital-transformation-models-of-complex-innovation-management/323522 DOI: 10.4018/978-1-6684-7416-7.ch004

Ali, M. B. (2021). Internet of Things (IoT) to Foster Communication and Information Sharing: A Case of UK Higher Education. In Ali, M. B., & Wood-Harper, T. (Eds.), *Fostering Communication and Learning With Underutilized Technologies in Higher Education* (pp. 1–20). IGI Global., https://www.igi-global.com/chapter/internet-of-things-iot-to-foster-communication-and-information-sharing/262718/ DOI: 10.4018/978-1-7998-4846-2.ch001

Ali, M. B., & Wood-Harper, T. (2022). Artificial Intelligence (AI) as a Decision-Making Tool to Control Crisis Situations. In *Future Role of Sustainable Innovative Technologies in Crisis Management*. IGI Global., https://www.igi-global.com/chapter/artificial-intelligence-ai-as-a-decision-making-tool-to-control-crisis-situations/298931 DOI: 10.4018/978-1-7998-9815-3.ch006

Ali, M. B., Wood-Harper, T., & Ramlogan, R. (2020). A Framework Strategy to Overcome Trust Issues on Cloud Computing Adoption in Higher Education. In Modern Principles, Practices, and Algorithms for Cloud Security (pp. 162-183). IGI Global. https://www.igi-global.com/chapter/a-framework-strategy-to-overcome-trust-issues-on-cloud-computing-adoption-in-higher-education/238907/

Chapter 3
The Influence of Social Media Influencers on College Students' Consumer Behavior: Exploring Digital Marketing Engagement

V. Mohana Sundari
https://orcid.org/0000-0003-3144-4600
SRM Institute of Science and Technology, India

ABSTRACT

This research explores the intricate dynamics between social media influencers and college students, focusing on the impact of digital marketing strategies on consumer behavior. In an era dominated by social media platforms, understanding the preferences and responses of college students to digital marketing content, especially that endorsed by influencers, becomes crucial for effective engagement. The study aims to analyze the effectiveness of social media influencers in promoting products/services to college students, examining factors influencing students' engagement, and identifying the broader impact on purchasing behavior and brand loyalty. Employing a mixed-methods approach, the research combines quantitative analysis of social media engagement metrics with qualitative insights gathered through surveys and interviews. The outcomes of this study are anticipated to contribute valuable insights for marketers seeking to tailor their digital marketing strategies to effectively resonate with and influence the consumer behavior of college students.

DOI: 10.4018/979-8-3373-0086-3.ch003

Copyright © 2025, IGI Global. Copying or distributing in print or electronic forms without written permission of IGI Global is prohibited.

I. INTRODUCTION

In an era dominated by digital connectivity, social media has transcended its initial purpose of connecting individuals and has become an integral part of everyday life, especially for college students. The ubiquity of smartphones and the proliferation of social media platforms have transformed how young adults communicate, interact, and consume information. Among college students, in particular, social media plays a central role in shaping not only their social lives but also their consumer behaviors.

Within this digital landscape, social media influencers have emerged as powerful agents of influence, wielding significant sway over the purchasing decisions of their followers. These influencers, often individuals who have amassed large followings on platforms such as Instagram, YouTube, and TikTok, have become key players in the realm of digital marketing. Brands recognize the potential of partnering with influencers to reach and engage with their target audiences in more authentic and impactful ways.

The influence of social media influencers on consumer behavior has been extensively studied across various demographics. However, the impact of these influencers on college students, a demographic characterized by its active online presence and susceptibility to peer influence, warrants specific attention. College students represent a lucrative market for brands, but they also pose unique challenges in terms of reaching and resonating with them amidst the noise of social media.

Understanding how social media influencers affect the consumer behavior of college students is not only academically intriguing but also practically relevant for marketers, educators, and policymakers. By unraveling the complex interplay between digital marketing, social media influencers, and college students' consumer behaviors, this study aims to shed light on an increasingly significant aspect of contemporary marketing dynamics.

A. Background

The pervasive use of social media platforms among college students has transformed the way they engage with information, brands, and each other. Platforms such as Instagram, TikTok, and YouTube have become virtual hubs where students not only socialize but also seek information and make purchasing decisions. Concurrently, the influence of social media influencers has soared, becoming a powerful factor in shaping the choices of the college demographic. As a result, understanding the dynamics of these influences is paramount for marketers seeking to establish meaningful connections with college students.

B. Research Problem

This study addresses the pressing need to comprehend the impact of digital marketing strategies, specifically those involving social media influencers, on the consumer behavior of college students. While the influence of social media influencers is acknowledged, there exists a significant gap in understanding the nuanced preferences and responses of college students to various digital marketing approaches. Unraveling these intricacies is essential for developing targeted and effective digital marketing strategies.

C. Objectives

- To evaluate the effectiveness of social media influencers in promoting products/services to college students.
- To investigate the factors that influence college students' engagement with digital marketing content on social media platforms.
- To identify Impact on Consumer Behavior: Explore and identify the broader impact of digital marketing on the purchasing behavior and brand loyalty of college students.

D. Significance of the Study

Understanding the influence of social media influencers on college students' consumer behavior has significant implications for marketers, educators, and policymakers. For marketers, insights from this study can inform more targeted and effective digital marketing strategies aimed at engaging with college students. Educators can use these findings to incorporate discussions on digital literacy and advertising ethics into their curriculum. Policymakers may also use this research to develop regulations to protect consumers, particularly vulnerable demographics like college students, from potentially harmful marketing practices on social media platforms.

By addressing these objectives, this study seeks to contribute to the existing body of knowledge on digital marketing, social media influencers, and consumer behavior while providing actionable insights for various stakeholders.

II. LITERATURE REVIEW

A. Digital Marketing Trends Among College Students

Overview of Digital Marketing Channels

College students, as digital natives, exhibit distinct preferences in their interaction with digital marketing channels. Social media platforms, email marketing, and mobile apps emerge as primary channels of engagement. Studies have indicated a growing reliance on visual content, such as videos and images, as a favored mode of communication, shaping the landscape of digital marketing strategies targeted at this demographic.

Factors Influencing Engagement

The engagement of college students with digital marketing content is a multi-faceted phenomenon. Personalization, authenticity, and relevance are identified as key factors influencing their interaction. Tailoring content to align with students' interests, values, and aspirations has been shown to significantly enhance engagement levels. Additionally, the timing and frequency of content delivery play a pivotal role in capturing and sustaining their attention.

B. Social Media Influencers and Their Role

Definition and Characteristics

Social media influencers wield a unique influence on the preferences and behaviors of college students. These individuals, often with a substantial following on platforms like Instagram, TikTok, and YouTube, possess the ability to shape opinions and purchasing decisions. Characteristics such as relatability, authenticity, and niche expertise contribute to their effectiveness as influential figures in the digital realm. Understanding these traits is crucial for comprehending the impact of influencer-led digital marketing.

Impact on Consumer Behavior

A body of previous research underscores the profound impact that social media influencers have on consumer behavior. Influencers serve as both content creators and trusted advisors, guiding their followers through purchasing decisions. Studies indicate that recommendations from influencers often carry a weight comparable to recommendations from peers, showcasing the transformative influence of these digital trendsetters on the consumer choices of college students.

C. College Students as a Target Market

Unique Characteristics and Preferences

College students represent a dynamic and diverse consumer group, shaped by factors such as age, lifestyle, and educational pursuits. Understanding their unique characteristics, including financial constraints, desire for experiences, and digital fluency, is pivotal for crafting effective marketing strategies. Tailoring campaigns to resonate with their aspirations and challenges is imperative for successful engagement.

Role of Peer Influence and Social Networks

Peer influence and social networks play a pivotal role in shaping the consumer behavior of college students. Social validation, recommendations from friends, and the shared experience of consumption contribute significantly to their decision-making processes. Social media platforms serve as not only a space for individual expression but also a communal arena where collective opinions and trends emerge, impacting the purchasing decisions of this interconnected demographic.

Recent literature on the effect of social media influencers (SMIs) on university students' customer conduct well-known shows a complicated interplay of factors that pressure engagement and purchasing choices. One of the most outstanding components is the perceived accept as true with and credibility of influencers, which substantially impacts purchaser behavior. Arora, Bansal, and Sharma (2021) emphasize that when influencers are viewed as actual and informed in a particular niche, they construct accept as true with their audience, making it much more likely for college students to follow their guidelines. This credibility often stems from long-time period engagement and consistency in content, creating a sense of familiarity and loyalty among fans.

Further research with the aid of Hwang and Zhang (2023) specializes in authenticity, noting that scholars are specially attracted to influencers who seem proper and relatable, instead of folks that are openly industrial. This aligns with the concept of parasocial relationships, in which followers feel a private reference to influencers, even if the relationship is one-sided. This emotional bond makes students much more likely to adopt the influencers' advised manufacturers or products, because it looks like a advice from a friend rather than a paid commercial.

Another significant subject matter in recent studies is the function of emotional engagement, particularly via storytelling, which has verified powerful in fostering a deeper connection between influencers and their audience. Lim, Tan, and Yeo (2022) highlight that influencers who use storytelling strategies now not most effective seize attention however additionally evoke emotions, making their followers much more likely to interact with the content and act on their hints.

The impact of social evidence on the formation of consumer behavior among college students is also important. When students let influencers use or endorse the product, it acts as a form of social loyalty. This increases the likelihood of buying through peer influence, as students are particularly sensitive to trends and shared ideas within their social circles (Kim, Lee, & Park, 2022).

Furthermore, the post-pandemic digital environment has further strengthened the role of influencers in marketing. With so many students spending so much time on social media, their reliance on influencers for awareness and brand engagement has increased. Micro-influencers in particular have gained traction due to their niche audience and perceived authenticity, which leads to greater engagement with smaller groups of followers (Sokolova & Kefi, 2020).

All of this literature focuses on the role of SMI in shaping college students' consumer behavior. By leveraging trust, authenticity, emotional engagement, and social proof, influencers are able to effectively drive digital marketing engagement and influence purchasing decisions in a way that traditional advertising often does cannot be done.

Ethical Concerns

Recent research highlights the ethical concerns and psychological impact of social media influencers (SMIs) on college students. The main ethical issue is the lack of transparency of sponsored resources. Many influencers do not disclose paid associations, resulting in deceptive marketing, which destroys trust and misleads students (Abidin, 2020; Campbell & Grimm, 2019). In addition, influencers often promote an inauthentic lifestyle, creating consumer pressure and materialism among students (Boerman et al., 2017).

From a psychological perspective, SMI can negatively impact students by promoting social comparisons, leading to low self-esteem and body image issues (de Vries & Kühne, 2015). The FOMO (Fear of Missing Out) effect can increase social anxiety and financial stress, as students feel pressured to adopt lifestyles and products promoted by influencers (Przybylski et al., 2013). This repetitive exposure can exacerbate mental health problems, especially when influencers model unattainable lifestyles or promotion.

III. RESEARCH METHODOLOGY

A. Research Design

This study employs a mixed-methods research design to comprehensively investigate the impact of digital marketing, particularly through social media influencers, on the consumer behavior of college students. The integration of quantitative and qualitative methods allows for a more nuanced understanding of engagement patterns and underlying motivations. Quantitative data will be collected to analyze engagement metrics, while qualitative insights will be gathered through interviews, offering a holistic perspective on the subject.

B. Sampling

The sampling strategy involves random selection of college students from diverse backgrounds and academic disciplines. This approach ensures a representative and varied sample, capturing a spectrum of perspectives and experiences. The inclusion of students with different interests, majors, and demographic characteristics contributes to the generalizability of findings.

C. Data Collection

Analysis of Social Media Engagement Metrics:

Social media platforms utilized by the target demographic will be identified.

Engagement metrics, including likes, shares, comments, and click-through rates, will be collected and analyzed.

Historical data will be examined to identify trends and patterns in engagement.

D. Data Analysis

Data analysis is a process of inspecting, cleaning, transforming, and modeling data with the goal of discovering useful information, drawing conclusions, and supporting decision-making. In the context of a study, data analysis is a crucial step that helps researchers to interpret the results and draw meaningful insights from the collected data.

Table 1. Descriptive analysis of the demographic variables

Gender	Frequency	Percentage
Female	130	34.21
Male	250	65.79
Total	380	100.00
Age		0.00
18-25	106	27.89
26-35	89	23.42
36-45	82	21.58
46-55	58	15.26
56 and older	45	11.84
Total	380	100.00
Marital Status		0.00
Married	98	25.79
Single	282	74.21
Total	380	100.00

In this study, the participant demographic is characterized by a gender distribution of 66% men and 34% women. In terms of age, the largest segment comprises individuals between 18-25 years old, constituting 27.89% of the respondents. Following closely, those aged between 26-35 make up 23%, while the 36-45 age group comprises 21.58%. Additionally, there are smaller cohorts within the age brackets of 46-55 (15.26%) and 56 and above (11.84%). Regarding marital status, the majority of participants identify as single, accounting for 74.21% of the respondents, while the remaining 25.79% report being married.

H1: The use of social media influencers significantly influences college students' perceptions based on gender

Table 2. T test

T test					
Brand Loyalty		**N**	**Mean**	**T**	**Sig.**
	Female	130	2.367	3.587	0.001
	Male	250	3.456		

The results of the t-test indicated that there was a significant difference between the male and female participants, as evidenced by the p-value of 0.001, which is less than the set significance level of 0.05. This finding supports the hypothesis

(H1) that there is statistically significant difference in terms of gender factor in the perception of social media influencers.

H2: There is no significant difference in the purchasing behavior and brand loyalty among different levels of exposure to digital marketing

Table 3. ANOVA

ANOVA					
Retro marketing strategies					
	Sum of Squares	**df**	**Mean Square**	**F**	**Sig.**
Between Groups	4290.229	27	158.897	15.159	0.002
Within Groups	4370.953	353	10.482		
Total	8661.182	380			

The results of the Anova test on the age status showed that there is a significant difference in the purchasing behavior and brand loyalty among different levels of exposure to digital marketing, with a p-value of 0.002, which is less than 0.05.

Regression Analysis for the Factors That Influence College Students' Engagement With Digital Marketing Content on Social Media Platforms

Table 4. Regression table summary

Coefficients[a]					
Model	**Unstandardized Coefficients**		**Standardized Coefficients**	**t**	**Sig.**
	B	**Std. Error**	**Beta**		
(Constant)	4.335	.735		6.313	<0.001**
Content relevance	1.334	.078	.613	17.567	<0.001**
Visual appeal	.731	.122	.230	5.112	<0.001**
Relatability	1.266	.089	.534	14.102	<0.001**

a. Dependent Variable: students engagement

The above coefficient table values indicate that the, independent variables of such as content relevance, visual appeal, and relatability, significantly influence college students' engagement with digital marketing content. The Linear Regression equation has the form Y= a + bX, where Y is the dependent variable (that's the variable that goes on the Y axis), X is the independent variable and, b is the slope of the line and a is the y-intercept.

The extracted regression equation is

Students engagement = -4.335+ 1.334 (content relevance) +.731 (visual appeal) + 1.266 (relatability)

IV. DISCUSSION

The demographic analysis revealed a gender distribution of 66% men and 34% women among study participants. The age distribution highlighted a substantial representation of individuals aged 18-25 (27.89%), followed by those aged 26-35 (23%) and 36-45 (21.58%). The majority of participants identified as single (74.21%), while 25.79% reported being married.

For the first hypothesis (H1), which posited that the use of social media influencers significantly influences college students' perceptions based on gender, the t-test results indicated a significant difference between male and female participants in terms of brand loyalty. The p-value of 0.001 was less than the set significance level of 0.05, supporting the hypothesis and suggesting that gender plays a statistically significant role in the perception of social media influencers.

Moving on to the second hypothesis (H2), which suggested there is no significant difference in purchasing behavior and brand loyalty among different levels of exposure to digital marketing, the ANOVA results contradicted this. The p-value of 0.002 was less than 0.05, indicating a significant difference in purchasing behavior and brand loyalty across various levels of exposure to digital marketing.

The regression analysis aimed at identifying factors influencing college students' engagement with digital marketing content on social media platforms. The coefficients table indicated that content relevance, visual appeal, and relatability significantly influenced students' engagement. The regression equation provided a quantitative representation of this relationship.

V. CONCLUSION

In conclusion, this study has shed light on the significant impact of gender on college students' perceptions of social media influencers, with females and males exhibiting distinct brand loyalty patterns. Additionally, exposure to digital marketing has proven to be a key determinant of purchasing behavior and brand loyalty among students.

The regression analysis has further delineated the influential factors affecting students' engagement with digital marketing content. Content relevance, visual appeal, and relatability emerged as critical elements shaping students' interactions with such content.

These findings offer valuable insights for marketers targeting college students, emphasizing the importance of tailoring digital marketing strategies based on gender and ensuring content aligns with students' preferences and interests. Researchers and practitioners can leverage these insights to optimize digital marketing campaigns and enhance their effectiveness among this demographic.

REFERENCES

Abidin, C. (2020). Influencer marketing: A critical review and research agenda. *Journal of Marketing Management*, 36(7-8), 681–695. DOI: 10.1080/0267257X.2020.1773367

Arora, A., Bansal, M., & Sharma, P. (2021). The impact of influencer credibility on brand loyalty: The role of social media marketing. *International Journal of Consumer Studies*, 45(5), 624–634. DOI: 10.1111/1470-6431.12651

Boerman, S. C., Willemsen, L. M., & Van Der Aa, E. (2017). Online influencers: A current state of research and future directions. *International Journal of Advertising*, 36(3), 261–284. DOI: 10.1080/02650487.2017.1329650

Campbell, C., & Grimm, P. E. (2019). Social media influencers: A new way to reach the college student market. *Business Horizons*, 62(6), 787–796. DOI: 10.1016/j.bushor.2019.07.002

de Vries, L. A., & Kühne, R. (2015). The influence of social media on consumer buying intention: A study among university students. *JMR, Journal of Marketing Research*, 2(4), 123–134. DOI: 10.11648/j.jmr.20150401.16

Hwang, K., & Zhang, D. (2023). The impact of social media influencers on consumer behavior: A systematic review. *International Journal of Advertising*, 42(1), 4–22. DOI: 10.1080/02650487.2022.2100571

Kim, J., Lee, Y., & Park, J. (2022). The role of social media influencers in shaping consumer behavior in the digital age: A comprehensive review. *Journal of Business Research*, 142, 524–538. DOI: 10.1016/j.jbusres.2021.12.035

Lim, H., Tan, Y., & Yeo, L. (2022). The role of storytelling in influencer marketing: Engaging consumers through narrative. *Journal of Marketing Communications*, 28(5), 551–566. DOI: 10.1080/13527266.2020.1784542

Przybylski, A. K., Murayama, K., & DeHaan, C. R. (2013). When boredom strikes: Affective, cognitive, and behavioral consequences of boredom. *Journal of Experimental Psychology. General*, 142(4), 1154–1163. DOI: 10.1037/a0033736

Sokolova, K., & Kefi, H. (2020). The role of micro-influencers in social media marketing: The effectiveness of influencer marketing on brand awareness and purchase intention. *Journal of Marketing Communications*, 26(3), 276–295. DOI: 10.1080/13527266.2018.1536860

ADDITIONAL READING

Ali, M. (2021). *Remote Work and Sustainable Changes for the Future of Global Business.* IGI Global. https://www.igi-global.com/book/remote-work-sustainable-changes-future/264375

Ali, M. (2022). *Future Role of Sustainable Innovative Technologies in Crisis Management.* IGI Global. https://www.igi-global.com/book/future-role-sustainable-innovative-technologies/281281

Ali, M. (2023). *Shifting Paradigms in the Rapidly Developing Global Digital Ecosystem: A GCC Perspective.* In Digital Entrepreneurship and Co-Creating Value Through Digital Encounters (pp. 145-166). IGI Global. https://www.igi-global.com/chapter/shifting-paradigms-in-the-rapidly-developing-global-digital-ecosystem/323525

Ali, M. (2023). T*axonomy of Industry 4.0 Technologies in Digital Entrepreneurship and Co-Creating Value.* In *Digital Entrepreneurship and Co-Creating Value Through Digital Encounters* (pp. 24–55). IGI Global., https://www.igi-global.com/chapter/taxonomy-of-industry-40-technologies-in-digital-entrepreneurship-and-co-creating-value/323520 DOI: 10.4018/978-1-6684-7416-7.ch002

Ali, M., & Wood-Harper, T. (2021). *Fostering Communication and Learning with Underutilized Technologies in Higher Education.* IGI Global. https://www.igi-global.com/book/fostering-communication-learning-underutilized-technologies/244593

Ali, M., Wood-Harper, T., & Kutar, M. (2023). Multi-Perspectives of Contemporary Digital Transformation Models of Complex Innovation Management. In *Digital Entrepreneurship and Co-Creating Value Through Digital Encounters* (pp. 79–96). IGI Global., https://www.igi-global.com/chapter/multi-perspectives-of-contemporary-digital-transformation-models-of-complex-innovation-management/323522 DOI: 10.4018/978-1-6684-7416-7.ch004

Ali, M. B. (2021). Internet of Things (IoT) to Foster Communication and Information Sharing: A Case of UK Higher Education. In Ali, M. B., & Wood-Harper, T. (Eds.), *Fostering Communication and Learning With Underutilized Technologies in Higher Education* (pp. 1–20). IGI Global., https://www.igi-global.com/chapter/internet-of-things-iot-to-foster-communication-and-information-sharing/262718/ DOI: 10.4018/978-1-7998-4846-2.ch001

Ali, M. B., & Wood-Harper, T. (2022). Artificial Intelligence (AI) as a Decision-Making Tool to Control Crisis Situations. In *Future Role of Sustainable Innovative Technologies in Crisis Management*. IGI Global., https://www.igi-global.com/chapter/artificial-intelligence-ai-as-a-decision-making-tool-to-control-crisis-situations/298931 DOI: 10.4018/978-1-7998-9815-3.ch006

Ali, M. B., Wood-Harper, T., & Ramlogan, R. (2020). A Framework Strategy to Overcome Trust Issues on Cloud Computing Adoption in Higher Education. In Modern Principles, Practices, and Algorithms for Cloud Security (pp. 162-183). IGI Global. https://www.igi-global.com/chapter/a-framework-strategy-to-overcome-trust-issues-on-cloud-computing-adoption-in-higher-education/238907/

Ali, M. B., & Wood-Harper, T. (2022). Artificial Intelligence (AI) as a Decision-Making Tool to Control Crisis Situations. In *Future Role of Sustainable Innovative Technologies in Crisis Management*. IGI Global., https://www.igi-global.com/chapter/

Chapter 4
Transforming Promotion Processes of University Foundations Using Social Media:
A Case Study on the HKU Foundation

Xiaoxu Lu
The University of Hong Kong, Hong Kong

Dickson K. W. Chiu
https://orcid.org/0000-0002-7926-9568
The University of Hong Kong, Hong Kong

ABSTRACT

Social media marketing has become essential for businesses of all sectors and sizes in the current digital world. However, many organizations encounter difficulties in promotion during their transformation. Thus, this chapter explores the possible problems affecting organizational performance in social media marketing using a case study of the University of Hong Kong Foundation under the lens of integrating the 5Es Usability Model (Effective, Efficient, Engaging, Error Torrelance, and Easy to Learn) and AIDA Marketing Communication Model (Awareness, Interest, Desire, and Action) models into a comprehensive framework. In the post-pandemic era, the reliance on digital marketing has intensified, making social media an even more pivotal tool for engagement. Furthermore, integrating Artificial Intelligence (AI) into social media marketing strategies has introduced new dynamics, offering predictive analytics, personalized content, and real-time engagement opportunities,

DOI: 10.4018/979-8-3373-0086-3.ch004

Copyright © 2025, IGI Global. Copying or distributing in print or electronic forms without written permission of IGI Global is prohibited.

which are critical for organizations like HKUF to stay competitive and relevant.

INTRODUCTION

Philanthropic foundations, such as the Bill & Melinda Gates Foundation, receive funds from all walks of life to support various charity activities. Among different categories of foundations, one specific type of foundation, the university foundation, aims to boost collaboration and development in universities. Many university foundations were established in the late 20th century to support their sustainable development. For example, in 1981, the president and deans of Harvard University established the Harvard Foundation for Intercultural and Race Relations to "improve relations among racial and ethnic groups within the University and to enhance the quality of our common life."

The COVID-19 pandemic has further emphasized the role of digital platforms in higher education, particularly as remote working and online engagement have become the norm (Carrigan & Jordan, 2022; Huang et al., 2021, 2022, 2023; P. Y. Yu et al., 2023). At the University of Hong Kong (HKU), the Foundation for Educational Development and Research (often known as the "HKU Foundation," HKUF) is the case study for its social media marketing on websites like WeChat, YouTube, Instagram, and Linked Forerunners envisioned developing the organization sustainably established HKUF in 1995 as a nonprofit organization, comprising benefactors who support the university's mission, both private and corporate. Since then, HKUF has used the proceeds from its investments to fund various initiatives to improve HKU's local and global communities. According to the intentions of the benefactors, gifts to the university may also be allocated for particular programs or departments. These contributions can support funding academic research, scholarships, bursaries, and development projects. A Board of Directors is responsible for the fund administration, while allocation is conducted through an annual Seed Grants exercise.

In the post-pandemic era, social media marketing has become even more indispensable for organizations to reach and engage with their target audience. It is a cost-effective way to build brand awareness, generate leads, and drive donations. However, social media marketing may waste time and resources if not used strategically (Lam et al., 2019, 2013). This study investigates various social media marketing techniques to determine their effectiveness in attracting donations for sustainable development. This chapter also provides simple yet effective solutions to improve the efficiency of social media marketing campaigns by reviewing the literature on social media marketing and identifying success factors. Next, this chapter enumerates the issues observed in HKUF marketing. Finally, this chapter develops pragmatic recommendations for HKUF to improve its social media marketing efforts based on the findings of the literature review and the analysis of the case study. The pandemic has forced many organizations, including HKUF, to rethink their engagement strategies, making digital platforms and AI-powered tools essential for fostering donor relationships.

This chapter contributes significantly to social media marketing by comprehensively analyzing the effectiveness of different social media marketing techniques for research development organizations. The recommendations can help organizations improve the efficiency and effectiveness of their social media marketing campaigns and raise more money for research. Moreover, integrating post-pandemic strategies and AI-driven insights offers a contemporary approach to addressing the evolving challenges of digital engagement in today's landscape.

LITERATURE REVIEW

Social Media Marketing

Social media (such as Facebook, Twitter, and Instagram) has become a fringe feature of academic life in less than a decade and a familiar presence for universities worldwide (Lam et al., 2023). This emerging technology has facilitated universities' communication with stakeholders (Jordan 2017; Stuart et al. 2019). The use of social media platforms, channels, and software for the creation, delivery, exchange, and communication of offerings that are valuable to an organization's stakeholders is known as social media marketing. Social media marketing is valuable because of its access to people and their functionality, especially when organizations desire to promote themselves with limited resources (Jiang et al., 2023; H.K.K. Yu et al., 2023). Businesses with well-defined public relations departments are more likely to embrace social media and use it to further their objectives.

Additionally, if social media platforms are credible to public relations practitioners, they are more inclined to employ them (Parveen et al., 2015). Social media marketing creates various benefits: brand association, brand knowledge, brand commitment, increased brand trust, consumer satisfaction, and positive attitudes and evaluations in online communities (Chiang et al., 2019). Data analytics and artificial intelligence (AI) increasingly drive social media strategies, facilitating more precise targeting and personalized content creation. AI tools now allow real-time adaptation in response to user behavior, significantly enhancing engagement and conversion rates (Yang, 2020; S. Li et al., 2023; Liu et al., 2023).

Digital Marketing

Digital marketing, a more general concept than social media marketing, emphasizes the method and concepts used to convey messages. In recent years, there has been a surge of research and literature exploring the various aspects of digital marketing, including social media marketing, search engine optimization (SEO), content marketing, email marketing, and influencer marketing (Lucid Advertising, 2023).

Digital marketing provides several advantages to companies that want to advertise their goods or services. The results' measurability and cost-effectiveness are two benefits. Marketers may increase return on investment and save costs by allocating their budget effectively and making frequent modifications with real-time data access. Furthermore, digital marketing offers countless alternatives for identifying the target demographic, enabling companies to hone their tactics and obtain insightful data. Digital marketing is made even more effective by its capacity to connect with consumers at several points in their buying process (S.M. Lee et al., 2023).

Moreover, the customization options available in digital campaigns allow businesses to minimize errors and make data-driven decisions. Enhanced consumer engagement through various digital platforms fosters loyalty and enables outreach to broader market segments. The post-COVID shift towards digital engagement has further accelerated the adoption of digital marketing techniques because businesses have adapted to the new normal of remote interaction and online consumer habits, especially targeting the younger generation (Leung et al., 2023). AI has played a significant role in this transformation, offering tools like predictive analytics, chatbots, and automated content creation to streamline processes and enhance customer experiences (Chin & Chiu, 2023; Lin et al., 2023). In particular, AI-driven digital marketing has revolutionized how businesses interact with consumers. From dynamic content personalization to AI-powered customer segmentation, these tools allow marketers to deliver highly relevant content to the right audience at the right time (Liu et al., 2023).

The COVID-19 pandemic has recently forced online service companies to maintain and build consumer relationships with their changed consumption habits (Alshurideh et al., 2021; Leung et al., 2023). Social media and ubiquitous mobile technologies have recently changed marketing practices, while the integration of artificial intelligence has further increased agility and customization (Victoria, 2019).

Overall, the literature on digital marketing provides valuable insights and best practices for businesses looking to succeed in the digital landscape. Organizations can develop effective digital marketing strategies that drive growth and success by creating engaging content, understanding their target audience, and tracking their results.

5E Usability Model

Usability, often equated to "easy to use," is a complex concept that requires a more accurate definition of five aspects: effective, efficient, engaging, error-tolerant, and easily learnable, to guide user-centered design tasks (Quesenbery, W., 2001). The five usability characteristics method helps comprehend user requirements and mental models for task transformation. Another article, 'Using the 5Es to understand users' (2023) in WQ Usability, also proposes a guideline on how to evaluate each aspect, which is as follows:

- Effective: Monitor each task's outcomes to note its frequency of correct completion and issues such as omitted information or mistakes.
- Efficient: Track the time and how long users take to complete each task. Look for areas where the navigation or screen layout makes the task more difficult than necessary.
- Engaging: Watch for indicators that the screens are hard to understand or confusing. Look for areas where the UI does not draw users into their jobs. Investigate how much they enjoyed the product and pay attention to any issues that prevented them from being happy with the whole experience.
- Error Tolerant: Construct a test where errors are expected to occur and assess the product's usefulness and users' ability to bounce back from setbacks. Monitor how often users encounter error messages and what actions may avoid them.
- Easy to Learn: Limit the guidance provided to test participants or invite seasoned users to take on particularly challenging, intricate, or infrequently used activities. Look for areas where the workflow or on-screen text assists or confuses users.

AIDA Marketing Communication Model

American advertising pioneer Elias St. Elmo Lewis first presented the AIDA paradigm in the late 1800s (Sriram et al., 2022), which has gained widespread adoption and is frequently cited in textbooks and marketing literature. The AIDA marketing communication model comprises four steps a customer takes before a purchase decision: Attention, Interest, Desire, and Action. Hanlon (2023) also proposes a clearer guideline on the application of AIDA to communicate the customers:

- *Awareness*: establishing a connection or awareness of a brand with its products or services.

- *Interest*: creating enough curiosity about the advantages of a product or service to persuade a potential customer to begin additional research.
- *Desire*: demonstrating the brand's personality through an "emotional connection" with the product or service - convert the customer from "liking" to "wanting" it.
- *Action*: Persuade the customer to contact the brand to proceed with some desirable actions, such as downloading a brochure, contacting you by phone, subscribing to your newsletter, starting a live chat, etc.

Marketing material should ideally achieve the following four aspects: raise brand awareness, spark interest in its products or services, pique people's curiosity, and encourage them to try them or take desirable actions (like discussion and sharing related information). Organizations can have more effective marketing on social media platforms via the AIDA approach (Jiang et al., 2023; Leung et al., 2023).

DETAILED ANALYSIS AND SOLUTIONS

Problem Identification

There are three categories of digital marketing strategies that HKUF is actively using: i) Promotion of events through emails with posters, ii) Content posts on multiple social media channels such as LinkedIn, Instagram, and Facebook, and iii) Scholarship promotion videos.

Although using posters and emails to promote events can be successful, the process transformation should consider several possible problems. The following are some typical difficulties that organizations could run across when implementing this promotion strategy:

> *Tracking and analytics*: Tracking the success and effectiveness of your promotional emails can be challenging when using posters as attachments. In online advertising, click-based performance indexes, e.g., clicks and click-through rate (CTR), reflect the relevance of advertisements from users' perspective (Yang & Zhai, 2022). Baer (2022) argues that organizations can focus on the performance of several key metrics, including but not limited to delivery rate, open rate, and click rate. It may be more difficult to track these key metrics since there are no functionalities in Google or Microsoft platforms to provide this information.

Email deliverability and spam filters: One of the biggest challenges in email marketing has always been getting past the spam filter (Dublino,2023). Emails with attachments, such as posters, may trigger spam filters or get flagged as potential spam. This can result in promotional emails not reaching the intended recipients' inboxes. Moreover, Internet Service Providers (ISPs) may block emails with abnormally low deliverability or sending rates (Dublino, 2023) — inadequate deliverability results in tremendous time, money, and effort loss.

Design and formatting limitations: Email is one of the most structured and professional ways to communicate with others, but its unique presentation style may be restricted to an antiquated format with text-oriented, lengthy-worded, and information-intensive characteristics.

Platform disparity: Organizations may encounter issues when sharing material across social media platforms like Facebook, Instagram, and LinkedIn (Lam et al., 2019; 2023). Social media is very active and fast-moving: what may be up-to-date today could have disappeared from the virtual landscape tomorrow. Thus, organizations should devise guidelines for various social media platforms to cater to different platform features, audience preferences, content formatting, and time concerns (Kaplan & Haenlein, 2010).

Inconsistent Branding: Content published across several platforms may have an inconsistent visual identity, tone of voice, and branding (Vestil, 2023). For a presence to be coherent and identifiable, keeping a consistent brand image across all channels is critical. For example, HKUF presents itself as a reliable and strategic partner that helps prospective contributors learn about the wide range of important work being done by HKU departments. It exemplifies teamwork, openness, and excellence and demonstrates the Foundation's dedication to creating significant giving possibilities. The Foundation portrays itself as a bridge between donors and departments and promotes a sense of shared purpose and impact by significantly emphasizing relationship-building and creating personalized proposals. It is rather challenging to maintain a consistent branding image should be consistent across the platforms due to different settings and limitations for the posts.

Hashtag and Tagging Mistakes: Influencers and organizations find this feature especially useful as it helps them capture and hold people's attention through strategic hashtag selection (Abidin, 2016). Semantic tagging is a crucial method for sorting, finding, and organizing content in digital media. It allows users to label and retrieve data in various ways, depending on an application's UI. For example, users can search the post using the tagging phrases. If people are interested in a post with a certain hashtag, the recommendation engine will suggest posts similar to the one they are viewing. Daer et al. (2014) also argued that metacommunication, a secondary tagging function, offers a user's thoughts on the post. #PackersGottaWinThis and #GirlsHelpsGirls are examples of how users utilize tagging to start the campaign. Misusing or neglecting to use relevant hashtags or tags can limit the visibility of your posts and make it difficult for users to discover your content. Loukianov et al. (2023) argue that in the discursive realm, strong relationships support themes in visibility. Because a specific subject cluster shows up regularly rather than infrequently in various feeds generated by hashtag search, it is easier to see as part of a narrative pattern. In contrast, if the hashtags and the content are less correlated, it is hard for the recommendation engine to deliver content to the targeted or potential audience will not be able to get the post by tagging-search.

Content-style Issues: Besides considering things from a branding perspective, examining the audience's preferences is crucial. The audience on each platform may have different preferences and expectations. Due to various groups of internet surfers separated by demographics, religions, and interests, the demand for media is somewhat different. For example, the culture on Instagram focuses more on photo sharing than copywriting. Therefore, posting content without much awareness of the importance of the expression of power in the pictures may cause a terrible result in which the audience regards the post as irrelevant and not engaging and chooses to swipe away the posts.

Content-size Issues: Sizing is a crucial aspect to consider when organizations present their content to their audiences. Each social media platform has its own formatting and display requirements. Content good for one platform may not appear properly or require adjustments on another, causing distorted images, broken links, or text formatting issues. The exponential rise in high-speed mobile networks and device technologies has massively expanded online video content (Leung et al., 2023; Wong et al., 2024). As people watch more and more videos online, marketing products and services have inevitably kept up with the medium (Boman & Raijonkari, 2017). Organizations may encounter several potential issues when using scholarship promotion videos as part of social media marketing. Here are a few to consider.

Misleading or false information: Regarding video marketing, organizations should follow several steps: scripting, filming, editing, and posting. The mobile environment of the 2020s is experiencing a vertical video revolution (Mulier et al.,2020). There is some crucial information on the sponsorship scheme for scripting, such as sponsor requirements and details. Once after scripting, information consistency throughout the process is essential. Thus, incorrect details about the scholarship or its eligibility criteria can confuse users and damage the organization's credibility.

Lack of engagement: Scholarship promotion videos may not always generate the desired level of engagement from the target audience. Creating compelling and engaging content that captivates viewers' attention and encourages them to take action, such as applying for a scholarship or sharing the video with others, is essential. However, video promotions often contain only the parts with the main character sharing personal experiences and feelings about the scholarship, lacking the vital parts, which may lead to failed video marketing.

Insufficient reach: Even with a well-produced video, it may not reach a wide enough audience. Besides inferior content, it may also be due to the account with inadequate exposure, focus, or followers. Therefore, even though the video content has all the correct information and requirements to be engaging and attractive, it may still fail.

Analyses Using the 5E Usability Model

During the process transformation, increasing HKUF's exposure and influence on social media is the goal, which can be guided by the 5Es usability model to understand the patrons better. This model helps analyze the usability of products and services through five dimensions: effectiveness, efficiency, engagement, error tolerance, and ease to learn, offering valuable recommendations to improve the products and services (Kaye & Haynes, 2023). Organizations can pair the elements in 5E with the problems suggested earlier in this chapter to strategically formulate more effective solutions addressing root causes.

Effectiveness

The current issue of promotion through emails and posters is less effective due to the lack of native support on Microsoft Outlook or Google Gmail for tracking and analytics. HKUF should leverage effective tracking and analytics from third-party platforms such as HubSpot to monitor the success of its email campaigns promoting events and initiatives. By analyzing key metrics such as open rates, click-through rates, and conversion rates, HKUF can gain valuable insights into the effectiveness of its messaging and targeting strategies (Farris et al., 2021). This data-driven approach allows HKUF to optimize its email campaigns continuously, ensuring they reach the target audience and achieve the desired results. By tracking and analyzing the performance of its email marketing efforts, the HKUF can identify areas for improvement, refine its messaging, and tailor its campaigns to its supporters' specific interests and preferences.

Besides email metrics analytics, organizations should also monitor the data on likes, comments, and views on social media platforms (Lam et al., 2019; Xue et al., 2024). For example, HKUF currently has around 100 likes on average for each post on Instagram, with some up to 500, while many Facebook posts less than ten. Thus, detailed analyses of the posts are necessary to identify successful and poor posts. The organization can replicate the post's success with the success factor identified. The result also means the same content does not fit on Facebook, thus requiring a customized design.

By reducing the pool of eligible candidates, insufficient distribution of scholarship advertising videos might compromise the effectiveness of scholarship programs. To solve this problem, HKUF can use sponsored advertising to draw in more viewers and expand the reach of its scholarship videos. By carefully targeting the videos to appeal to particular interest groups and demographics, strategically placing them on pertinent websites and social media channels, and producing captivating and educational content, HKUF may greatly expand its audience for its scholarship promotion initiatives. This will eventually add to the success of the scholarship programs by drawing in more eligible applications.

Efficiency

The efficient aspect focuses more on user experience. One efficiency issue may happen when content, such as images, is not properly optimized for different social media platforms. Each platform has its own recommended sizing and aspect ratios for images; otherwise, it can result in inefficient content display and user experience (Lynch et al., 2016). For instance, an image may be cropped or deformed when displayed on some social networking platforms if it is too big or has the incorrect aspect ratio. This may result in crucial text omission or presented erratically, reducing the content's usefulness. To address this issue, one possible solution is to create an internal version of the content that is properly optimized for each social media platform. This internal version should be shared with a small group for testing in advance to identify and resolve any issues with image sizing or formatting before releasing the content. This approach ensures that the content is visually appealing and effectively conveys its intended message on all targeted social media platforms, enhancing the overall efficiency of the content distribution process.

Engagement

The Engage phase serves as the initial touchpoint for information sharing for digital marketing to pique the target audience's interest, motivating them to seek more information actively. However, current issues, such as content-related issues in content post-marketing, hinder engagement with the client. For example, the focus of HKUF's Instagram posts is misplaced in the copywriting of the main character's life path and experiences, such as selfies and group photos. While the content may demonstrate the donation's help to the recipients, it often lacks a persistent and engaging theme. Moreover, the content is mainly about the main character's background without the clear message HKUF wants to express. Thus, all the post cover pages should use images with similar style, color tone, or editing text. Creating some mottos or infographics on the cover page can enhance the expression of the characteristics (Chu et al., 2024), providing the power to speak and engage the audience while encouraging comments.

Error Tolerance

For scholarship promotion videos, misleading or false information can lead to confusion and miscommunication with the audience. For instance, if the scripting of a video contains errors regarding the application deadline, it can create significant confusion among viewers who may rely on the provided information. A possible solution could involve responsible staff cross-checking the content before publishing by reviewing the script and the information accuracy.

Additionally, leveraging AI language models can be useful in the content review process. These models can be trained to check the content against inaccuracies or inconsistencies. The review process can be further enhanced and streamlined by utilizing AI technology, reducing the chances of misleading or false information being included in the scholarship promotion videos. Yet, final human inspections of AI-powered solutions are necessary for ensuring correct and trustworthy information (Lin et al., 2023).

Easy to Learn

One of the issues is that HKUF makes mistakes in hashtag and tagging strategies on social media platforms such as Instagram, which may lead to potential confusion about a post's theme. Thus, a solution should involve researching effective tagging strategies for specific topics relevant to HKUF's content. This research can use AI tools to generate potential hashtag candidates based on the content's theme or keywords. Subsequently, manual research can analyze the popularity and usage of these hashtags, considering factors such as the number of posts and engagement they have received. With optimization based on popularity and relevancy, HKUF can include these well-considered hashtags in their postings. This strategy boosts the possibility of reaching a larger audience and clearly explaining things to individuals who actively follow or look up those hashtags. It makes HKUF's material easier to find and guarantees the target audience can comprehend the main idea.

Analyses Using the AIDA Marketing Communication Model

While the 5Es model provides insights into the problems' core and establishes a framework to propose a detailed solution, the AIDA marketing communication model can provide more guidelines.

> *Attention*: First, several strategies can be implemented to enhance awareness of the branding of HKU Foundation. Firstly, HKUF can leverage social media platforms to engage with its target audience actively by regularly posting informative and visually appealing content highlighting the foundation's mission, projects, and impact (Xue et al., 2024), which is currently unsatisfactory considering the current performance of the existing posts. Utilizing storytelling techniques and sharing the success stories of beneficiaries (which can now be facilitated with generative AI) can effectively create an emotional connection with the audience, leading to increased awareness and interest in HKUF's work. Additionally, HKUF can collaborate with influencers or partner with other organizations, such as official HKU social media accounts, to extend their reach and tap into new networks (Wong et al., 2024). HKUF may establish itself as a thought leader and increase its exposure among important stakeholders by staging webinars, virtual events, and active participation in pertinent online conversations. Targeted advertising efforts on social media platforms can also aid HKUF in expanding its audience and enhancing brand awareness. Through regular application of these tactics, HKUF can effectively raise awareness and build a solid rapport with its intended audience.
>
> *Interest*: HKUF should highlight the distinctive benefits and significant projects to spark interest in the organization. One strategy is to post engaging content showcasing HKUF's contributions to community development, research, and education, such as results of ground-breaking research projects funded by HKUF, promoting community outreach initiatives, or telling the tales of students who have benefited from HKUF's grants or scholarships. Effectively conveying the advantages and concrete benefits of sponsoring HKUF increases the likelihood that prospective contributors and supporters would be interested in discovering more (Jiang et al., 2023). Moreover, organizing webinars or virtual

events with well-known speakers or professionals in related fields can draw interest and keep the audience interested (Lu et al., 2024). These gatherings can offer insightful viewpoints that pique interest in HKUF's work even more. HKUF can effectively pique the attention and curiosity of its target audience and encourage them to investigate the foundation's programs and become more involved by regularly publishing informative and engaging information.

Desire: Demonstrating the essence of the HKUF and its contribution is crucial to arousing desire and cultivating an emotional bond with the organization. Sharing moving testimonies and anecdotes from people who have directly benefited from HKUF's activities is one powerful approach to accomplish this. Emphasizing the individual experiences and transformations made feasible by the foundation can elicit empathy and a desire to contribute to the cause from potential donors and supporters. A desire to support HKUF's purpose can also be motivated by highlighting the organization's successes and landmarks through aesthetically appealing content, such as influential movies or infographics (Chu et al., 2024; Wong et al., 2024). Moreover, highlighting the distinctive value proposition of HKU, such as its dedication to excellence in research and education, can motivate people to support the foundation's objectives and connect themselves with its mission (Cheung et al., 2021; Xue et al., 2024). The foundation may cultivate desire and transform people from liking the cause to actively wanting to help and make a significant impact by continuously highlighting the emotional and concrete benefits of supporting HKUF.

Action: Using strong calls-to-action (CTAs) on social media is essential to promoting action and getting people to interact with HKUF. These CTAs should encourage users to take action and participate in the foundation's objectives. For example, HKUF may utilize eye-catching buttons or links in their social media postings to take viewers to their website, where they can learn more about the foundation and how they can become involved. This can involve donating money, volunteering, or subscribing to newsletters to be informed about the events and initiatives of HKUF. Adding interactive elements, such as online forms or live chat assistance, can facilitate communication between interested parties and HKUF personnel. Using social media, HKUF can also motivate people to share their tales or experiences linked to the organization's mission, fostering a sense of community and motivating others to take the initiative. By routinely examining engagement and performance indicators on social media, HKUF can determine which call-to-actions are most successful and make wise improvements to encourage even more action. This can involve donating money, volunteering, or subscribing to newsletters to be informed about the events and initiatives of HKUF. Adding interactive elements, such as online forms or live chat assistance, can facilitate communication between interested parties and HKUF personnel. Using social media, HKUF can also motivate people to share their tales or experiences linked to the organization's mission, fostering a sense of community and motivating others to take the initiative. By routinely examining engagement and performance indicators on social media, HKUF can determine which call-to-actions are most successful and make wise improvements to encourage even more action.

DISCUSSION

The post-pandemic era has significantly accelerated the shift towards digital engagement, as many organizations, including HKUF, should have transformed their processes with emerging technologies. Social media has become even more critical for maintaining donor connections when in-person events are less frequent. As a result, AI's digital engagement strategies are more focused on personalization and real-time interactions, making it easier to nurture long-term relationships efficiently. Further, generative AI can facilitate easy content creation. Building and sustaining long-term donor relationships through social media engagement cannot be overstated. Social media allows for continuous interaction and engagement, which is essential for fostering trust and loyalty among donors. The importance of digitally sustaining donor relationships lies in maintaining regular communication so donors feel connected and appreciated, increasing the likelihood of continued support over time.

Using the 5Es and AIDA models to assess the issues in HKUF's social media marketing offers significant insights for organizational performance improvement. These models provide a structured and systematic approach to evaluate and analyze the effectiveness of current strategies. By applying the 5Es model, HKUF gains insights into the various stages of engagement, from examination to evaluation, allowing them to identify areas of improvement and develop targeted solutions. Similarly, the AIDA model helps HKUF understand the customer journey and develop compelling content that generates awareness, interest, desire, and actions. The actionable strategies based on these models offer practical steps for HKUF to implement and enhance its social media marketing efforts. These strategies can range from content optimization to audience targeting, enabling HKUF to engage effectively with its target audience and achieve its marketing objectives.

Despite the advantages offered by the use of the 5E models and AIDA models, there are some limitations to consider. One limitation is that these models provide a framework for analysis and strategy development but do not guarantee immediate results. Implementing the proposed strategies and observing the desired outcomes takes time and consistent effort. Additionally, the effectiveness of these models and strategies may vary depending on the specific context and target audience of HKUF. It is essential to continuously monitor and analyze the results, making adjustments and refinements as needed. Another limitation is the word limit constraint, which limits the depth and breadth of examples provided. While the transformation strategies outlined are generally applicable, it is crucial to consider the unique characteristics and requirements of each organization and platform to ensure optimal performance. While social media is a valuable tool for building impact for organizations like HKUF, in addition to the strategies mentioned above, exploring opportunities for fostering relationships through in-person, face-to-face interactions for a more comprehensive engagement approach is also necessary.

CONCLUSION

This chapter analyzes the marketing process transformation strategies using social media for the HKU Foundation based on the 5Es usability model and the AIDA marketing communication model. It assesses their current application on different platforms like Facebook and Instagram in terms of follower numbers, posting frequency, and content types. While HKU Foundation's social media channels are wide-reaching, there is room for improvement in content and updating regularity. Specifically, their performance in the exposure and engagement stages of the 5Es model could be strengthened. The post-pandemic era highlights the need for more dynamic online engagement, where AI-driven tools can help automate and enhance these stages through personalized content and predictive analytics. Under the lens of the AIDA model, the *interest* and *desire* elements should be further transformed for improvement. AI can support these elements by using data analytics to predict user intent and tailor content to evoke stronger emotional responses.

In conclusion, with enhanced strategic social media management focusing on audience targeting and engagement metrics, HKUF can further amplify its impact and mission online. Regular evaluation of key performance indicators would also help optimize the strategy, which is our immediate follow-up study. We are also interested in the social media analytics of organizations for marketing purposes, particularly how AI can further drive efficiencies and results in the post-pandemic digital landscape.

REFERENCES

Abidin, C. (2016). Visibility labour: Engaging with influencers' fashion brands and #OOTD advertorial campaigns on Instagram. *Media International Australia, Incorporating Culture & Policy*, 161(1), 86–100. DOI: 10.1177/1329878X16665177

Advertising, L. (2023, September 26). The benefits of digital marketing. https://www.lucidadvertising.com/benefits-digital-marketing/

Alshurideh, M. T., Hassanien, A. E., & Masa'deh, R. (2021). *The Effect of Coronavirus Disease (COVID-19) on Business Intelligence* (1st ed. 2021, Vol. 334). Springer International Publishing AG. DOI: 10.1007/978-3-030-67151-8

Anderson, E. (2010). *Social media marketing game theory and the emergence of collaboration*. Springer. DOI: 10.1007/978-3-642-13299-5

Baer, J. (2022, May 31). *7 email marketing problems and 9 medicines to fix them*. Convince & Convert. https://www.convinceandconvert.com/digital-marketing/7-email-marketing-problems-9-medicines-fix/

Bin-Nashwan, S. A., & Al-Daihani, M. (2021). Fundraising campaigns via social media platforms for mitigating the impacts of the COVID-19 epidemic. *Journal of Islamic Marketing*, 12(3), 576–597. DOI: 10.1108/JIMA-07-2020-0200

Boman, K., & Raijonkari, K. (2017). Online Video as a Marketing Tool: A quantitative survey on video marketing habits.

Carrigan, M., & Jordan, K. (2022). Platforms and Institutions in the Post-Pandemic University: A Case Study of Social Media and the Impact Agenda. *Postdigital Science and Education*, 4(2), 354–372. DOI: 10.1007/s42438-021-00269-x

Chen, Y., & Chiu, D. K. W. (2023). Digital Marketing and Service Strategies for Sustainable Development of Visual Culture: A Case Study of M+ Museum. In Gigauri, I., Palazzo, M., & Ferri, M. A. (Eds.), *Handbook of Research on Achieving Sustainable Development Goals With Sustainable Marketing* (pp. 68–91). IGI Global. DOI: 10.4018/978-1-6684-8681-8.ch004

Cheng, Y., & Jiang, H. (2022). Customer–brand relationship in the era of artificial intelligence: Understanding the role of chatbot marketing efforts. *Journal of Product and Brand Management*, 31(2), 252–264. DOI: 10.1108/JPBM-05-2020-2907

Cheung, T. Y., Ye, Z., & Chiu, D. K. W. (2021). Value chain analysis of information services for the visually impaired: A case study of contemporary technological solutions. *Library Hi Tech*, 39(2), 625–642. DOI: 10.1108/LHT-08-2020-0185

Chiang, I. P., Wong, R., & Huang, C. H. (2019). Exploring the benefits of social media marketing for brands and communities. *International Journal of Electronic Commerce Studies*, 10(2), 113–140. DOI: 10.7903/ijecs.1547

Chin, G. Y. L., & Chiu, D. K. W. (2023). RFID-based Robotic Process Automation for Smart Museums with an Alert-driven Approach. In Tailor, R. (Ed.), *Application and Adoption of Robotic Process Automation for Smart Cities* (pp. 1–27). IGI Global. DOI: 10.4018/978-1-6684-7193-7.ch001

Chu, S. T., Chiu, D. K. W., & Ho, K. K. W. (2024). Using infographics in disseminating healthy lifestyle information on social media is likely to increase uptake and sharing. *Health Information and Libraries Journal*, 41(3), 246–266. DOI: 10.1111/hir.12526 PMID: 38554025

Constantinides, E. (2014). Foundations of Social Media Marketing. *Procedia: Social and Behavioral Sciences*, 148, 40–57. DOI: 10.1016/j.sbspro.2014.07.016

Daer, A. R., Hoffman, R., & Goodman, S. (2014, September). Rhetorical functions of hashtag forms across social media applications. In *Proceedings of the 32nd ACM International Conference on the Design of Communication CD-ROM* (pp. 1-3). DOI: 10.1145/2666216.2666231

Diwanji, V. S., Lee, J., & Cortese, J. (2022). Deconstructing the role of artificial intelligence in programmatic advertising: at the intersection of automation and transparency. *Journal of Strategic Marketing, ahead-of-print*(ahead-of-print), 1–18. DOI: 10.1080/0965254X.2022.2148269

Dublino, J. (2023, October 31). *The 6 biggest email marketing challenges and how to fix them.* business.com. https://www.business.com/articles/6-email-marketing-challenges-and-how-to-overcome-them/

Evans, D., & McKee, Jake. (2010). *Social media marketing the next generation of business engagement* (1st ed.). Wiley Technology Pub.

Farris, P. W., Bendle, N., Pfeifer, P., & Reibstein, D. (2021). Marketing metrics: The manager's guide to measuring marketing performance. FT press.

Giridharadas, A. (2018). *Winners take all : the elite charade of changing the world* (1st ed.). Alfred A. Knopf.

Hanlon, A. (2023, March 20). *The AIDA model.* Smart Insights. https://www.smartinsights.com/traffic-building-strategy/offer-and-message-development/aida-model/

Huang, P. S., Paulino, Y., So, S., Chiu, D. K. W., & Ho, K. K. W. (2021). Editorial - COVID-19 Pandemic and Health Informatics (Part 1). *Library Hi Tech*, 39(3), 693–695. DOI: 10.1108/LHT-09-2021-324

Huang, P.-S., Paulino, Y. C., So, S., Chiu, D. K. W., & Ho, K. K. W. (2022). Guest editorial: COVID-19 Pandemic and Health Informatics Part 2. *Library Hi Tech*, 40(2), 281–285. DOI: 10.1108/LHT-04-2022-447

Huang, P.-S., Paulino, Y. C., So, S., Chiu, D. K. W., & Ho, K. K. W. (2023). Guest editorial: COVID-19 Pandemic and Health Informatics Part 3. *Library Hi Tech*, 41(1), 1–6. DOI: 10.1108/LHT-02-2023-585

Jiang, X., Chiu, D. K. W., & Chan, C. T. (2023). Application of the AIDA model in social media promotion and community engagement for small cultural organizations: A case study of the Choi Chang Sau Qin Society. In Dennis, M., & Halbert, J. (Eds.), *Community Engagement in the Online Space* (pp. 48–70). IGI Global. DOI: 10.4018/978-1-6684-5190-8.ch004

Jockey Club Announces Institute of Philanthropy - bringing together local, regional and global thought leadership for the betterment of society - corporate news - about HKJC - The Hong Kong jockey club. (n.d.). https://corporate.hkjc.com/corporate/corporate-news/english/2023-09/news_2023091101328.aspx?b_cid=EWHPJSC_PACM_CORPNEWSsep-2023_

Jordan, K. (2017). Examining the UK Higher Education sector through the network of institutional accounts on Twitter. *First Monday*, 22(5), 5. DOI: 10.5210/fm.v22i5.7133

Kaplan, A. M., & Haenlein, M. (2010). Users of the world, unite! The challenges and opportunities of Social Media. *Business Horizons*, 53(1), 59–68. DOI: 10.1016/j.bushor.2009.09.003

Kazi, B. U., Shaikh, M. S. I., & Munna, A. S. (Eds.). (2023). *Contemporary approaches of digital marketing and the role of machine intelligence*. IGI Global., DOI: 10.4018/978-1-6684-7735-9

Lam, A. H. C., Ho, K. K. W., & Chiu, D. K. W. (2023). Instagram for student learning and library promotions? A quantitative study using the 5E Instructional Model. *Aslib Journal of Information Management*, 75(1), 112–130. DOI: 10.1108/AJIM-12-2021-0389

Lam, E. T. H., Au, C. H., & Chiu, D. K. W. (2019). Analyzing the use of Facebook among university libraries in Hong Kong. *Journal of Academic Librarianship*, 45(3), 175–183. DOI: 10.1016/j.acalib.2019.02.007

Leung, Y. L., Chan, R., Chiu, D. K. W., & Tian, R. (2023). (in press). Investigating the Consumption Behavior of Young Adults Using Online Food Delivery Platforms during the COVID-19 Pandemic. *Aslib Journal of Information Management*. Advance online publication. DOI: 10.1108/AJIM-05-2023-0177

Lewis, E. S. E. (1899). Side talks about advertising. *The Western Druggist*, 21(2), 65–66.

Li, S., Xie, Z., Chiu, D. K. W., & Ho, K. K. W. (2023). Sentiment Analysis and Topic Modeling Regarding Online Classes on the Reddit Platform: Educators versus Learners. *Applied Sciences (Basel, Switzerland)*, 13(4), 2250. DOI: 10.3390/app13042250 PMID: 39354955

Li, S. M., Lam, A. H. C., & Chiu, D. K. W. (2023). Digital transformation of ticketing services: A value chain analysis of POPTICKET in Hong Kong. In Santos, J. D., & Pereira, I. V. (Eds.), *Management and Marketing for Improved Retail Competitiveness and Performance* (pp. 156–179). IGI. Global.

Lin, C.-H., Chiu, D. K. W., & Lam, K. T. (2022). Hong Kong Academic Librarians' Attitudes Towards Robotic Process Automation. *Library Hi Tech*, 42(3), 991–1014. DOI: 10.1108/LHT-03-2022-0141

Liu, Y., Chiu, D. K. W., & Ho, K. K. W. (2023). Short-Form Videos for Public Library Marketing: Performance Analytics of Douyin in China. *Applied Sciences (Basel, Switzerland)*, 13(6), 3386. DOI: 10.3390/app13063386

Loukianov, A., Burningham, K., & Jackson, T. (2023). The patterning of the discursive space in search for the# goodlife: A network analysis of the co-occurrence of Instagram hashtags. *The Information Society*, 39(1), 62–78. DOI: 10.1080/01972243.2022.2125604

Lu, S. S., Tian, R., & Chiu, D. K. W. (2023). Why do people not attend public library programs in the current digital age? *Library Hi Tech*, 42(4), 1237–1265. DOI: 10.1108/LHT-04-2022-0217

Lv, B., Deng, Y., Meng, W., Wang, Z., & Tang, T. (2024). Research on digital intelligence business model based on artificial intelligence in post-epidemic era. *Management Decision*, 62(9), 2937–2957. DOI: 10.1108/MD-11-2022-1548

Lynch, P. J., Horton, S., & Marcotte, E. (2016). *Web style guide: foundations of user experience design* (4th ed.). Yale University Press.

Mulier, L., Slabbinck, H., & Vermeir, I. (2021). This Way Up: The Effectiveness of Mobile Vertical Video Marketing. *Journal of Interactive Marketing*, 55(1), 1–15. DOI: 10.1016/j.intmar.2020.12.002

Parveen, F., Jaafar, N. I., & Ainin, S. (2015). Social media usage and organizational performance: Reflections of Malaysian social media managers. *Telematics and Informatics*, 32(1), 67–78. DOI: 10.1016/j.tele.2014.03.001

Quesenbery, W. (2001). *What Does Usability Mean: Looking Beyond 'Ease of Use.'* WQ Usability. https://www.wqusability.com/articles/more-than-ease-of-use.html

Reis, L., Carvalho, L. C., Silveira, C., & Brasil, D. X. (2022). *Digitalization As a Driver for Smart Economy in the Post-COVID-19 Era* (1st ed.). IGI Global. DOI: 10.4018/978-1-7998-9227-4

Role of Artificial Intelligence in Social Media Marketing. (2019). *International Journal of Recent Technology and Engineering, 8*(4S3), 66–69. https://doi.org/DOI: 10.35940/ijrte.D1001.1284S319

Sands, S., Campbell, C. L., Plangger, K., & Ferraro, C. (2022). Unreal influence: Leveraging AI in influencer marketing. *European Journal of Marketing*, 56(6), 1721–1747. DOI: 10.1108/EJM-12-2019-0949

Sriram, K. V., Poojary, A. A., Jawa, V., & Kamath, G. B. (2022). Return on investment and return on ad spend at the action level of AIDA using last touch attribution method on digital advertising platforms. *International Journal of Internet Marketing and Advertising*, 17(1-2), 111–132. DOI: 10.1504/IJIMA.2022.125145

Stuart, E., Thelwall, M., & Stuart, D. (2019). Which image types do universities tweet? *First Monday*, 24(3). Advance online publication. DOI: 10.5210/fm.v24i3.9225

Vestil, M. (2023, May 19). *Developing a consistent brand voice across social media channels*. Agility PR Solutions. https://www.agilitypr.com/pr-news/public-relations/developing-a-consistent-brand-voice-across-social-media-channels/

Wong, I. H. S., Fan, E. C. H., Chiu, D. K. W., & Ho, K. K. W. (2024). Internet Celebrities' Influence on Youths' Diet Behaviors: A Gender Study on Social Media. *Aslib Journal of Information Management*, 76(5), 778–799. DOI: 10.1108/AJIM-11-2022-0495

Xue, B., Yao, R., Ye, Z., Chan, C.-T., Chiu, D. K. W., & Zhong, Z. (2024). Social Media Analytics for Academic Music Library: A Case Study of CUHK Center for Chinese Music Studies. *Library Hi Tech*. Advance online publication. DOI: 10.1108/LHT-12-2023-0616

Yang, Y., & Zhai, P. (2022). Click-through rate prediction in online advertising: A literature review. *Information Processing & Management, 59*(2), 102853-. https://doi.org/DOI: 10.1016/j.ipm.2021.102853

Yang, Z. (2020). Development of Online Marketing During Coronavirus Epidemic. *E3S Web of Conferences, 218*, 1020-. DOI: 10.1051/e3sconf/202021801020

Yu, H. H. K., Chiu, D. K. W., & Chan, C. T. (2023). Resilience of symphony orchestras to challenges in the COVID-19 era: Analyzing the Hong Kong Philharmonic Orchestra with Porter's five force model. In Aloulou, W. (Ed.), *Handbook of Research on Entrepreneurship and Organizational Resilience During Unprecedented Times* (pp. 586–601). IGI Global.

Yu, H. Y., Tsoi, Y. Y., Rhim, A. H. R., Chiu, D. K. W., & Lung, M. M. W. (2022). Changes in habits of electronic news usage on mobile devices in university students: A comparative survey. *Library Hi Tech*, 40(5), 1322–1336. DOI: 10.1108/LHT-03-2021-0085

Zheng, J., Lam, A. H. C., & Chiu, D. K. (2023). Evaluating the effectiveness of learning commons as third spaces with the 5es usability model: The case of Hong Kong University of Science and Technology Library. In *Third-Space Exploration in Education* (pp. 123–143). IGI Global.

ADDITIONAL READING

Ali, M. (2021). *Remote Work and Sustainable Changes for the Future of Global Business.* IGI Global. https://www.igi-global.com/book/remote-work-sustainable-changes-future/264375

Ali, M. (2022). *Future Role of Sustainable Innovative Technologies in Crisis Management.* IGI Global. https://www.igi-global.com/book/future-role-sustainable-innovative-technologies/281281

Ali, M. (2023). *Shifting Paradigms in the Rapidly Developing Global Digital Ecosystem: A GCC Perspective.* In Digital Entrepreneurship and Co-Creating Value Through Digital Encounters (pp. 145-166). IGI Global. https://www.igi-global.com/chapter/shifting-paradigms-in-the-rapidly-developing-global-digital-ecosystem/323525

Ali, M. (2023). T*axonomy of Industry 4.0 Technologies in Digital Entrepreneurship and Co-Creating Value.* In *Digital Entrepreneurship and Co-Creating Value Through Digital Encounters* (pp. 24–55). IGI Global., https://www.igi-global.com/chapter/taxonomy-of-industry-40-technologies-in-digital-entrepreneurship-and-co-creating-value/323520 DOI: 10.4018/978-1-6684-7416-7.ch002

Ali, M., & Wood-Harper, T. (2021). *Fostering Communication and Learning with Underutilized Technologies in Higher Education*. IGI Global. https://www.igi-global.com/book/fostering-communication-learning-underutilized-technologies/244593

Ali, M., Wood-Harper, T., & Kutar, M. (2023). Multi-Perspectives of Contemporary Digital Transformation Models of Complex Innovation Management. In *Digital Entrepreneurship and Co-Creating Value Through Digital Encounters* (pp. 79–96). IGI Global., https://www.igi-global.com/chapter/multi-perspectives-of-contemporary-digital-transformation-models-of-complex-innovation-management/323522 DOI: 10.4018/978-1-6684-7416-7.ch004

Ali, M. B. (2021). Internet of Things (IoT) to Foster Communication and Information Sharing: A Case of UK Higher Education. In Ali, M. B., & Wood-Harper, T. (Eds.), *Fostering Communication and Learning With Underutilized Technologies in Higher Education* (pp. 1–20). IGI Global., https://www.igi-global.com/chapter/internet-of-things-iot-to-foster-communication-and-information-sharing/262718/ DOI: 10.4018/978-1-7998-4846-2.ch001

Ali, M. B., & Wood-Harper, T. (2022). Artificial Intelligence (AI) as a Decision-Making Tool to Control Crisis Situations. In *Future Role of Sustainable Innovative Technologies in Crisis Management*. IGI Global., https://www.igi-global.com/chapter/artificial-intelligence-ai-as-a-decision-making-tool-to-control-crisis-situations/298931 DOI: 10.4018/978-1-7998-9815-3.ch006

Ali, M. B., Wood-Harper, T., & Ramlogan, R. (2020). A Framework Strategy to Overcome Trust Issues on Cloud Computing Adoption in Higher Education. In Modern Principles, Practices, and Algorithms for Cloud Security (pp. 162-183). IGI Global. https://www.igi-global.com/chapter/a-framework-strategy-to-overcome-trust-issues-on-cloud-computing-adoption-in-higher-education/238907/

Chapter 5
Competition in an Age of Ecosystems:
Implications for Strategy

John Loonam
Dublin City University, Ireland

ABSTRACT

Organisations are increasingly looking beyond the firm to seek value creating opportunities. In particular, with the rise of digital technologies a new era of platforms, and business models, has enabled organisations, and respective strategists, to rethink how they compete. Greater openness and collaboration are redrawing organisational and industry boundaries, allowing opportunities within ecosystems. This chapter seeks to explore how competition has evolved over the past decades culminating in a new era of ecosystems competition. The author provides a framework to support strategists in mapping the competition landscape with a series of strategic insights offering academic and practitioner reflections.

1. INTRODUCTION

The nature of competition is changing. Increasingly, organisations are looking beyond their industries to seek out new opportunities for growth. The rise of digital natives (or born digital) enterprises has introduced a new way of thinking about competition. Buoyed by the successes attributed to digital native enterprises, traditional organisations are beginning to look beyond 'supply-side' economies of scale and focus upon 'demand-side' economies of scale. The traditional approach to competition, where products and services moved from left to right along the value chain is being transformed. The demand-side economies of scale, through the use of platforms

DOI: 10.4018/979-8-3373-0086-3.ch005

Copyright © 2025, IGI Global. Copying or distributing in print or electronic forms without written permission of IGI Global is prohibited.

(as opposed to value chains), powered by network effects transforms organisations' approach to thinking about competition. Instead of resources and processes being created with the customer in mind, value is created through community participation via network effects which in turn creates ecosystem value. This chapter begins with a recap on strategy and competition, introducing the information technology that has helped to transform organisations. The rise of ecosystem competition is next explored, where a framework is provided to illustrate the evolutionary steps competition has journeyed on. The chapter concludes with a review of key implications for strategy.

2. ON COMPETITION

The concept of competition, and the important role of business strategy, began to take root during the 1950s. As organization's started to grow, primarily driven by opportunities to rebuild after the global interruption of World War II, many organisations began to increase economies of scope as a result of new technologies associated with mass production. Equally, economies of scale also increased, as advantages learned during the mobilisation efforts associated with a world war were harnessed into the global distribution of goods and services. Naturally, such a rise in the opportunities to trade into global markets brought firms into increased competition with one another. Initial strategic thinking, in reflecting on how organisations might more effectively compete within such a macro-environment, adopted both an outside and inside organisational approach to strategy. Igor Ansoff, who is often referred to as the 'father of strategic management', took aim at the external landscape and in his publication titled 'Corporate Strategy' (1965) sought to develop a series of plans and techniques for managers to help tame this macro environment, culminating with the Ansoff Matrix which sought to support managers in mapping product and market growth opportunities. These strategic insights were advanced by other authors such as_Andrews, whose publication titled 'the concept of Corporate Strategy' (1971), proposed attention be given to both external macro-environmental opportunities and threats but equally matched to an organization's internal strengths and weaknesses. An approach that came to be referred to as SWOT analysis for strategic thinking. Kiechel reminds us of strategy's practice-centric orientation, where initial interest came from the management consulting firms, particularly in the North-Eastern part of the United States. Consultants working in firms such as McKinsey, Bain, and the Boston Consulting Group (BCG) and in collaboration with academic faculty within Harvard Business School and MIT Sloan, were at the vanguard of the strategy and competition conversation (2010). In particular, BCG's 'the experience curve' allowed executives to think differently about their environmental positioning and respective competition. As Kiechel notes, "businesses should expect their costs.......to decline systematically, at a rate that can be accurately predicted. With each doubling of experience, costs and prices should decline by a predictable amount, typically between 15 and 25 percent. Secondly, ...BCG posited a direct relationship between a company's position on the experience curve—and hence its costs—and its market share" (2010: 34). The experience curve was revolutionary in its insights, as it provided strategists with data on how their organisations were performing in terms of costs but perhaps more importantly it provided insights on competitors and their costs, market share and invariably position within an industry. Central to the experience curves approach was the belief that there could only ever be one or two key players that would dominate any industry. Magretta notes that "if rivals all pursue the "one best way" to compete, they will find themselves on a collision course. Companies will benchmark each other's practices and products. Competing to be the best leads inevitably to a destructive, zero-sum competition that no one can win" (2012: 35).

Before moving on to discuss competitive strategy and the rise of ecosystem competition, it is firstly important to introduce the technology that has shaped this evolution. As identified in Figure 1.1. below, four key evolutionary stages have occurred over the past four decades in relation to understanding business competition. In particular, information technology has played a key part in enabling this evolutionary process, with enterprise systems (and their influence on integrating value chain activities in support of attaining competitive advantage for respective products and services), the Internet (and in particular the Internet of Things (IoT) (referred to by Porter & Hepplemann as systems for smart, connected products) has put data at the centre of understanding competitive strategy, disruptive technologies (Christensen et al, 2013) and the associated market innovations brought about by reimagining the customers experience, and finally digital transformation and the associated big data and artificial intelligence applications have led to the emergence of digital platforms and new ways of viewing competition. Five of the world's top companies by market capitalization are digital natives (i.e., Apple, Microsoft, Amazon, Alphabet, and Meta with a combined valuation of over $8 trillion. Increasingly, digital natives have shown that platforms offer enormous potential in shaping competition. Therefore, traditional organisations are now seeking to play like the digital natives. According to a McKinsey survey, the author estimates "that by 2025 IoT will have a potential total economic impact of as much as $11.1 trillion per year. In fact, IoT will be the biggest source of value of all disruptive technologies, ahead of mobile Internet, knowledge-work automation, cloud computing, and advanced robotics" (Menard, 2017: 32). Central to the functioning and operation of IoT are the interconnections products and systems can make in establishing ecosystems. This new adaptation is transforming how organisations think about competition and the respective business models deployed to yield value-creation.

3. THE RISE OF ECOSYSTEM COMPETITION

As a consequence, strategy has come to focus on two key perspectives in exploring competition, i.e. *capturing and creating value*. Figure 1 below provides a framework that introduces these approaches from a competition perspective. The framework introduces capturing and creating value as opposing entities (hence a 2*2 Matrix) in order to illustrate their development over time and the current rise of ecosystem competition. Each perspective is presented along two axis (y-axis represents capturing value while the x-axis represents creating value), both which span low/high dimensions. Four quadrants help to illustrate the evolutionary nature of business competition. Commencing at the bottom left quadrant, we see competitions' primary focus was on industry products and services. With the rise of information technology and smart, connected products organisations started to seek greater value through data-centric competition. A schism in the approaches to viewing competition appears between Porter's (1980) competitive strategy and Kim and Mauborgne's (2005) blue ocean strategy thinking (although as Magretta (2012) points out this is less a schism and more a misinterpretation on Porter's definition of of 'being unique' from a strategy perspective). Finally, with the rise of digital platforms, which enabled scale and scope at exponential levels, strategists looked to the power of network effects to shape their thinking around ecosystem competition. Each of these quadrants will now be further discussed.

Figure 1. Competition in an age of ecosystems

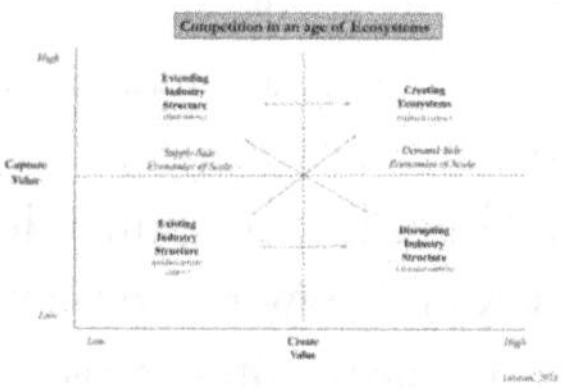

The first quadrant adapts a firm and industry structure lens onto competition where the primary focus is on product/service value add. This represents the classical Porterian view of competitive strategy, where Industry Structure is identified as the primary source for strategic analysis. The focus for strategists, using such tools as the five forces and value chain frameworks, is to explore where industry profit resides and how the organization can position itself to capture such unmet value (Loonam, 2021). A focus on industry structure reveals that profit realization must consider the interplay between the forces of suppliers, customers, new entrants, substitutes, and rivalry intensity. Each force is central to understanding industry competition and helps to explain the industry economics of average prices and costs, and therefore the average industry profitability incumbents are trying to beat (Porter, 1980). From the framework we see that industry structure is primarily focused on capturing value through strategic positioning. The 'industry' is, therefore, the key unit of analysis, where value is captured from within respective industries rather than created. However, since the advent of the Internet, which Porter & Hepplemann refer to as the second wave of information technology-driven competition (2014), many strategists have begun to view industry structure as a more porous entity. The Internet's primary effect on industry structure was its ability to reduce the reliance buyers and suppliers had on third agents, a concept referred to as 'disintermediation' (Porter, 2001). Previously, many business transactions required a third party that would facilitate an exchange for services or products between customers and suppliers. For example, many airlines hired travel agents to liaise with prospective customers in the sale of seats and packaged holidays. The Internet often removed this dependency on third party transactional agents and enabled strategists to liaise directly with their customers. Apart from increasing revenue for comparative transactions, strategists also began to 'get closer to their customers'. This became the real strategic opportunity for many organisations, where new avenues began to be explored into capturing new value.

The second quadrant illustrates this progression in strategic thinking towards competition. Existing industry structure, which the framework portrays as low both in terms of capturing and creating value in an ecosystem era, influenced by the rise in information technology began to push towards the top left quadrant, of extending industry structure. This quadrant was particularly influenced with the rise of the third wave of information technology-driven competition (Porter & Hepplemann, 2014) during the mid-2000s, where organisations looked to digital technologies to enhance product/service optimisation and co-create value (Prahalad & Ramaswamy, 2004) by becoming more data-centric. Two computing challenges, in particular, were resolved which enabled strategists to explore new forms of value capture. For decades, many organisations were limited in terms of data storage and processing capacity. The rise of cloud computing and big data analytics respectively, resolved these dilemmas and gave rise to an era of smart connected products (also referred to as The Internet of Things). This generation of "smart, connected products not only reshape competition within industries but expand industry boundaries. This occurs as the basis of competition shifts from discrete products to product systems consisting of closely related products, to systems of systems that link an array of product systems together" (Porter & Hepplemann, 2014: 74). Porter and Hepplemann note that industry structure is influenced by these smart connected products, specifically focusing on the five forces that shape industry profitability. For example, these digital technologies move competition away from focusing on price alone and enable greater product differentiation, which "enhances a company's ability to segment customers, customize products, set prices to better capture value, and extend value-added services" (2014: 72). This additional value capture helps to mitigate or reduce the bargaining power of buyers and thus strengthen an organization's competitive advantage. Once again, the ability to customize products through customer segmentation, migrates rivalry away from price alone and allows organisations to differentiate their offerings. In fact, some product-centric organizations can even start to focus on service offerings as a result of new data insights, thus creating new forms of value. Accordingly, new entrants are confronted with significant challenges when competing with incumbents embracing digitised products. Specifically, the complexity associated with products with sensors, software and supporting IT infrastructure raises fixed costs of incumbents. New entrants would need to match these costs in order to offer comparative products, which becomes a significant barrier to entry. The increased usage of data within products creates a new generation of product design and broadens product scope and definition, again making it difficult for new entrants to compete. Finally, "barriers to entry also rise when agile incumbents capture critical first-mover advantages by collecting and accumulating product data and using it to improve products and services and to redefine after-sale service" (Porter & Hepplemann, 2014: 73). The authors further note that smart, connected products can offer superior performance, customisation, and customer value that reduce substitution threats and improve industry growth and profitability. Finally, digitalisation is reshaping the bargaining power of suppliers. As products become more software enabled, the dependency on physical components for supply and repair reduces as software monitors and maintains product performance, therefore reducing the bargaining power of traditional suppliers. (Porter & Hepplemann, 2014: 74). However, one significant unintended consequence of digitalisation is the rise in new types of suppliers, such as "providers of sensors, software, connectivity, embedded operating systems, and data storage, analytics, and other parts of the technology stack" (Porter & Hepplemann, 2014: 74). These new suppliers, such as Google, Apple, and Amazon have increased their leverage and will play a significant role in our fourth quadrant of growing ecosystem competition.

The third quadrant speaks to the rise of value innovation as an approach to competition. This approach has evolved to include two broad competition variations, (i) disruptive innovation (Christensen et al, 2013) and (ii) blue ocean strategy (Kim & Mauborgne, 2005). Similarities exist between the variations, in particular the focus they have on creating new value opportunities and emphasising the customer as the key unit of analysis (rather than the competition) in reflecting on strategic insights. The key difference relates to the types of new market space opportunities and respective approaches to attaining these. As Leavy noted, "blue ocean strategy tends to focus on value innovation that uncovers new aggregations of demand by redefining the category, like Cirque du Soleil –entertainment that merges circus and theater – while disruptive innovation tends to concentrate on new demand-creation that expands the current served market, like Southwest and Ryanair in low-price air travel" (2018: 11). By focusing on value innovation (where both cost and differentiation are not viewed as trade-offs but potentially as complements) firms can expand their respective strategic choices to focus on the current underserved market, such as Ryanair, or create a wholly new customer experience, such as Cirque du Soleil. The focus on the customer as the key unit of analysis allows strategists to cut loose of the confines associated with industry structures and to think more creatively about respective industry products and services.

The fourth quadrant introduces the current era of ecosystem competition. Porter and Hepplemann highlight the growing bargaining power of new suppliers such as Google, Amazon, and Apple in this digitalized era, where their respective capabilities around software, cloud computing, data analytics, and increasingly artificial intelligence, give them significant leverage when participating in product 'systems of systems' (2014). Creating ecosystem competition differs from extending industry structure or disrupting industry structure as the primary unit of analysis, i.e. the organisation, is expanded to include a more holistic structural entity, the ecosystem. Strategists begin to explore future value opportunities within the ecosystem rather than just within the organisation. Many terms have been used to describe this phenomenon, namely, platform strategy, platform ecosystems, digital ecosystems or digital enterprises. Platform strategies promise to move the organization away from traditional 'make one, sell one' business models and support the introduction of networking ecosystems, where co-opetition becomes a key strategic approach. Organizations are increasingly looking to move away from such 'pipeline' thinking and embrace opportunities afforded by 'platform' strategies, where 'complex relationships are formed in which producers, consumers, and the platform itself- connect and conduct interactions with one another using the resources provided by the platform (Parker et al, 2016: 6-7). As Bjorkdahl et al noted, 'digital platforms are currently reshaping almost every sector of the economy. These platforms commonly create new ecosystems, connecting different types of users and/or complementary products and services. By leveraging the value created by such connections, successful platform ecosystems have repeatedly managed to compete with and disrupt existing value chains' (2024: 27-28).

Therefore, for strategists, capturing value becomes less about linear value chain thinking, with greater emphasis placed on new value opportunities across the platform (Loonam & O' Regan, 2022). As Van Alstyne et al note, 'Information Technology (IT) has enabled platforms to build scale quickly, to reach exponential growth in terms of user participation, and allow for real-time data capture that strengthens the platform network effect and increased potential value propositions'

(2016). Participant engagement within the ecosystem creates a two-sided network, which differs to traditional value chains where value moves from left (costs) to right (revenues) (Li et al, 2022). Within the ecosystem, "cost and revenue are both to the left and the right, because the platform has a distinct group of users on each side. The platform incurs costs in serving both groups and can collect revenue from each. The two groups are attracted to each other-a phenomenon that economists call the "network effect". With two-sided network effects, the platform's value to any given user largely depends on the number of users on the network's other side. Value grows as the platform matches demand from both sides" (Eisenmann et al, 2006: 94). Therefore, the unit of analysis for exploring competition becomes the ecosystem rather than the firm or industry. As Jacobides notes, "the firm and even the industry have ceased to be meaningful units of strategic analysis. We must focus instead on competition between digitally enabled designed ecosystems that span traditional industry boundaries and offer complex and customizable product-service bundles" (2019: 132).

4. IMPLICATIONS FOR STRATEGY

As a consequence, competition within an era of ecosystems has significant implications for strategy. From the framework above, and as noted by Menz et al (2021) and Holgersson et al (2022), five key insights emerge, namely (i) a blurring of industry boundaries, (ii) a move away from value capture towards greater value creation, (iii) an increase in a diverse approach to business models, (iv) the rise of ecosystems that shape vertical and horizontal scope, and (v) ecosystems structure can change over time and are a balance between centripetal and centrifugal forces.

Perhaps the most significant outcome of ecosystem competition has been the fraying of industry boundaries. While this has been a phenomenon since the emergence of blue ocean thinking in the early 2000s (Kim & Mauborgne, 2005), digitalisation has significantly disrupted the concept of firm and industry boundaries. From the framework above we see that increasingly traditional industries are looking for growth opportunities either through disruptive breakthroughs or new value creating revenue. For many traditional manufacturing organisations, for example John Deere, digitalization is a preferred option as it builds 'smartness' into its current suite of products that consequently enable new value creating opportunities. Yet, this path is not simple and as Porter and Hepplemann (2014) note, traditional organisations pursuing this route require a 'technology stack' that will enable digital transformation. The technology stack is typically composed of an Enterprise System, which integrates all organisational data into a central database. Digital technologies then feed into this enterprise system to enable data to be stored, processed, and analysed

(Loonam, 2021). Such an approach requires significant transformation from participating organisations, with a new suite of digital capabilities required to support data-driven value creation (Wormald et al, 2023). Successful implementation of digital technologies breaks the reliance on traditional industry competition. Instead, product-centric organisations fuelled with new insights into product usage, monitoring, analytics, and disposal can develop a suite of additional services to expand revenue and open opportunities in alternative industries. John Deere has begun this journey with an array of additional agri-business services now possible from a data-centric approach.

The second key insight from a strategy perspective, emerges as industry boundaries become more porous. Organisations begin to compete less in terms of 'capturing value' within an industry and start to explore avenues for creating value (Schreieck et al, 2024). From the framework above, we see that traditional organisations somewhat straddle both value seeking options as they move towards data-driven competition (from bottom left quadrant to top left quadrant). As Menz et al note, "both the market-based/industry structure and resource-based views of the firm traditionally focused on the ways firms could capture value, whether through building barriers to entry or through the inimitability of resource stocks. However, in today's digital business world the most talked-about firms are often not capturing any value (even though incumbents often aim to capture additional value through digital technologies)" (2021: 1701). Instead, the focus is on creating value opportunities. Central to creating ecosystem value are strategic approaches to network effects (customers), co-opetition (rivals), and partnerships (suppliers/stakeholders). Data becomes the key unit of analysis in facilitating success in collaborating with customers, rivals, and suppliers/stakeholders. Data, therefore, becomes the central mechanism through which new value is created, where strategists need to explore the type of data required and the suite of digital capabilities that can harness advantage to maximise the value of organisational offerings. Porter and Hepplemann note that "for companies seeking leadership in the product system (systems of systems), there is a need to invest in capturing and analyzing more-extensive data across multiple products and the external environment, even for products the company does not produce. For example, a smart, connected product system might need to capture traffic data, weather conditions, and fuel prices at different locations for an entire fleet of vehicles" (2014: 81).

The variety and diversity of business models on offer, has been one of the more profound influences of digitalization and is the third key strategic insight (Wang et al, 2024). In fact, digitalization has created two types of organisations, which has influenced the delivery of respective business models, traditional organisations, and digital natives. Traditional organisations pursue competitive advantage by controlling scarce and valuable resources where value moves from costs to revenue across the value chain with business models reflective of this dynamic. Organisations that are extending industry structures to capture additional value, develop novel insights from customer data to shape their business models. Digitalization enables traditional organisations to move beyond the 'make one-sell one' approach to a 'product-as-a-service' business "in which the manufacturer retains ownership and takes full responsibility for the costs of product operation and service in return for an ongoing charge (Porter & Hepplemann, 2014: 84). A consequence of moving to such a business model approach requires traditional organisations to rethink their structures, systems, and processes. Moving from product-centric to product and service-centric is not a simple business model switch but rather will require significant capability transformation and execution (Xu et al, 2023). Finally, digital natives, on the other hand, 'support asset-lite business models of those like Uber and Airbnb that allow customers to share physical assets by creating a market for underutilized capacity' (Menz et al, 2021: 1701). Such business models require platforms to enable such transactions, where the stronger the network effect the more easily it becomes for the platform to scale up (Zhu & Iansiti, 2012).

The fourth strategic insight leads on from a focus on network effects and platforms with the pursuit of vertical and horizontal scope as a consequence of ecosystem competition. From the framework above we see that both disruptive innovation (bottom right quadrant) and extending industry structure (top left quadrant) progress towards creating ecosystem competition. In fact, the quadrants (and respective lines and double-sided arrows) illustrate that a symbiotic relationship can exist between all three perspectives. Traditional organisations, whether embracing a blue ocean strategy or a digitalization of its products, can move over time to orchestrate (or participate) within an ecosystem. The pace of such 'strategic intent' influences vertical and horizontal scope aspirations. However, Menz et al note, that the "ecosystem effect appears to lead to a reduction in firm scope, because market-based transactions are more efficient" (2021: 1703). The key question then for organisations that decide to play within an ecosystem is whether it should expand its scope or continue as is. Porter and Hepplemann note that two strategic choices are presented with this scenario, "the first is whether a company should expand into related products or other parts of the system of systems (ecosystem). The second is whether a company should seek to provide the platform that connects the related products and information, even if it does not make or control all the parts (2014: 86). The key to supporting an effective decision is for organisations to ensure product/service quality which in turn will enhance network effects and platform scale.

The final strategic insight focuses on the nature of ecosystem structure. Unlike industry structure, which maintains relative stability over time, 'ecosystems are seldom stable but often in a state of flux…….and are a result of a delicate balance between centripetal forces that push economic activities toward integration, and centrifugal forces that pull economic activities out onto the market' (Holgersson et al, 2022: 5-6). According to the authors, two key complementarities shape ecosystem structure and value creation, namely technological innovation, and new management techniques and as a consequence influence competition and strategy. Technological innovations within the ecosystem, which are the main source of centripetal force, are dynamic and may be commoditized, generalized, or standardized over time. Commoditization occurs as substitutes are introduced for a given component, causing complements to lose their 'uniqueness' and as a consequence devaluing respective products. Components are specialized to a particular ecosystem and as the number of substitutes increase, they compete for the same market. Alternatively, generalization occurs when 'the complement may remain equally valuable in one ecosystem while becoming increasingly valuable in other ecosystems' (Holgersson et al, 2022: 10). Finally, the third centripetal force is that of standardization, which shares elements of both commoditization and generalization and often focuses primarily on 'the interface to enable interoperability of multiple alternative components' (Holgersson et al, 2022: 11). The second force that causes ecosystem change, and invariably shapes strategy, relates to management and coordination techniques. A primary focus of organisational and management theory over the past century has been to explore the allocation of resources across markets and where to position firm boundaries to coordinate activities (Shi et al, 2024). Managerial practices such as open innovation, which allows organisations to access talent pools, and as a consequence knowledge flows, beyond their own structural confines has further supported ecosystem collaboration and co-opetition. Kapoor and Lee noted, 'as value creation takes place across actors in ecosystems, firms need to find new business models to enable distributed value creation while capturing sufficient value. Hence, value creation and value capture in ecosystems lead into a specific coordination challenge, namely, that of balancing cooperation and competition' (2013). Therefore, the evolutionary nature of ecosystems, where a balance between centripetal forces, which push economic activities into a single firm, and centrifugal forces, which pull economic activities out onto the market, shapes strategy and has important insights for competition.

5. CONCLUSION

This chapter points to a changing landscape when exploring competition, where strategists move between product, customer, data, and network-centric perspectives of competition. The rise of platform systems has enabled ecosystem users to participate in the creation of value. Organisations are no longer just stand-alone entities driven by supply-side economies of scale in delivering 'make one sell one' business models within their respective industries. This chapter seeks to explore lessons from the digital natives, which by creating demand-side economies of scale through network effects promises to open new value creating opportunities for ecosystem participants. The framework above provides both academics and practitioners with a more holistic approach to reflecting on value capture and value creation. From a scholarship perspective, future research could explore the interconnected relationships between the quadrants with particular focus on organisations' evolutionary development of embracing ecosystem competition opportunities. From a managerial perspective, the framework provides a practical approach to reflecting on strategy across four key analytical approaches, i.e., products/services, data, customers, and networks), which seeks to support organisations in preparing for greater ecosystem competition.

REFERENCES

Andrews, K. R. (1971). *The concept of Corporate Strategy*. R.D. Irwin.

Ansoff, H. I. (1965). *Corporate Strategy: An Analytic Approach to Business Policy for Growth and Expansion*. McGraw-Hill.

Björkdahl, J., Holgersson, M., & Teece, D. J. (2024). Digital Platform Grafting: Strategies for Entering Established Ecosystems. *California Management Review*, 66(3), 27–46. DOI: 10.1177/00081256241238453

Christensen, C., Raynor, M. E., & McDonald, R. (2013). *Disruptive innovation*. Harvard Business Review.

Eisenmann, T., Parker, G., & Van Alstyne, M. W. (2006). Strategies for two-sided markets. *Harvard Business Review*, 84(10), 92.

Holgersson, M., Baldwin, C. Y., Chesbrough, H., & Bogers, M. L. (2022). The forces of ecosystem evolution. *California Management Review*, 64(3), 5–23. DOI: 10.1177/00081256221086038

Jacobides, M. G. (2019). In the ecosystem economy, what's your strategy? *Harvard Business Review*, 97(5), 128–137.

Jacobides, M. G., Cennamo, C., & Gawer, A. (2018). Towards a theory of ecosystems. *Strategic Management Journal*, 39(8), 2255–2276. DOI: 10.1002/smj.2904

Kapoor, R., & Lee, J. M. (2013). Coordinating and competing in ecosystems: How organizational forms shape new technology investments. *Strategic Management Journal*, 34(3), 274–296. DOI: 10.1002/smj.2010

Kiechel, W. (2010). *Lords of strategy: The secret intellectual history of the new corporate world*. Harvard Business Press.

Kim, W. C. (2005). Blue ocean strategy: From theory to practice. *California Management Review*, 47(3), 105–121. DOI: 10.1177/000812560504700301

Leavy, B. (2019). Value innovation and how to successfully incubate "blue ocean" initiatives. *Strategy and Leadership*, 46(3), 10–20. DOI: 10.1108/SL-02-2018-0020

Li, H., Zhang, C., & Kettinger, W. J. (2022). Digital Platform Ecosystem Dynamics: The Roles of Product Scope, Innovation, and Collaborative Network Centrality. *Management Information Systems Quarterly*, 46(2), 739–770. DOI: 10.25300/MISQ/2022/15444

Loonam, J. (2021). Towards Digital Transformation: Implications for Strategic Change. In Reviving Businesses With New Organizational Change Management Strategies (pp. 56-70). IGI Global.

Loonam, J., & O'Regan, N. (2022). Global value chains and digital platforms: Implications for strategy. *Strategic Change*, 31(1), 161–177. DOI: 10.1002/jsc.2485

Magretta, J., 2012. Understanding Michael Porter: The essential guide to competition and strategy. Harvard business press.

Menard, A. (2017). *How can we recognize the real power of the Internet of Things?* McKinsey Consulting.

Menz, M., Kunisch, S., Birkinshaw, J., Collis, D. J., Foss, N. J., Hoskisson, R. E., & Prescott, J. E. (2021). Corporate Strategy and the Theory of the Firm in the Digital Age. *Journal of Management Studies*, 58(7), 1695–1720. DOI: 10.1111/joms.12760

Parker, G. G., Van Alstyne, M. W., & Choudary, S. P. (2016). *Platform revolution: How networked markets are transforming the economy and how to make them work for you.* WW Norton & Company.

Porter, M. E. (1980). *Competitive Strategy.* The Free Press.

Porter, M. E. (2001). Strategy and the Internet. *Harvard Business Review*, 79, 62–78. PMID: 11246925

Porter, M. E., & Heppelmann, J. E. (2014). How smart, connected products are transforming competition. *Harvard Business Review*, 92(11), 64–88.

Prahalad, C. K., & Ramaswamy, V. (2004). Co-creating unique value with customers. *Strategy and Leadership*, 32(3), 4–9. DOI: 10.1108/10878570410699249

Schreieck, M., Huang, Y., Kupfer, A., & Krcmar, H. (2024). The Effect of Digital Platform Strategies on Firm Value in the Banking Industry. *Journal of Management Information Systems*, 41(2), 394–421. DOI: 10.1080/07421222.2024.2340825 PMID: 38974483

Shi, X., Liang, X., & Ansari, S. (2024). Bricks without straw: Overcoming resource limitations to architect ecosystem leadership. *Academy of Management Journal*, 67(4), 1084–1123. DOI: 10.5465/amj.2021.1440

Van Alstyne, M. W., Parker, G. G., & Choudary, S. P. (2016). Pipelines, platforms, and the new rules of strategy. *Harvard Business Review*, 94(4), 54–62.

Wang, Y., Yue, L. Q., Rajagopalan, N., & Wu, B. (2024). The entry-deterring effects of synergies in complementor acquisitions: Evidence from Apple's digital platform market, the iOS app store. *Strategic Management Journal*, smj.3639. DOI: 10.1002/smj.3639

Wormald, A., Shah, S. K., Braguinsky, S., & Agarwal, R. (2023). Pioneering digital platform ecosystems: The role of aligned capabilities and motives in shaping key choices and performance outcomes. *Strategic Management Journal*, 44(7), 1653–1697. DOI: 10.1002/smj.3475

Xu, L., Yang, S., Liu, Y., Newbert, S. L., & Boal, K. (2023). Seeing the forest and the trees: Exploring the impact of inter-and intra-entrepreneurial ecosystem embeddedness on new venture creation. *Academy of Management Journal*, 66(6), 1954–1982. DOI: 10.5465/amj.2021.0791

Zhu, F., & Iansiti, M. (2012). Entry into platform-based markets. *Strategic Management Journal*, 33(1), 88–106. DOI: 10.1002/smj.941

ADDITIONAL READING

Ali, M. (2021). *Remote Work and Sustainable Changes for the Future of Global Business*. IGI Global. https://www.igi-global.com/book/remote-work-sustainable-changes-future/264375

Ali, M. (2022). *Future Role of Sustainable Innovative Technologies in Crisis Management*. IGI Global. https://www.igi-global.com/book/future-role-sustainable-innovative-technologies/281281

Ali, M. (2023). *Shifting Paradigms in the Rapidly Developing Global Digital Ecosystem: A GCC Perspective*. In Digital Entrepreneurship and Co-Creating Value Through Digital Encounters (pp. 145-166). IGI Global. https://www.igi-global.com/chapter/shifting-paradigms-in-the-rapidly-developing-global-digital-ecosystem/323525

Ali, M. (2023). T*axonomy of Industry 4.0 Technologies in Digital Entrepreneurship and Co-Creating Value*. In *Digital Entrepreneurship and Co-Creating Value Through Digital Encounters* (pp. 24–55). IGI Global., https://www.igi-global.com/chapter/taxonomy-of-industry-40-technologies-in-digital-entrepreneurship-and-co-creating-value/323520 DOI: 10.4018/978-1-6684-7416-7.ch002

Ali, M., & Wood-Harper, T. (2021). *Fostering Communication and Learning with Underutilized Technologies in Higher Education*. IGI Global. https://www.igi-global.com/book/fostering-communication-learning-underutilized-technologies/244593

Ali, M., Wood-Harper, T., & Kutar, M. (2023). Multi-Perspectives of Contemporary Digital Transformation Models of Complex Innovation Management. In *Digital Entrepreneurship and Co-Creating Value Through Digital Encounters* (pp. 79–96). IGI Global., https://www.igi-global.com/chapter/multi-perspectives-of-contemporary-digital-transformation-models-of-complex-innovation-management/323522 DOI: 10.4018/978-1-6684-7416-7.ch004

Ali, M. B. (2021). Internet of Things (IoT) to Foster Communication and Information Sharing: A Case of UK Higher Education. In Ali, M. B., & Wood-Harper, T. (Eds.), *Fostering Communication and Learning With Underutilized Technologies in Higher Education* (pp. 1–20). IGI Global., https://www.igi-global.com/chapter/internet-of-things-iot-to-foster-communication-and-information-sharing/262718/ DOI: 10.4018/978-1-7998-4846-2.ch001

Ali, M. B., & Wood-Harper, T. (2022). Artificial Intelligence (AI) as a Decision-Making Tool to Control Crisis Situations. In *Future Role of Sustainable Innovative Technologies in Crisis Management*. IGI Global., https://www.igi-global.com/chapter/artificial-intelligence-ai-as-a-decision-making-tool-to-control-crisis-situations/298931 DOI: 10.4018/978-1-7998-9815-3.ch006

Ali, M. B., Wood-Harper, T., & Ramlogan, R. (2020). A Framework Strategy to Overcome Trust Issues on Cloud Computing Adoption in Higher Education. In Modern Principles, Practices, and Algorithms for Cloud Security (pp. 162-183). IGI Global. https://www.igi-global.com/chapter/a-framework-strategy-to-overcome-trust-issues-on-cloud-computing-adoption-in-higher-education/238907/

Chapter 6
Economic Dimensions of Competition in the Indian Telecom Sector:
A Study on the Impact of Reliance Jio on the Telecom Sector and Consumers

Karun Sanjaya
Symbiosis Law School, Nagpur, India & Symbiosis International University (Deemed), Pune, India

Neha Agarwal
HRDC Economics, University of North Bengal, Siliguri, India

ABSTRACT

Reliance Jio has created a revolution in the Indian telecom industry. The success of Jio in the industry can be attributed to the strategies it adopted to penetrate the market and the use of the same at the right time. It is not surprising to see that Reliance Jio is the only other player in the telecom industry apart from Bharti Airtel, which has launched 5G services in India. The paper attempts to analyze the strategies adopted by Reliance Jio and their impact on the industry and the consumers. The chapter is divided into five parts. The first part provides background information on the competition in the Indian telecom sector. The second part analyzes the market gap that allowed Reliance Jio to enter and penetrate the market successfully. The third part examines how Reliance Jio's entry affected other players in the telecom sector. The fourth part discusses the impact of Reliance Jio on consumers' lifestyles. Finally, the chapter concludes with the study's findings and suggests the way forward.

DOI: 10.4018/979-8-3373-0086-3.ch006

Copyright © 2025, IGI Global. Copying or distributing in print or electronic forms without written permission of IGI Global is prohibited.

I. INTRODUCTION

India has the second-largest telecommunication market in terms of subscriber base. Until the mid-1980s, the telecom sector was government-aided. It was only after 1981 that liberalization of the telecom industry began when the honourable Prime Minister "Indira Gandhi signed contracts with Alcatel CIT of France to merge with the state-owned Telecom Company (ITI), in an effort to set up 5,000,000 lines per year" (Dash, 2005). The actual evolution began after 1985 when the "Department of Post and Telegraph" was separated and a new "Department of Posts" and the "Department of Telecommunications" (DoT) was formed. The formulation of the National Telecom Policy, 1994, played a crucial role as it encouraged investments, foreign and domestic, in the Indian telecom sector. However, participation of private companies was not allowed in 'national long-distance (NLD) and international long-distance (ILD) services'. Subsequently, in 1997 TRAI (Telecom Regulatory Authority of India) was set up by the government to reduce its intrusion in the decision-making of the telecom sector. The real milestone came in 1999 through New Telecom Policy (NTP) 1999, under which ILD and NLD were allowed even to the private sector. It was in the year 2002 that the government "opened its doors to private players, allowing the likes of Reliance Communication, Jio, Tata Indicom, Vodafone, Loop Mobile, Airtel, Idea, etc., to enter the telecom, broadband, Internet, and enterprise services market" (Lakshminarasimha & Abraham, 2021).

Before the entry of Reliance JIO in the telecom market, there were ten wireless providers, which included operators like Reliance Communications, Tata Teleservices, Aircel, Telenor, Sistema, and Videocon (Singh, 2019). The fact that telecom service providers like Videocon, Hutch Essar, Telstra, and Escotel were forced out of the industry even before Reliance JIO's entry shows that the major players like Airtel, Vodafone, and Idea created a hostile environment for the sustenance of small players in the telecom industry. With the entry of Reliance JIO in 2016, companies like Reliance Communications and Airtel faced so much revenue loss that they had to shut down due to bankruptcy. Bharti Airtel, one of the leading private units, and BSNL ('Bharat Sanchar Nigam Ltd.'), one of the largest & leading public sector units in the telecom industry, also faced substantial loss in terms of revenue and customers. Now, there are only three private companies (Airtel and Vodafone-Idea), including JIO and two state-run operators, BSNL and MTNL. However, a merger of MTNL with BSNL was proposed in the later quarter of 2019 (Kurup, 2019).

II. THE ENTRY OF RELIANCE JIO

Mukesh Ambani very well knew that in the21st century data would become the new oil. After the death of Dhirajlal Harichand Ambani (popularly known as Dhirubhai), it was his wife, Kokilaben Ambani, who brokered the deal between her two sons. The new age economies, which included Reliance Infocomm, Reliance Energy and Reliance Capital, went to Anil Ambani and the old age economies, which included Reliance Industries and IPCL, went to Mukesh Ambani. There was a ten-year no-compete agreement that stated that the two would not be permitted to enter each other's sectors. However, due to the continuous efforts of Mukesh Ambani, it was scrapped in 2010. "The boards of Mukesh Ambani-controlled Reliance Industries Ltd (RIL) and Reliance-Anil Dhirubhai Ambani (R-Adag) group firms approved and signed an agreement cancelling the non-compete arrangement they had entered in January 2006" (Shrivastava et al., 2010). This meant that Mukesh Ambani now got an opportunity to enter the telecom market. Without wasting any time, he made an entry into this market. Accordingly, on 1st September 2016, Reliance JIO was launched, which disrupted the whole telecom industry. Reliance JIO refined and revolutionized the Indian telecom sector (Himanshi Lohchab, 2024). Aggressive plans were followed to make a stand in the fastest-growing sector of India. The services included discounted plans like free transfer of 4G internet connectivity and free voice and roaming till 31st December. In addition to this, there was easy access to SIMS, i.e., 8 SIMS would be provided to a single AADHAR card which would take fifteen minutes to be activated, unlike other SIMS, which took twenty-four hours. For this, a massive investment of Rs 1,50,000 was made (Abbas, 2016). The question arises as to why would Mukesh Ambani invest so much in a plan that would not yield any profits to him? The answer is -to capture the telecom market using the "loss-leading strategy". Under this strategy, the companies sell a product at a lower price than the market price with the purpose of acquiring customers from their rival firms. This is precisely what Mukesh Ambani successfully did. He applied the growth hacking strategy to expand his business and conquer the telecom industry. However, there was a fear that as soon as the offer ended on 31st December, people might not use Reliance JIO. Hence, in order to retain its customers, Reliance JIO came up with a plan better known as the 'Happy new year plan', extending the date of discount till 30th March. With this, Reliance JIO became the first organisation that provided free data and calls to its customers for a stretch of six months. According to a report published by the Telecom Regulatory Authority of India (TRAI), "the subscriber base of telecom companies in India in October 2017 for Bharti Airtel stood at 285 million, followed by Vodafone at 208 million, Idea Cellular at 191 million, and Reliance Jio at 145.9 million making Reliance JIO the fourth largest telecom operator in India within a span of one year" (Press Trust of India, 2017). Reliance JIO tried its best to provide good services to its customers so that its customers would unknowingly promote Reliance JIO. This strategy is known as referral generation. It means when a customer turns into a promoter. Thus, in this way, with the help of the growth hacking strategy of acquisition, activation, retention, and referral, Reliance JIO ultimately reached the final and the most critical stage of revenue generation. Reliance JIO, rather than trying to beat the competition, made the competition irrelevant through the implementation of the blue ocean strategy. Under this strategy, a company explores a new market space where there has been no competition. In other words, rather than trying to grab a market share of demand, Reliance JIO created new and innovative market demand. The wise decision of implementing the blue ocean strategy is what attributes to the outstanding success of JIO in the telecom industry.

III. IMPACT OF JIO ON THE TELECOM INDUSTRY

India, the second-largest telecom market, was stirred after the entry of the giant telecom player Reliance JIO. The new entrant was no less than a curse for other existing companies. The aggressive strategies and plans made by Reliance JIO made it tough for other players like Idea, Vodafone, BSNL, and Airtel to survive in the market. The effect of Reliance JIO on the Indian telecom sector was evident from the very first day of its inception when Number 1 telecom operator Bharti Airtel lost its share price by 6.4% on the Bombay Stock Exchange. Even other telecom operators like Idea Cellular and Reliance Communications, who at that time were ranked Number 2 and 3 respectively, saw a fall in their share prices by 10.5% and 8.8% respectively (ET Bureau, 2016). On the one hand, in order to drive the competitors strategically out of the market, and on the other, to attract customers, the strategy of predatory pricing was followed. A price below average variable cost (AVC) was set, which obviously would lead to huge losses.

Reliance JIO was prepared to take such risks as these losses would be borne but only in the short run. It was a long-term perspective of earning maximum profits in the long -run. But what about other companies? They were bound to revise their plans as sticking to the existing schemes implied losing their market share. Airtel, India's largest telecommunication service provider, reduced its pre-paid data tariffs (Business Standard, 2016) and also launched 4G data pack that could match the high-speed data provided by Reliance JIO. The impact of pricing strategy was so adverse that it led to some companies shutting down and others struggling for their survival. Reliance communications, headed by Anil Ambani, decided to shut most of its wireless operations, and the employees of Reliance Communications had been put on notice period. Reliance communication blamed Reliance JIO for having brought the "creative destruction" (Sengupta, 2017).

The existence of a price and data war forced Idea and Vodafone to join hands. On 20th March 2017, the Board of Directors of Vodafone India and Idea jointly announced the merger, which was approved on 31st August 2018. The merged company was known as Vodafone-idea limited. The merger would have dual benefits- firstly, it would support both these companies striving for survival. Secondly, it will help them deal with the dominance faced due to the new entrant "Reliance JIO" in the telecom sector. However, the announcement of the merger also created a negative image in public. The Idea prices started to drop and the share price of Idea declined from Rs.97.70 on 20th March 2017 to Rs. 81.81 on 6th September 2017 (Thekeepitsimple, 2021). The big game-changer was achieving success in terms of the customer base as well. It is known that the cost of acquiring a new customer is more than the cost of retaining the existing customer. Reliance JIO was triumphant in not only having new customers subscribing to its services but also gaining customers from its rivals. This implies that other companies were losing their subscribers. Vodafone-Idea lost eight crores of its subscribers till early 2019, pushing it to the position of number 3 (Singh & Garg, 2010). "According to a report from Statista released in February 2020, the subscriber base of Reliance Jio is 370 million and is the largest in the country and third-largest in the world as of December 2019. The other telecom operators in the country are Vodafone-Idea (332M), Bharti Airtel (327.3M), BSNL (118.12M), MTNL (3.38 M) and Reliance (0.02M)". The point to be noted is that these operators have been a part of the telecom industry for more than ten years, yet they were unable to withstand JIO, which is not even four years old (Madhavan & Chirputkar, 2020). According to recent data released by the Telecom Regulatory Authority of India (TRAI), "Vodafone Idea lost over 40 lakh subscribers in June 2021. On the other hand, rival Indian telecom companies such as Airtel and Jio have gained about 38 lakh and 54 lakh subscribers in the same period" (Mehrotra, 2021).

The other players were well aware that innovative ideas are a prerequisite for a solid subscriber base. Companies started using catchy slogans and hiring celebrities to endorse their products. Reliance JIO hired Shah Rukh Khan as its brand ambassador and A.R Rahman to host the launch function. Both of them had earlier been associated with its rival, Airtel. Some among others were Idea's slogan, "An idea can change your life," which had Abhisekh Bachchan as its brand ambassador. Vodafone's slogans 'Wherever you go our network follows' signified the importance of network coverage, and another slogan, 'Happy to Help,' was used to show the care towards the customer (Kalyani, 2016). Hence, we can say that Reliance JIO is a game-changer in the telecom industry. It dominated the 4G market by its early mover advantage. The rivals faced difficulties to such an extent that some had to shut down while some formed mergers. The prices of shares like that of BSNL and Idea started to fall. Revision of schemes and plans by telecom companies had become a common feature in the market. Of course, how to gain a customer base was another concern for them which was done through advertisement and innovative ideas. However, Reliance JIO was the one who ultimately emerged out as a winner as they made customers realise that they are still the king of the market.

IV. IMPACT OF JIO ON CONSUMERS

A war was raging between different telecom operators since the entry of Reliance JIO. The war, no doubt, created disruptions and disturbances in the industry. However, the consumers evolved as the absolute winners even without having been a part of it. It has been very rightly said that "Customer is defined as the king of the market and also known as the Blackhole because it is not an easy task to understand the need and demand of the customer" (Singh & Garg, 2010). Having said this, it will not be incorrect if we say that Mukesh Ambani, the brain behind Reliance JIO, to a large extent knew what Indians actually needed. Making data as the primary source of revenue and voice calls as its secondary source leaves no question on the strategic moves. The impact of JIO on consumers can be seen from various aspects, viz.

Speed: The dream of every Indian to have high internet speed was turned into reality by Reliance JIO. According to a report published by TRAI My speed Portal in February 2018, "Reliance JIO had the highest 4G download average speed of about 20.3Mbps in India compared to other networks" (Joy and Bahl, 2018). According to the Telecom Regulatory Authority of India (TRAI), "Reliance JIO maintained its top position with the highest average data download speed of 24.1 megabits per second among 4G service providers" (Press Trust of India, 2021).

Budget Friendly Data Plans: Vodafone customers had to spend on an average Rs 3861 for 13 G.B of data for a year. Similarly, BSNL and Idea customers paid approximately Rs 2574 for 13 GB for a year and Rs 3,237 for 13 GB for a year, respectively. Contrary to it, Jio announced free voice and data till December 2016 (Kumar, 2016). Even after announcing paid "Prime" plans in March 2017, the average cost per GB of data remained low at almost 11 per GB (Mehta, 2017). The growing insecurities among the operators led to the revision of their plans. For instance, Airtel came out with several recharge plans, and the cheapest amongst them was Rs 8 plan. Under this plan, the offer included Local plus STD mobile calls at 30 paisa/minute for 56 days (Saha,

2017). As a result of competition among operators, the prices came down through which the customer benefitted.

Endorsement and Sponsorship: Advertisement has been the prime factor that affects the consumer of any product. What would have been more advantageous for Reliance JIO when the honourable Prime Minister, Narendra Modi himself, endorsed its offerings. He also called the Reliance JIO's services and products "Revolutionary" (Bhatia & Palepu, 2017). This implies that consumers' trust in any product was already instilled in them. Jio also tied up with the TV quiz-based reality show Kaun Banega Crorepati (KBC), which increased its subscriber base and simultaneously made the customers engage in it (Datta and Majumdar, 2019). In order to prove its product superiority and maintain status stature, Reliance JIO also sponsored some of the programs, namely "Filmfare, a set of movie awards presented by The Times Group, the Mumbai Film Festival, Pro-Kabaddi League team Jaipur Pink Panthers, and the Rio-bound Indian Olympics contingent in 2016, among others, besides KBC" (Jha, 2017).

Low-Cost Smartphones: Reliance JIO became the first telecom operator in India to provide mobile phones named LYF at very affordable prices. The phones came with free sim cards and preloaded JIO apps like My JIO, JIO Chat, JIO news express, and others. The rural population who could not initially afford expensive phones could also purchase these phones, which had the latest 4G technology due to its cheap rates. As a result, Reliance JIO also gained control over the rural and middle-class people whose contribution is directly proportional to Reliance JIO's success (Joy & Bahl, 2018).

Bundled Entertainment Services: Reliance JIO was able to bridge the digital gap prevalent in India through its storehouse of JIO apps like JIO cinema, JIO Wallet, JIO Meet, JIO TV, to name a few. All these apps increased consumers' satisfaction and had positive responses. In a world of digitalization, having a variety of apps at one's doorsteps is no less than a blessing. This blessing was bestowed by the giant player Reliance JIO on its customers that too without any additional charges.

Subscriptions: Reliance JIO joined hands with DISNEY+HOTSTAR to provide a free one-year subscription of DISNEY+HOTSTAR to its prepaid users. According to the information available on the website, "The Rs. 499 prepaid recharge gets a validity of 28 days with daily 2GB high-speed data limit. Once the limit is crossed, users will get only 64kbps of speed. Other benefits include unlimited voice calls and 100 SMS messages per day" (Khare, 2022).

Endowment Effect: The addiction to data consumption is as harmful as addiction of any other kind. An individual has become so dependent on the internet and his smartphone that life seems to come to a halt without these.

Initially, by giving free internet services to the customers, Reliance JIO has made us so used to using it that from making payments to buying groceries, for studying to being entertained, all required data. Reliance JIO takes advantage of this. It has now announced a tariff hike as it knows that now customers would be ready to pay even a higher price in order to continue with the services of Reliance JIO. The reason is that the product which the customer has used for a certain period becomes more valuable to them. This is known as the endowment effect. At present, the basic necessities of life for a person are food, cloth, shelter, and data.

5G Technology- the latest technology, i.e., 5G, has been recently launched in India. In order to win the bid for the 5G spectrum, a considerable investment was required. So, Reliance JIO like its rivals, Airtel and Vodafone-Idea, has increased its tariff plans too. This is done to increase their Average Revenue Per User (ARPU) so that profits can increase and required finance can be accumulated. This means that customers will have to face a hike in their plans which means paying more for the same plans. However, the price rise can be compensated by better services by the telecom operators.

The customers are the 'king of the market' is completely relevant and correct. For any business to reach the desired heights of success, it requires the positive response of the consumers. Reliance JIO, through its affordable tariff plans, low-cost smartphones, attractive advertisement, sponsorships, diversification in apps bundled with various subscriptions, was able to win over the customers. As far as the consumers were concerned, they were quite satisfied with Reliance JIO. What would 'digital India' want more when they were getting data at low prices not only through Reliance JIO but other operators too. The credit can be attributed to Reliance JIO and their plans, which shook the telecom sector. Earlier, every MB of data was not less precious than a drop of water for a person in the desert. Now data has become an addiction that people cannot even imagine living without. Reliance JIO has successfully won the game, which had started way back in 2010. However, the news about the launch of 5G in the near future has resulted in tariff hikes.

V. SUMMARY OF FINDINGS

1. Even before the entry of Reliance JIO, the Indian telecom industry was dominated by major players like Airtel, Idea, and Vodafone.
2. Soon after the entry of Reliance JIO, it was able to capture the telecom market within a short span of time with the help of the growth hacking strategy.

3. Reliance JIO's entry into the telecom sector caused the shutdown, merger, and loss of subscriber base of other telecom service providers, including Airtel and Vodafone-Idea.
4. The data pricing policy of Reliance JIO, along with its other attractive offers, has resulted in highly contented customers.
5. Reliance JIO's predatory pricing policy forced the other telecom players to revise their pricing strategies, ultimately benefiting the customers.
6. With its irresistible schemes, JIO could become the largest mobile network operator in India and the third-largest in the world.
7. Though Reliance JIO has hiked its tariffs, there is no significant loss of subscriber base. The same can be attributed to two reasons: a) endowment effect and b) penetration pricing.
8. The huge investment that was required for the 5G spectrum is a factor that contributed to the tariff hike by 20-25%.

VI. SUGGESTIONS

The study puts forth the following suggestions:

1. The government should fix the floor price for the telecom sector, which will enable every player to cover their total cost and earn a minimum profit required to sustain in the market.
2. The mobile operators should try to compete not only in terms of pricing but also in terms of services. If the quality offered by them is satisfactory, then the differences in prices will not affect their customer base to a large extent.
3. The Competition Commission of India (CCI) should monitor the mobile operators to see that the existing dominant players do not form cartels and create entry barriers for other players.
4. The relief package announced for the telecom sector needs to be implemented properly and efficiently to encourage more players, which will lead to consumer sovereignty.
5. Due to the hike in tariff rates, for having cost-effective data plans, customers can install wifi at their homes and can have minimum recharge just for calls.

VII. CONCLUSION

To conclude, we can say that the evolution of the Indian telecom industry has a long history with several twists and turns. It was only after 1981 that private companies were allowed to operate in the telecom market. Earlier, the market was dominated by public telecom operators, mainly BSNL and MTNL. The liberalization policy and other developments like the setting up of TRAI and formulation of the New Telecom Policy brought major changes in the telecom market. However, it was the giant entrant Reliance JIO that changed the entire game of the telecom market. The 'JIO EFFECT' was like a tsunami that washed away the hopes of the then-dominant players like Airtel, Vodafone, Idea, and BSNL to establish themselves as the leader of the telecom market. Reliance JIO made the environment in the telecom market so antagonistic that some companies like Reliance Communications and Aircel had to cease their operation while others like Vodafone with Idea and Telenor India with Bharti Airtel formed mergers. The ongoing conflict between telecom service providers proved most advantageous to the customers, especially in terms of speed and cost of data. The customers were content with the services provided by Reliance JIO, implying that the main objective of having a maximum subscriber base was achieved by this game-changer.

The growing debt faced by telecom operators has led to an increase in their tariff rates due to a decline in profits. It was Airtel who first increased their price to raise their Average Revenue Per User (ARPU) for a healthy, sustainable competition. This was followed by Vodafone-Idea and then Reliance JIO. According to them, in order to sustain the competition, especially after the launch of 5G, tariff hike was necessary. Thus, it can be seen that telecom operators have been increasing the prices, which may further increase in the future so that they can keep their profit level intact and raise the huge finance needed for making an investment in the 5G spectrum.

The million-dollar question is whether the Reliance JIO made huge investments for the benefit of its customers or it actually used the customers as an investment for its benefit?

REFERENCES

Abbas, M. (2016). *Reliance Jio is world's largest startup with Rs 150,000 crore investment: Mukesh Ambani*. The Economic Times. https://economictimes.indiatimes.com/industry/telecom/reliance-jio-is-worlds-largest-startup-with-rs-150000-crore-investment-mukesh-ambani/articleshow/51613248.cms?from=mdr

Bhatia, J., & Palepu, A. R. (2016). Reliance Jio: Predatory Pricing or Predatory Behaviour? *Economic and Political Weekly*, 51(41), 33–39. https://www.jstor.org/stable/44165786

Bureau, E. T. (2016, September). *Mukesh Ambani ushers in telecom revolution, Reliance Jio to launch services on September 5*. The Economic Times; Economic Times. https://economictimes.indiatimes.com/news/company/corporate-trends/mukesh-ambani-ushers-in-telecom-revolution-reliance-jio-to-launch-services-on-september5/articleshow/53970531.cms

Business Standard. (2016, July 17). *Airtel cuts pre-paid data tariffs giving up to 67% more data*. Business Standard; Business Standard. https://www.business-standard.com/article/companies/airtel-cuts-pre-paid-data-tariffs-giving-up-to-67-more-data-116071700348_1.html

Dash, K. C. (2005). *Veto Players and the Deregulation of State-Owned Enterprises: The Case of Telecommunications in India*. Archive.org. https://web.archive.org/web/20080911040829/http://www.thunderbird.edu/wwwfiles/publications/magazine/fall2005/pdf-files/Telecom_RevJune27AS__1.pdf

Datta, A., & Majumdar, S. (2019). *Inside Reliance Jio's content factory*. Www.fortuneindia.com. https://www.fortuneindia.com/enterprise/inside-reliance-jios-content-factory/103723

Himanshi Lohchab. (2024, September 5). *Jio's disruptive entry revolutionised India's telecom market*. The Economic Times; Economic Times. https://economictimes.indiatimes.com/industry/telecom/telecom-news/et-graphics-jios-disruptive-entry-revolutionised-indias-telecom-market/articleshow/113104507.cms?from=mdr

Jha, L. (2017, October 11). *Reliance Jio's expenditure on sponsorship deals pegged at Rs300 crore*. Mint. https://www.livemint.com/Companies/vD8Xvm0RUotYwuS69CksBM/Reliance-Jio-spend-on-sponsorship-deals-pegged-at-Rs300-cror.html

Joy, T., & Bahl, S. (2018). Disruption by Reliance Jio in Telecom Industry. *International Journal of Pure and Applied Mathematics*, 118(20), 43–49. https://www.acadpubl.eu/hub/2018-118-21/articles/21a/6.pdf

Kalyani, P. (2016). An Empirical Study on Reliance JIO Effect, Competitor's Reaction and Customer Perception on the JIO'S Pre- Launch Offer. *Journal of Management Engineering and Information Technology*, 3(5), 18–36. DOI: 10.5281/zenodo.183437

Khare, S. (2022, January 6). *Jio Rs. 499 Prepaid Recharge Plan With 1-Year Disney+ Hotstar Subscription Revived: All the Details*. Gadgets 360. https://gadgets360.com/telecom/news/jio-rs-499-prepaid-recharge-plan-revived-disney-plus-hotstar-28-days-validity-2gb-high-speed-data-benefits-2692228

Kumar, R. P. (2016, August 30). *Reliance Jio effect: Data charges slashed, here's a comparison for the best deal*. The Economic Times; Economic Times. https://economictimes.indiatimes.com/news/company/corporate-trends/reliance-jio-effect-data-charges-slashed-heres-a-comparison-for-the-best-deal/articleshow/53926255.cms?utm_source=contentofinterest&utm_medium=text&utm_campaign=cppst

Kurup, R. (2019, July 29). *MTNL to be a BSNL subsidiary*. Business Line. https://www.thehindubusinessline.com/info-tech/mtnl-to-be-a-bsnl-subsidiary/article28749551.ece

Lakshminarasimha, K., & Abraham, K. J. (2021). *Forbes India - Telecom In India–propelling Digital Growth*. Forbes India. https://www.forbesindia.com/blog/enterprise/does-indias-telecom-sector-still-need-restrictive-policies/

Madhavan, P. M., & Chirputkar, A. (2020). ANALYSIS OF THE IMPACT OF RELIANCE JIO INFOCOMM LTD ON INDIAN ECONOMY: A CASE STUDY. *PalArch's Journal of Archaeology of Egypt / Egyptology, 17*(6), 4452–4461. https://archives.palarch.nl/index.php/jae/article/view/1695

Mehrotra, S. (2021). *Vodafone Idea loses over 4 million subscribers, Jio and Airtel dominate market share: TRAI*. Republic World. https://www.republicworld.com/technology-news/mobile/vodafone-idea-loses-over-4-million-subscribers-jio-and-airtel-dominate-market-share-trai.html

Mehta, I. (2017, June 1). *Reliance Jio Is Driving Indian Internet Growth, Says The Mary Meeker Report*. HuffPost. https://www.huffpost.com/archive/in/entry/reliance-jio-is-driving-indian-internet-growth-says-the-mary-me_a_22120777

Press Trust of India. (2017, December 25). *Reliance Jio subscriber base touches 160 million*. ETTelecom.com; PTI. https://telecom.economictimes.indiatimes.com/news/reliance-jio-subscriber-base-touches-160-million/62237555

Saha, S. (2017). *Airtel and Jio offer Rs 149, Rs 349 and Rs 399 plans: What all you get and which one is better*. India Today. https://www.indiatoday.in/technology/news/story/airtel-reliance-jio-offer-rs-149-rs-349-and-rs-399-tariff-plans-which-one-is-better-1037312-2017-09-04

Sengupta, D. (2017, October 25). *RCom may shut its wireless business in next 30 days, employees put on notice period*. The Economic Times; Economic Times. https://economictimes.indiatimes.com/news/company/corporate-trends/first-on-et-rcom-may-shut-its-wireless-business-in-next-30-days-employees-put-on-notice-period/articleshow/61213636.cms

Shrivastava, B., John, S., Kalesh, B., & Bhaskar, U. (2010, May 24). *Ambanis scrap non-compete agreements*. Livemint. https://www.livemint.com/Home-Page/fKCkWOUMUIEW8v78AJfL2M/Ambanis-scrap-noncompete-agreements.html

Singh, G., & Garg, S. K. (2020, April 1). *Consumer Retention Policies Followed by Telecom Companies- A Post Jio Scenario*. Papers.*ssrn*.com. https://papers.ssrn.com/sol3/papers.cfm?abstract_id=3565769

Singh, H. (2019, November 27). *Vodafone Idea: Everything to know about India's ailing private telco*. ETTelecom.com; ETTelecom. https://telecom.economictimes.indiatimes.com/news/vodafone-idea-everything-to-know-about-indias-ailing-private-telco/72258027

Thekeepitsimple. (2021, April 8). *Vodafone Case Study Of Vodafone & Idea Merger-Reasons, Analyses*. t K Itsim . https://www.thekeepitsimple.com/vodafone-case-study/

ADDITIONAL READING

Ali, M. (2021). *Remote Work and Sustainable Changes for the Future of Global Business*. IGI Global. https://www.igi-global.com/book/remote-work-sustainable-changes-future/264375

Ali, M. (2022). *Future Role of Sustainable Innovative Technologies in Crisis Management*. IGI Global. https://www.igi-global.com/book/future-role-sustainable-innovative-technologies/281281

Ali, M. (2023). *Shifting Paradigms in the Rapidly Developing Global Digital Ecosystem: A GCC Perspective*. In Digital Entrepreneurship and Co-Creating Value Through Digital Encounters (pp. 145-166). IGI Global. https://www.igi-global.com/chapter/shifting-paradigms-in-the-rapidly-developing-global-digital-ecosystem/323525

Ali, M. (2023). T*axonomy of Industry 4.0 Technologies in Digital Entrepreneurship and Co-Creating Value.* In *Digital Entrepreneurship and Co-Creating Value Through Digital Encounters* (pp. 24–55). IGI Global., https://www.igi-global.com/chapter/taxonomy-of-industry-40-technologies-in-digital-entrepreneurship-and-co-creating-value/323520 DOI: 10.4018/978-1-6684-7416-7.ch002

Ali, M., & Wood-Harper, T. (2021). *Fostering Communication and Learning with Underutilized Technologies in Higher Education.* IGI Global. https://www.igi-global.com/book/fostering-communication-learning-underutilized-technologies/244593

Ali, M., Wood-Harper, T., & Kutar, M. (2023). Multi-Perspectives of Contemporary Digital Transformation Models of Complex Innovation Management. In *Digital Entrepreneurship and Co-Creating Value Through Digital Encounters* (pp. 79–96). IGI Global., https://www.igi-global.com/chapter/multi-perspectives-of-contemporary-digital-transformation-models-of-complex-innovation-management/323522 DOI: 10.4018/978-1-6684-7416-7.ch004

Ali, M. B. (2021). Internet of Things (IoT) to Foster Communication and Information Sharing: A Case of UK Higher Education. In Ali, M. B., & Wood-Harper, T. (Eds.), *Fostering Communication and Learning With Underutilized Technologies in Higher Education* (pp. 1–20). IGI Global., https://www.igi-global.com/chapter/internet-of-things-iot-to-foster-communication-and-information-sharing/262718/ DOI: 10.4018/978-1-7998-4846-2.ch001

Ali, M. B., & Wood-Harper, T. (2022). Artificial Intelligence (AI) as a Decision-Making Tool to Control Crisis Situations. In *Future Role of Sustainable Innovative Technologies in Crisis Management.* IGI Global., https://www.igi-global.com/chapter/artificial-intelligence-ai-as-a-decision-making-tool-to-control-crisis-situations/298931 DOI: 10.4018/978-1-7998-9815-3.ch006

Ali, M. B., Wood-Harper, T., & Ramlogan, R. (2020). A Framework Strategy to Overcome Trust Issues on Cloud Computing Adoption in Higher Education. In Modern Principles, Practices, and Algorithms for Cloud Security (pp. 162-183). IGI Global. https://www.igi-global.com/chapter/a-framework-strategy-to-overcome-trust-issues-on-cloud-computing-adoption-in-higher-education/238907/

Chapter 7

Digital Infrastructure Challenges for Techno-Entrepreneurs in Rural Areas: The Need for Capacity Building

Kasturi Srinivasa Vijaya Sekhar
https://orcid.org/0000-0002-6246-8966
International Institute of Information Technology, Hyderabad, India

ABSTRACT

This chapter discusses the importance of capacity building and the role of digital infrastructure in delivering citizen services, focusing on the challenges entrepreneurs face. In the pre-digital era, when computers were not part of public service delivery, the government's internal procedures were cumbersome. Citizens encountered several challenges viz., standing in long queues, filling out lengthy forms, carrying documents, and making multiple trips to various departments, — these all forced them to incur additional costs. To address this, governments have introduced entrepreneurs into the system. Mainly, rural areas suffer from inadequate physical and electronic infrastructure, such as unreliable electricity supply, limited internet connectivity, and outdated computers and other faded equipment. These constraints contribute significantly to the digital divide, where certain populations lack access to digital services and benefits. To mitigate this divide, especially in the public sector, concerted efforts are needed from the outset of ICT initiatives.

DOI: 10.4018/979-8-3373-0086-3.ch007

Copyright © 2025, IGI Global. Copying or distributing in print or electronic forms without written permission of IGI Global is prohibited.

1. INTRODUCTION

The primary objectives of utilizing Information and Communication Technologies (ICTs) are to reduce transaction costs, improve the quality of customer interactions, enhance service reach, deliver high-quality public services, and increase transparency, efficiency, and productivity, thereby ensuring equitable distribution of benefits. With the advent of Information and Communication Technologies (ICTs), the government started delivering public services through web portals accessible via personal computers, laptops, and mobile phones. These technologies collectively constitute ICTs to streamline the process of public service delivery. However, these objectives are often undermined by the tendency to merely computerize and digitize outdated processes in delivering public services. For ICT to effectively reach beneficiaries, there must be a comprehensive effort to conduct awareness and training programs on the latest technological developments. This approach is essential for empowering those who have not yet benefited from digital advancements thereby promoting digital inclusion and equity. To overcome such challenges the Government of India has set up about a lakh Common Service Centers (CSCs). An entrepreneur who set up a kiosk with minimum digital infrastructure viz., a computer, a printer with an internet connection etc., was brought into the system for delivering public services, efficiently and effectively.

1.1 Context Setting

Innovative technologies are often expensive and difficult to procure besides this, technical skills are crucial for driving innovation, a trait that distinguishes successful entrepreneurs who navigate both internal and external challenges (Ying & Yenchun, 2019). However, technology adoption faces significant barriers - poor network connectivity and slower communication networks hinder technology penetration and contribute to maintenance issues. Additionally, there is a shortage of human resources with technical skills, compounded by a lack of training facilities dedicated to new technologies. Those who adopt technical skills have a greater potential for higher income compared to those who lag in utilizing technical knowledge (Cristina et al., 2022). Furthermore, a substantial portion of the rural population lacks basic literacy skills, let alone proficiency in computer usage. Digital illiteracy further exacerbates their challenges, complicating access to ICT-based services. Moreover, many beneficiaries of these services do not speak English, rendering non-vernacular web pages inaccessible. Even if the government were to design web pages in vernacular languages, this marginalized group would still face barriers unless services are explained, made accessible, and delivered through voice interaction modes.

1.2 Problem Statement

The rapid evolution of advanced technologies poses significant challenges for local entrepreneurs aiming to establish efficient ecosystems for the delivery of services. Basic infrastructure like desktop computers, printers, internet access, and scanners is becoming increasingly outdated. There is a growing need for awareness and adoption of advanced technologies such as blockchain, cybersecurity measures, Internet of Things, and effective computer skills. Before the introduction of computers in administrative processes, turnaround times were notably cumbersome. In essence, digital transformation simplifies this - an entrepreneur 'A' having ordinary infrastructure such as basic computer equipment, an ordinary printer, modest network bandwidth, and minimal hardware with outdated software. In contrast, another entrepreneur 'B' utilizes sophisticated technologies like smartphones, cameras, fingerprint devices, webcams, IoT-configured hardware, and the latest 5G network bandwidth including advanced software. Comparing the speed and accessibility of services provided by entrepreneur 'A', another entrepreneur 'B' demonstrates the advantages that he enjoys. The investments in and returns from advanced technologies are more favorable for citizens approaching entrepreneur 'B' due to the enhanced service speed and citizen satisfaction. Another crux is that the 'B' entrepreneur has specialized skills while using several mobile applications can deliver speedy services at the counters (Zhi & Yueyi, 2025).

1.3 Objective

The importance of having an entrepreneur is evident across various domains where tasks are undertaken on a larger scale. For example, an agricultural landlord employs laborers to cultivate crops, while a homeowner engages masons and their teams to build houses. In governmental contexts, entities like the postal department, with its extensive network, outsource specific tasks such as delivering postal letters, courier parcels, and money orders in remote and hilly areas. These tasks are implemented only with the help of another partner / entrepreneur. In the government sector, a partner is an authorized entity entrusted with specific tasks aligned with achieving governmental objectives. In India, governments leverage partnerships to enhance the delivery of public services to rural areas, thereby optimizing resource utilization.

1.4 Need for Capacity Building

The introduction of ICTs has significantly enhanced the scalability of entrepreneurs using electronic devices, enabling them to offer services more effectively. Government departments that are looking to integrate into this digital spectrum provide basic training to entrepreneurs. During these trainings, subject matter experts demonstrate how services, traditionally managed through manual processes, are streamlined using online systems. The methodology used in the training programs can be adapted to the different departments and profiles in which it is required, depending on the needs of the respective departments, allowing its replication and adaptation as required. This training highlights the simplification and increased efficiency gained from transitioning to digital service delivery. The objectives of these capacity-building programs are:

- To create awareness of how a manual service is aligned with a software to the entrepreneurs
- To provide information about statutory charges and timelines for delivering a service to the citizens by the entrepreneurs
- To deliver effective and efficient public services while using ICT applications to the citizens

2. BACKGROUND

2.1 Overview of Rural Entrepreneurship

Delivering public services has significant challenges, primarily due to the country's vast landscape comprising over six lakh villages. Approximately two-thirds of the population reside in rural regions across various States and Union Territories. While some states, such as Andhra Pradesh, have implemented numerous welfare schemes and development programs, the effectiveness of these initiatives is hindered by internal challenges, hierarchical disagreements, and lengthy administrative procedures. In contrast, the increasing population exacerbates the strain on manual service delivery processes, leading to inefficiencies and, in some cases, corruption. Rajiv Gandhi famously remarked that only 16 paise out of every rupee allocated for public services reaches the common man, highlighting the pervasive issue of leakage and inefficiency in service delivery. To address these challenges and improve service delivery outcomes, there has been a growing emphasis on leveraging Information and Communication Technologies (ICTs) within government operations, particularly in realm of public service delivery. ICTs are seen as essential tools to enhance efficiency, transparency, and accessibility in governance and to ensure that welfare benefits reach intended recipients more effectively.

2.2 Digital Infrastructure in Rural Areas

In India, 72% of the population uses the Internet out of a total population of 1.44 billion, approximately 33% reside in urban areas, leaving the rest in rural areas. Despite the global presence of 5.3 billion computer users, rural population in India face significant challenges in accessing online services, contributing to a digital divide exacerbated by limited technology awareness. Rural citizens often rely on nearby kiosks (CSCs) due to geographical constraints, highlighting the need for strategically located setups to address these limitations. Several initiatives have played pivotal roles in the evolution of ICT-based service delivery. Common Service Centers (CSCs) were established as part of the National eGovernance Program (NeGP). The primary objective was to make government services accessible to every citizen through local service delivery outlets. These CSCs are integral to 34 Mission Mode Projects (MMPs) that are characterized by specific timelines and goals aimed at achieving measurable outcomes in service delivery efficiency, transparency, and reliability. To bridge the gap in service delivery capacity, the government's authorized agent Village Level Entrepreneur (VLE) was involved in operating the scheme. This scheme was introduced to meet the needs of over six lakh villages through one lakh kiosks. These centers are owned and operated by a local entrepreneur who assists citizens by processing their service requests, assists in filling out online application forms, and uploading necessary documents about a specific service etc., Government mandates to various departments have facilitated the recognition of electronic documents, thereby reducing reliance on paper-based transactions and ink signatures.

Entrepreneurs operating Common Service Centers (CSCs) are authorized to deliver a wide array of government services, encompassing over 320 services from 18 departments including Revenue, Agriculture, Education, Property tax, Passport, and Utility Payments. The income generated by CSC operators is derived from a portion of the statutory fees associated with each service they facilitate. Their profits are directly tied to the number of transactions processed in each month. This financial incentive motivates operators to increase transaction volumes, sometimes at the expense of accuracy, leading to errors in data entry thereby it is required to implement value for money to bring effectiveness into public-private partnerships (Bhatia, 2010). Consequently, citizens may need to revisit government offices to rectify document errors, or operators themselves may liaise with government officials to resolve such issues on behalf of their clients. However, many people, particularly in rural areas, are unaware of how to access technology-based services. Additionally, entrepreneurs often lack orientation and awareness of the latest technologies.

2.3 Importance of Technology for Entrepreneurs

The Common Service Center (CSC), referred to as MeeSeva in this context, operates on a three-tier model. At the top level, the State Government establishes a high authority known as the State Designated Agency (SDA), which selects a private partner called the State Center Agency (SCA). This agency identifies and recruits local entrepreneurs to set up these centers that provide public services, with the entrepreneurs assuming the financial risk. Any individual who has completed at least the 10th grade and is 18 years or older can establish a kiosk, provided they have the necessary infrastructure, including a computer, printer, internet connection, and scanners. These entrepreneurs act as government-authorized agents. Graduates and postgraduates are also encouraged to participate, and 10% of kiosks are reserved exclusively for women to empower them and enhance their community impact. The selection criteria for entrepreneurs are based on education, prior experience, and familiarity with computer usage, among other factors. Those without sufficient computer knowledge can participate in specialized training programs to improve their skills. Accessibility and availability of operators or entrepreneurs in these centers are critical considerations (Eriksson et al., 2024). Throughout the history of ICT-based service delivery, several initiatives have been implemented to enhance government information dissemination via electronic devices.

These initiatives include:

Public Call Office (PCO): Introduced in the early 1990s, PCOs served as communication channel interactive over the telephones located across cities, towns, districts, and mandals.

Tele-centers: Launched in the mid-1990s, tele-centers marked the introduction of computers equipped with Internet connections to facilitate basic government services. These centers were established by private individuals within their localities to act as a government-authorized agent.

Service Delivery Points: Tele-centers evolved into service delivery points, expanding their range of services to include activities such as selling mobile recharge coupons and remitting electric bill payments and water cess bills etc.

Rajiv Internet Village Centers (RaJiv Centers): Formerly known as service delivery points, these centers further extended to include private services like issuing bus, air and train tickets.

These successive initiatives underscored a trend toward greater accessibility and efficiency in government service delivery through ICTs. They also facilitated public familiarity and proficiency in using computers for basic transactions leaving rural citizens aside.

3. CHALLENGES IN DIGITAL INFRASTRUCTURE

The International Telecommunication Union (ITU) releases an annual Measuring Information Society report that assesses the ICT readiness of economies based on the ICT Development Index (ITU, 2023). One objective of the report is to monitor progress in ICT development in both developed and developing countries and to measure the evolution of the global digital divide. According to these statistics, India ranked 131st out of 167 countries. The report identified several areas requiring special attention, including a lack of ownership, lack of implementing infrastructure, lack of visionary leadership, and lack of cohesiveness. One key difference between developing and developed countries is that, in developing nations, women are 16% less likely than men to use internet-based services whereas the gender gap is only 2% in developed countries (ITU). Effective governance minimizes unnecessary interference from multiple layers and depends on a strong infrastructure, supported by local processes and parameters, to enable governments to reach end beneficiaries.

3.1 International Movements

The tele-center movement began in the 1980s with the global use of computers. Originally, tele-centers were public telephone booths equipped with computers to deliver basic government services. The term "tele" refers to distance, while computers provide information, and networks transmit that information. The convergence of these three ICTs sparked the information revolution. In the 1970s, the United States introduced tele-centers in the government sector, and India followed suit in the late 1990s. Renowned organizations such as the International Development Research Centre (IDRC) in Canada, UNESCO, the United Nations Development Program (UNDP), and the World Bank supported the tele-center movement to help achieve the Millennium Development Goals (MDGs). These goals aimed to eliminate poverty and provide universal education by 2014. These organizations believed that tele-centers had the potential to create knowledge hubs and stimulate economic growth, particularly in developing countries (UNDP, 2005). To achieve these goals, a large-scale common platform was required, which tele-centers provided. In the early days, the centers focused on delivering essential information related to agriculture, telemedicine, health, education, and government services to rural communities. These centers are known by various names in different countries, such as Public Internet Access Centres (PIAPs), Village Knowledge Centres (VKCs), Community Technology Centres (CTCs), Community Multimedia Centres (CMCs), and Common/Citizen Service Centres (CSCs) etc.

3.2 High Costs and Affordability

Observing these outcomes, Chief Ministers of other states, bureaucrats, government authorities, NGOs, private agencies, and political leaders implemented several ICT-based government services in their respective states. The computer revolution was widely utilized in government welfare schemes and development programs, benefiting the government and citizens. To strengthen the tele-center movement in Andhra Pradesh, these centers were converted into service delivery points by providing computer and internet facilities. The government recognized the potential of these kiosks to deliver digital services, and, for ease of administration, these service delivery points were classified into rural and urban categories to meet diverse needs (IT&C, GoAP, 2003). Existing telephone booths across the 1,040 mandals were converted into service delivery points, enhancing the telecenters. These delivery points provided information services such as agricultural commodity prices, weather data, seasonal pest control advice for farmers, and more. They also offered employment opportunities for rural youth, internet browsing, and email services. Government services such as birth and death registrations, income certificates, municipal permission applications, online sales tax return filing, and utility services were integrated. Additionally, utility bill payments, insurance premiums, land title (patta) services, vehicle registrations, travel reservations (bus, train, airlines), and school and college admission fees were facilitated in the next phase. However, delivering such a wide range of services requires basic infrastructure and sufficient bandwidth. To address this, modems, Uninterrupted Power Supplies (UPS), printers, internet-enabled computers, and smart card readers were made available at the outlets. A local entrepreneur, acting as a government-authorized agent, managed these outlets, and the service charges on transactions became a source of income. Unemployed individuals took advantage of this initiative and started their businesses in many localities, in addition to providing standard telephone services. It is not an exaggeration to say that most of these centers are operated and run by local entrepreneurs.

3.3 Technological Literacy Gap

RAJiv – RAJiv Internet Village was an upgraded version of service delivery points, established to bring the government closer to the people with enhanced infrastructure, requiring additional investment of 50,000 from entrepreneurs (IT&C, GoAP, 2007). The scheme was launched in Chiluvuru, a village in Duggirala Mandal of Guntur District, in August 2004. Krishna Prasad Katragadda, an Indian-origin professional who had lived in the United States for three years, returned to India to serve the nation. He was inspired by A. P. J. Abdul Kalam's dream initiative, the Providing Urban Amenities in Rural Areas (PURA) model (GoAP, 2004). The objective of the PURA model is to identify a nodal village that provides basic infrastructure to meet the needs of at least six surrounding villages. This includes facilities like high schools, colleges, hospitals, health services, roads, transport, electricity, and reliable communication networks (ADB, 2013). If these infrastructures are established at a nodal village, they can revamp rural potential by covering the needs of surrounding areas.

RAJiv centers were established following these principles, providing financial support to entrepreneurs through a payback method. These centers offer various services, including prepaid recharge coupons, mobile phone SIM card sales, national agriculture insurance (Rain Insurance), internet browsing, job portal registration, astrology services, Bharat Matrimony, and railway ticketing etc. Other essential services include land record details, Pattadar passbooks, ration cards, bank loans, health records, and crop insurance information for farmers. Additionally, mandatory services encompass utility payments, electricity bills, passport applications, and student-related services.

3.4 Government and Policy Gaps

The Second Industrialization Policy emphasizes the need to stabilize industries to achieve rapid economic growth. Currently, over 30% of the state's IT workforce comprises women. The policy includes provisions to encourage women entrepreneurs by offering incentives if they hold at least 51% of the shares in ICT companies. These incentives include 100% reimbursement of stamp duty and registration fees on sale/lease deeds, rebates on industrial financial deeds and mortgages etc. For Scheduled Caste/Scheduled Tribe women, there are direct rebates on land costs for setting up Special Economic Zones (SEZs) or Information Technology Parks, whether private or public. Additional policies include reservations for built-up office space, providing water facilities and subsidies on power bills etc (GoAP).

Working from home is another feature that enables talented and physically challenged individuals to participate in the workforce. Work norms are also relaxed for those with young children, allowing them to work from home due to household responsibilities. The government aims for women to take the lead in the ICT industry and has implemented several measures to promote her participation. Several women already occupy roles in call centers and the Information Technology Enabled Services (ITeS)/Business Process Outsourcing (BPO) sectors. As a result, they are prepared to work 24/7/365 on a shift basis whereas in Common Service Centers, only 10% of kiosks were reserved for women operators.

4. FEEDBACK ON IMPACT OF DIGITAL INFRASTRUCTURE

4.1 Socio-Economic Impact

Another feature is Service Centre Verification Report, which was introduced to audit the monthly performances of the kiosks. A similar exercise was carried out by the Government of Andhra Pradesh Rural Poverty Reduction Project (APRPRP) using Citizen Score Cards (CSC) in 2006 (Velugu, 2004). The project, which ran from 2003 to 2011 under the World Bank, aimed to audit and collect citizen feedback on primary healthcare centers. However, many kiosks are limiting their income levels by refusing certain services for instance, operators often decline the Swasthya Tablet, a health checkup service that performs 12 medical tests for 85 and gives operators 45 in income, because it takes more than two hours to complete a single transaction. In villages, customers often have limited writing skills, so they rely on the operator's assistance, which consumes a lot of time. Operators with prior experience in government organizations are becoming kiosk owners, and their knowledge of various processes is extensive. If a kiosk wants to earn more income, it should consider accepting additional private services such as Western Union transfers, and rail and bus ticket bookings etc.,

4.2 Barriers to Innovation and Growth

Building trust and accepting successful outcomes bring social change, creating awareness and fostering networking (Obare, 2020). Newly established kiosks are often dissatisfied with their current income, as some centers fail to meet the required number of transactions each month. One major issue is the slow diffusion of technology, particularly computer applications. Some operators are charging excessive user fees, ignoring citizen charter norms. While e-Government is a one-way communication protocol, e-Governance requires two-way communication, and the lack of awareness and insufficient training programs further reduce kiosk productivity. Although literacy rates are improving, acquiring ICT skills is becoming an additional burden for operators. Some are so dissatisfied with their income that they plan to close their centers, despite going through a lengthy shortlisting process to become entrepreneurs whereas others are starting alternative businesses where they feel more confident.

4.3 Limited Financial Inclusion

Before setting up CSCs, the initial investment for entrepreneurs ranged from 1.50 to 2.00 lakhs. However, they later encountered unforeseen direct costs, such as hardware maintenance, transportation, installation, training program attendance, and kiosk modifications. There are indirect costs, such as website maintenance, operator salaries, security applications, computer repairs, and electricity outages. Some services require significant top-up balances but offer low commissions in return. Handling cash transactions also poses risks, as processing is simple, but the income from each transaction is higher when compared with other services. Implementing separate visiting hours for women, children, and men might help but would be challenging to enforce (IT for Change, 2007). Other issues that incur additional penalties include malfunctions, legal costs from allegations, piracy, theft, and software modifications after initial trials. These factors should be included in initial investment plans and policy documents. Operators are required to complete a minimum number of transactions daily to ensure a sufficient monthly income. Initially, operators had the flexibility to offer private services like desktop publishing, photocopying, and scanning. However, due to the increasing demand for government services, authorities have restricted these private services, causing some loss of income.

On the other hand, internet penetration in India is steadily increasing, and people are gradually becoming accustomed to using online services. As a result, citizens are beginning to access government websites directly to avail themselves of services, which may further reduce the income of operators (Sekhar & Bagga, 2012). Often, private partners prioritize profit over providing services that yield lower returns (Mazzucato, 2015). Accountability is maintained through Service Center Verification Reports and Citizen Scorecard audits (Velugu, 2004). Tech-savvy District Managers play a critical role in supporting entrepreneurs by addressing technical issues, supplying authorized stationery, and conducting performance reviews. The new technologies in rural areas have underscored the vital role of coordinators or mediators in service delivery, such as private operators at public telephone booths or qualified individuals offering internet-based services.

5. CAPACITY BUILDING: A PATHWAY TO OVERCOME CHALLENGES

Often, government policies affect an entrepreneur's business income for instance, registration deeds have recently been attached to CSCs, which is the job of a notary writer. In response to this drastic decision by the government, notary writers have gone on agitation, demanding to delink these services from CSCs (Sakshi, 2013). This situation has led to unknown differences between the entrepreneurs' and notary writers' associations. Kiosks that adhere to a set of standards expect motivation and encouragement from the government to survive in the business. Whether the income is high or low, certain promotions and incentives can be planned that provide social respect in society, representing an upliftment in terms of social conditions.

5.1 Importance of Capacity Building

At CSCs, communicating with senior citizens and specially challenged individuals consumes a significant amount of time; however, operators manage such cases very gently due to their respectful attitude towards elderly citizens (Sonali, 2009). The government has directed that all CSCs be set up on the ground floor to benefit physically challenged citizens. However, some of these kiosks have been established on the first or second floors of buildings in certain locations. It is the operator's responsibility to stay updated on such policies. For example, property tax regulations in Panchayat localities and Municipal Corporations differ from each other, following different bands and slab systems, which makes familiarization with such calculations a challenge. Sometimes, pressures from economically disadvantaged individuals to avail themselves of such services create apprehensions and cause business losses for kiosks thus people tend to avoid experimenting with new faces, and therefore new operators do not receive much business. In some centers, manual couriers are being utilized; to overcome this, there is a requirement for 25% more operators at the counters, which leads to additional expenses for the entrepreneurs (Sakshi, 2013).

5.2 Types of Capacity Building

For administrative convenience, CSCs are categorized into two types: Push and Pull. Push services, such as telephone, water, and electricity bill payments, are delivered instantly over the counter. In contrast, pull services - like ration cards, passports, driving licenses, caste certificates, and income certificates - require background checks and take more time. Before the widespread use of computers in public administration, processing these services took much longer. However, with the adoption of Information and Communications Technologies (ICTs), the turnaround time has significantly reduced to about seven days. For instance, passports are now delivered within five working days.

5.3 Role of Government, NGOs, and Private Sector

When a department adds a new service to CSCs, relevant officers conduct basic training programs for the entrepreneurs. These sessions, led by subject matter experts, demonstrate how manual processes have been simplified and how the online system can streamline service delivery. The training sessions are recorded and made available on the CSC website, allowing operators to access them whenever needed. Government has also published an exclusive User Manual that includes detailed information on approximately 320 services, covering service descriptions, statutory charges, delivery timelines, and more. This manual employs pictorial representations to guide operators in troubleshooting issues at the centers. There is a guarantee that entrepreneurs have access to quality training for their employment, thus contributing to exercising their right to work and occupation.

This compendium also covers process details from around 36 departments, including Aadhaar, Revenue, Agriculture, Education, Property Tax, Factories, Healthcare, and Social Welfare. The aim is to equip entrepreneurs with the knowledge and comfort they need to deliver online services efficiently. Beyond government services, entrepreneurs are given the flexibility to offer private and social services from their CSCs, providing them with an opportunity to earn additional income. It is up to the entrepreneurs to decide how they wish to offer these services after undergoing the training programs, considering their local community needs thereby it is practical, fast, and accessible guidance and well-versed dynamic training so that entrepreneurs can apply them immediately to their economic activity in their profession.

5.4 Successful Models

The smart operators, who possess computer knowledge and strong educational skills, are earning more. Although the government has stopped manual services, a few departments are still offering parallel services that affect kiosk income volumes. For document validation, kiosk owners must visit the parent government office, leading to repeated travel and additional costs. In the case of a single operator, this situation can force them to shut down their kiosk whereas a few centres are planning to recruit an assistant to liaise with such departments in government. Setting up an exclusive help desk with a designated person to usher visitors to multiple counters is a positive step.

> *APOnline*: Introduced as a joint venture between Tata Consultancy Services and the Government, which focused primarily on utility services such as collecting telephone, electricity, and water bills covering all mandals across the state emphasizing widespread accessibility.

eSeva: Evolving from APOnline, eSeva aimed to integrate and expand service delivery further. However, its implementation was limited to approximately 250 to 300 centers concentrated in major towns and cities. Despite the smaller number of centers, eSeva pioneered advancements in service delivery mechanisms.
Common Service Centers (CSCs): Launched as a flagship project under public-private-partnership (PPP) in 2006, aim to deliver government, private, and social services, with a primary focus on rural areas. These centers are operated by local entrepreneurs, facilitating community-level access to essential services.

6. RECOMMENDATIONS

6.1 Policy Interventions

There are incentive plans for entrepreneurs who conduct a higher volume of transactions to encourage the delivery of exceptional services. To encourage them to excel in their profession and familiarize themselves with automation technologies, the government introduced an online examination aimed at creating awareness among the operators. The examination is multiple-choice based, and upon clearing it, operators receive a signed certificate from the respective District Collector or Joint Collector. The objective of this online test is to reduce complaints from citizens and enhance knowledge about departmental services. The certification is classified into bronze, silver, and gold categories: Bronze is for understanding basic services, Silver is for the next level of services, and the final exam, Gold, covers all the services.

Substantial questionnaires have already been prepared, and all operators are required to attend the examination compulsorily. Two free attempts are provided to operators in case they do not pass; if they fail after these attempts, a final test will be administered to determine the fate of the center. The examination helps officials assess operators' awareness levels regarding various services, and upon successful completion, a certificate must be displayed at the centers. Kiosk infrastructure, citizen comfort levels, and the number of transactions are basic indicators based on which operator performance can be measured. It is necessary to encourage those who are not earning adequate income and planning to quit the scheme. The Centre for Good Governance (CGG) of Andhra Pradesh instituted the Parishramika Vijetha Awards to recognize entrepreneurs in their respective fields, introduced sometime back in 2003 (CGG, 2003). The ranking methodology could be developed by governments and regularly carried out by private partners, universities, or research institutes in conjunction with the Department of IT in each state. Such rankings would ensure healthy competition among entrepreneurs, and the findings should be widely publicized.

Advantages: The integration of Information and Communication Technologies (ICTs) in government service delivery offers numerous benefits.

Time and Cost Savings: ICTs streamline service delivery, saving customers valuable time and money spent on transport expenses. By offering a wide range of services from a single location, ICTs eliminate the need for repeated trips to government offices.

Enhanced Convenience: Citizens can interact with government services digitally, reducing the necessity for physical visits. This shift has transformed how people engage with government entities, promoting efficiency and accessibility.

Efficiency and Resource Management: ICT-enabled paperless transactions save significant resources thereby reducing the need for paper and associated administrative costs. Digital records can be easily retrieved and reused, which saves time for both governments and customers.

Environmental Impact: The transition to paperless operations through ICTs contributes to environmental conservation by reducing paper consumption and saving trees.

Transparency and Equity: ICT-based services are designed to be transparent and user-friendly, ensuring equal access and treatment for all citizens regardless of their socioeconomic status (Jon et.al., 2024).

This approach promotes fairness and inclusivity in service delivery. Overall, ICTs have revolutionized government service delivery by enhancing efficiency, reducing costs, promoting environmental sustainability, and ensuring equitable access to services. As technology continues to advance, its role in governance is poised to further optimize service effectiveness and citizen satisfaction.

6.2 Outcomes

The integration of Information and Communication Technologies (ICTs) has revolutionized inter-departmental communication and operational efficiencies within governments. Key advancements include:

Enhanced Communication: Departments now utilize emails, websites, and mobile phones for seamless communication, overcoming previous challenges. This integration has fostered collaboration and information sharing among departments.

Automation and Efficiency: This shift has decentralized operations and implemented better monitoring systems, significantly enhancing employee productivity and operational cost-effectiveness.

Speedy and accountability: Departments have streamlined service delivery processes, offering faster, simpler, and more transparent services. This transformation allows personnel to allocate more time to core responsibilities, improving overall service quality and accountability.

Nationwide adoption: While some states have embraced ICT advancements and made significant progress, others still face challenges in adopting and integrating ICTs into their day-to-day functions.

Overall, ICTs have become indispensable in modernizing government operations, enabling efficient communication, automating processes, and delivering accountable services. As more states continue to leverage ICTs, the potential for further advancements in governance and service delivery remains promising.

Benefits: The involvement of private partners has been instrumental in the success of government initiatives, particularly in leveraging expertise from both the public and private sectors to address emerging national needs. Key aspects include:

Enhancing Digital Transformation: Private partners bring specialized skills and resources to support entrepreneurial teams in mastering digital transformation. This collaboration fosters innovation and sustains enterprise success in a knowledge-driven society (Burkhard & Gregor, 2023).

Financial and Operational Advantages: Partnering with private entities allows governments to mitigate financial investments and risks, as highlighted by the World Bank. Partners also assist in recruiting and managing sufficient manpower to achieve project objectives effectively.

Partnership Models: Various partnership models such as Build-Own-Operate-and-Transfer (BOOT), Build-Own-and-Operate (BOO), and lease agreements enable governments to pay partners based on unit usage or long-term project viability (Sachdeva, 2006). These models ensure financial sustainability while allowing partners to collect user charges and reinvest profits as needed.

Historical and Global Context: Partnerships in infrastructure began during the late 19th century globalization era and have since expanded into complex social sector projects. Partnerships evolve alongside government priorities, reducing risks and ensuring continuity until joint goals are met.

Flexibility and Renewal: Partnerships are typically structured with flexibility for contract extension or discontinuation based on mutual agreement after the initial term expires. This approach supports ongoing collaboration aligned with evolving needs and objectives.

Overall, partnerships between governments and private entities play a crucial role in enhancing operational efficiency, reducing risks, and achieving sustainable development goals (Egnew, et.al., 1998). As globalization continues to influence collaboration models, effective partnerships remain pivotal in driving innovation and achieving shared success.

6.3 Capacity Building Programs

India has been producing numerous IT professionals for the last two decades and has the potential to build the next Google in the future (Eric, 2013). Citizens' aspirations are also increasing day by day; hence, IT infrastructure needs to be doubled to meet such demands. The government is also investing in training programs for operators and concerned partners. What should have been done two decades ago is now being implemented, indicating a delay in effective solutions within the administration process. The forefathers did not anticipate the technological needs of the present generation, but the next generation must not repeat these mistakes (Vithal et al., 2013). The advantage of the next generation is that they are well-versed in using ICTs and are ready to reap the benefits.

At the time of tele-centers, Service Delivery Points, and Rajiv centers, the number of services offered was very few, resulting in limited income. However, Common Service Centres are now providing a substantial range of services. This requires significant financial investment, and it has been observed that individuals with the financial capacity are becoming owners and succeeding in their businesses. The government also intends to give preference to experienced operators, considering their previous track records, and to hold them responsible for the success or failure of the business. In this way, credibility plays a crucial role for entrepreneurs to excel in their businesses (Jovanna, 2021). As a matter of fact, International Telecommunication Union (ITU) has come out with a blueprint on digital innovation ecosystem. The accelerators indicates that these are the enablers that are going to bring in significant changes to the digital transformation (ITU, 2024).

Upon becoming authorized entrepreneurs, operators of Common Service Centers (CSCs) are entrusted with delivering three types of services: government, private, and social. For administrative convenience, the operators undergo training programs facilitated by the relevant department authorities to ensure efficient service delivery across varied categories. These training sessions are scheduled before introducing a new service into the scheme. Operators can enhance their income potential by diversifying service offerings and improving efficiency. Some kiosks have implemented fixed-income models for CSC owners, ensuring stable monthly earnings, such as the Khidmat Centers in Jammu & Kashmir (Jamwal, 2013). There is significant demand for photocopying services and other non-network services, which CSCs can capitalize on to increase revenue and expand their service portfolios. When operator unable to attend these training sessions physically, they can access video lectures available on the CSC websites. A comprehensive user manual, which includes details on each service description, statutory charges, and processing time frames, has been published. This manual serves as a ready reference, enabling operators to deliver services smoothly and effectively, especially when handling internet-based services where caution is paramount.

However, the entrepreneurship sector lacks standardized training and education, resulting in operators entering the business without fully understanding the operational complexities and potential costs involved (Li & Bu, 2024). Overall, the training and support mechanisms provided by CSCs not only equip operators with the necessary skills and knowledge but also incentivize them to maintain high standards of service delivery, thereby enhancing customer satisfaction and operational efficiency. The government incentivizes operators to excel in their businesses (Jain et al., 2010). District collectors also acknowledge outstanding performance by awarding cash prizes and other forms of recognition.

6.4 Entrepreneur's Etiquette – A Key Aspect of the Business

One major operational challenge faced by Common Service Centers (CSCs) is the difficulty internet service providers have in delivering reliable and uninterrupted connectivity. This issue contributes to delays in providing timely services to customers. Consequently, operators often prioritize services that yield immediate income, such as earning commissions on electricity payments and offering rapid information on train and bus ticket availability. These income streams are directly beneficial to CSCs, frequently resulting in a preference for them over government services.

While CSC operators play a crucial role in delivering a wide range of government services to citizens, their operational focus sometimes shifts toward maximizing transaction volumes and income generation. This shift can potentially impact the accuracy and reliability of service delivery. Therefore, addressing connectivity issues and balancing service priorities is essential for enhancing overall CSC efficiency and customer satisfaction. CSCs also provide a variety of services that do not rely on internet connectivity, including photocopying, data entry, scanning documents, and offering basic information verbally. These services are especially vital in areas with unreliable electricity supply and frequent internet slowdowns, which are common in rural regions. Customer satisfaction surveys indicate a preference for non-network services due to their faster turnaround times and simplicity, making them appear quicker and more accessible than their network-based counterparts. As a result of these challenges, entrepreneurs operating CSCs often focus on generating income from non-network services. Their income levels depend significantly on customer satisfaction, particularly regarding time and cost savings. Non-network services typically require less time and are perceived as more convenient by customers compared to network-dependent services like online transactions or digital submissions.

In conclusion, while non-network services provide a reliable income stream for CSC operators in areas facing infrastructure challenges, balancing these with essential network-dependent services remains crucial. Addressing operational challenges and leveraging the benefits of digital transformation are key to enhancing service delivery effectiveness and ensuring sustainable CSC operations in rural and underserved areas. Digital transformation, while advantageous, introduces its own set of challenges. Issues such as data protection, potential job losses due to automation, and debates over the effectiveness of e-learning are frequently discussed (Aschemann, 2017; Ezat et al., 2019). These factors underscore the complexity and multifaceted impact of ICT adoption in service delivery. In response, governments have imposed regulations that prioritize the delivery of essential government services through CSCs, ensuring that critical public services reach citizens efficiently, even amidst challenges like slow internet and electricity shortages.

6.5 Socio-Economic Impact

The Common Service Centre (CSC) initiative exemplifies an effective scheme designed under a Public-Private Partnership (PPP) model, showcasing commendable efforts by entrepreneurs and operators. While ICT projects have led to significant improvements in various areas, their impact has not kept pace with the rapid growth of the IT industry. It is crucial to extend the benefits of IT to remote and underserved areas, as this can help bridge the digital divide and foster social inclusion.

Strong government initiatives are essential to mitigate the disparity between the affluent and the underprivileged by formulating comprehensive and accessible policies. Additionally, leveraging the skills of Indian computer scientists to customize generic software for local conditions and needs is vital, as their expertise has predominantly been focused on meeting the demands of international markets. Without ensuring that ICT benefits reach rural and marginalized populations—who constitute two-thirds of the nation—our advancements in technology will fall short of creating meaningful change.

According to Julia et al. (2024), involving private partners in the delivery of government services can sometimes be detrimental. These private partners may prioritize financial gains over service quality, which can compromise the objectives of public service delivery. To streamline operations, states have been divided into zones, with specific private partners allocated to each zone. While this zoning system aims to enhance administrative efficiency and service delivery effectiveness, certain centers face geographical disadvantages.

Revenue generated from statutory charges for each service is shared among three stakeholders—the government, private partner, and entrepreneur—based on a predefined revenue-sharing model. This model ensures that each party receives a portion of the income commensurate with their role and contribution to service delivery. However, many entrepreneurs have raised concerns regarding the transparency of their earnings. Revenue shares are credited directly into the respective bank accounts monthly, reflecting transactions and services delivered, which can complicate reconciliation yet guarantees the timely income for entrepreneurs.

6.6 Leveraging Emerging Technologies

Since the liberalization of the Indian economy in 1991, the Information Technology (IT) sector has witnessed remarkable growth, driven primarily by software exports, with a compounded annual growth rate (CAGR) that reflects this momentum. The sector is poised for further expansion due to increased computer usage within government operations and the implementation of IT policies at both the state and central levels. The Indian IT industry is delivering global solutions that adhere to international standards at an accelerated pace and at lower costs.

The growth of software revenues can be attributed to a heightened focus on electronic governance adopted by various governments. The IT industry collaborates closely with public agencies to enhance software and IT-enabled services across states. Most state governments have implemented IT policies, establishing special task forces to nurture new technologies and address cybersecurity challenges. Within the framework of Common Service Centers, data ownership rests with the respective departments, and the data is stored at the State Data Center (SDC). Applications undergo security audits by CERT-IN and the Standardisation Testing and Quality Certification (STQC), with deficiencies promptly addressed. The departmental servers, accessible via the internet, are safeguarded by routers or firewalls approved by the Department of Information Technology and Communications.

These initiatives, developed over approximately three decades, mark significant progress in leveraging ICTs for effective service delivery. They highlight ongoing debates and perspectives regarding the scalability, inclusivity, and efficiency of ICT-based models in enhancing public service accessibility.

6.7 Sustainability of CSCs

Entrepreneurs operating CSCs face numerous challenges beyond service delivery, including promoting awareness about available services, managing operational logistics (ensuring uninterrupted power supply through Uninterruptible Power Supply systems and Generator Sets), and handling seasonal fluctuations in service demand.

To ensure consistent service delivery, many entrepreneurs invest in solar power systems, despite the additional financial burden this entails. These investments are essential for emergency services and ensuring operational continuity. Additionally, entrepreneurs are tasked with promoting CSC services within their communities, Viz., employing strategies like distributing pamphlets, advertising in newspapers, and engaging in community-driven initiatives. Such efforts aim to bolster public awareness and utilization of CSC services (Inge et al., 2024). Despite these initiatives, the digital ecosystem, encompassing electronic devices and digital transformation, faces inherent contradictions and challenges.

During peak periods, such as exam result announcements, the surge in transactions can overwhelm internet bandwidth and data servers, leading to delays and decreased service efficiency. Operators frequently manage multiple applications simultaneously, exacerbating bandwidth limitations and operational slowdowns. Evaluating the complexity and dynamics of competition among operators within this ecosystem is critical, given the evolving industry landscape and technological disruptions (Kimura et al., 2019). While entrepreneurs undergo training programs to enhance their IT proficiency and operational readiness, focusing on basic computer skills for effective service delivery, the unexpected expenditures and investments pose challenges to their economic viability, despite the significant business opportunities presented.

7.CONCLUSION

In summary, while the three-tier revenue-sharing model aims to optimize service delivery and incentivize stakeholders, challenges such as the motivations of private partners and concerns about service quality highlight the need for robust governance and oversight. This oversight is crucial for maintaining service standards and public trust. Effectively addressing these challenges is essential for the sustainable success of Common Service Centers (CSCs) in meeting the needs of citizens across various regions and service categories.

Operators often provide free information and services that do not generate revenue, impacting profitability. Maintaining positive relationships with government offices is vital, though it may not always yield tangible returns. Additionally, some government services are still delivered manually, which limits CSCs' income potential from digital transactions. Efforts to integrate all services digitally can help mitigate this issue. New entrepreneurs may encounter difficulties in gaining citizens' trust, particularly when handling cash transactions, posing a risk to business sustainability. These operators should cultivate qualities such as knowledge of broader market outreach, cost-effectiveness, and an understanding of network effects, as these factors can significantly influence their performance (Magaji & Xinbo, 2023).

In conclusion, while CSCs offer entrepreneurs opportunities to contribute to digital service delivery and community development, it is crucial to address infrastructure challenges, promote service awareness, and ensure adequate support from government authorities for sustainable operation and growth in the digital era. The entrepreneurs (kiosk owners) seek basic infrastructure facilities, incremental revenue with minimal costs, equitable treatment from governments and private partners, and fair distribution of additional services. Unlimited internet bandwidth and a consistent power supply are essential for their daily operations. They invest considerable effort into their endeavors, anticipating that this will lead to increased business opportunities. With the addition of new services, their revenue potential should ideally expand.

7.1 Key Findings

Operator Experience and Performance: Operators with previous experience in aponline, eSeva, telecenters, and other service-oriented roles tend to perform better. However, they often use outdated systems that struggle to meet current demands [Kasturi and Pallavi, 2014].

Impact of Qualifications and Technical Skills: Operators with higher qualifications and technical problem-solving abilities tend to earn more income. Training programs, particularly those focused on troubleshooting, play a significant role in enhancing their performance and efficiency (Kehrbusch & Engels, 2023).

Potential for Innovation: There is a recognition of India's potential to innovate and develop technologies akin to global giants like Google, highlighted by Eric Schmidt's statement (James, 2013). This underscores the importance of leveraging technological advancements in governance and service delivery.

Exploring the option of engaging liaison persons to commute between government offices and households for door-to-door service delivery is an idea worth considering. To build trust, keeping multiple currency denominations and using two-side monitor methods can assist operators.

7.2 Future Implications

Technological Advancements: To address current challenges like internet connectivity issues and server overloads during peak times, there is a need for upgraded infrastructure and higher bandwidth internet connections. This will support the efficient handling of tasks like document scanning, uploading and navigating multiple web portals at a time.

Expansion and Integration: Other government departments should collaborate and integrate their services with CSC to provide a unified platform for citizens. This would streamline service delivery and enhance user experience.

Workforce Development: There is a need for a techno-savvy workforce in civil services to effectively implement e-governance initiatives. Addressing the shortfall in skilled personnel, as observed is critical for the successful implementation of digital governance projects.

7.3 Summary

During seasonal peaks, Common Service Centers (CSCs) create temporary employment opportunities by hiring additional staff to manage increased service demands. This not only supports local employment but also enhances service delivery capacity. However, there are unavoidable costs associated with this approach. To maximize income generation, some CSCs adopt strategic business hours, offering government services during the day and private services during late hours. While this strategy aims to boost revenue, it can also impact operational efficiency. Despite financial challenges, many CSC operators find satisfaction and social respect in their roles within their communities, which motivates them to sustain their businesses (Sharma et al., 2023). However, operators may discontinue services that do not provide adequate financial incentives, particularly when support and encouragement from government authorities are lacking. This situation underscores the need for consistent engagement and robust support mechanisms.

CSC operations are typically constrained by fixed working hours, which limit income potential compared to more flexible work arrangements permitted under labor laws (Swamy, 2007). Many centers are in remote areas, and entrepreneurs should have the option to relocate to commercial localities to enhance their business prospects. Frequent performance checks and feedback mechanisms are essential for understanding challenges and improving service delivery. The entrepreneur's efficient model in Common Service Centers (CSCs) minimizes bureaucratic hurdles while maximizing citizen convenience. The evolution towards digital governance is pivotal in meeting the increasing demands of citizens and ensuring effective service delivery. Achieving this goal necessitates proactive infrastructure development and a skilled workforce capable of navigating technological advancements to deliver quality services seamlessly.

Information and Communication Technologies (ICTs) have witnessed rapid growth over the past three decades, resulting in the formulation of policies that align with national requirements across several countries (Trebon, 2005). Since India's economic liberalization in 1991, the ICT sector has experienced significant expansion, primarily driven by software exports and technological advancements.

These developments highlight the transformative role of ICTs in governance, service delivery, and economic development on a global scale. The growing popularity of CSCs reflects a shift towards digital governance and an increasing public demand for efficient, transparent, and corruption-free services. Integrating various government services with CSCs is crucial for meeting evolving citizen expectations and enhancing administrative efficiency.

REFERENCES

Anaf, J., Freeman, T., & Baum, F. (2024). Privatisation of government services in Australia: What is known about health and equity impacts. *Globalization and Health*, 20(1), 32. DOI: 10.1186/s12992-024-01036-w PMID: 38627788

Aschemann, B. (2017). The Digital Readiness of Adult Education. The EBmooc for adult educators. *Magazin Erwachsenenbildung.at*: Vol. 11. *Issue, 30*. Springer Publications.

Bhatia, A. (2010). *Approach Paper on Defining Public-Private Partnerships*. Ministry of Finance, Department of Economic Affairs, Government of India. Para 6.3. https://www.pppinindia.gov.in/assets/doc/20181/22330/33_pppacMinutes.pdf

Biernacki, M., Luśtyk, A., & Wisła, R. (2023). Differentiation of the digital economic development in Europe. Edited By Judyta Lubacha, Beata Mäihäniemi, Rafał Wisła. In *The European Digital Economy - Drivers of Digital Transition and Economic Recovery* (pp. 45–60). Routledge. DOI: 10.4324/9781003450160-5

Centre for Good Governance (2003). A Report.

Cervantes-Guzmán, J. N. (2021, April-June). [2021]. *Evolution of Entrepreneur Women from Traditional Companies to E-Business*. (In). *International Journal of Business Strategy and Automation*, 2(2), 32. DOI: 10.4018/IJBSA.20210401.oa3

Egnew, R. C., & Baler, S. G. (1998). Developing principles, goals, and models for public/private partnerships. *Administration and Policy in Mental Health*, 25(6), 571–580.

Eriksson, J., Calling, S., Jakobsson, U., Wolff, M., Bolmsjö, B. B., & Nymberg, V. M. (2024). Inequity in access to digital public primary healthcare in Sweden: A cross-sectional study of the effects of urbanicity and socioeconomic status on utilization. *International Journal for Equity in Health*, 23(1), 72. DOI: 10.1186/s12939-024-02159-7 PMID: 38622678

Ezat, A., Neumann, L., Sievert, S., Robra-Bissantz, S., Helmholz, P., & Perl, A. (2019). Herausforderungen im Datenschutz an der Hochschule. Generierung von Lösungsvorschlägen für Forschung und Lehre. In S Robra-Bissantz, O Bott, N Kleinefeld, K Neu, K Zickwolf: Teaching Trends 2018. Die Präsenzhochschule und die digitale Transformation (pp. 182-188). Waxmann.

Fernandes, C., Ferreira, J. J., Veiga, P. M., Kraus, S., & Dabić, M. (2022). Digital entrepreneurship platforms: Mapping the field and looking towards a holistic approach. *Technology in Society*, 70, 101979.

Hsieh, Y.-J., & Wu, Y. J. (2019). Entrepreneurship through the platform strategy in the digital era: Insights and research opportunities, *Computers in Human Behavior*, Volume 95, Pages 315-323, ISSN 0747-5632, https://doi.org/DOI: 10.1016/j.chb.2018.03.033

Inge Panneels, Susan Lechelt, Alessandra Schmidt, Aykut Coşkun (2024). Data-driven innovation for sustainable practice in the creative economy - Ecological, social, and cultural aspects (In) Data-Driven Innovation in the Creative Industries. Edited By *Melissa Terras, Vikki Jones, Nicola Osborne, Chris Speed. pp.243-266. Routledge.* International Telecommunications Union (ITU). https://www.itu.int/en/ITU-D/Innovation/Pages/Digital-Transformation-Accelerators.aspx accessed on 26.9.2024.

Jain, A. Bagga, R.K. and Vijaya Sekhar K.S., (2010) 'Capacity Building for eGovernance: Learning by Doing Methodology' in Gupta et al (Eds.) *Enablers of Change: Selected e-Governance Initiatives in India*, ICFAI University Press. pp 52-62.

James, M. (Interviewer), & Eric, Schmidt. (Interviewee). (2013). *Reimagining India: A Conversation with Eric Schmidt* [Interview transcript]. McKinsey & Company.

Jamwal, J. (2013). *Khidmat Center – An initiative of J&K Bank: Bridging the Digital Divide in Jammu and Kashmir.* 10 September, Locally Published. pp 11.

Kehrbusch, B., & Engels, G. (2023). Digital Transformation-Towards Flexible Human-Centric Enterprises. In Vogel-Heuser, B., Wimmer, M., & Vieweg, S. (Eds.), *Digital Transformation: Core Technologies and Emerging Topics from a Computer Science Perspective* (pp. 497–526). DOI: 10.1007/978-3-662-65004-2_20

Kimura, R., Reeves, M., & Whitaker, K. (2019). *The new logic of competition.* Boston Consulting Group Report.

Li, S., Bu, Y., Zhang, Z., & Huang, Y. (2024). Digital entrepreneurship intention and digital entrepreneurship behavior: The mediating role of managing learning and entrepreneurship education. *Education + Training*.

Mazzucato, M. (2015). *The Entrepreneurial State Debunking Public vs. Private Sector myths.* Public Affairs.

Obare, S. O. (2020). Successful STEM Women of Color Must Network Differently. In Leggett-Robinson, P., & Villa, B. (Eds.), *Overcoming Barriers for Women of Color in STEM Fields: Emerging Research and Opportunities* (pp. 1–18). IGI Global., DOI: 10.4018/978-1-7998-4858-5.ch004

Quan, Z., & Zhang, Y. (2025). A Historical Review on Learning with Technology: From Computers to Smartphones. In *Encyclopedia of Information Science and Technology*, Sixth Edition. DOI: DOI: 10.4018/978-1-6684-7366-5.ch004

Sachdeva, S. (2006). *'Twenty-Five Steps to Successful e-Governance', I-WAYS, Digest of Electronic Government Policy and Regulation 29*. IOS Press.

Sharma, R., Kamble, S., Gupta, S., Belhadi, A., Rana, N. P., & Kumar, K. (2023). Interlinkages Between Digital-Social Entrepreneurship and Technological Capabilities for Sustainable Value Creation. [JGIM]. *Journal of Global Information Management*, 31(1), 1–26. DOI: 10.4018/JGIM.328515

Swamy, M. (2007). *Exploring New Horizons through ICTs: A Handbook for Women's organizations in Karnataka*. IT for Change.

Trebon, K. (2005) *Citizen Service Levels Interagency Committee (CSLIC)*, USA Services e-Gov Program. 202-501-1802.

United Nations Development Programme. (2005). *Trends and Challenges in Public Administration Reform in Asia and the Pacific*. Keen Publishing.

Usman, M. A., & Sun, X. (2023). The impact of digital platforms on new startup performance: Strategy as moderator. *Heliyon*, 9(12).

Vijaya Sekhar, K. S., & Bagga, R. K. (2012). Citizen's experiences of eGovernance with Technology as Focus: A case study on eSeva in Andhra Pradesh. Proceedings of International Conference on Public Policy and Governance (PPG-2012), IISc, Bangalore. Excel India Publishers. Vol. II, Pp. 521-528.

Vijaya Sekhar, K. S., & Pallavi, K. (2014) 'ICT based Opportunities for women entrepreneurs in Andhra Pradesh' In *Building Bridges: Contemporary Research in Gender Studies*, University of Hyderabad, March 24-26, 2014.

Vithal, D. V. R., Bagga, R. K., & Vijaya Sekhar, K. S. (2013). Thirty Years of eGovernance in CSI. In Kapoor, S., Gollamudi, P., Bhatt, N., & Iyer, H. P. (Eds.), *Inclusive Growth through eGovernance* (pp. 39–50). Universities Press.

ADDITIONAL READING

Ali, M. (2021). *Remote Work and Sustainable Changes for the Future of Global Business*. IGI Global. https://www.igi-global.com/book/remote-work-sustainable-changes-future/264375

Ali, M. (2022). *Future Role of Sustainable Innovative Technologies in Crisis Management*. IGI Global. https://www.igi-global.com/book/future-role-sustainable-innovative-technologies/281281

Ali, M. (2023). *Shifting Paradigms in the Rapidly Developing Global Digital Ecosystem: A GCC Perspective.* In Digital Entrepreneurship and Co-Creating Value Through Digital Encounters (pp. 145-166). IGI Global. https://www.igi-global.com/chapter/shifting-paradigms-in-the-rapidly-developing-global-digital-ecosystem/323525

Ali, M. (2023). T*axonomy of Industry 4.0 Technologies in Digital Entrepreneurship and Co-Creating Value.* In *Digital Entrepreneurship and Co-Creating Value Through Digital Encounters* (pp. 24–55). IGI Global., https://www.igi-global.com/chapter/taxonomy-of-industry-40-technologies-in-digital-entrepreneurship-and-co-creating-value/323520 DOI: 10.4018/978-1-6684-7416-7.ch002

Ali, M., & Wood-Harper, T. (2021). *Fostering Communication and Learning with Underutilized Technologies in Higher Education*. IGI Global. https://www.igi-global.com/book/fostering-communication-learning-underutilized-technologies/244593

Ali, M., Wood-Harper, T., & Kutar, M. (2023). Multi-Perspectives of Contemporary Digital Transformation Models of Complex Innovation Management. In *Digital Entrepreneurship and Co-Creating Value Through Digital Encounters* (pp. 79–96). IGI Global., https://www.igi-global.com/chapter/multi-perspectives-of-contemporary-digital-transformation-models-of-complex-innovation-management/323522 DOI: 10.4018/978-1-6684-7416-7.ch004

Ali, M. B. (2021). Internet of Things (IoT) to Foster Communication and Information Sharing: A Case of UK Higher Education. In Ali, M. B., & Wood-Harper, T. (Eds.), *Fostering Communication and Learning With Underutilized Technologies in Higher Education* (pp. 1–20). IGI Global., https://www.igi-global.com/chapter/internet-of-things-iot-to-foster-communication-and-information-sharing/262718/ DOI: 10.4018/978-1-7998-4846-2.ch001

Ali, M. B., & Wood-Harper, T. (2022). Artificial Intelligence (AI) as a Decision-Making Tool to Control Crisis Situations. In *Future Role of Sustainable Innovative Technologies in Crisis Management.* IGI Global., https://www.igi-global.com/chapter/artificial-intelligence-ai-as-a-decision-making-tool-to-control-crisis-situations/298931 DOI: 10.4018/978-1-7998-9815-3.ch006

Ali, M. B., Wood-Harper, T., & Ramlogan, R. (2020). A Framework Strategy to Overcome Trust Issues on Cloud Computing Adoption in Higher Education. In Modern Principles, Practices, and Algorithms for Cloud Security (pp. 162-183). IGI Global. https://www.igi-global.com/chapter/a-framework-strategy-to-overcome-trust-issues-on-cloud-computing-adoption-in-higher-education/238907/

KEY TERMS AND DEFINITIONS

NeGP: National eGovernance Programme was initiated in 2006 to deliver all public services through a common service centre covering over six lakh villages from about one lakh CSCs.

CSC: Common Service Center is a kiosk owned and operated by an entrepreneur who delivers several public and private services acting on behalf of the government.

VLE: Village Level Entrepreneur is a typical 10th-grade pass-outs, who manage CSC kiosks equipped with essential infrastructure like computers, printers, internet, and scanners to deliver public and private services from a locality.

MMP: Mission Mode Projects are timebound projects that are confined to government services such as passport delivery, postal delivery, and issuing citizen-cantered services promptly.

Chapter 8
Unlocking the Future of Education:
Factors Influencing the Adoption of Mobile Learning in Higher Education

Khem Chand
https://orcid.org/0000-0001-7879-5198
Lovely Professional University, India

Sapna Jangra
Maharshi Dayanand University, India

Anjali Gupta
https://orcid.org/0000-0003-1825-6568
Maharshi Dayanand University, India

Rajesh Tiwari
https://orcid.org/0000-0002-5345-2508
Graphic Era University (Deemed), India

Pradeep Kumar
Raffles University, India

ABSTRACT

Contemporary societies are witnessing an unprecedented surge in technological advancements across various domains, with education being no exception. In alignment with this evolving landscape, educational institutions are increasingly incorporating information and communication technology (ICT) as an integral tool for facilitating

DOI: 10.4018/979-8-3373-0086-3.ch008

Copyright © 2025, IGI Global. Copying or distributing in print or electronic forms without written permission of IGI Global is prohibited.

teaching and learning processes. In a manner reminiscent of learning organizations, academic establishments prioritize the integration of state-of-the-art technologies, particularly in the realm of education and instruction. This study focuses on the implementation of mobile learning among higher education students, recognizing the growing role of technology in education. The research collected data from 100 students and used PLS-SEM for analysis. Key findings indicate that factors like social influence, self-efficacy, perceived ease of use, and usefulness significantly influence the intention of students to use mobile learning. This research can assist developers, designers, and educational institutions in improving mobile learning systems.

1. INTRODUCTION

In the contemporary era, societies worldwide are witnessing an unprecedented proliferation of technology across diverse domains and education is no exception to this transformative wave. Consequently, educational settings are increasingly harnessing the power of information and communication technology as an essential tool for enhancing both teaching and learning experiences (Matimbwa & Anney (2016). Much like learning organizations, academic institutions prioritize the integration of cutting-edge technologies to drive progress, having particular attention on enhancing the realm of teaching and learning (Balash et al., 2011). Another noteworthy technological development and educational movement is mobile learning, which offers teachers and students many alternatives (İlçi, 2014). The use of mobile technology in education is expanding the potential for effective and efficient instruction (Abidin & Tho, 2018); (Sanga, et al., 2016). It is because of benefits arising from mobile learning which may include knowledge sharing without any restrictions of time and space, critical thinking development, problem solver, communication skills development and participatory learning (Abidin & Tho, 2018).

The meaning of the "Mobile Learning" concept is still not clear and continues to change frequently due to the multiplication of digital mobile devices (DMD) applications and continuous development in the education field. To describe mobile learning (Traxler, J., 2007) identifies a few important concepts including personal, spontaneous, place, private and portable. Using mobile and internet technologies, learners can access instructional materials at their convenience, regardless of location (Lan & Sie., 2010). Mobile devices often boast affordability, portability and flexibility, making them exceptionally appealing and valuable tools for the learning journey.

Digital mobile devices provide a variety of programs that can help teach and learn in education such as Word, Excel and PowerPoint as well as specialized apps for learning languages and problem solution (Alzaza & Yaakub, 2011). The distinctive feature of mobile learning is its emphasis on mobility, setting it apart from other educational systems. Notwithstanding the advantages mentioned earlier, it is important to recognize that mobile education will never be able to completely replace the traditional education system. However, when used properly, it may serve as complementary to current learning methods.

Due to the rapid development of digital mobile devices, it may take time to assess the potential of digital mobile devices in the classroom (Gawelek et al. 2011; Cano, E. V., 2012). Ongoing development in the arena of digital mobile devices in the education domain opens up a wide range of opportunities in this field. To foster the knowledge required to take decisions regarding the use of technological processes and use the same to improve the capacity to work to achieve better results (Bertschy et al. 2009; Murphy, G., 2011).

1.1 Mobile Learning

Mobile learning denotes the method of acquiring knowledge or skills through the use of a mobile device (Crompton & Burke, 2018) "The use of Mobiles, laptops, tablets, PC technologies to provide training, education and teaching" (Sarrab et al., 2018). Through the use of technology and the internet, students can learn at their convenience regardless of location. Mobile learning has great potential for learners along with accessing required material information (Fan et al., 2022). It is a valuable technology that might have a substantial effect on teaches (Tossell et al., 2015) due to its widespread market penetration and rapidly evolving technological capabilities (Yip et al., 2021). The accomplishment of mobile learning platforms relies significantly on the endorsement and adoption by both students and educators (Hamidi & Chavoshi, 2018; Almaiah et al., 2021). Mobile phones provide a distinctive learning experience by making it possible for students to obtain the required information for learning.

The Indian context has witnessed multiple successful models and case studies, which demonstrate the achievements and struggles of mobile learning usage. The DigiLocker platform of the Government of India was initially conceived as a digital document storage service. However, it grew into a means of mobile learning in higher education. Universities have integrated DigiLocker for this purpose as well, providing students with easily accessed educational materials on their mobile devices by digitally giving certificates, degrees, and other academic documents. This particular project has shown a new way of learning access through the government platforms. Earlier, students and faculty hesitated because of a lack of digital literacy and the habit of using regular paper in it (Girijan, 2024). After that, there has been more acceptance of it, especially as universities like Delhi University and IGNOU began to include it. In areas where the internet is not available students experienced problems trying to get their papers processed. Hence, the service was provided but the students did not get the opportunity to use it because of the slow internet connectivity. During the COVID-19 pandemic, BYJU's, which is a well-known education technology company in India, turned into a great example of mobile learning in the country. The platform included video lessons, interactive quizzes, and live classes, all of which could be accessed through mobile phones. However, despite the good outcome BYJU's faced, difficulties in rural areas due to limited access to mobile devices, unstable internet, and power issues were still prevalent. Besides, the high cost of data plans was a major challenge for families with low incomes. For starters, the students and parents were a bit skeptic about the effectiveness of these materials because mobile apps learning was a new thing. The traditional stereotype of education was a major concern as parents took a pass at it. Many parents showed reservations regarding quality and efficiency of mobile-based education. Some students felt less involved because of the self-paced nature of mobile learning and they thought that without the regular classroom sessions they were less motivated. The absence of peer interaction was a further important contributing factor (Ray et al., 2024).

1.2 Benefits of Mobile Learning

Creating one-to-one teaching situations and techno-savvy classrooms to reduce the cost for the institutions and allow students to save money on notebooks. M-Learning helps in making students more engaged and involved due to active tutors. For making the learning process effective. Teachers can teach their students regarding how to collaborate, be creative and social networking skills if they have access to their own mobile devices. Incorporating the relevant skills among students will help them in making their demand high in the future job market. In the current scenario, learning is not limited to classrooms. It has crossed the boundaries due to students' continuous engagement. They can expand their learning outside the classroom as per their comfort zone. Giving students their own mobile devices encourage them to be accountable for both their learning and the ongoing upkeep and security of their equipment. Learning is becoming more individualized thanks to the app revolution and the abundance of productivity applications for students. This is the major and notable advantage of mobile learning. Students will develop higher levels of independence that will foster lifelong learning when they are learning anywhere, anytime and more responsibly. Moments, locations, and any chance to study impulsively, as best suited to their welfares and requirements, may all be taken advantage of with m-learning's emphasis on spontaneity and opportunity.

1.3 Challenges

Every student cannot buy the same equipment which leads to the issue of device equity. This may create a line of difference among students which may put wealthier students ahead of less fortunate ones. Diversification of learning material is required to enable personalized learning. IT interface varies as per different platforms which may create an additional burden on instructors to assist students with the platform environment. Access to a trustworthy Wi-Fi network is required for making mobile learning successful. Device safety needs to be addressed to increase awareness of the fact that it is the student's responsibility to keep their gadgets safe. Another concern for schoolchildren, but one that has less of an impact on college students is e-safety (online safety). Students' gadgets' accessibility to gaming and other forms of entertainment as well as their connectedness to the outside world may cause distractions constantly.

There are very challenging cultural and technological obstacles, in conjunction with student resistance and many other factors (Quraishi et al., 2024). Diverse views on education, contact, and communication with technological gadgets may limit the usage of mobile learning in some cultural areas. In certain places, the educational system is so much fixed on conventional teaching methods that it becomes a hardship for both students and educators to switch to mobile-based learning as an authentic educational tool. Likewise, the society's attitudes towards education technology, gender roles, and the level of digital literacy can further complicate the seamless integration of mobile learning solutions. The ultimate of mobile learning largely hinges on having access to reliable technology, the major battle of which is the poor infrastructure in some areas. Limited internet connection, inadequate access to smart devices, and inconsistent technical support are the difficulties encountered by both students and teachers. Besides, the wide disparities among digital literacy and the great costs of technological resources are the big divide to the teaching of mobile learning through which one of the student groups certainly cannot have any access to. Many students object to mobile learning because of the fact that they are not familiar with it or they like the traditional classroom atmosphere. While some students feel uncomfortable with the self-directed nature of mobile learning and other are having the mobile devices as the distraction in the class. Also, a lack of motivation or doubt in the efficacy of mobile learning in comparison with face-to-face interaction can also be a factor (Hakimi et al., 2024). Overcoming these issues through a holistic approach requires the involvement of varied steps such as increasing awareness, strengthening the digital ecosystem, delivering training, and making accessible mobile learning platforms that are friendly to the diversities of students (Asimoah et al., 2024). The implementation of mobile learning has many social and economic challenges. Social Challenges consists of digital divide, technological literacy, privacy concerns and cultural resistance (Saikat et al., 2021). Not all students have equal access to mobile devices and reliable internet connections, leading to disparities in learning opportunities. Both students and educators may lack the necessary skills to use mobile learning efficiently. There can be resistance to adopting new technologies due to cultural preferences for traditional learning methods. Ensuring the privacy and security of students' data is a significant Concern. Economic Challenges includes cost of devices, training cost, maintenance and upgrades. The initial outlay for mobile devices and infrastructure might be heavy. Continual costs of maintaining and upgrading technological systems can be a drain to educational budgets. Besides the direct costs of licenses and equipment, there is also the need for additional financial resources for providing educator training sessions (UNESCO, 2009).

1.4 Research Gap

There appears to be little consideration of the drivers triggering the student's utilization of mobile applications. To meet students' needs and improve their perceptions of mobile learning acceptance, it is vital to particularly examine the acceptance of students concerning the use of mobiles for learning. The current study may help developers, designers, and higher education institutions to advance their mobile learning systems. This research was conducted to explore the main drivers that drive the adoption of mobile learning, aiming to address a research gap and enhance the overall educational experience and performance of students. The current study endeavored to pinpoint the crucial factors that impact students' willingness to embrace mobile learning within the higher education context.

2. PROPOSED MODEL

2.1 Perceived Usefulnes

The primary factors affecting the usage and acceptance of mobile learning have been evaluated in numerous researches in the literature. It was Highlighted the potential application and drawbacks of technology in M-learning (Liu et al., 2010). The authors argue that mobile learning necessitates self-reliance and a learner's readiness to actively engage in the learning process. This, in turn, can foster increased student engagement with the provided activities and information. They emphasize that people who use technology may think that "perceived usefulness" and "perceived ease of use" are vital factors in influencing their attitudes and intention to utilize m-learning services and systems. The extent to which a user thinks employing technology will support in attaining an improved job or academic performance is known as perceived usefulness (Venkatesh et al., 2003; Akbar, 2013). It is a reliable predictor of the desire to use technology applications in a range of settings. In addition, studies have revealed that "perceived usefulness" is a robust predictor of students' behavioral intention to use mobile learning (Avci & Askar, 2012; Joo, 2016; Han & Shin, 2016; Teo et al., 2016).

H1: "Perceived usefulness positively affects the behavioral intention of students to adopt Mobile learning."

2.2 Perceived Ease Of Use

Perceived ease of use is "The level of ease associated with the use of the system" (Venkatesh et al., 2003). The receipt and practice of Mobile learning by learners were found to be directly correlated with perceived simplicity of use (Lee & Lee, 2008; Sanchez & Hueros, 2008). The intent to apply mobile learning increased the positive perception of students regarding its simple use and easily accessible content (Liu, et al., 2010). Categorize it into long-term and short-term. If mobile learning is perceived to be useful in the long run, then it indicates results in the future whereas short-term usefulness indicates instant results. The personal innovativeness of persons and their willingness to try new information technology influence how they use mobile learning. The superior the level of innovativeness, the greater will be the propensity to have positive beliefs and thereby affecting their behavioral intention (Agarwal & Prasad, 1997; Liu, et al., 2010; Hameed et al., 2024).

H2: "Perceived ease of use positively influences the behavioral intention of students to adopt mobile learning."

2.3 Social Influence

It can be defined as the extent to which a person believes that important people in their life endorse or expect them to take a specific action, such as utilizing the system or technology (Venkatesh & Davis, 2000). Social influence has a major impact on the behavioral intention of students to adopt mobile learning (Venkatesh & Davis, 2000; Šumak et al., 2010; Akbar, 2013; Han, & Shin, 2016). Additionally, parties other than the user themselves, such as the users' peers, can have an impact on how valuable they believe a technology or system to be (Claar et al., 2014).

H3: "Social Influence positively influences the behavioral intention of students to adopt mobile learning."

2.4 Mobile Self-Efficacy

It denotes a person's confidence in his skills to effectively plan, implement, and accomplish a detailed set of tasks or actions to attain particular levels of performance (Compeau & Higgins (1995;Pituch & Lee, 2006). Mobile system efficacy refers to the efficiency of mobile systems and related applications which enable students to readily access and participate in lessons without interruption. Study included computer self-efficacy and mobile self-efficacy. It is logical to suppose that students' intent to use the technology would be positively impacted by their sense of self-efficacy as m-learning necessitates greater individual autonomy. Research from the past has demonstrated this concept in e-learning settings (Pituch & Lee, 2006). The following relationship was generated as hypothesis:

H4: "Mobile Self-Efficacy positively influences the behavioral intention of students to adopt mobile learning."

3. RESEARCH METHODOLOGY

Quantitative analysis is applied in this study to establish the links between underlying construct (Bell, & Bryman, 2007). This is a highly recognized approach to methodically compiling information (Smith, 2012). Underlying constructs are measured by adapting the items for previous studies. Previous studies were taken to ensure content validity. Five-point Likert scale was employed in which respondents rated their agreement level, with 1 indicating "strongly disagree" and 5 representing "strongly agree." The questionnaire included items related to various factors such as Personal Ease of Use, Social Influence, Perceived Usefulness, Behavioral Intention and Self-efficacy. Data has been collected through convenience sampling method from college and university students in Rohtak. 100 responses provided base for the analysis. CFA was performed on underlying factors for validation. Relationships between underlying constructs were measured by applying Structural Equation Modelling (SEM) through Smart PLS.

4. DATA ANALYSIS

4.1 Overview

PLS-SEM is superior to AMOS for estimating composite models. As a result, we believed that the PLS-SEM method of variance-based structural equation modeling was the most suitable for analyzing the model. Additionally, PLS-SEM is the best method to use to estimate multiple relationships between latent constructs, and it also performs exceptionally well when the sample size is small (Hair et al., 2017). These factors all contributed to our decision to use this technique. So, applying Smart-PLS, the model was examined.

The factor analysis loadings values lies between 0.835 to 0.937 as indicated in Table 1. At the 0.05 level, all loadings were significant. Convergent validity and internal consistency were tested using the average variance extracted (AVE) and composite reliability (CR) calculations (Fornell & Larcker, 1981). Convergent reliability and internal consistency were established by the fact that every research variable had AVE values greater than 0.5 and CR values greater than 0.70.

Table 1. Factor loadings, AVE, Alpha value and CR

	Loadings	AVE	Cronbach's Alpha	Composite Reliability
Perceived ease of use (PEU)		.888	.937	.960
PEU1	.909			
PEU2	.927			
PEU3	.937			
Social Influence (SIN)		.923	.958	.973
SIN1	.935			
SIN2	.884			
SIN3	.891			
Self-Efficacy (SEY)		.858	.959	.968
SEY1	.835			
SEY2	.866			
SEY3	.853			
SEY4	.896			
SEY5	.899			
Usefulness (USE)		.927	.961	.974
USE1	.845			
USE2	.903			
USE3	.885			
Behavioral Intention (BIN)		.926	.960	.974
BIN1	.889			
BIN2	.893			
BIN3	.907			

Source: Author's survey

Discriminant validity was assessed through two distinct tests. The initial test, known as the Fornell and Larcker rule, evaluates the square root of the AVE with the intercorrelations between variables. As shown in Table 2, the data met the requirement for discriminant validity, as the square root of AVE exceeded the intercorrelation values.

Additionally, we employed the Heterotrait-Monotrait Ratio (HTMT) to further substantiate the presence of discriminant validity. The outcomes presented in Table 3 indicate that all HTMT values are less than the recommended threshold of 0.85, as suggested by (Hulland, 1999). This observation confirms the discriminant validity of the components.

Table 2. Fornell-Larcker criterion

	BIN	**PEU**	**SIN**	**SEY**	**USE**
BIN	**.962**				
PEU	.462	.943			
SIN	.684	.366	.926		
SEY	.642	.256	.467	.961	
USE	.775	.415	.690	.703	.963

Source: Author's survey

Table 3. HTMT ratio

	Perceived ease of use	**Social Influence**	**Self-Efficacy**	**Usefulness**	**Behavioral Intention**
Perceived ease of use					
Social Influence	0.271				
Self-Efficacy	0.385	0.487			
Usefulness	0.439	0.732	0.719		
Behavioral Intention	0.485	0.669	0.711	0.807	

Source: Author's survey

The R-squared (R2) value for Behavioral Intention in the structural model was computed as 0.683. According to Chin (1998) recommendations, this value is considered acceptable.

4.2 Hypothesis Results

The outcomes of the direct path analysis are shown in Table 4 below. According to the findings: Perceived Usefulness was positively associated to the behavioral intention of learners to implement Mobile learning (ß = 0.377, t = 2.907, p = 0.004), PEU positively influence the intention of students to implement mobile learning (ß = 0.152, t = 2.229, p = 0.026). SE have a positive effect on the Behavioral intention of students (ß = 0.213, t = 2.739, p = 0.006). Lastly, SI is positively linked to the behavioral intention of students (ß = 0.269, t = 2.639, p = 0.009). The findings are consistent with H_1, H_2, H_3 and H_4.

Table 4. Path analysis

Relationship	Path Coefficient	SD	t-value	95CI	P-value	Hypothesis	Result
PEU -- > BI	0.152	0.068	2.229	0.004-0.280	0.026	H_2	Spt
SI -- > BI	0.269	0.102	2.639	0.079-0.461	0.009	H_3	Spt
SE -- > BI	0.213	0.078	2.739	0.028-0.373	0.006	H_4	Spt
USE -- > BI	0.377	0.130	2.907	0.121-0.648	0.004	H_1	Spt

Source: Author's survey

5. DISCUSSION

The current empirical study focuses on factors associated with behavioral intention of students to adopt mobile learning among university students. Four constructs were identified after thorough review of literature. PLS-SEM was employed to assess the influence of these four constructs on behavioral intention of students to apply mobile learning and path coefficients were estimated. Findings revealed that all the four hypotheses were accepted. Perceived ease of use, perceived usefulness, Self-efficacy, and social influence were found to be significantly influencing Behavioral intention of students to adopt mobile learning. These results align with previous study findings, indicating consistency and agreement between the current research outcomes and prior research results (Hsu, 2012); (Saroia & Gao, 2019); (Tan & Chou, 2008); (Venkatesh & Morris, 2000). Both theoretical and practical ramifications of this investigation are substantial. This is one of the earliest research projects on the variables influencing learners' behavioral intentions on the theoretical contributions of using mobile learning in higher education. It appears that the alternative model used in our study has proven to be a more effective explanation for the formation of intentions compared to the Technology Acceptance Model.

Additionally, our conclusions suggest that cultural factors play a noteworthy role in shaping these intentions. This connection between cultural factors and intention formation may warrant further investigation, potentially using Hofstede's Cultural Dimensions as a framework for deeper exploration and understanding (Bhagat, 2002). Engagement of policy holders is crucial for attainment of the outcomes (Tiwari et al., 2020). If end users get satisfaction from the technology, they will use it for long term (Tiwari, 2022). Technology driven delivery can enhance access of services for the economically backward sections of society (Tiwari et al., 2021). The architecture of the system has to be outcome driven with optimum efficiency (Karthick, 2023). Integrated fusion teaching offers the potential to unleash the creative power of youth (Tiwari et al., 2023). Low cost of internet usage has made it feasible to offer services through online medium in India (Chand et al., 2023). Wasteful activities in the operations need to be eliminated, to improve effectiveness and efficiency (Padmalosan et al., 2023). Employees are the crucial factor for long term success of the organization. Unless they are given fair treatment, their involvement will never be optimal (Chand et al., 2023).

The current research, supported by robust theoretical foundations and data analysis, offers practical implications for the creation and promotion of mobile apps for higher education that are pertinent to educators, library service providers, and app developers. These implications are in line with earlier studies, indicating a degree of consistency and reliability in the recommendations. Furthermore, our study's results hold the potential to provide valuable insights for mobile learning and application developers, particularly in the context of university students in the Asia Pacific region. Given the rapid expansion of mobile technology in this region, our research could inform the development of the next generation of apps tailored to the specific needs and preferences of students in this environment. This aligns with the rising standing of mobile technology in education and need to adapt to evolving technological trends.

6. CONCLUSION

Mobile e-learning involves adapting existing e-learning methods to leverage wireless and mobile technology, enabling access to previously existing learning management systems (LMS) via mobile devices. Data for the research consist of university students in Rohtak, aiming to analyze the aspects persuading mobile learning adoption. The study introduces an alternative model drawing from the Technology Acceptance Model and Unified Theory of Acceptance and Use of Technology, emphasizing the impact of users' cultural backgrounds on the adoption process. This research highlights the practical implications of mobile and wireless technologies in real-world, including the use of laptops, tablets, and wireless networks to enhance flexibility in classrooms. Moreover, it underscores the probable of mobile learning to assist the field personnel training and reach marginalized and remote communities, along with special needs groups, using widely accessible mobile technologies like cell phones. The study identifies four significant factors— perceived ease of use, self-efficacy, social influence, and perceived usefulness—that significantly influence students' behavioral intentions to adopt mobile learning. Ultimately, this research yields practical insights for the creation and promotion of mobile apps for higher education that are pertinent to educators, library service providers, and app developers.

REFERENCES

Abidin, N. Z., & Tho, S. (2018). The development of an innovative resonance experiment using smartphones with free mobile software applications for tertiary education. *International Journal of Education and Development using ICT, 14*(1).

Agarwal, R., & Prasad, J. (1997). The role of innovation characteristics and perceived voluntariness in the acceptance of information technologies. *Decision Sciences*, 28(3), 557–582. DOI: 10.1111/j.1540-5915.1997.tb01322.x

Akbar, F. (2013). *What affects students' acceptance and use of technology*. Dietrich College of Humanities and Social Sciences.

Almaiah, M. A., Almomani, O., Al-Khasawneh, A., & Althunibat, A. (2021). Predicting the acceptance of mobile learning applications during COVID-19 using machine learning prediction algorithms. *Emerging technologies during the era of COVID-19 pandemic*, 319-332.

Alzaza, N. S., & Yaakub, A. R. (2011). Students' awareness and requirements of mobile learning services in the higher education environment. *American Journal of Economics and Business Administration*, 3(1), 95–100. DOI: 10.3844/ajebasp.2011.95.100

Asamoah, D. A., Dinsmore, J. B., & Swani, K. (2024). Benefits, barriers, and facilitators of developing B2B mobile applications. *Journal of Business and Industrial Marketing*, 39(3), 537–552. DOI: 10.1108/JBIM-10-2022-0457

Avci, U., & Askar, P. (2012). The comparison of the opinions of the university students on the usage of blog and wiki for their courses. *Journal of Educational Technology & Society*, 15(2), 194–205.

Balash, F., Yong, Z., & Bin Abu, B. (2011). Lecturers and educational technology: Factors affecting educational technology adoption in teaching. In *2nd International Conference on Education and Management Technology IPCSIT* (Vol. 13).

Bell, E., & Bryman, A. (2007). The ethics of management research: An exploratory content analysis. *British Journal of Management*, 18(1), 63–77. DOI: 10.1111/j.1467-8551.2006.00487.x

Bertschy, K., Cattaneo, M. A., & Wolter, S. C. (2009). PISA and the Transition into the Labour Market. *Labour*, 23(s1), 111–137. DOI: 10.1111/j.1467-9914.2008.00432.x

Bhagat, R. S. (2002). Culture's consequences: Comparing values, behaviors, institutions, and organizations across nations.

Cahyana, U., Lestari, I., Irwanto, I., & Suroso, J. (2024). Development of a mobile learning network for science with augmented reality and its impact on students' literacy and numeracy. *International Journal of Innovative Research and Scientific Studies*, 7(2), 576–586. DOI: 10.53894/ijirss.v7i2.2685

Cano, E. V. (2012). Mobile learning with Twitter to improve linguistic competence at secondary schools. *The New Educational Review*, 29(3), 134–147.

Chand, K., Jangra, S., Singh, P. C., Tiwari, R. S., & Tiwari, R. (2023). Sustainability of Mobile Wallets in the Era of Low Cost Data Usage in India. In *Data-Driven Approaches for Effective Managerial Decision Making* (pp. 102–126). IGI Global. DOI: 10.4018/978-1-6684-7568-3.ch005

Chand, K., Tiwari, R., & Bhardwaj, K. (2021, December). Impact of Welfare Measures on Job Satisfaction of Employees in the Industrial Sector of Northern India1. In *Presented at IIF International Research Conference & Award Summit (November*. Claar, C., Portolese Dias, L., & Shields, R. (2014). Student acceptence of learning management systems: A study on demographics. *Issues in Information Systems*, 15(1).

Compeau, D. R., & Higgins, C. A. (1995). Computer self-efficacy: Development of a measure and initial test. *Management Information Systems Quarterly*, 19(2), 189–211. DOI: 10.2307/249688

Crompton, H., & Burke, D. (2018). The use of mobile learning in higher education: A systematic review. *Computers & Education*, 123, 53–64. DOI: 10.1016/j.compedu.2018.04.007

Fan, M., Ndavi, J. W., Qalati, S. A., Huang, L., & Pu, Z. (2022). Applying the time continuum model of motivation to explain how major factors affect mobile learning motivation: A comparison of SEM and fsQCA. *Online Information Review*, 46(6), 1095–1114. DOI: 10.1108/OIR-04-2021-0226

Fornell, C., & Larcker, D. F. (1981). Evaluating structural equation models with unobservable variables and measurement error. *JMR, Journal of Marketing Research*, 18(1), 39–50. DOI: 10.1177/002224378101800104

Gawelek, M. A., Spataro, M., & Komarny, P. (2011). Mobile perspectives: On iPads—why mobile? *EDUCAUSE Review*, 46(2), 28–30.

Girijan, K. P. (2024). Digital India Initiative: The Road Towards Sustainable Development. *Journal Commedies*, 1(1), 5–8.

Hair, J. F.Jr, Matthews, L. M., Matthews, R. L., & Sarstedt, M. (2017). PLS-SEM or CB-SEM: Updated guidelines on which method to use. *International Journal of Multivariate Data Analysis*, 1(2), 107–123. DOI: 10.1504/IJMDA.2017.087624

Hakimi, M., Katebzadah, S., & Fazil, A. W. (2024). Comprehensive Insights into E-Learning in contemporary Education: Analyzing trends, challenges, and best practices. [JETL]. *Journal of Education and Teaching Learning*, 6(1), 86–105. DOI: 10.51178/jetl.v6i1.1720

Hameed, F., Qayyum, A., & Khan, F. A. (2024). A new trend of learning and teaching: Behavioral intention towards mobile learning. *Journal of Computers in Education*, 11(1), 149–180. DOI: 10.1007/s40692-022-00252-w

Hamidi, H., & Chavoshi, A. (2018). Analysis of the essential factors for the adoption of mobile learning in higher education: A case study of students of the University of Technology. *Telematics and Informatics*, 35(4), 1053–1070. DOI: 10.1016/j.tele.2017.09.016

Han, I., & Shin, W. S. (2016). The use of a mobile learning management system and academic achievement of online students. *Computers & Education*, 102, 79–89. DOI: 10.1016/j.compedu.2016.07.003

Hsu, H. H. (2012). The acceptance of Moodle: An empirical study based on UTAUT. *Creative Education*, 3(8), 44–46. DOI: 10.4236/ce.2012.38B010

Hulland, J. (1999). Use of partial least squares (PLS) in strategic management research: A review of four recent studies. *Strategic Management Journal*, 20(2), 195–204. DOI: 10.1002/(SICI)1097-0266(199902)20:2<195::AID-SMJ13>3.0.CO;2-7

İlçi, A. (2014). *Investigation of pre-service teachers' mobile learning readiness levels and mobile learning acceptance levels* (Master's thesis, Middle East Technical University).

Joo, Y. J., Kim, N., & Kim, N. H. (2016). Factors predicting online university students' use of a mobile learning management system (m-LMS). *Educational Technology Research and Development*, 64(4), 611–630. DOI: 10.1007/s11423-016-9436-7

Karthick, M., Somesh, V., Gudadhe, N., Boopathi, B., Padmanabhan, S., Tiwari, R., & Sharma, A. (2023). Structural analysis of motorcycle spokes design using finite element analysis with alloy materials. *Materials Today: Proceedings*. Advance online publication. DOI: 10.1016/j.matpr.2023.04.380

Lan, Y. F., & Sie, Y. S. (2010). Using RSS to support mobile learning based on media richness theory. *computers & education, 55(2)*, 723-732.

Lee, J. K., & Lee, W. K. (2008). The relationship of e-Learner's self-regulatory efficacy and perception of e-Learning environmental quality. *Computers in Human Behavior*, 24(1), 32–47. DOI: 10.1016/j.chb.2006.12.001

Liu, Y., Li, H., & Carlsson, C. (2010). Factors driving the adoption of m-learning: An empirical study. *Computers & Education*, 55(3), 1211–1219. DOI: 10.1016/j.compedu.2010.05.018

Matimbwa, R., & Anney, V. N. (2016). Teachers' and students' perceptions of self-driven acceptance of mobile phone use as an ICT teaching tool. *Journal of Emerging Trends in Educational Research and Policy Studies*, 7(2), 91–106.

Murphy, G. (2011). Post-PC devices: A summary of early iPad technology adoption in tertiary environments. *E-Journal of Business Education & Scholarship of Teaching*, 5(1), 18–32.

Padmalosan, P., Vanitha, S., Kumar, V. S., Anish, M., Tiwari, R., Dhapekar, N. K., & Yadav, A. S. (2023). An investigation on the use of waste materials from industrial processes in clay brick production. *Materials Today: Proceedings*. Advance online publication. DOI: 10.1016/j.matpr.2023.01.238

Pituch, K. A., & Lee, Y. K. (2006). The influence of system characteristics on e-learning use. *Computers & Education*, 47(2), 222–244. DOI: 10.1016/j.compedu.2004.10.007

Quraishi, N. T., Bayani, B. M., Yashar, N. S., Daudzai, N. M., Salamzada, N. R., Amini, N. M., & Hakimi, N. M. (2024). Integration of Mobile Learning Technologies in Afghanistan Universities: Opportunities and Challenges. *Education Specialist*, 2(1), 1–14. DOI: 10.59535/es.v2i1.227

Ray, S., Jain, K., Birru, P., & Mohata, R. (2024). A case study of BYJU'S failure. *World Journal of Advanced Research and Reviews*, 21(3), 674–689. DOI: 10.30574/wjarr.2024.21.3.0765

Saikat, S., Dhillon, J. S., Ahmad, W. F. W., & Jamaluddin, R. A. (2021). A Systematic Review of the Benefits and Challenges of Mobile Learning during the COVID-19 Pandemic. *Education Sciences*, 11(9), 459. DOI: 10.3390/educsci11090459

Sánchez, R. A., & Hueros, A. D. (2010). Motivational factors that influence the acceptance of Moodle using TAM. *Computers in Human Behavior*, 26(6), 1632–1640. DOI: 10.1016/j.chb.2010.06.011

Sanga, C., Mlozi, M., Haug, R., & Tumbo, S. (2016). Mobile learning bridging the gap in agricultural extension service delivery: Experiences from Sokoine University of Agriculture, Tanzania. *International Journal of Education and Development using ICT*, 12(3).

Saroia, A. I., & Gao, S. (2019). Investigating university students' intention to use mobile learning management systems in Sweden. *Innovations in Education and Teaching International*, 56(5), 569–580. DOI: 10.1080/14703297.2018.1557068

Sarrab, M., Al-Shihi, H., Al-Manthari, B., & Bourdoucen, H. (2018). Toward educational requirements model for mobile learning development and adoption in higher education. *TechTrends*, 62(6), 635–646. DOI: 10.1007/s11528-018-0331-4

Smith, L. (2012). Biographical method. *J. Goodwin. Biographical research Volume one: Biographical research: starting points, debates and approaches*, 1-36..

Šumak, B., Polancic, G., & Hericko, M. (2010, February). An empirical study of virtual learning environment adoption using UTAUT. In *2010 Second international conference on mobile, hybrid, and on-line learning* (pp. 17-22). IEEE.

Tan, F. B., & Chou, J. P. (2008). The relationship between mobile service quality, perceived technology compatibility, and users' perceived playfulness in the context of mobile information and entertainment services. *International Journal of Human-Computer Interaction*, 24(7), 649–671. DOI: 10.1080/10447310802335581

Teo, T., Zhou, M., Fan, A. C. W., & Huang, F. (2019). Factors that influence university students' intention to use Moodle: A study in Macau. *Educational Technology Research and Development*, 67(3), 749–766. DOI: 10.1007/s11423-019-09650-x

Tiwari, R. (2022). *Effect of Perception and Satisfaction on Preference for Mobile Wallet. Chand K, Tiwari R., & Sapna (2022). Effect of Perception and Satisfaction on Preference for Mobile Wallet.* FIIB Business Review.

Tiwari, R., Agrawal, P., Singh, P., Bajaj, S., Verma, V., & Chauhan, A. S. (2023). Technology Enabled Integrated Fusion Teaching for Enhancing Learning Outcomes in Higher Education. *International Journal of Emerging Technologies in Learning*, 18(7), 243–249. DOI: 10.3991/ijet.v18i07.36799

Tiwari, R., Chand, K., & Anjum, B. (2000). Crop insurance in India: A review of pradhan mantri fasal bima yojana (PMFBY). *FIIB Business Review*, 9(4), 249–255. DOI: 10.1177/2319714520966084

Tiwari, R., Chand, K., Bhatt, A., Anjum, B., & Thirunavukkarasu, K. (2021). Agriculture 5.0 in India: Opportunities and Challenges of Technology Adoption. *A Step Towards Society 5.0*, 179-198..

Tossell, C. C., Kortum, P., Shepard, C., Rahmati, A., & Zhong, L. (2015). You can lead a horse to water but you cannot make him learn: Smartphone use in higher education. *British Journal of Educational Technology*, 46(4), 713–724. DOI: 10.1111/bjet.12176

Traxler, J. (2007). Defining, discussing, and evaluating mobile learning: The moving finger writes and having writ. *International Review of Research in Open and Distance Learning*, 8(2), 1–12. DOI: 10.19173/irrodl.v8i2.346

United Nations Educational, Scientific and Cultural Organization. (2009). EFA global monitoring report 2009: Overcoming inequality: Why governance matters. UNESCO. https://unesdoc.unesco.org/ark:/48223/pf0000192144

Venkatesh, V., & Davis, F. D. (2000). A theoretical extension of the technology acceptance model: Four longitudinal field studies. *Management Science*, 46(2), 186–204. DOI: 10.1287/mnsc.46.2.186.11926

Venkatesh, V., & Morris, M. G. (2000). Why don't men ever stop to ask for directions? Gender, social influence, and their role in technology acceptance and usage behavior. *Management Information Systems Quarterly*, 24(1), 115–139. DOI: 10.2307/3250981

Venkatesh, V., Morris, M. G., Davis, G. B., & Davis, F. D. (2003). User acceptance of information technology: Toward a unified view. *Management Information Systems Quarterly*, 27(3), 425–478. DOI: 10.2307/30036540

Yip, K. H. T., Lo, P., Ho, K. K., & Chiu, D. K. (2021). Adoption of mobile library apps as learning tools in higher education: A tale between Hong Kong and Japan. *Online Information Review*, 45(2), 389–405. DOI: 10.1108/OIR-07-2020-0287

ADDITIONAL READING

Ali, M. (2021). *Remote Work and Sustainable Changes for the Future of Global Business*. IGI Global. https://www.igi-global.com/book/remote-work-sustainable-changes-future/264375

Ali, M. (2022). *Future Role of Sustainable Innovative Technologies in Crisis Management*. IGI Global. https://www.igi-global.com/book/future-role-sustainable-innovative-technologies/281281

Ali, M. (2023). *Shifting Paradigms in the Rapidly Developing Global Digital Ecosystem: A GCC Perspective.* In Digital Entrepreneurship and Co-Creating Value Through Digital Encounters (pp. 145-166). IGI Global. https://www.igi-global.com/chapter/shifting-paradigms-in-the-rapidly-developing-global-digital-ecosystem/323525

Ali, M. (2023). T*axonomy of Industry 4.0 Technologies in Digital Entrepreneurship and Co-Creating Value*. In *Digital Entrepreneurship and Co-Creating Value Through Digital Encounters* (pp. 24–55). IGI Global., https://www.igi-global.com/chapter/taxonomy-of-industry-40-technologies-in-digital-entrepreneurship-and-co-creating-value/323520 DOI: 10.4018/978-1-6684-7416-7.ch002

Ali, M., & Wood-Harper, T. (2021). *Fostering Communication and Learning with Underutilized Technologies in Higher Education*. IGI Global. https://www.igi-global.com/book/fostering-communication-learning-underutilized-technologies/244593

Ali, M., Wood-Harper, T., & Kutar, M. (2023). Multi-Perspectives of Contemporary Digital Transformation Models of Complex Innovation Management. In *Digital Entrepreneurship and Co-Creating Value Through Digital Encounters* (pp. 79–96). IGI Global., https://www.igi-global.com/chapter/multi-perspectives-of-contemporary-digital-transformation-models-of-complex-innovation-management/323522 DOI: 10.4018/978-1-6684-7416-7.ch004

Ali, M. B. (2021). Internet of Things (IoT) to Foster Communication and Information Sharing: A Case of UK Higher Education. In Ali, M. B., & Wood-Harper, T. (Eds.), *Fostering Communication and Learning With Underutilized Technologies in Higher Education* (pp. 1–20). IGI Global., https://www.igi-global.com/chapter/internet-of-things-iot-to-foster-communication-and-information-sharing/262718/ DOI: 10.4018/978-1-7998-4846-2.ch001

Ali, M. B., & Wood-Harper, T. (2022). Artificial Intelligence (AI) as a Decision-Making Tool to Control Crisis Situations. In *Future Role of Sustainable Innovative Technologies in Crisis Management*. IGI Global., https://www.igi-global.com/chapter/artificial-intelligence-ai-as-a-decision-making-tool-to-control-crisis-situations/298931 DOI: 10.4018/978-1-7998-9815-3.ch006

Ali, M. B., Wood-Harper, T., & Ramlogan, R. (2020). A Framework Strategy to Overcome Trust Issues on Cloud Computing Adoption in Higher Education. In Modern Principles, Practices, and Algorithms for Cloud Security (pp. 162-183). IGI Global. https://www.igi-global.com/chapter/a-framework-strategy-to-overcome-trust-issues-on-cloud-computing-adoption-in-higher-education/238907/

Chapter 9
FinTech Startups: What Are the Critical Success Factors?

Mongi Elloumi
https://orcid.org/0009-0006-5856-6009
NOVA Information Management School, Portugal

Amira Sghari
https://orcid.org/0000-0001-6121-9645
University of Tunisia, Tunisia

ABSTRACT

Entrepreneurship is gaining significant interest worldwide, with countries encouraging young people to launch startups. Research studies on the success of startups have grown substantially over time. However, the success factors for fintech startups, remain underexplored. This research aims to determine the critical success factors of fintech startups. To achieve this, a qualitative approach using multiple case studies was conducted on four Tunisian fintech startups, examining their development processes. The development is divided into three stages: seed phase, early phase, and growth phase. The results revealed three categories of success factors: essential and complementary (shared by all four startups) and specific factors unique to each startup. The influence of these factors varies across the different life cycle stages.

INTRODUCTION

The continuous evolution of Information and Communication Technologies (ICT) accelerates digital transformation, fostering the emergence of new industries that blend traditional sectors with digital technologies (Denoo and Yli-Renko, 2019).

DOI: 10.4018/979-8-3373-0086-3.ch009

Copyright © 2025, IGI Global. Copying or distributing in print or electronic forms without written permission of IGI Global is prohibited.

In the financial services industry, digital technologies are reshaping the value proposition of existing services (Swacha-Lech, 2017) by accelerating innovations and driving rapid development of modern financial solutions. As a result, a new field, Financial Technology (Fintech), is emerging.

Thakor (2020) described three phases in the evolution of Fintech:

- **Phase 1 (1866-1967):** Marked by the laying of the first trans-Atlantic cable and telegraph, which enabled the rapid transmission of financial information, transactions, and payments.
- **Phase 2 (1967-2008):** Defined by the introduction of electronic payments, clearing systems, ATMs, and online banking, as well as the adoption of information technology by traditional financial institutions to enhance products and services.
- **Phase 3 (2008-present):** Characterized by the emergence of new entrants using technology to offer non-intermediated financial services directly to customers, leading to a transformed competitive landscape for financial institutions."

Consequently, the digital revolution has redefined entrepreneurship globally, creating new business ventures and digital startups integrating cutting-edge technologies into their core business models and operations (Elia et al., 2020). Digitalization has transformed the financial sector, leading to the rise of innovative ventures like Fintech startups, which utilize new technologies to develop advanced financial solutions.

According to Arner et al. (2015), the global financial crisis of 2008 was a pivotal moment for the emergence of Fintech startups. The crisis served as a crucial catalyst for their rise, as regulatory restrictions on banks, the public's loss of trust in the financial system, and technological advancements created an ideal environment for Fintech growth. Arner et al. (2015) describe this era as Fintech 3.0, during which new startups and established tech companies began offering innovative financial solutions and products directly to companies and particular consumers.

Although financial technology (Fintech) is recognized as one of the most important innovations in the financial industry and is evolving rapidly, driven by the sharing economy, favorable regulations, and advancements in information technologies (Lee and Shin, 2018), it continues to grow at an impressive rate. According to the Global Fintech Adoption Index 2019, the adoption of Fintech services increased from 16% in 2015 to 36% in 2017, and then to 64% in 2019. Globally, awareness of the Fintech concept is very high, with 96% of consumers knowing at least one alternative Fintech solution for transferring money or making payments. Another study by KPMG (Pulse of Fintech 2018) shows significant growth in total investment in the Fintech industry, reaching a record $111.8 billion in 2018, an increase of 120%

compared to $50.8 billion in 2017. This data underscores the rapid expansion of the Fintech sector.

Interest in fintech has been growing steadily across countries. The United Arab Emirates (UAE) has become the largest fintech startup hub in the Middle East and North Africa (Limna and Tanpat, 2022). Several investment funds have emerged in recent years, playing a crucial role in the global fintech investment ecosystem (Limna and Tanpat, 2022). Since late 2017, six funds have been established in Bahrain and the UAE, focusing on partnerships with other ventures or directly investing in innovative firms (Limna and Tanpat, 2022). Collectively, these funds have raised approximately $1.5 billion in capital, and many are now shifting their focus from external opportunities to emerging regional ones (Al Suwaidi et al., 2022).

In India, fintech has grown rapidly over the last five years and is projected to expand further in the coming years (Sharma et al., 2022). Similarly, in Thailand, fintech startups have better chances of growth and development when collaborating with companies in both related and unrelated industries (Limna and Tanpat, 2022). Additionally, fintech presents a transformational opportunity for China's financial system (Allen et al., 2022). In Tunisia, research on Fintech startups remains at an embryonic stage (Bouaziz and Sghari, 2021).

Studying the key critical success factors of fintech startups is of paramount importance in a context where technological innovation is constantly reshaping financial services. Understanding these factors not only helps anticipate the challenges inherent to each phase of a startup's lifecycle but also identifies the strategic levers that drive sustainable growth. Fintechs, as engines of disruption, introduce innovative solutions that meet the evolving needs of consumers and businesses. By examining these factors, entrepreneurs and investors can optimize decisions related to financing, operational strategy, risk management, and partnerships. This also contributes to creating an ecosystem conducive to the growth of fintechs, particularly in emerging markets where financial inclusion and service efficiency are priorities.

Despite the importance of key critical success factors of fintech startups, there is a notable lack of work in the academic literature addressing this subject (Milian et al., 2019). Considering the global growth of Fintech startups and their impact on the traditional financial sector, this study aims to explore the critical success factors at each stage of a startup's life cycle. Essentially, we seek to answer the question: What are the critical success factors for a Fintech startup in each phase of its life cycle?

To answer this question, a qualitative study was conducted with four Tunisian fintech startups. The results showed the existence of three categories of success factors: essential and complementary (shared by all four startups) and specific factors unique to each startup. The influence of these factors varies across the different life cycle stages (seed phase, early phase, and growth phase).

1. LITERATURE REVIEW

1.1 Critical Success Factors of Fintech Startups

As many factors determine success, it is necessary to identify the critical factors and focus on those decisive to provide a growing and successful entity. To limit the critical success factors of Fintech startups, we regroup the factors based on two criteria:

- Number of citations: one factor must be cited in at least two research studies.
- Meaning/similarities sharing: grouping of factors that do not have the same name assigned by the authors, however, they reflect the same meaning.

Thus, 24 critical factors summarized in Table 1 below are identified:

Table 1. Critical success factors of Fintech startups

Factor	Definition	References
Technology innovation	Technological innovation is at the core of developing a startup's products and services.	Lee and Osteryoung, (2001); Balboni *et al.* (2014); Almakenzi *et al.* (2015); Azimzadeh *et al.* (2015); Guzmán and Lussier (2015); Santisteban and Mauricio (2017); Lampadarios *et al.* (2017); Kim *et al.* (2018); Werth *et al.* (2019).
Startup management experience	An entrepreneur's management experience facilitates the launch of a startup and helps mitigate risks based on past experiences.	Sammut (2001); Song *et al.* (2008); Kessler and Rank (2009); Balboniet *al.* (2014); Santisteban and Mauricio (2017); Lampadarios *et al.* (2017).
Action Plan / Business Plan	A business plan involves strategic planning where founders set objectives, strategies, and organizational structures, while an action plan outlines how to execute and transform the business plan into reality.	Chorev and Anderson (2006); Song *et al.* (2008); Balboniet *al.* (2014); Guzmán and Lussier (2015); Lampadarios *et al.* (2017).
Regulatory Framework	Startups often face challenges with regulatory frameworks, especially when using advanced technology, while some governments attempt to adjust their laws to accommodate these new startups.	Kessler and Rank (2009); Balboniet al. (2014); Balboniet *et al.* (2014); Azimzadeh *et al.* (2015); Santisteban and Mauricio (2017); Werth *et al.* (2019).

continued on following page

Table 1. Continued

Factor	Definition	References
Risk	Due to market competitiveness, startups are more vulnerable to failure compared to established companies because of their limited resources. Therefore, founders should carefully consider risks and work proactively to mitigate them.	Sammut (2001); Kessler and Rank (2009); Kim *et al.* (2018).
Market exploitation and growth	The capability of a startup to align with the market depends on thorough market analysis, an effective market penetration strategy, and the extent to which these efforts increase profitability.	Sammut (2001); Lee and Osteryoung (2001); Chorev and Anderson (2006); Song *et al.* (2008); Balboni *et al.* (2014); Lampadarios *et al.* (2017); Santisteban and Mauricio (2017); Kim *et al.* (2018); Nalintippayawong *et al.* (2018); Werth *et al.* (2019).
Industry experience	Industry experience is crucial for gathering information and acquiring knowledge about a specific industry to prevent potential risks.	Song *et al.* (2008); Guzmán and Lussier (2015).
Financial resources (Initial financing or startup capital)	It involves covering the startup's initial expenses.	Sammut (2001); Kessler and Rank (2009); Balboni *et al.* (2014); Guzmán and Lussier (2015); Santisteban and Mauricio (2017); Lampadarios *et al.* (2017); Kim *et al.* (2018); Werth *et al.* (2019).
Venture capital	It represents a long-term investment in the startup's capital, offering growth potential and contributing to financial stability.	Almakenzi *et al.* (2015); Santisteban and Mauricio (2017). Kim *et al.* (2018).
Startup fundraising	It is an investment made at specific stages of the startup's lifecycle, targeting specific objectives such as marketing, acquiring customers, and developing services.	Lee and Osteryoung (2001); Chorev and Anderson (2006); Kim *et al.* (2018); Nalintippayawong *et al.* (2018).
Employee competencies and technical capabilities in the industry	Employees with industry experience and technical skills, such as proficiency in technology manipulation, facilitate the development of products/services that create a competitive advantage for the startup.	Sammut (2001); Chorev and Anderson (2006); Almakenzi *et al.* (2015); Lampadarios *et al.* (2017); Santisteban and Mauricio (2017); Kim *et al.* (2018); Werth *et al.* (2019).
Entrepreneur attitude and personality	These are the characteristics and skills of the entrepreneur that facilitate the management of the startup and enable the team to achieve its objectives.	Chorev and Anderson (2006); Kessler and Rank (2009); Balboni *et al.* (2014); Azimzadeh *et al.* (2015); Almakenzi *et al.* (2015); Lampadarios *et al.* (2017); Santisteban and Mauricio (2017); Kim *et al.* (2018); Werth *et al.* (2019).

continued on following page

Table 1. Continued

Factor	Definition	References
Marketing (experience, capabilities, intensity)	By understanding the market and customer needs and drawing upon the team's experience, they formulate a strategic plan to attract customers and successfully sell products/services.	Lee and Osteryoung (2001); Chorev and Anderson (2006); Song *et al.* (2008); Balboni *et al* (2014); Almakenzi *et al.* (2015); Lampadarios *et al.* (2017); Santisteban and Mauricio (2017).
Customer management	It primarily focuses on targeting the right customer segments, meeting their needs, and establishing effective distribution channels for products/ services to satisfy customer demands.	Chorev and Anderson (2006); Almakenzi *et al.* (2015); Lampadarios *et al.* (2017); Nalintippayawong *et al.* (2018); Werth *et al.* (2019).
R&D (experience, investment, alliances)	For developing innovative products/ services, the team requires experience in research and development (R&D), and the top management is committed to investing in and forming alliances within the field.	Song *et al.* (2008); Balboni *et al.* (2014); Santisteban and Mauricio (2017).
Product Quality	The product should meet customer expectations regarding quality and durability.	Lee and Osteryoung (2001); Chorev and Anderson (2006).
External environment	The startup is impacted by the rapid pace of dynamic changes in the external environment, including political, socio-cultural, and economic factors.	Lee and Osteryoung (2001); Song *et al.* (2008); Balboni *et al.* (2014); Santisteban and Mauricio (2017); Lampadarios *et al.* (2017).
Network	Having a strong network can help in finding talented employees with industry experience and facilitates forming partnerships.	Chorev and Anderson (2006); Kessler and Rank (2009); Balboni *et al.* (2014); Almakenzi *et al.* (2015); Lampadarios *et al.* (2017); Nalintippayawong *et al.* (2018); Werth *et al.* (2019).
Partnership	It is an arrangement between startups and organizations to establish either a financial or strategic partnership.	Sammut (2001); Song *et al.* (2008); Balboni *et al.* (2014); Guzmán and Lussier (2015); Santisteban and Mauricio (2017).
Professional support system	It is a support system providing guidance and mentoring from professional expert advisors in a specific industry, such as accelerator programs, incumbents, and mentors.	Sammut (2001); Guzmán and Lussier (2015); Nalintippayawong *et al.* (2018). Werth *et al.* (2019).
Motivation	The team is committed to achieving and meeting the startup objectives.	Chorev and Anderson (2006); Kessler and Rank (2009). Balboni *et al.* (2014); Kim *et al.* (2018).
Patent protection	Protection of the product/service and technology process.	Song et al. (2008); Balboni *et al.* (2014).
Competition intensity	Strengthen inter-firm competition within the industry.	Song et al. (2008); Balboni *et al.* (2014).
B2B focus	Some startups target the B2B sector, which includes mature organizations seeking to enhance their digitization and innovation capabilities.	Werth *et al.* (2019).

1.2 Startup Life Cycle

The early foundational stages of any business launch are critical to its existence and evolution, as startups are considered sensitive and fragile organizations (Salamzadeh and Kesim, 2017). Startups are designed to experiment with business models based on innovative ideas proposed by co-founders or team members (Salamzadeh and Kesim, 2017). The literature identifies several stages in the life cycle of a startup. According to Santisteban and Mauricio (2017), the lifecycle stages of an IT startup consist of four stages: Seed, Early, Growth, and Expansion. This study focuses on the first three stages because Tunisia lags in Fintech development (Bouaziz and Sghari, 2021). Consequently, having been founded recently, Tunisian Fintech startups have not yet reached the final stage. The lifecycle is presented as follows (Salamzadeh and Kesim, 2017):

The seed Stage (or the Idea Phase), is characterized by:

- Formation of the founding team
- Development of the prototype (product/service)
- Determination of the initial capital to start the business

This stage is known for its high uncertainty (Salamzadeh and Kesim, 2017).

Early Stage (or the Young Stage), is characterized by:

- The product is in the market while working on attracting more clients
- Product innovation
- The necessity of investment

Growth Stage (or the Development Stage), is characterized by:

- Perfecting the business model
- Receiving investment funds specialized for startup development
- Increasing competitiveness through expanding market share

Literature does not clearly state the existence of success factors specific to each phase of a startup's life cycle, nor the importance of these factors throughout the creation and post-creation processes. Therefore, this research aims to identify and analyze success factors for each phase of the life cycle of a fintech startup.

2. RESEARCH METHODOLOGY

As the aim of the study is to explore and understand the critical success factors for Fintech startups in the Tunisian ecosystem, we opted for a qualitative approach with multiple case studies. This choice is motivated by the fact that qualitative research with case studies allows for consideration of the complexity of phenomena (Miles *et al.*, 2003). Data collection was carried out through semi-structured interviews and documentary analysis. The collected data was structured and subsequently subjected to content analysis.

Primary data collection was carried out through retrospective semi-structured interviews. This approach is justified by our aim to understand the evolution of a phenomenon over time, specifically the study of success factors throughout the life cycle stages of a Fintech startup. We are focusing only on the first three phases, as the Fintech industry is a relatively new concept in the Tunisian ecosystem. The interview guide (Appendix 1) is structured into three parts:

- An introductory question to identify the participant and their current position.
- Three sets of questions for each lifecycle phase: defining and describing each phase, identifying the important factors for success in each phase, and exploring potential obstacles.
- Finally, the participant is invited to evaluate the Fintech industry in Tunisia.

The interviewee sample is diverse, including CEOs of startups, sales operation managers, and technology developers who have worked on Fintech products. **CEOs** provide a strategic overview of the company, as they are responsible for resource management, strategic decision-making, and the long-term direction of the startup. Their insights are essential for understanding the success factors from a managerial and entrepreneurial standpoint.

Technology developers are at the heart of implementing innovative solutions. Their technical expertise is critical for grasping the challenges related to the development of fintech products, the integration of new technologies, and the continuous innovation needed to remain competitive in a fast-evolving market.

Finally, the **Head of Sales Operations** offers a market-oriented perspective focused on growth and performance. This profile is crucial for understanding how fintech solutions are positioned and sold, and for identifying the key factors related to commercialization, sales development, and customer satisfaction. By combining these three perspectives, strategic, technical, and commercial, the study provides a more comprehensive and nuanced understanding of the success factors that influence the development of fintech startups.

We conducted interviews with six participants, as presented in Table 2 below. It is important to emphasize that the number of interviews conducted is limited, primarily due to difficulties in accessing participants. However, despite this limitation, the discussions held have provided valuable and in-depth perspectives on the subject studied. These interviews, although limited in number, have yielded significant insights that enrich our understanding of the challenges faced by fintech startups.

Table 2. Sample presentation

Participant	Startup ID	Position	Fintech sector
Mr. A	Startup CHY	Head of Sales Operation	Payment Solution
Mr. B	Startup YOT	CEO	Digital Payment Solution
Mr. C	Startup RYM	CEO	Digital Accounting Solution
Mrs. D	Startup SAM	Technology Developer	Digital Tax Solution
Mrs. E	Startup SAM	Technology Developer	

All interviews lasted between one and two hours and were immediately recorded and transcribed. The collected data were subject to content analysis (Bardin, 1998).

As recommended by Miles et al. (2003), the data was condensed by thematic coding. A code start list from a literature review was established (see Table 1). This coding system has been modified as and when considering all the data during the categorization. Two types of coding were performed (Miles et al., 2003):

- A multiple coding is carried out by the researcher to ensure the internal coherence of the coding. All interviews were coded a second time a month later. The confrontation between the first coding and the second coding has defined a reliability coefficient of 97%.
- multiple coding carried out by a second researcher to check the reliability of the coding: extracts taken at random from the interviews were coded by a second researcher in management sciences. The reliability coefficient calculated between encoders is 92%. The coefficients found are greater than 80%. They ensure a good reliability of the results (Miles et al., 2003).

3. RESULTS

In this section, we first present the results found for each case studied. Then, we provide a synthesis of these results.

3.1. Intra-Case Analyzes

3.1.1. Case of the Fintech Startup CHY

CHY is a Tunisian Fintech startup founded in 2018 and obtained a label in April 2019. Its first product aimed to innovate mobile peer-to-peer (P2P) payments in Tunisia and integrate electronic signatures to facilitate remote access to government services. CHY offers financial services directly to customers by enabling them to open bank accounts remotely through a digital process. Their second product is designed to automate processes within the banking infrastructure. The primary mission of CHY is to promote financial inclusion by leveraging data science.

Critical Success Factors During the Seed Stage

The first step in establishing a startup is to validate the idea and its market adaptation (**market investigation**). This investigation reveals whether the idea is suitable for banks or financial institutions and identifies if a competitor is already promoting a similar product or service. After validating the idea, the next step is to determine the **innovative technology** that will be used in the product's development, which also serves as a tool for creating new financial solutions. Therefore, the **team** responsible for developing the technological solution must possess skills in both the new technology and the financial ecosystem.

The subsequent step involves planning and executing the **business model** to establish the strategic approach and set objectives. For example, the startup determined its pricing model early on, considering that Tunisian customers often distrust the banking system due to high taxes. Their strategy was to charge banks for transactions between a bank and a user and to share the charges for transactions between two users.

To support the above steps, financial backing is crucial. The founders, having studied at a prestigious university in the U.S., were able to convince **business angels** to invest in the startup. Another critical factor, as suggested by the interviewee, is understanding the **regulatory framework**, or **REGTECH**. Since FinTech is an emerging field and the financial sector is governed by specific regulations and laws that can present barriers or challenges, the founders signed a **partnership** with a bank to create a compliant operating system.

Critical Success Factors During the Early Stage

The early stage begins with **attracting customers**, aiming to find and convince early adopters to test the product. Following this, the development of the **Minimum Viable Product (MVP)** takes place; this prototype includes the essential features needed for early customers to use and provide feedback. This feedback is crucial for adjusting the final product to meet customer needs. When asked about financial resources, the interviewee emphasized the importance of **fundraising** during the creation phase, as it provides financial stability. The interviewee also noted that financial support is not a barrier for FinTech startups, as there are many investors ready to invest in this sector, as illustrated in the following interview excerpt:

To succeed in this phase, *"I think one of the critical success factors is perseverance, that you resist against all the challenges"*. This phase is challenging, encompassing everything from product development to market introduction and sales operations.

Critical Success Factors During the Growth Stage

The growth stage is when the startup introduces its product to the market. At this point, **customer attraction** involves approaching new clients and convincing them to purchase the product. Successful customer acquisition leads to the scalability of the startup, which is its ability to grow as sales increase. This stage determines the startup's **market positioning** relative to its competitors. An interviewee stated, *"Knowing your market positioning is important to understand other competitors, such as payment institutions and other FinTech startups that offer similar products. We are not alone in the market. What makes the customer choose my product over others? We need to offer features ranging from security to a user-friendly experience also suited to the Tunisian culture."*

Table 3. Critical success factors of CHY

Seed stage	Early stage	Growth stage
• Market understanding • New technology • Team • Business model • Business angels • Regulatory framework • Partnership	• Fundraising • MVP development • Customer attraction	• Customer attraction • Market Positioning

3.1.2. Case of the Fintech Startup YOT

YOT is a Tunisian startup founded in 2018, which recently expanded its office to Paris in 2021. The startup offers two main types of activities:

- The first activity involves guiding customers to innovate and create value using new technology through training sessions for companies, consultancy, application development, and benchmarking.
- The second key activity is providing a solution consisting of a mobile wallet and a digital platform, leveraging Blockchain technology to make microfinance more accessible and socially inclusive.

An interview was conducted with the founder and CEO of YOT. The critical success factors in each stage of YOT's lifecycle are presented below.

Critical Success Factors During the Seed Stage

The **network** is a critical factor in validating ideas and gathering methodological and technical advice. This is illustrated in the following interview excerpt: *"You will encounter a lot of people that will enrich you with quality insights that will guide you to finish your idea."* These exchanges and shared experiences help mitigate risks. According to the CEO of YOT, *"After 10 years of working on management and information systems in a consultancy firm, I decided to launch my startup because I was passionate about Blockchain technologies."* His **industry experience** enabled him to meet the requirements to launch a startup utilizing a technology he understands. This expertise also facilitated the creation of new services aimed at supporting financial inclusion.

Choosing technology for product creation is crucial, as it provides the necessary tools for the expected product. Subsequently, the founder should seek a qualified **co-founder** with complementary skills. For instance, the founder of YOT, who has a technical background, needed a co-founder to handle administrative and management tasks. The process of creating a startup requires **entrepreneurial skills** to manage multiple functions and overcome challenges. **Perseverance** is essential for turning an idea into reality. *"Persevere! Persevere! Persevere!"* emphasizes the CEO.

Critical Success Factors During the Early Stage

This stage begins with forming a **team** comprising individuals with diverse profiles to share ideas and divide tasks. Technological skills are essential, especially for working with blockchain technology. Next, conducting a **market investigation** is crucial to understand market needs, assess competitors' products, and determine if the proposed product will fit within the market. Following that, a **customer approach** is necessary to pitch the idea to potential clients, gather their feedback, and identify their needs to adapt the product accordingly.

Critical Success Factors During the dGrowth Stage

The "growth stage," also known as the "selling stage" or "**customer attraction** stage," is when the team focuses on attracting clients and building trustworthy customer relationships. As the founder explains, *"All we have to do is prospect a first project until they trust us, then prospect a second one and a third one, showing them our previous projects, and it progresses gradually."* At this stage, it is essential to continue **developing the product** by adjusting and correcting errors. Additionally, "maintaining team motivation becomes crucial, as effective human **management** is key", as cited by the CEO.

Table 4. Critical success factors of YOT

Seed stage	Early stage	Growth stage
• Perseverance • Industry experience • Network • Co-founder • Technology choice • Entrepreneur skills	• Market investigation • Customer approach • Team	• Customer attraction • Product development • Team management

3.1.3. Case of the Fintech Startup RYM

RYM is a Tunisian cloud accounting service startup founded in 2016, which received a label in 2019. Its main mission is to provide an accounting solution that allows micro-enterprises and small and medium enterprises to publish their invoices, quotes, and purchase orders with one click, and to access real-time key performance indicators of their financial situation. An interview was conducted with the founder of RYM to gain insights and perceptions about the startup. The results are presented below.

Critical Success Factors During the Seed Stage

"Mainly you need to search for your co-founders and their specialties" affirms the founder when asked about the success factors in the seed stage. A **co-founder** should bring complementary skills that the other founder lacks, creating a supportive environment. For idea validation, it is beneficial to leverage your **network** or approach experts in relevant fields to gather feedback and professional advice for adjusting and revising the idea. Subsequently, the next step is forming a **team** with diverse and skillful profiles capable of handling technologies and possessing financial and management knowledge.

Critical Success Factors During the Early Stage

At this stage, the founder considers enrolling in **accompaniment programs** that support startups through their launch phase and help them understand the entrepreneurial ecosystem, from developing the business model to launching the product. These programs can include incubation programs, training sessions, or participation by expert coaches in specific fields. Conducting a **market investigation** is mandatory at this stage. As the founder mentioned, *"We need to analyze the market and understand its ecosystem by identifying our competitors and their position in the market."* The goal is to understand market needs, determine what kind of product fits the market, and analyze the stakeholders related to the startup. Finally, the **Minimum Viable Product (MVP)**, a prototype to test with potential customers, is developed.

Critical Success Factors During the Growth Stage

Customer attraction is a crucial factor for this startup. It involves creating a marketing or communication plan to promote the product in the market and attract new customers. The founder also emphasizes the importance of **flexibility** in understanding customer and market needs. Based on this understanding, adjustments to the product's quality and pricing model can be made as needed.

Table 5. Critical success factors of RIM

Seed stage	Early stage	Growth stage
• Co-founder • Team • Network	• MVP • Market investigation • Accompaniment programs	• Customer attraction • Flexibility

3.1.4. Case of the Fintech Startup SAM

SAM is a Tunisian startup founded in 2018 and labeled in 2020. SAM offers a web-based cloud solution for invoice processing and payment, helping micro, small, and medium enterprises manage their invoices digitally and collect payments electronically. Two technology developers were interviewed: one who joined the startup at its inception and the other who was recruited during its growth stage. The results are presented below.

Critical Success Factors During the Seed Stage

The founders begin by securing **initial financing** for the startup's feasibility studies. **Market investigation** is crucial for understanding the market ecosystem and identifying competitors. One technology developer emphasized, '*We need a thorough market analysis to understand its dynamics... This will guide our sales strategy and help us define our competitors' strategies.*' Consulting with the **network** gathers feedback to validate the idea. Once validated, **forming a team** with diverse technical skills is crucial for establishing the startup's infrastructure, especially when leveraging **new technologies** for a competitive advantage.

Critical Success Factors During the Early Stage

A second crucial enhancement in the early stages involves **fundraising**, described by a technology developer as "*crucial for boosting team support and product development*". It proposes a **product specification booklet** that outlines tasks with specific descriptions tailored to customer feedback and team needs: '*Before starting development, we should establish clear product guidelines with detailed task descriptions and time limits.*' This approach aims to guide the development of the **Minimum Viable Product (MVP)**, prototype launch, and client testing to ensure adjustments meet market needs.

Critical Success Factors During the Growth Stage

After product development, **attracting customers** becomes essential for successfully commercializing the product in the market. This involves prospecting new customers and persuading them to adopt the product. Furthermore, implementing a **B2B communication strategy** enables the startup to engage with business clients such as banks, insurance companies, and financial institutions to promote the product, as emphasized by an interviewee: '*We should rely on a B2B communication strategy to attract new clients.*'

Table 6. Critical success factors of SAM

Seed stage	Early stage	Growth stage
• Initial financing • Market investigation • Team formation • Technology • Network	• Fundraising • MVP • Product specification booklet	• Attraction phase • B2B communication strategy

3.2. Inter-Case Analysis

The inter-case analysis involves identifying similarities and discrepancies among the results across different stages of the startup's lifecycle. Comparing the studied cases reveals common Critical Success Factors (CSFs), and unique CSFs specific to individual startups. The analysis is based on the frequency of citations of these factors across the four cases:

- Core factors are essential for success and are cited in at least three startups.
- Complementary factors support success but are less critical than core factors, cited in at least two startups.
- Specific factors are unique to each case studied.

3.2.1. Seed Stage

The critical success factors for the four cases studied during the seed stage are presented in Table 7 below.

Table 7. Critical success factors in the Seed stage

CHY	YOT	RYM	SAM
• Market investigation • Technology • Team • Business model • Business angels • Regulatory framework • Partnership	• Perseverance • Industry experience • Network • Co-founder • Technology • Entrepreneur skills	• Co-founder • Team • Network • Idea validation	• Initial financing • Market investigation • Team • Technology • Network

Team, **technology**, and **network** emerged as common factors across three startups, establishing them as core elements essential for the seed stage's success. This observation can be attributed to the founder's need to gather feedback and expert advice from their network to validate or refine their startup idea. Once the idea's feasibility is confirmed, entrepreneurs focus on identifying suitable technology solutions and assembling a skilled team to execute the startup's product vision.

Therefore, team, technology, and network play pivotal roles in the seed stage of a Fintech startup. Additionally, we identified **co-founder**, **initial financing**, and **market investigation** as common success factors present in the two startups, serving as complementary elements that enhance the success rate. The importance of a **co-founder** is highlighted by CEOs, who emphasize the value of partnering with individuals possessing complementary skills, as illustrated in this interview excerpt: *'Mainly, I need to find co-founders with specialized expertise.* **Initial fi-**

nancing (SAM case), or **business angels** (CHY case) are significant, though some interviewees note that fundraising for Fintech startups in certain regions does not present challenges: *'Today, fundraising isn't a significant issue in Africa, especially in Fintech... In 2020, investments exceeded $1 billion. In Tunisia, however, we only access a small fraction of this total.'* Lastly, **market investigation** complements network feedback by validating the idea's viability through empirical data.

While not as critical as the core and complementary factors, the business model, business angels, regulatory framework, partnerships, perseverance, industry experience, entrepreneurial skills, and idea validation still play a significant role in promoting the success of the seed stage.

3.2.2. Early Stage

The critical success factors for the four cases studied during the early stage are presented in Table 8 below.

Table 8. Critical success factors in the Early stage

CHY	YOT	RYM	SAM
• Fundraising • MVP development • Customer attraction	• Market investigation • Customer approach • Team	• MVP development • Market investigation • Accompaniment programs	• Fundraising • MVP development • Product specification booklet

The **MVP development**, a core factor, involves creating a prototype of the startup's product to be tested in the market and used by customers to gather valuable feedback and reactions. This process helps understand customer preferences and their interest in purchasing the product. Based on the collected data, adjustments will be made to refine and launch the final product.

Complementary factors include two main elements: **fundraising**, necessary for MVP development and covering product development costs; and **market investigation**, conducted to understand the startup's market position and plan a market penetration strategy.

Each Fintech startup has specific factors. For example, the startup RYM recommends enrolling in an accompaniment program, such as an incubator, to receive step-by-step guidance from a professional coach.

3.2.3. Growth Stage

The critical success factors for the four cases studied during the growth stage are presented in Table 9 below.

Table 9. Critical success factors in the Growth stage

CHY	YOT	RYM	SAM
• Customer attraction • Market Positioning	• Customer attraction • Product development • Team management	• Customer attraction • Flexibility	• Customer attraction • B2B communication strategy

The **customer attraction** factor, cited by all four startups, is a core factor for this stage. It involves the ability to approach and convince new clients to purchase the launched product. Specific factors unique to each startup include:

- **Market positioning:** Understanding the startup's position relative to its competitors.
- **Product development:** Continuously enhancing the product to maintain and improve its quality.
- **Flexibility:** Adapting to market changes.
- **Communication strategies:** Tailoring communications to different customer segments, such as B2B clients.
- **Team management:** Managing diverse profiles and ensuring the continuous motivation of the team.

4. DISCUSSION

The results indicate the presence of several Critical Success Factors (CSFs) across the three lifecycle stages of Fintech startups. Due to the limited number of studies specifically addressing Fintech success factors, this discussion incorporates findings from research on general startup success factors.

In the seed stage, the primary CSF to consider is the **network**. A founder cannot establish a startup in isolation; the idea development stage relies heavily on the environment to gather information and validate the idea through interactions with others (Sammut, 2001; Van Gelderen et al., 2006; Chorev and Anderson, 2006; Kessler and Rank, 2009; Balboni *et al.*, 2014; Lampadarios et al., 2017; Nalintippayawong et al., 2018; Werth et al., 2019). The **choice of technology** is another critical factor for Fintech startups, as it provides a competitive advantage over banks and financial institutions (Balboni et al., 2014; Santisteban and Mauricio, 2017; Kim et al., 2018; Werth et al., 2019). Achieving this technological advantage requires a **team** with diverse profiles and experience in finance and technology development (Chorev and Anderson, 2006; Kessler, 2007; Song et al., 2008; Kessler and Rrank, 2009; Balboni et al., 2014; Santisteban and Mauricio, 2017; Werth et al., 2019).

These factors represent the core elements for the success of the first stage. Additionally, other complementary factors were identified in two different startups, starting with a **market investigation**. This factor is crucial not only for FinTech but for all seed-stage startups (Sammut, 2001; Chorev and Anderson, 2006; Song et al., 2008; Almakenzi et al., 2015; Santisteban and Mauricio, 2017; Nalintippayawong et al., 2018; Werth et al., 2019). The process involves analyzing the market, identifying competitors and customer segments, and assessing customer willingness to accept and use the product.

Two interviewees emphasized the necessity of selecting a compatible **co-founder** with the right qualifications and skills. **Initial financing** or capital is also crucial for covering initial expenses. However, according to Santisteban and Mauricio (2017), the amount of initial capital does not significantly influence startup success.

In addition, the results highlight the importance of specific factors for two startups:

- For the startup CHY, **partnership** is considered crucial. An interviewee mentioned that shortcomings in the regulatory framework necessitated forming a partnership, making it significant for this startup, though it may not be as critical for others. Studies in various contexts indicate that the regulatory framework and laws play a central role, especially for new entrepreneurs (Temtime and Pansiri, 2007; Azimzadeh et al., 2013; Balboni et al., 2014; Santisteban and Mauricio, 2017; Werth, 2019).
- Concerning startup YOT, three factors were identified. Firstly, **perseverance** is necessary for success in this phase. This aligns with several studies that emphasize the importance of motivation and the willingness to succeed in business (Van Gelderen et al., 2006; Chorev and Anderson, 2006; Kessler and Rank, 2009; Kim et al., 2018). Secondly, **industry experience** is significant as it helps build a network within the sector. Additionally, technical experience and skills facilitate the launch and help prevent potential errors (Van Gelderen et al., 2006; Song et al., 2015; Guzman and Lussier, 2015; Santisteban and Mauricio, 2017). Finally, **entrepreneurial skills** are crucial for success, corroborating the findings of Chorev and Anderson (2006), Almakenzi et al. (2015), and Santisteban and Mauricio (2017). These studies highlight the im-

portance of the knowledge, attitude, and skills required for an entrepreneur to effectively manage a startup.

In the early stage, the core factor is the **Minimum Viable Product (MVP)**. According to Ries (2011), the MVP is the first version of the product, allowing the team to collect maximum validated information and knowledge about customers with minimal effort. Two complementary factors are identified:

- The first is **fundraising** capital, such as venture capital, which provides financial stability to the startup despite its high potential and risk (Almakenzi et al., 2015; Santisteban and Mauricio, 2017; Kim et al., 2018).
- The second is the **market investigation**, which took place in the second phase for YOT and RYM, unlike SAM and CHY.

Specific factors show varying results, some of which are common with the first phase:

- For the CHY startup, **customer attraction** is crucial. This finding aligns with Werth et al. (2019), highlighting the importance of acquiring and attracting new customers in a competitive market.
- For the YOT startup, the **team** and **regulatory framework** are vital in this stage. Werth et al. (2019) identified the team as the most critical element in a Fintech startup and emphasized the necessity of a regulatory framework. The regulatory challenges distinguish Fintech startups from general startups.
- For the RYM startup, enrolling in an **accompaniment program** is important at this stage. These support programs assist with funding, shared business experience, and business model development (Nalintippayawong et al., 2018).
- For the SAM startup, the interviewee suggests developing a **product specification booklet** detailing the tasks for each team member, with descriptions that vary based on customer feedback and needs. This factor has not been proposed in previous studies.

In the growth stage, the only core factor is **customer attraction**. It is considered the most important and necessary element, as it enables the acquisition of new customers. This aligns with Werth et al. (2019), who emphasize that Fintech startups must compete with large institutions like banks and financial organizations. There are no complementary factors, but specific ones were identified:

- For the CHY startup, **market positioning** relative to competitors and their products is crucial. It ensures an understanding of market size and access strategies, which is related to customer attraction and may explain its absence in previous studies.
- For the YOT startup, **product development** based on data collected from the MVP is essential, though it has not been proposed in previous research.
- For the RYM startup, **flexibility** is key, meaning continuous adjustment of the product based on customer needs and feedback. This factor has not been proposed in previous work, possibly due to regulatory rigidity in the Tunisian context.
- For the SAM startup, which operates with a B2B approach, the use of a **B2B communication strategy** to attract corporate customers is vital (Werth et al., 2019).

5. CONCLUSION

This exploratory study aims to understand how to successfully set up a FinTech startup. Our research focused on investigating and analyzing the critical success factors (CSFs) for FinTech startups at each stage of their life cycle. We conducted a qualitative study using multiple case studies, interviewing four FinTech startups based in Tunisia. Data was collected through semi-structured interviews.

The theoretical contribution of this book chapter lies in its dynamic vision, presenting success factors across the three stages of the Fintech lifecycle. During the seed stage, the most important factors are technology choice, network, and team. In the subsequent stages, each has a single core factor: MVP development for the early stage and customer attraction for the growth stage. Complementary factors in the seed stage include the regulatory framework, initial financing, market investigation, and the co-founder. For the early stage, the two complementary factors are fundraising and market investigation.

On a managerial level, the results of this research can help Fintech owners or entrepreneurs by providing better visibility on the critical and less critical factors for success during each phase of the Fintech startup implementation process.

Despite its contributions, this research has some limitations. The small sample size of interviewees is due to the limited number of startups and staff in this emerging industry in Tunisia. Additionally, the health crisis has discouraged participation. Future research could include interviews with Fintech startups utilizing common technologies such as Blockchain, AI, crowdfunding platforms, and robotic process automation to identify more specific critical success factors for each type of technology used.

The Fintech sector is a booming industry that has significantly reshaped the traditional financial system. However, it still faces challenges, particularly regarding the regulatory framework and laws related to the establishment of Fintech startups. Nearly all interviewees mentioned regulatory issues as a major barrier to Fintech development in Tunisia. One interviewee expressed frustration, exclaiming: *"Tunisia is so behind on what's going on the other side of the world. The government and laws are based on a traditional and classic system"*.

Despite these challenges, the government has proposed solutions such as SANDBOX, a regulatory initiative within the central bank. This initiative brings together various participants from the financial ecosystem to test and supervise Fintech start-ups, and to adjust laws for their legal establishment. While the sandbox represents a potential solution, it is a lengthy process. Nonetheless, Fintechs are expected to persist and adapt to upcoming changes in the sector, making it a fascinating field for further research.

REFERENCES

Al-Mudimigh, A., & Anshari, M. (2020). Financial Technology and Innovative Financial Inclusion. *Financial Technology and Disruptive Innovation in ASEAN*, 119-129.

Al Suwaidi, M. E. Y. M., Sidek, S. B., & Al-Shami, S. A. (2022). A Conceptual Framework of Fintech Laws and Regulations on the Risk Management of Financial Institutions in UAE. *Mathematical Statistician and Engineering Applications*, 71(3), 01-07.

Allen, F., Gu, X., & Jagtiani, J. (2022). Fintech, Cryptocurrencies, and CBDC: Financial Structural Transformation in China. *Journal of International Money and Finance*, 124, 1–38. DOI: 10.1016/j.jimonfin.2022.102625

Almakenzi, S., Bramantoro, A., & Rashideh, W. (2015). A Survivability Model for Saudi ICT Startups. *International Journal of Computer Science and Information Technologies*, 7(2), 145–157. DOI: 10.5121/ijcsit.2015.7213

Arner, D. W., Barberis, J. N., & Buckley, R. P. (2015). *The Evolution of Fintech: A New Post-Crisis Paradigm?* (SSRN Scholarly Paper 2676553). https://doi.org/ DOI: 10.2139/ssrn.2676553

Balboni, B., Bortoluzzi, G., Tivan, M., Tracogna, A., & Venier, F. (2014). The Growth Drivers of Start-up Firms and Business Modelling: A First Step toward a Desirable Convergence. *Management*, 9(2), 131–154. https://ideas.repec.org//a/mgt/youmng/v9y2014i2p131-154.html

Bardin, L. (1998). *L'analyse de contenu*. Librairie Eyrolles.

Bouaziz, F., & Sghari, A. (2021). FinTech's Interpretations and Tunisian Ecosystem Analysis. In *Influence of FinTech on Management Transformation* (pp. 167–190). IGI Global., DOI: 10.4018/978-1-7998-7110-1.ch008

Bouaziz, F., & Sghari, A. (2021), "FinTech's Interpretations and Tunisian Ecosystem Analysis", In **Sghari**, A and Mezghani, K. (2020), Chapter 8 (pp. 167-190), *Influence of FinTech on Management Transformation*, Edited by IGI Global. DOI: DOI: 10.4018/978-1-7998-7110-1.ch008

Denoo, L., & Yli-Renko, H. (2019). Entrepreneurship in a new digital industry: The emergence and growth of mobile health. In Baierl, R., Behrens, J., & Brem, A. (Eds.), *Digital Entrepreneurship* (pp. 79–98). Springer., DOI: 10.1007/978-3-030-20138-8_4

Elia, G., Margherita, A., & Passiante, G. (2020). Digital entrepreneurship ecosystem: How digital technologies and collective intelligence are reshaping the entrepreneurial process. *Technological Forecasting and Social Change*, 150, 119791. Advance online publication. DOI: 10.1016/j.techfore.2019.119791

Guzmán, J. B., & Lussier, R. (2015). *Success Factors for Small Businesses in Guanajuato, Mexico*. https://www.semanticscholar.org/paper/Success-Factors-for-Small-Businesses-in-Guanajuato%2C-Guzm%C3%A1n-Lussier/330a63d5d4069dde9b3f7ec5c70721733d922cb3

Kessler, A. (2007). Success factors for new businesses in Austria and the Czech Republic. *Entrepreneurship and Regional Development*, 19(5), 381–403. https://ideas.repec.org//a/taf/entreg/v19y2007i5p381-403.html. DOI: 10.1080/08985620701439959

Kessler, A., & Frank, H. (2009). Nascent Entrepreneurship in a Longitudinal Perspective: The Impact of Person, Environment, Resources and the Founding Process on the Decision to Start Business Activities. *International Small Business Journal*, 27(6), 720–742. DOI: 10.1177/0266242609344363

Kim, B., Kim, H., & Jeon, Y. (2018). Critical Success Factors of a Design Startup Business. *Sustainability (Basel)*, 10(9), 9. Advance online publication. DOI: 10.3390/su10092981

Lampadarios, E., Kyriakidou, N., & Smith, G. (2017). Towards a new framework for SMEs success: A literature review. *International Journal of Business and Globalisation*, 18(2), 194. DOI: 10.1504/IJBG.2017.081954

Lee, I., & Shin, Y. J. (2018). Fintech: Ecosystem, business models, investment decisions, and challenges. *Business Horizons*, 61(1), 35–46. DOI: 10.1016/j.bushor.2017.09.003

Lee, S. S., & Osteryoung, J. S. (2001). A Comparison of Determinants for Business Start-Up in the U.S. and Korea. *Journal of Small Business Management*. https://www.tandfonline.com/doi/abs/10.1111/1540-627X.00018

Limna, P., & Kraiwanit, T. (2022). The Rise of Fintech: A Review Article. *STOU Academic Journal of Research and Innovation*, 2, 35–46.

Miles, M. B., Huberman, A. M., & Saldana, J. (2013). *Qualitative Data Analysis: A Methods Sourcebook*. SAGE Publications.

Milian, E. Z., Spinola, M. M., & Carvalho, M. M. (2019). Fintechs: A literature review and research agenda. *Electronic Commerce Research and Applications*, 34, 100833. DOI: 10.1016/j.elerap.2019.100833

Nalintippayawong, S., Waiyawatpattarakul, N., & Chotipant, S. (2018). Examining the Critical Success Factors of Startup in Thailand Using Structural Equation Model. *10th International Conference on Information Technology and Electrical Engineering (ICITEE)*, Bali, Indonesia, 2018, pp. 388-393, DOI: 10.1109/ICITEED.2018.8534854

Salamzadeh, A., & Kawamorita Kesim, H. (2017). The enterprising communities and startup ecosystem in Iran. *Journal of Enterprising Communities: People and Places in the Global Economy*, 11(4), 456–479. DOI: 10.1108/JEC-07-2015-0036

Sammut, S. (2001). Processus de démarrage en petite entreprise : Système de gestion et scénarios. *Revue de l'Entrepreneuriat / Review of Entrepreneurship, 1*(1), 61-76. https://doi.org/DOI: 10.3917/entre.011.0061

Santisteban, J., & Mauricio, D. (2017). Systematic Literature Review of Critical Success Factors of Information Technology Startups. *Academy of Entrepreneurship Journal, 23*(2), 0-0. https://www.abacademies.org/articles/systematic-literature-review-of-critical-success-factors-of-information-technology-startups-6638.html

Sharma, S., Srivastav, S., Gupta, A., & Manglick, A. (2022). Application of Technology and Innovation in Fintech and Its Adaptability in India. 2nd *International Conference on Innovative Practices in Technology and Management*, 2, 305-311. IEEE.

Song, M., Podoynitsyna, K., Van Der Bij, H., & Halman, J. I. M. (2008). Success factors in new ventures: A meta-analysis. *Journal of Product Innovation Management*, 25(1), 7–27. DOI: 10.1111/j.1540-5885.2007.00280.x

Swacha-Lech, M. (2017). The main challenges facing the retail banking industry in the era of digitalization. Journal of Insurance. *Financial Markets and Consumer Protection*, 26(4), 94–116.

Thakor, A. V. (2020). Fintech and banking: What do we know? *Journal of Financial Intermediation*, 41, 100833. DOI: 10.1016/j.jfi.2019.100833

Van Gelderen, M., Thurik, R., & Bosma, N. (2006). Success and Risk Factors in the Pre-Startup Phase. *Small Business Economics*, 24(4), 365–380. DOI: 10.1007/s11187-004-6994-6

Werth, O., Cardona, D. R., Nowatschin, J., Werner, M., Guhr, N., & Breitner, M. H. (2019). Challenges of the Financial Industry—An Analysis of Critical Success Factors for FinTechs. *AMCIS 2019 Proceedings*. https://aisel.aisnet.org/amcis2019/ebusiness/ebusiness/4

ADDITIONAL READING

Ali, M. (2021). *Remote Work and Sustainable Changes for the Future of Global Business.* IGI Global. https://www.igi-global.com/book/remote-work-sustainable-changes-future/264375

Ali, M. (2022). *Future Role of Sustainable Innovative Technologies in Crisis Management.* IGI Global. https://www.igi-global.com/book/future-role-sustainable-innovative-technologies/281281

Ali, M. (2023). *Shifting Paradigms in the Rapidly Developing Global Digital Ecosystem: A GCC Perspective.* In Digital Entrepreneurship and Co-Creating Value Through Digital Encounters (pp. 145-166). IGI Global. https://www.igi-global.com/chapter/shifting-paradigms-in-the-rapidly-developing-global-digital-ecosystem/323525

Ali, M. (2023). T*axonomy of Industry 4.0 Technologies in Digital Entrepreneurship and Co-Creating Value.* In *Digital Entrepreneurship and Co-Creating Value Through Digital Encounters* (pp. 24–55). IGI Global., https://www.igi-global.com/chapter/taxonomy-of-industry-40-technologies-in-digital-entrepreneurship-and-co-creating-value/323520 DOI: 10.4018/978-1-6684-7416-7.ch002

Ali, M., & Wood-Harper, T. (2021). *Fostering Communication and Learning with Underutilized Technologies in Higher Education.* IGI Global. https://www.igi-global.com/book/fostering-communication-learning-underutilized-technologies/244593

Ali, M., Wood-Harper, T., & Kutar, M. (2023). Multi-Perspectives of Contemporary Digital Transformation Models of Complex Innovation Management. In *Digital Entrepreneurship and Co-Creating Value Through Digital Encounters* (pp. 79–96). IGI Global., https://www.igi-global.com/chapter/multi-perspectives-of-contemporary-digital-transformation-models-of-complex-innovation-management/323522 DOI: 10.4018/978-1-6684-7416-7.ch004

Ali, M. B. (2021). Internet of Things (IoT) to Foster Communication and Information Sharing: A Case of UK Higher Education. In Ali, M. B., & Wood-Harper, T. (Eds.), *Fostering Communication and Learning With Underutilized Technologies in Higher Education* (pp. 1–20). IGI Global., https://www.igi-global.com/chapter/internet-of-things-iot-to-foster-communication-and-information-sharing/262718/ DOI: 10.4018/978-1-7998-4846-2.ch001

Ali, M. B., & Wood-Harper, T. (2022). Artificial Intelligence (AI) as a Decision-Making Tool to Control Crisis Situations. In *Future Role of Sustainable Innovative Technologies in Crisis Management*. IGI Global., https://www.igi-global.com/chapter/artificial-intelligence-ai-as-a-decision-making-tool-to-control-crisis-situations/298931 DOI: 10.4018/978-1-7998-9815-3.ch006

Ali, M. B., Wood-Harper, T., & Ramlogan, R. (2020). A Framework Strategy to Overcome Trust Issues on Cloud Computing Adoption in Higher Education. In Modern Principles, Practices, and Algorithms for Cloud Security (pp. 162-183). IGI Global. https://www.igi-global.com/chapter/a-framework-strategy-to-overcome-trust-issues-on-cloud-computing-adoption-in-higher-education/238907/

APPENDIX I

Interview Guide

Introductory Question

1. Could you introduce yourself, tell me about your startup, and explain your position within the startup?

Questions Related to Phase 1

1. Could you describe what actions you took during the idea phase, just before the official creation of your startup?
2. What factors do you consider crucial for the success of this phase?
3. What obstacles or barriers may have hindered progress during this phase?

Questions Related to Phase 2

1. Could you describe the key activities during the creation phase of your startup?
2. What factors do you consider important for the success of this phase?
3. What obstacles or barriers may have posed challenges during this phase?

Questions Related to Phase 3

1. Could you describe what you did after the creation of your startup, particularly during the launch and development of your products or services?
2. What factors do you consider crucial for the success of this phase?
3. What obstacles or barriers may have hindered progress during this phase?

Conclusion

1. In your opinion, how would you assess the emergence of fintech startups in Tunisia?
2. What recommendations would you suggest for the development of this sector?

Chapter 10

Managing Cyber Security Risks and Cyber Hygiene in Organizations:

Improving Cyber Resilience

Tuğçe Karayel
https://orcid.org/0000-0002-5556-225X
Duzce University, Turkey

Adem Akbıyık
https://orcid.org/0000-0001-7634-4545
Sakarya University, Turkey

ABSTRACT

The rate and volume of cyber attacks increases every year, causing additional costs to organizations. Especially in recent years, new generation cyber attacks against government organizations, private companies and service providers have become increasingly complex with the use of artificial intelligence tools. Since the new generation of cyber attacks are much more complex than the previous ones, corporate managers and employees lack expertise and awareness in taking counter-measures. Studies are needed to support organizations in order to increase cyber resilience in this area. This chapter focuses on cybersecurity risk management and individual cyber hygiene practices as a solution to cyber attacks. Well-developed cybersecurity risk management and strong cyber hygiene behaviors will make it easier for organizations to take measures against advanced cyber attacks. It will also increase the cyber resilience of organizations and provide a line of defense against potential threats.

DOI: 10.4018/979-8-3373-0086-3.ch010

Copyright © 2025, IGI Global. Copying or distributing in print or electronic forms without written permission of IGI Global is prohibited.

INTRODUCTION

On a global scale, organizations of all sizes and in every sector face cyber security risks. The rate and volume of cyber-attacks increases every year, causing additional costs to organizations. It is predicted that the costs of cybercrime worldwide will be 10.5 trillion dollars by 2025. In recent years, next-generation cyber-attacks targeting government organizations, private companies, and service providers have become increasingly complex with the use of artificial intelligence tools. Since these new-generation cyber-attacks are much more sophisticated than previous ones, there is a lack of expertise and awareness among institution managers and employees in taking countermeasures. In this field, there is a need for efforts that will support organizations in enhancing cyber resilience.

Organizations spend significant amounts on technological measures to protect their digital assets against cyber-attacks. However, they still fail to secure their digital assets. This is because cybersecurity is a multidisciplinary field that involves the human element. In this field, user behavior is critically important in combating cyber risks. According to a study, it was revealed that 95% of cyber security incidents are caused by user error. For example, last September, Airbus was hacked when an employee downloaded malware onto the corporate computer. This incident reminded us once again that the weakest link in cyber security is the human element. Users intentionally or negligently cause major threats to information security. Sharing account information with friends, downloading software from unreliable sites, writing passwords on sticky paper and putting them on the computer screen, using ID numbers as usernames or passwords are examples of user errors. Poor cyber hygiene behaviors such as negligence, ignorance and unconsciousness of users are often the main causes of security breaches. At this point, importance should be given to cyber hygiene practices in order to raise information security awareness to users and prevent poor cyber hygiene behaviors. Cyber hygiene is the actions that can be implemented to protect data and devices from cyber risks. Even though organizations take technological measures for cyber security, they will become the target of cyber-attacks unless the cyber hygiene behavior of their employees is improved. Cyber hygiene activities help increase cyber resilience in organizations. More precisely, cyber resilience cannot be mentioned without cyber hygiene.

For organizations to be prepared for cyber-attacks, identify potential attack risks, enhance their incident response capabilities when an attack occurs, and quickly return to normal operations afterwards—in other words, to increase their cyber resilience—cyber hygiene practices are of critical importance. Cyber hygiene practices create a strong line of defense against cyber threats. It also helps organizations ensure cyber security. Another way to increase cyber resilience is to manage cyber security risks. Cyber security risk management is the process of identifying potential risks to important data systems and networks, evaluating the impact of these risks, and planning actions to be taken in response to possible attacks in case they occur. The cyber security risk management process consists of five steps. To manage cyber security risks, a risk assessment must first be made. During the risk assessment process, a digital asset inventory is created, potential threats are identified and security vulnerabilities in the system are identified. In the second stage, security policies and procedures need to be designed. At this stage, the rules that all employees and stakeholders must comply with are determined, authorization and access control are made regarding who will access digital assets and how, and the activities to be carried out during and after cyber-attack events are determined. In the third stage, technological measures are taken. These include using intrusion detection and prevention systems, keeping firewalls open and up to date, enabling multi-factor encryption techniques, and using antivirus software. The fourth stage is to carry out awareness activities regarding the training and awareness of employees. At this stage, relevant training should be given under the subheadings of cyber hygiene factors. For example, it is necessary to provide training and assistance to employees on how to perform software updates, how to scan a USB memory or external disk for viruses, how to keep virus protection software up to date, how to enable two-factor or multi-factor authentication, and how to enable firewalls. In the fifth and final stage, continuous monitoring and control should be carried out. Cyber resilience is a dynamic process that demands continuity and requires adapting to the changing nature of technology, threats and business needs. At this stage, it is necessary to constantly monitor network traffic to detect system anomalies, keep track of whether software and systems are up to date, and perform security tests at regular intervals. Additionally, at this stage, awareness tests and games should be prepared to measure employees' cyber hygiene levels. Next, informing users about their level of cyber hygiene will help them understand where they are lacking, what they are good at, and how their actions harm or contribute to the security of the organization. As a result, managing cybersecurity risks requires a rational and proactive approach.

This chapter focuses on cybersecurity risk management and individual cyber hygiene practices as a solution to cyber-attacks that are becoming more complex with artificial intelligence tools. Well-developed cyber security risk management and strong cyber hygiene behaviors will make it easier for organizations to take precautions against advanced cyber-attacks. It will also increase the cyber resilience of organizations and provide a line of defense against potential threats. The content of the section first explains the current status of cyber security risks and the basic stages of cyber security risk management. Next, the role of cyber hygiene in managing cyber security risks is examined from the perspective of case studies. To build cyber resilience, five principles are described, each corresponding to a set of cyber hygiene activities. At the end of the study, cyber security risk factors for organizations are revealed and measures that can be taken regarding cyber hygiene to increase cyber resilience are included.

CYBER SECURITY

The main purpose of cyber security, also known as information technology (IT) security, is to protect the information technology infrastructure of organizations and the information necessary for their daily operations. Since organizations transfer important information through systems while doing work, they may lose their data and customers and be subject to some penalties due to any cyber threat. Global cyber threats continue to grow rapidly, with data breaches increasing every year. Security reports reveal that billions of personal and corporate data are compromised by malicious attackers every year due to data breaches, especially in recent years. In this regard, cyber security provides solutions to protect organizations information, information processing or storage systems (Tam vd., 2021).

Kaspersky cyber security is defined as protecting computers, mobile devices, servers, networks, electronic systems and data, in short, all IT assets from cyber attacks by malicious individuals (Kaspersky, 2019). The International Telecommunication Union (ITU) defines cybersecurity as follows: "The International Telecommunication Union (ITU) defines cybersecurity as follows: Cybersecurity means the tools, policies, security concepts, security measures, guidelines, risk management approaches, actions, training, best practices, assurance that can be used to protect the cyber environment, the institution and the user's assets. and the sum of technologies. The organization's and user's assets include networked computing devices, personnel, infrastructure, applications, services, telecommunications systems, and the sum of information transmitted and/or stored in cyberspace. Cyber security is to ensure that the institution's and user assets are secured against relevant security risks in the cyber environment and to strive to maintain this security." (ITU, 2008).

In the Oxford dictionary, cybersecurity is defined as the state of protection against criminal or unauthorized use of electronic data, or the measures taken to achieve this (ENISA, 2015). According to Merriam Webster dictionary, cyber security is defined as measures taken to protect a computer or computer system against unauthorized access or attack (R. Solms & Niekerk, 2013).

Cybersecurity refers to the security of cyberspace. Cyberspace is defined as the set of connections and relationships between objects that can be accessed through a telecommunications network, or the set of objects that provide interfaces that allow remote access to data. Therefore, cyber security is a concept that provides the confidentiality, integrity and accessibility of relationships and objects in cyberspace and provides the same paradigm for protecting the privacy of legal entities (ENISA, 2015). In summary, cyber security is about how organizations and individuals combat and reduce cyber risks.

Cyber Security and Artificial Intelligence

The overall impacts of Artificial Intelligence (AI) on cybersecurity are both positive and negative. Attackers use AI technologies to find weaknesses in cybersecurity technologies. On the other hand, automations using machine learning algorithms are used to prevent attackers from attacking systems with AI (Ansari et al., 2022). It has been proven that attacks against companies are becoming increasingly dangerous. As AI technology continues to evolve, the volume and sophistication of frauds is increasing. Deepfake, an AI technology, is increasingly spreading worldwide. The growing wave of deepfake fraud is causing companies worldwide to lose millions of dollars. For example, $25 million was stolen in a deepfake attack in 2024. A Hong Kong financial employee transferred more than $25 million to fraudsters posing as his colleagues using deepfake technology in a video call (Butts, 2024).

In another case, a deepfake voice was used. This AI-generated voice caused a UK-based energy company to lose US$ 243,000. The cybercriminals pretended to be the CEO of the parent company, called the CEO of the UK company, and demanded a large wire transfer to get their hands on the large sum of money. Deepfake, or fake audio and video fraud, is a new type of cyberattack that highlights how artificial intelligence can be misused. Preventing such AI-powered attacks requires a concerted effort by both business personnel and business partners to exercise vigilance and increase security awareness within the organization (Trendmicro, 2024).

In addition, organizations can develop strong security protection by integrating Deepfake detection software that uses algorithms that use artificial intelligence to detect Deepfakes and prevent identity fraud into user behavior. However, employees need to be trained on how to use AI-enabled security tools, how to interpret the results of these tools, and how to adapt to these technologies (Bioid, 2024). In order to determine what is real and what is fake in deepfakes, personnel can be practiced with simulated or gamified case examples. These practices will help improve employees' intuition and increase their degree of cyber hygiene.

On the other hand, AI technology has contributed to reducing cybercrime. AI technology has enabled faster detection of system failures, as its monitoring activities are much more powerful than those of humans. AI technology can be developed by cyber attackers to produce computer viruses (Ansari et al., 2022). Organizations and their employees need to be vigilant against these new types of malwares. AI systems can be trained to detect cyber threats and malware, making them more effective in cybersecurity. On the other hand, AI is a powerful technology that helps cybersecurity teams automate repetitive tasks, accelerate threat detection and response, and improve the accuracy of their actions to strengthen their security posture against cyberattacks. In addition, AI helps organizations protect against cyberattacks by rapidly analyzing millions of events to anticipate the problem and take action (Kaur et al., 2023).

Cyber Risk

In the literature, the concept of cyber risk is defined in different ways by many authors. Gordon et al. (2003) define cyber risk as work risks arising from being connected to the internet. Biener et al. (2015) risks affecting the confidentiality, availability or integrity of information or information systems, in short, it defines it as operational risks towards digital assets. According to Eling & Schnell (2016), cyber risk is defined as risks arising from the use of IT that compromise the confidentiality, availability or integrity of data or services. Cyber risks generally affect all types of organizations of all sizes and regardless of business models (Lloyd, 2020).

Exposure to cyber risks largely depends on the security vulnerabilities of the organization. Therefore, existing vulnerabilities in IT security increase cyber risks (Marotta et al., 2017). However, researchers agree that even if there is a high level of IT security, organizations cannot completely prevent losses from cyber risks (Camillo, 2017). This is because cyber security is a multidisciplinary subject. It is stated that cyber attacks do not only occur from technological or technical errors, but also arise from human actions, unsuccessful business processes and external events (Cebula & Young, 2010). Indeed, it is stated in the literature that the majority of cyber incidents are caused by human errors, not technological vulnerabilities (Alanazi et al., 2022; Biener et al., 2015; Pollock, 2017). For example, a report prepared by IBM found that 95% of information security incidents are caused by human error (Howarth, 2014). According to ENISA, approximately 77% of data breaches are caused by human vulnerability (ENISA, 2022). Verizon (2024) analyzed 30,458 cyber security incidents and found that 68% of the incidents were caused by human error. As a result, cyber risk management is too important an issue to be delegated only to the IT department (Verizon, 2024).

Emerging technologies such as Industry 4.0, social media, cloud computing, smartphone technology, IoT and artificial intelligence are leading to new attack patterns, further increasing the complexity of effectively dealing with these threats (Loonam et al., 2022). Because of these new technologies and the rapid development of information systems, the cyber risk environment is constantly evolving. Attack techniques are constantly changing and can be carried out easily and cheaply. According to the Allianz Risk Report, more than 2700 risk management experts from 102 countries and regions stated that cyber incidents are recognized as the most important business risk. Cyber risks continue to increase day by day. Organizations are facing an increasing number of new challenges, including larger and more expensive data breaches, the rise in ransomware, as well as the possibility of litigation after a cyber incident. As a result, many organizations recognize that cyber risk is an important component of enterprise risk management, and their main goal is to increase cyber resilience.

Cyber Risk Assessment

The cyber risk assessment phase consists of eight topics. In the first phase, it is determined how users are harmed by cyber vulnerabilities. In the second phase, IT managers design a Spear Phishing penetration test. In the third phase, the basis for pen testing is created. In the fourth phase, the pen test is applied on users in the organization. In the fifth phase, a two-question cyber risk questionnaire is administered. In the sixth phase, vulnerabilities are identified, and the causes of security weaknesses are diagnosed. Using the cyber risk questionnaire, users' performance in the pen test is analyzed. In the seventh stage, a cyber resilience score is obtained for the organization. The score is obtained by subtracting the percentage of high-risk users from the percentage of low-risk users. The value of the metric theoretically ranges from -100 to +100. A low number indicates increased vulnerability, while a high number indicates higher resilience. For example, if 70 percent of the organization's users are assessed as high risk based on the cyber risk score and 30 percent are assessed as low risk, the resulting cyber resilience score would be 40 (70-30). A cyber resilience score close to 100 indicates that the organization is fully resistant to phishing. Conversely, a score close to zero indicates that the organization is not resilient, while a negative number indicates high vulnerability. The eighth stage involves sharing the results with stakeholders. The cyber resilience score should be shared with all users in the organization, not just senior management. To achieve cyber resilience, everyone needs to participate in the process, especially the users who are the weakest link and pose the greatest risk to the organization (Vishwanath, 2022, p. 170).

Figure 1. Cyber risk assessment phase (Vishwanath, 2022, p. 170)

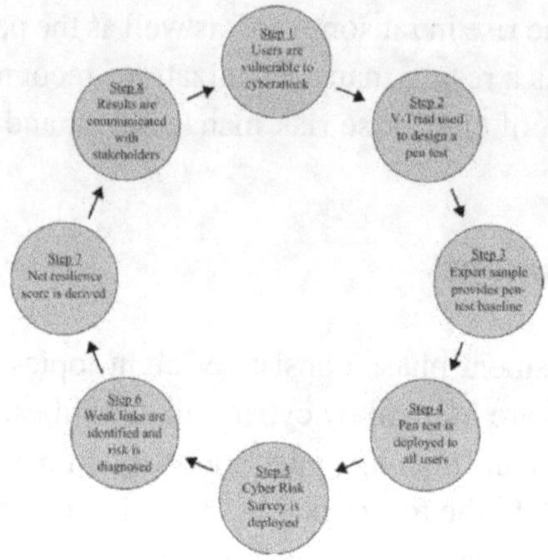

Cyber Security Risk Management

Cybersecurity has become an essential priority for today's organizations. As threats in the digital world evolve rapidly, a robust cyber security risk management (CSRM) program is essential for organizations to cope with these threats. The key to cyber risk management is the identification, development and implementation of a risk management program. Globally, researchers are focusing more intensively on how organizations manage their cyber risks, how they establish their risk tolerance, whether they apply this tolerance, and whether this approach is appropriately audited (Allen et al., 2023).

Cyber security studies started in the late 1960s and first developed under different names such as computer security and information security. Cyber security refers to protecting the confidentiality, integrity and availability of information in complex environments consisting of the interaction of people, software and services on the internet using technological devices and networks (ISO/IEC, 2012). As more and more devices are connected to each other, the potential for cyber attacks has increased significantly, so cyber security has become an important issue for all organizations (Lee, 2021). The lack of active measures taken in this area not only increases the possibility of cybercriminals accessing sensitive data but also causes the entire information technologies (IT) infrastructure of organizations to be disrupted (Miller & Bossomaier, 2024). Therefore, cybersecurity risk management, also called cyber risk management, is defined as the process of identifying, analyzing and managing an organization's IT security risks to prevent ongoing cyber threats and future cyber attacks (IBM, 2024).

Cybersecurity risk management encompasses all the processes of detecting, analyzing, evaluating and taking measures against cyber threats. Today, cyber risk management has become an indispensable issue, especially for organizations that carry out their business processes using digital channels. Cyber security risk management is the process of identifying, analyzing and taking precautions against threats to which the digital assets of the organization may be exposed. In this process, potential security vulnerabilities, the likelihood of cyber threats and the damages that may occur if these threats materialize are evaluated. The aim is to minimize cyber risks and strengthen the organization's cyber security profile.

Organizations are under pressure to demonstrate that they have effective processes and controls in place to manage cyber security threats, detect, respond to, mitigate and recover from security breaches and other security incidents. At this point, it is important for organizations to take precautions against and manage these risks. Cybersecurity risk management focuses on identifying risks to information assets and creating actions to mitigate or eliminate these risks.

Cyber security risk management consists of four basic stages;

1) Risk assessment: In this stage, an inventory of digital assets is created, potential threats and vulnerabilities in the system are identified.
2) Creating risk management strategies: At this stage, security policies and procedures need to be designed. At this stage, the rules that all employees and stakeholders must comply with are determined, authorization and access control are made regarding who will access digital assets and how, and the activities to be carried out during and after cyber attack events are determined.
3) Risk monitoring and taking precautions: At this stage, technological measures should be taken. These include using intrusion detection and prevention systems, keeping firewalls open and up to date, enabling multi-factor encryption techniques, and using antivirus software. Additionally, at this stage, precautions must be taken regarding employee behavior. Employees need to be educated and conscious, in short, work should be done on employees' cyber hygiene.
4) Risk control: At this stage, continuous improvement and auditing should be carried out. Systems and employees should be inspected at regular intervals. The risk management process should be reviewed and any problems that arise should be corrected. In addition, continuous improvement activities need to be carried out in this department. Emerging cyber attacks should

be investigated and the risk management process should be updated. As a result, the cybersecurity risk management process is a dynamic process. This process should be revised according to the requirements of technology and the time period we are in.

Cybersecurity risk management involves a series of key stages aimed at identifying, assessing and mitigating potential threats to the organization's digital assets. The process typically begins with risk identification, where potential risks are recognized and categorized based on their potential impact on the integrity, availability, and confidentiality of the organization başlar (Orlando, 2021). A comprehensive assessment of these risks is then conducted to understand their likelihood of occurrence and potential consequences (Hariharan, 2021). This assessment phase is crucial for prioritizing risks and effectively allocating resources to address them. Following the risk assessment, organizations move on to the stage of determining risk management strategies, where they develop strategies to manage and reduce the identified risks. This phase involves implementing security controls, protocols, and measures to reduce the likelihood of a cyber attack and minimize its impact if it occurs. To effectively plan and implement risk management strategies, it is important for organizations to conduct thorough research on vulnerabilities in their systems and potential damage costs (Frantti & Korkiakoski, 2022). Cybersecurity risk management also includes the process of constantly monitoring and reviewing measures implemented to ensure their effectiveness and suitability in the face of advanced cyber threats. Regular risk assessments and audits are essential to keep up with the dynamic nature of cyber risks and adapt risk management strategies accordingly (Hart et al., 2020). In conclusion, the basic stages of cyber security risk management include risk identification, assessment, strategy development, risk monitoring and risk control. By following these stages meticulously, organizations can increase their cyber resilience against cyber threats and effectively protect their digital assets.

Cyber Resilience

Cyber resilience includes the ability to return a system's performance to pre-cyber-attack levels, recover the system and improve system performance. Cybersecurity focuses on preparing for, protecting against and detecting cyber attacks. Cyber resilience is about protecting against and responding to cyber attacks. When designing a resilient system, it is important to plan for the restoration of the system after cyber incidents. Cyber resilience aims to maintain the system's ability to achieve the intended results (Singh et al., 2024).

According to Ayoub et al. (2017), cyber resilience refers to the ability to prevent and protect against cyber attacks. For organizations, cyber resilience is defined as the ability to defend against, prevent, detect and respond to cyber attacks (Ayoub et al., 2017). Cyber resilience is a fundamental concept that focuses on the ability of systems to withstand cyber-attacks or system outages, adapt to security policies, and recover from cyber-attacks. It also encompasses several dimensions, such as the ability to improve system performance after a cyber-attack or the ability to perform daily functions despite adverse cyber events (Flammini et al., 2024; Linkov & Kott, 2018).

Cyber resilience is measured by a combination of the ability of systems and organizations to withstand cyber incidents, average time to failure, and average time to recovery (Orlando, 2021). A comprehensive framework for measuring cyber resilience includes the ability to identify and prepare for system problems, troubleshoot problems, improve functionality, and adapt to increase cyber resilience (Ligo et al., 2021). This framework emphasizes the importance of protecting critical services and assets during cyber incidents, restoring functionality after the incident, and evolving to become more resilient over time. Moreover, cyber resilience covers all phases from proactive to reactive cyber resilience. It involves the development of cyber resilience frameworks to enhance and improve cyber resilience by ensuring that systems can effectively cope with and recover from cyber incidents (Bagheri et al., 2023). In summary, cyber resilience is a multifaceted concept that encompasses the ability of systems to withstand, adapt to, and recover from cyber threats.

Cyber resilience is a new paradigm that emphasizes an organization's business ability to recover from cyber threats (Bei, 2019; Buchmann et al., 2020). In contrast, cybersecurity is described as a set of policies, strategies and programs to protect cyber systems (Craigen et al., 2014). The ultimate goal of cybersecurity and cyber resilience approaches is to protect organizations against cyber threats. Cyber resilience helps organizations prepare for and improve their ability to recover from cyber risks and hazards. Therefore, a cyber resilient system not only protects against cybercrime, but also considers responses before, during and after a cyber incident (Roege et al., 2017).

Cyber problems cannot be solved by technical decision makers alone. In addition to IT staff and managers, business staff and managers need to be involved (Orozco et al., 2015). Despite the important role of business managers in cybersecurity decision-making, studies show that business managers lack the appropriate level of knowledge on cybersecurity and cyber resilience, leading to conflict between organizational cyber goals and business objectives. To overcome this problem, a common cybersecurity and cyber resilience perspective is needed between senior

IT and business managers in different functional roles (Johnson, 2009). As both roles are key to effective decision making to address cyber threats, harmonizing the perspectives of the two groups will strengthen organizational cyber resilience (Bagheri et al., 2023).

Cyber Hygiene and Case Studies

Cyber hygiene activities that make organizations resistant to cyber attacks help to build cyber resilience. In the literature, five principles have been identified to build cyber resilience, each corresponding to a cyber hygiene activity. The first principle, building cyber resilience requires awareness. Awareness is necessary to deal with each threat appropriately, but awareness alone is not enough. The second principle requires knowledge to build cyber resilience. Users need cyber hygiene knowledge related to their tasks and mission requirements. The third principle is that building cyber resilience is a process. Cyber resilience is a process that builds over time, gradually and incrementally changing the way users behave and think. The fourth principle is that building cyber resilience requires measurement. What is lacking and what is succeeding needs to be measured and tracked. Fifth, cyber resilience requires accountability. Accountability occurs when robust and objective measurements are consistently and fairly applied and shared with users across the organization. These five principles show that achieving cyber resilience goes beyond awareness and knowledge (Vishwanath, 2022).

An integral element of users' cyber risk involves examining cyber hygiene. In order to improve users' cyber hygiene, many issues need to be addressed by organizations, ranging from awareness training, pen testing, patch management, VPN usage, strong password usage, two-factor authentication and antivirus usage. The analysis of some case studies according to cyber hygiene is shown in Table 1.

Table 1. Case studies according to cyber hygiene sub-dimensions

Item	Case Study
Updating latest operating system, software update or patch	Equifax serves as a leading credit reporting agency in the United States. In 2017, the company suffered a massive data breach. As a result of this breach, the personal information (social security numbers, dates of birth, addresses and, in some cases, driver's licenses) of 147 million American citizens was stolen. This was because an Equifax internal audit in 2015 found that there were numerous vulnerabilities that needed to be patched and that Equifax was not following its own timelines for doing so (Portman & Carper, 2019). Updates are critical to close vulnerabilities and add new features.
Managing privacy settings on social media platforms	The Cambridge Analytica scandal is a data privacy scandal that erupted in 2018 and raised serious concerns about Facebook's misuse of user data. At the center of the incident was the unauthorized collection of Facebook users' data by Cambridge Analytica, a British data analytics firm, and its use for political purposes (Cadwalladr & Graham-Harrison, 2018). This incident marked an important turning point in data protection and privacy issues.
Running a virus scan on any new USB or External Storage device	Stuxnet is one of the most famous examples of cyber-attacks involving the use of USB drives to spread malware. The computer worm, delivered via USB drive, caused serious damage to the Iranian nuclear facility (Fruhlinger, 2022). Scanning a USB drive or external storage device for viruses is an effective way to prevent cyber attacks.
Keeping virus protection updated	WannaCry is a ransomware crypto worm cyber attack targeting computers running the Microsoft Windows operating system. The WannaCry ransomware worm has spread to more than 200,000 computers in more than 150 countries. It caused serious damage to computers without virus protection programs or outdated ones (Tunggal, 2024). Up-to-date virus protection software plays a critical role in mitigating the effects of such attacks.
Enabling the firewall on the computer	In 2023, Airbus faced a cyber-attack and security breach when a Turkish Airlines employee turned off the firewall and downloaded an infected program to his computer (Pandagle, 2023). An effective firewall can prevent such attacks.
Enabling two-factor or multi-factor authentication for logins	In 2020, Twitter suffered a major security breach where the accounts of high-profile individuals and companies were compromised in an attempt to promote a cryptocurrency scam. Among the political accounts attacked were respected leaders such as Barack Obama and Joe Biden. The main reasons for these attacks stem from not using multi-factor authentication methods (Witman & Mackelprang, 2022). A major attack on Twitter accounts has once again highlighted the importance of multi-factor authentication.
Changing default passwords on all Internet enabled devices	Mirai Botnet is a malware that infects smart devices and turns them into remotely controlled bots. It has turned thousands of poorly secured IoT devices into a botnet that launches Distributed Denial of Service (DDoS) attacks (Cloudflare, 2024). This case study highlights the critical need to secure IoT devices. Hacking of IoT devices has made it clear that users need to change their default passwords and use strong passwords.

continued on following page

Table 1. Continued

Item	Case Study
Checking an incoming email's header	In 2018, a phishing attack was launched targeting Netflix ID subscribers. Users received fake emails claiming there was a problem with their Netflix account and redirecting them to a fake login page. The fake web page collected usernames, passwords, and payment details, exploiting trust in the Netflix brand (Tressler, 2018). Awareness of checking the email header is an effective way to prevent email-based cyber attacks by improving users' cyber hygiene.
Checking to see if email requests have grammatical or typographical errors	Phishing scams targeting PayPal users captured user information by instructing users to verify their identity by clicking on the link in the sent e-mail (ManageEngine, 2024). Phishing attacks often take advantage of users' carelessness or ignorance. Users should carefully review suspicious emails, avoid clicking on unknown links, and always access their accounts using the official website or app.

The table summarizes recent case studies related to the statements of some dimensions of cyber hygiene. Regular updating of software and systems and keeping the firewall open, which are sub-expressions of the device security dimension of the cyber hygiene inventory, ensure that security gaps are closed. The WannaCry attack, Equifax cyber incident and Airbus cyber-attack incidents described in the table are case studies where updates were not made, the firewall was not activated/turned off and precautions were not taken regarding security vulnerabilities. Cyber hygiene helps prevent threats to systems by increasing user awareness and knowledge on these issues. Enabling two-factor or multi-factor authentication, an expression of the authentication dimension of cyber hygiene, increases the security of user accounts. In 2020, the social engineering attack on the Twitter social media application, which was carried out by compromising high-profile accounts, is an example of a cyber attack caused by the lack of adequate measures regarding authentication hygiene. Checking the email header and spelling mistakes, which are expressions of the email hygiene dimension of cyber hygiene, are factors that increase user awareness in preventing cyberattacks via email. In this context, the cyber-attacks targeting Paypal and Netflix users detailed in the table are examples of cyber-attacks caused by lack of email hygiene. The case studies in this table illustrate why each cyber hygiene practice is important and how it can protect against security risks that can be encountered in daily life. Different cybersecurity threats and hygiene practices are discussed to provide a broad perspective.

CONCLUSION

While traditional security systems can be slow and inefficient, AI techniques can improve their overall security performance and provide better protection against a growing number of complex cyber threats. How AI's capabilities, such as automated threat detection and anomaly monitoring, can be integrated into user behavior to create strong security protection in a way that improves cyber hygiene. If available, employees should be taught how to use AI-supported security tools, how to interpret the results of these tools and how to adapt to these technologies through relevant trainings and use cases.

The malicious use of artificial intelligence, social engineering attacks such as deepfake, and its impact on automated cyberattacks can be prevented through cyber hygiene practices. Cyber hygiene practices will ensure that users gain awareness and security consciousness. In the context of cyber hygiene, it is important to conduct training programs and awareness-raising campaigns that can improve users' ability to recognize and deal with AI-generated threats. For example, organizations can provide practical training to employees to improve their ability to recognize deepfake videos.

Cyber hygiene plays an important role in enhancing cyber resilience by focusing on preventive measures and sound security practices. Through the Cyber Hygiene Inventory methodology, organizations can assess their employees' cyber hygiene levels, take proactive and reactive measures and raise security standards to increase their cyber resilience against potential cyber threats. Regular training, awareness raising, and technical measures minimize the impact of cyber attacks and ensure the operational sustainability of organizations.

This chapter focuses on cybersecurity risk management and individual cyber hygiene practices as a solution to cyber-attacks, which are increasing in speed, complexity and volume every day and are becoming more complex with the use of artificial intelligence tools. All sectors on a global scale and all organizations, no matter how small or large, are under cyber risks. Cyber attacks increase significantly every year, causing additional costs to organizations. Organizations must respond proactively to cyber attacks, restore their systems quickly and increase their cyber resilience against new attacks that may occur. Accordingly, well-developed cyber security risk management and strong cyber hygiene behaviors will make it easier for organizations to take measures against advanced cyber attacks. It will also increase organizations' cyber resilience and provide a line of defense against potential threats.

FUTURE RESEARCH

Just like every study, this study also has some limitations. The study focuses on cyber hygiene practices for cyber security risk management. Cybersecurity risk management is a comprehensive topic consisting of four items. Similarly, the critical role of cyber hygiene in enhancing cyber resilience is examined and other topics are excluded. Moreover, this study examined a limited number of case studies on cyber hygiene practices due to time constraints.

For future studies, it is recommended to examine the case studies from a broader perspective. It is also suggested that all stages of cyber security risk management should be examined and explained in detail.

REFERENCES

Alanazi, M., Freeman, M., & Tootell, H. (2022). Exploring the factors that influence the cybersecurity behaviors of young adults. *Computers in Human Behavior, 136*(December 2021), 107376. DOI: 10.1016/j.chb.2022.107376

Allen, B., Bapst, B., & Hicks, T. A. (2023). Building a Cyber Risk Management Program. In *O'Reilly Media Inc.* https://learning.oreilly.com/library/view/building-a-cyber/9781098147785/

Ayoub, R. M., Firth, C., & Nayaz, M. (2017). Cyber Resilience in the Digital Age. *EY & World Government Summit.* https://worldgovernmentsummit.org/api/publications/document?id=24717dc4-e97c-6578-b2f8-ff0000a7ddb6

Bagheri, S., Ridley, G., & Williams, B. (2023). Organisational Cyber Resilience: Management Perspectives. *AJIS. Australasian Journal of Information Systems*, 27, 1–28. DOI: 10.3127/ajis.v27i0.4183

Bei, H. (2019). *Problems of Cybersecurity in the Context of Becoming and Development of the New Economy*. 454–464.

Biener, C., Eling, M., & Wirfs, J. H. (2015). Insurability of cyber risk: An empirical analysis. *The Geneva Papers on Risk and Insurance. Issues and Practice*, 40(1), 131–158. DOI: 10.1057/gpp.2014.19

Buchmann, R. A., Polini, A., Johansson, B., & Karagiannis, D. (2020). Perspectives in Business Informatics Research. *19th International Conference on Business Informatics Research, BIR 2020, Vienna, Austria, September 21–23, 2020, Proceedings (Vol. 398):* Cadwalladr, C., & Graham-Harrison, E. (2018). *Revealed: 50 million Facebook profiles harvested for Cambridge Analytica in major data breach.* https://www.theguardian.com/news/2018/mar/17/cambridge-analytica-facebook-influence-us-election

Camillo, M. (2017). Cyber risk and the changing role of insurance. *Journal of Cyber Policy*, 2(1), 53–63. DOI: 10.1080/23738871.2017.1296878

Cebula, J. J., & Young, L. R. (2010). A Taxonomy of Operational Cyber Security Risks. *Carnegie-Mellon Univ Pittsburgh Pa Software Engineering Inst*, (December), 1–47.

Cloudflare. (2024). *What is Mirai?*https://www.cloudflare.com/learning/ddos/glossary/mirai-botnet/

Craigen, D., Diakun-Thibault, N., & Purse, R. (2014). Defining Cybersecurity. *Technology Innovation Management Review*, 4(10), 13–21. DOI: 10.22215/timreview/835

Eling, M., & Schnell, W. (2016). What do we know about cyber risk and cyber risk insurance? *The Journal of Risk Finance*, 17(5), 474–491. DOI: 10.1108/JRF-09-2016-0122

ENISA. (2022). *ENISA threat landscape report 2018 : 15 top cyber- threats and trends.*https://op.europa.eu/en/publication-detail/-/publication/6373c334-574d - 11e9-a8ed-01aa75ed71a1/language-en

Flammini, F., Alcaraz, C., Bellini, E., Marrone, S., Lopez, J., & Bondavalli, A. (2024). Towards Trustworthy Autonomous Systems: Taxonomies and Future Perspectives. *IEEE Transactions on Emerging Topics in Computing, XX*(Xx), 1–13. DOI: 10.1109/TETC.2022.3227113

Frantti, T., & Korkiakoski, M. (2022). Security Controls for Smart Buildings with Shared Space. *2022 6th International Conference on Smart Grid and Smart Cities, ICSGSC 2022*, 156–165. DOI: 10.1109/ICSGSC56353.2022.9963114

Fruhlinger, J. (2022). *Stuxnet explained: The first known cyberweapon*. https://www.csoonline.com/article/562691/stuxnet-explained-the-first-known-cyberweapon.html

Gordon, L. A., Loeb, M. P., & Sohail, T. (2003). A framework for using insurance for cyber-risk management. *Communications of the ACM*, 46(3), 81–85. DOI: 10.1145/636772.636774

Hariharan, N. K. (2021). *Cyber-risk management: identification, prevention, and mitigation techniques. September 2020.*

Hart, S., Margheri, A., Paci, F., & Sassone, V. (2020). Riskio: A Serious Game for Cyber Security Awareness and Education. *Computers & Security*, 95, 101827. Advance online publication. DOI: 10.1016/j.cose.2020.101827

Howarth, F. (2014). The role of human error in successful security attacks. *IBM Security Intelligence Website*, 1–6. https://securityintelligence.com/the-role-of-human-error-in-successful-security-attacks/

IBM. (2024). *What is cyber risk management?*https://www.ibm.com/topics/cyber-risk-management

Johnson, A. M. (2009). Business and Security Executives Views of Information Security Investment Drivers: Results from a Delphi Study. *Journal of Information Privacy and Security*, 5(1), 3–27. DOI: 10.1080/15536548.2009.10855855

Kaspersky. (2019). What is Cyber Security? | Definition, Types, and User Protection | Kaspersky. In *Www.Kaspersky.Co.Uk* (p. Home/Resource Centre/Definitions). https://www.kaspersky.com.au/resource-center/definitions/what-is-cyber-security

Klimburg, A. (2012). *NATIONAL CYBER SECURITY FRAMEWORK MANUAL.*

Ligo, A. K., Kott, A., & Linkov, I. (2021). How to Measure Cyber-Resilience of a System with Autonomous Agents: Approaches and Challenges. *IEEE Engineering Management Review*, 49(2), 89–97. DOI: 10.1109/EMR.2021.3074288

Linkov, I., & Alexander Kott. (2018). Fundamental Concepts of Cyber Resilience: Introduction and Overview Motivation: Why Cyber Resilience? *Cyber Resilience of Systems and Networks.*

Lloyd, G. (2020). The business benefits of cyber security for SMEs. *Computer Fraud & Security*, 2020(2), 14–17. DOI: 10.1016/S1361-3723(20)30019-1

Loonam, J., Zwiegelaar, J., Kumar, V., & Booth, C. (2022). Cyber-Resiliency for Digital Enterprises: A Strategic Leadership Perspective. *IEEE Transactions on Engineering Management*, 69(6), 3757–3770. DOI: 10.1109/TEM.2020.2996175

ManageEngine. (2024). *PayPal users targeted in a phishing scam.*https://www.manageengine.com/log-management/phishing-attacks/paypal-phishing-email-scam.html

Marotta, A., Martinelli, F., Nanni, S., Orlando, A., & Yautsiukhin, A. (2017). Cyber-insurance survey. *Computer Science Review*, 24(December), 35–61. DOI: 10.1016/j.cosrev.2017.01.001

Miller, S., & Bossomaier, T. (2024). *Cybersecurity, Ethics, and Collective Responsibility.* Oxford University Press. DOI: 10.1093/oso/9780190058135.001.0001

Orlando, A. (2021). Cyber risk quantification: Investigating the role of cyber value at risk. *Risks*, 9(10), 184. Advance online publication. DOI: 10.3390/risks9100184

Orozco, J., Tarhini, A., Masa'deh, R., & Tarhini, T. (2015). A Framework of IS/ Business Alignment Management Practices to Improve the Design of IT Governance Architectures. *International Journal of Business and Management*, 10(4), 1–12. DOI: 10.5539/ijbm.v10n4p1

Pandagle, V. (2023). *Airbus Cyber Attack: Work of USDoD Hacker, Linked to Turkish Airlines Employee Account Hack.* CyberExpress. https://thecyberexpress.com/airbus-cyber-attack-usdod-turkish-airlines/

Pollock, T. (2017). *Reducing human error in cyber security using the Human Factors Analysis Classification System (HFACS).* https://digitalcommons.kennesaw.edu/ccerp%0Ahttp://digitalcommons.kennesaw.edu/ccerp/2017/research/2

Portman, R., & Carper, T. (2019). *How Equifax Neglected Cybersecurity and Suffered a Devastating Data Breach.*

Roege, P., Collier, Z., Chevardin, V., & Chouinard, P. (2017). Bridging the Gap from Cyber Security to Resilience. In *Resilience and Risk* (pp. 383–414). DOI: 10.1007/978-94-024-1123-2_14

Singh, J., Patel, C., & Chaudhary, N. K. (2024). Resilient Risk-Based Adaptive Authentication and Authorization (RAD-AA) Framework. *Lecture Notes in Electrical Engineering, 1075 LNEE*, 371–385. DOI: 10.1007/978-981-99-5091-1_27

Tam, T., Rao, A., & Hall, J. (2021). The good, the bad and the missing: A Narrative review of cyber-security implications for australian small businesses. In *Computers and Security* (Vol. 109, p. 102385). DOI: 10.1016/j.cose.2021.102385

Tressler, C. (2018). *Netflix phishing scam: Don't take the bait*. https://consumer.ftc.gov/consumer-alerts/2018/12/netflix-phishing-scam-dont-take-bait

Tunggal, A. T. (2024). *What is the WannaCry Ransomware Attack?*https://www.upguard.com/blog/wannacry#:~:text=WannaCry exploited a known vulnerability,months prior to the attack.

Verizon Business. (2024). 2024 Data Breach Investigations Report. *Verizon Business Journal*, 1–60. file:///C:/Users/Edward S. Forde/Downloads/rp_Verizon-DBIR-2014_en_xg.pdf

Vishwanath, A. (2022). *The weakest link How to Diagnose, Detect, and Defend Users from Phishing*. MIT Press., DOI: 10.7551/mitpress/14653.001.0001

Witman, P. D., & Mackelprang, S. (2022). The 2020 Twitter Hack – So Many Lessons to Be Learned. *Journal of Cybersecurity Education. Research and Practice*, 2021(2). Advance online publication. DOI: 10.62915/2472-2707.1089

ADDITIONAL READING

Ali, M. (2021). *Remote Work and Sustainable Changes for the Future of Global Business.* IGI Global. https://www.igi-global.com/book/remote-work-sustainable-changes-future/264375

Ali, M. (2022). *Future Role of Sustainable Innovative Technologies in Crisis Management.* IGI Global. https://www.igi-global.com/book/future-role-sustainable-innovative-technologies/281281

Ali, M. (2023). *Shifting Paradigms in the Rapidly Developing Global Digital Ecosystem: A GCC Perspective.* In Digital Entrepreneurship and Co-Creating Value Through Digital Encounters (pp. 145-166). IGI Global. https://www.igi-global.com/chapter/shifting-paradigms-in-the-rapidly-developing-global-digital-ecosystem/323525

Ali, M. (2023). T*axonomy of Industry 4.0 Technologies in Digital Entrepreneurship and Co-Creating Value*. In *Digital Entrepreneurship and Co-Creating Value Through Digital Encounters* (pp. 24–55). IGI Global., https://www.igi-global.com/chapter/taxonomy-of-industry-40-technologies-in-digital-entrepreneurship-and-co-creating-value/323520 DOI: 10.4018/978-1-6684-7416-7.ch002

Ali, M., & Wood-Harper, T. (2021). *Fostering Communication and Learning with Underutilized Technologies in Higher Education.* IGI Global. https://www.igi-global.com/book/fostering-communication-learning-underutilized-technologies/244593

Ali, M., Wood-Harper, T., & Kutar, M. (2023). Multi-Perspectives of Contemporary Digital Transformation Models of Complex Innovation Management. In *Digital Entrepreneurship and Co-Creating Value Through Digital Encounters* (pp. 79–96). IGI Global., https://www.igi-global.com/chapter/multi-perspectives-of-contemporary-digital-transformation-models-of-complex-innovation-management/323522 DOI: 10.4018/978-1-6684-7416-7.ch004

Ali, M. B. (2021). Internet of Things (IoT) to Foster Communication and Information Sharing: A Case of UK Higher Education. In Ali, M. B., & Wood-Harper, T. (Eds.), *Fostering Communication and Learning With Underutilized Technologies in Higher Education* (pp. 1–20). IGI Global., https://www.igi-global.com/chapter/internet-of-things-iot-to-foster-communication-and-information-sharing/262718/ DOI: 10.4018/978-1-7998-4846-2.ch001

Ali, M. B., & Wood-Harper, T. (2022). Artificial Intelligence (AI) as a Decision-Making Tool to Control Crisis Situations. In *Future Role of Sustainable Innovative Technologies in Crisis Management*. IGI Global., https://www.igi-global.com/chapter/artificial-intelligence-ai-as-a-decision-making-tool-to-control-crisis-situations/298931 DOI: 10.4018/978-1-7998-9815-3.ch006

Ali, M. B., Wood-Harper, T., & Ramlogan, R. (2020). A Framework Strategy to Overcome Trust Issues on Cloud Computing Adoption in Higher Education. In Modern Principles, Practices, and Algorithms for Cloud Security (pp. 162-183). IGI Global. https://www.igi-global.com/chapter/a-framework-strategy-to-overcome-trust-issues-on-cloud-computing-adoption-in-higher-education/238907/

Chapter 11
Digital Supply Chain Management in Transformation in Business Economic Development, Success, and Risk Factors:
Concept on Performance, Order, and Strategic Management

Zuber Peermohammed Shaikh
Savitribai Phule Pune University, India

ABSTRACT

Digital supply chain is a supply chain whose foundation is built on web-enabled capabilities. Many supply chains use a mix of paper-based and IT-enabled processes. A true digital supply chain goes far beyond this hybrid model to fully capitalize on connectivity, system integration and the information-producing capabilities of smart components. The ultimate goal of the digital supply chain is to enable insights for increased efficiencies, facilitating greater profits. Companies with a digital supply chain are better able to move resources, assets, people and inventory to where they are needed at any given time in order to reduce costs by responding proactively to transportation and manufacturing risks. The potential payoffs of a fully realized digital supply chain include savings in every area, from resources, time, and money to a reduced environmental footprint. These Review Chapter focuses on right tool

DOI: 10.4018/979-8-3373-0086-3.ch011

Copyright © 2025, IGI Global. Copying or distributing in print or electronic forms without written permission of IGI Global is prohibited.

that can help you to automate the transition to a digital supply chain.

INTRODUCTION

Digital Supply Chain Management

To better understand digital supply chains, it will be helpful to first examine traditional supply chains. In a traditional supply chain, items travel linearly. Each link in the supply chain is dependent on the success of the functions completed in the previous link. While this linear model seems simple enough, its success is ultimately determined by how well each step in this process is performed. Most of the time, when an error does occur at one stage in the chain, discovering that mistake can take days or weeks. In this model, a single error could result in missed deadlines and unhappy customers. A digital supply chain is a set of processes that use advanced digital technologies so that businesses can make better decisions about supplies they need, the demand for their products, and all of the relationships in between.

Where traditional supply chains function in a linear fashion, digital supply chains function more like networks. And unlike traditional supply chains, digital supply chains can provide real-time visibility into the performance of each step along the chain. This visibility into supplier performance and customer needs allows a business to develop more relationships with more suppliers, and better protects the company against disruptions when they occur. Digital supply chains work by integrating internal systems and data with external information, both structured and unstructured. Using new technologies to collect, monitor, and analyse data, a digital supply chain can help you make predictions and recommend actions in real-time.

However, integrating your legacy supply chain management technologies can be a complicated task. It will involve mining data from business processes, as well as retooling your equipment using sensors and monitors so that you can audit manufacturing or logistics processes. Configuring your equipment is just one aspect of digitizing your supply chain. Once you have the sensors and monitors in place (typically using Internet of Things (IoT) technology, you'll need advanced analytics to consume all that data you produce and to use it to make predictions about outcomes. The complexity of this data will only grow as the number of suppliers, parts, distributors, and customers that you have grows. This is where "digital twin" technology can help. A digital twin is a virtual model of a physical product or process. It allows a business to make a digital copy of its supply chain and use that copy to model potential scenarios.

With machine learning algorithms, this technology uses predictive modelling and makes recommendations on how businesses should respond to changing conditions. Digitizing your supply chain will transform your business into a more responsive organization, one that allows you to predict and prescribe actions to take before disruptions occur. Now, let's take a closer look at some of the other benefits you can expect from a digital supply chain. Despite having great potential, digital technologies are not applied in all companies to the same extent and have different levels of effectiveness due to varying levels of development and alignment. This is demonstrated in the hype cycle, which is developed by Gartner annually. Thus, in 2019, the main trends and driving forces behind the changes in operations and business models are presented by blockchain, quantum computing, augmented analytics and artificial intelligence. At the same time, at a company level, the following dynamics are observed. According to a survey of 4,600 business leaders from 42 countries, which was conducted by Dell company, there are five distinct areas in which companies invest in digital transformation: cybersecurity, Internet of Things, multi-cloud environment, artificial intelligence, compute centric approach. (Farahani P, 2015b)

LITERATURE REVIEW

Current Context of Research on Supply Chain Digitalization

The business models of some companies (e.g. Google, Amazon, Alibaba, Airbnb, Uber) are fundamentally built on digital technologies. Other companies, whether they have existed for five, ten, twenty or even one hundred years, are forced to transform and embrace digital technologies in order to compete. This process has various names such as digitization, digitalization or digital transformation. We will now define these terms in detail. Digitization is the process of creating digital versions of analogue/physical things such as paper documents, microfilm images, photographs, sounds, and more. Thus, it is simply converting something non-digital (other examples include signals, health records, location data, identity cards, etc.) into a digital format which can then be used by a computing system for numerous possible purposes. As a result, we are getting continuous information flows in a digital form, leading to the acceleration and improvement of operations accuracy and a reduction in the staff required. The digitization creates the ground for operations automation and digitalization.

Digitalization means adding digitality to interactions, communications, business functions and business models, which often leads to a mix of digital and physical, such as in omni-channel customer service, integrated marketing or smart manufacturing with a mix of autonomous, semi-autonomous and manual operations. Thus, digitalization is the improvement of functions and business processes with digital technologies and digital data. The basis for digital processes is the use of detailed analytics for the managing of company operations. We can talk about the digitalization of production or the digitalization of marketing, which means that many functions and operations will be carried out automatically without human participation. Digitalization lays the groundwork for transition to digital business. Digital transformation is a transition to digital business: a complex transformation of business activities, processes, models and employees' competences to fully exploit digital opportunities. Very often, digital transformation leads to the emergence of new markets, new consumers, and a new business. Generally speaking, digitalization and digital transformation are aimed at achieving the following objectives: Use of information in the digital form, Sensory interaction with devices, Managing customer experience, Providing cybersecurity, Automation of operations and decision-making, Usage of external and internal social networks.

A Digital Supply Chain (DSC) is a smart, value-driven, efficient process to generate new forms of revenue and business value for organizations and leverage new approaches with novel technological and analytical methods. DSC is not about whether goods and services are digital or physical; it is about how supply chain processes are managed with a wide variety of innovative technologies, e.g. unmanned aerial vehicles, cloud computing, and Internet of Things, among others. (Gimpel, Henner,2015)

BACKGROUND

Digital Technologies in Supply Chain Management

In supply chain optimization, a wide range of instruments of varying complexity and costs are employed, for instance, software products for efficient supply chain design, providing systemic integration, such as SAP, Oracle etc. Supply chain management traditionally applies scenario and simulation modelling, operations research, production and inventory control. It is clear that the greatest efficiency is achieved through the joint application of digital and information systems. For example, electronic procurement and automated vendor search are instruments that use digital technologies and Internet applications in combination with ERP systems, which allow the automation of both internal and global business processes. Procurement specialists worldwide can easily share information to simplify the process and to save time and money without a negative impact on product quality and standards.

The variety of technologies can be grouped into three large areas: data analytics and visualization technologies; technologies for operations automation and equipment management; technologies providing communications between supply chain participants. The key objective is to efficiently generate, collect, store and analyse information on each product design and composition, specifics of use, location, disassembly capabilities, various ways of recycling, etc. All this is necessary to create multiple product lifecycles in the later stages after initial use. Previously, the lack of up-to-date information in all parts of the chain did not allow effective closed loop supply chains, but now the spread of digital technologies ensures the development of the closed product life cycle. Thus, cyberphysical systems allow access to information on products in all stages of production and use, impact on the environment of all processes and product handling. This reduces the information asymmetry as producers reveal information on products' components and materials while consumers' use of the product is also monitored.

Sensors track down, in real time, the exact location of the product at the end of its use. Big Data analytics is transferred to companies utilizing used products as core production resources. The optimization of primary resources' demand and supply according to waste and recyclables amounts is revolutionized with digital platforms, which form the markets for used products, with application of IoT sensors. These sensors provide data on the products' composition and indicate possibilities for their further application. As a result, recycled resources are getting cheaper and more price competitive than primary resources and materials. Thus, digital markets for recycling products and waste are emerging.

Key processes, consolidating products, components, materials and resources within the supply chain, enable the extension of the product life cycle, by reusing, repairing and refurbishing a used product to achieve the quality of a new product, or save resources, through processing and extrusion of new materials, energy and fertilizers. It should be noted that digital technologies have varying degrees of relevance for individual processes generating reverse flows. It represents the product life cycle in phases: from extraction of raw materials and energy resources necessary for production, to its disposal at end of use. Each process in the reverse flow returns a product to a certain life cycle stage, e.g. reprocessing returns the material flow to Stage 2 - Manufacturing of details and components. Here, the processes of energy generation by burning waste and its disposal do not participate in the closed loop supply chains, as they are not intended to conserve resources inside the supply chain and so should be minimized. (Hoberg P, 2015)

Table 1. Digital technologies in supply chain management

Goal	Functions	Information and automation systems and technologies	Digital technologies
Data analysis and visualization	Navigation of business processes, electronic catalogues data unification, integration of information systems, monitoring supply chain, real time planning of enterprise activity, administration of product data and events, data processing, predictive analytics	SCOR, ISO и CALS-standards, ERP, PIM, SCEM, TMS, SCMo, Real-time Factory Scheduling	Big Data, artificial intelligence, cloud computing and storage, quantum computing, S&OP platforms, smart warehouse, wearables
Communication between supply chain participants	Automated supplier search, electronic procurement, e - commerce, supply chain processes synchronization, supply chain transparency, communication between supply chain elements	CRM, SRM, CSRP, AMS, Single Window, EDI, EANCOM, EDIFACT, digital signiture	Automated e-sourcing, omni-channel Smart Fulfilment Solution, blockchain, social media marketing, feedback loop, social networks, industrial cloud
Automation of processes and asset management	Flexible automation of production, digital production processes, digital product quality, digital reverse engineering, virtual analogues for physical products/production	Robots, automatic production lines, WMS, Flexible Factory automation, RFID	Digital twins, 3D-seal, sensors, driverless vehicles mixed and augmented reality, industrial IoT, additive manufacturing, intelligent robots

We will now consider how technologies are used in closed loop supply chains, focusing both on direct and reverse material, components and goods flows. These processes, including the activities related to the product or its post-sale maintenance, with the aim of optimizing, improving service efficiency, reducing costs and saving environmental resources, are known as reverse logistics.

METHODOLOGY

Trends in Supply Chain Management

Industry 4.0 creates a disruption and requires companies to rethink the way they design their supply chain. Several technologies have emerged that are altering traditional ways of working. On top of this, mega trends and customer expectations change the game. Besides the need to adapt, supply chains also have the opportunity to reach the next horizon of operational effectiveness, to leverage emerging digital supply chain business models, and to transform the company into a digital supply chain. Several mega trends have a heavy influence on supply chain management: there is a continuing growth of the rural areas worldwide, with wealth shifting into regions that have not been served before. Pressure to reduce carbon emissions as well as regulations of traffic for socioeconomic reasons add to the challenges that logistics are facing. But changing demographics also lead to reduced labour availability as well as increasing ergonomic requirements that arise as the workforce age increases. At the same time customer expectations are growing: the online trend of the last years has led to increasing service expectations combined with a much stronger granularization of orders. There is also a very definite trend towards further individualization and customization that drives the strong growth of and constant changes in the SKU portfolio. The online-enabled transparency and easy access to a multitude of options regarding where to shop and what to buy drives the competition of supply chains. To build on these trends and cope with the changed requirements, supply chains need to become much faster, more granular, and much more precise. (Rutkowsky, S.,2015)

Figure 1. Digital supply chain transformation

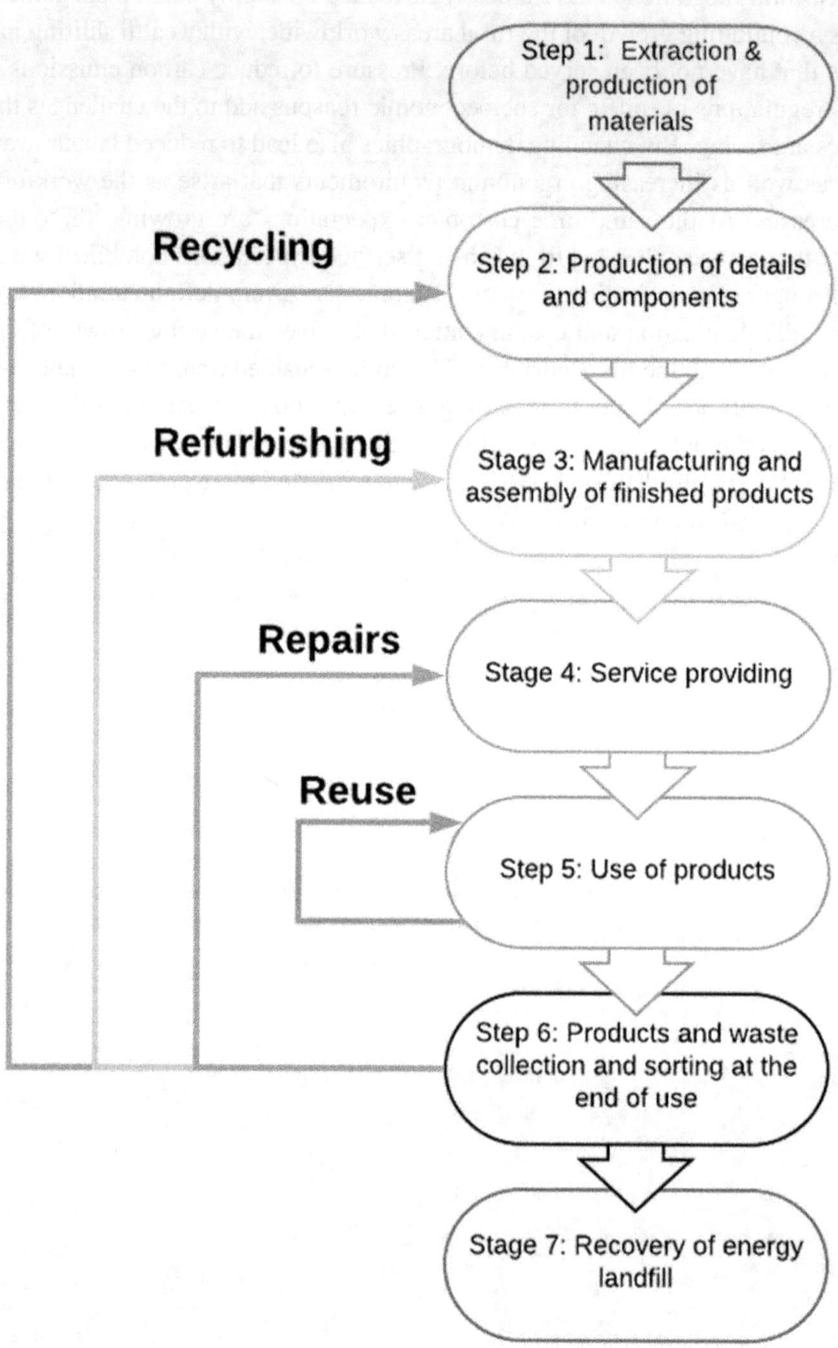

Steps Involved in Digital Supply Chain Transformation

Stage 1: Consumption and use of primary materials is minimized by Industry 4.0 technologies, with the flagship being 3D-printing, which not only allows the personalization of products and the reduction of consumption but also the recycling of 3D waste and conversion back into usable filament.
Stage 2: Manufacturing of elements and components includes the selection of materials that are most suitable for future recycling, including biodegradables. Also, any eco-design product should have a long life cycle and, where applicable, the possibility to repair or refurbish it. Big Data and high-performance computing, vendor search automation and digital twins provide a vast range of opportunities to advance eco-design.
Stage 3: Products are designed to allow future automated disassembly with minimal manual labour. Particular attention is paid to the labelling and certification of individual items for future recycling. Thus, Michelin fit IoT sensors directly into their tyres to allow real time monitoring of tyres. When critical wear levels are reached, vehicles are recalled to the factory for restoration of tyres, with the reconstruction costs being around half the cost of raw materials required to manufacture a new product.
Stage 4: Offering services and goods for temporary use is actively developing as an alternative to goods ownership. Mass customization prevails over mass standardization, and the permanent improvement of products for customer requirements is implemented through feedback loops and predictive analytics systems. For example, Hello Tractor company from Nigeria uses mobile technology to provide 250,000 small farmers with access to tractors at a convenient time, improving their food security and optimizing costs. Instead of buying and maintaining the tractor, a farmer rents it. In addition, tractors are equipped with M2M technology to share information about the vehicle and its efficiency, which in turn maximizes its use and extends the life of the tractor.
Stage 5: In the process of use, products are controlled by manufacturers, and when exhausted, or broken, or obsolete, they are effectively disposed of in the most eco-friendly way. The use of automation technologies and predictive analytics is extremely relevant at this stage. Thus, a robot for the disassembly of the Apple iPhone has 29 hands and is able to decompound a used iPhone in 11 seconds and divide its components into useful materials. To date, Apple has extracted 61 million pounds of materials that can be used in future products, including 2,204 pounds of gold, worth 40 million dollars.
Stage 6: The collecting and sorting of waste and used products is highly effective with IoT, feedback platforms and Big Data. Location, quality and product ownership monitoring as well as defining actors responsible for dis-

posal are extremely important. For instance, in the U.S. the cloud-based Big Data analytics platform Rubicon connects waste producers with a network of independent waste carriers in 50 U.S. and Canadian states, as well as in 18 other countries. This provides higher recycling rates, a tailored approach to waste reuse, optimized transport routes and detailed analysis of waste data (Yang, M.,2021)

RESULTS

Importance of Digital Supply Chains

Unlike a traditional supply chain, a digital supply chain is one that functions in real-time, is dynamic, and can adapt to changing circumstances. Digital supply chains integrate information from information technology (IT) systems and operational technology (OT) systems to optimize profit and service levels. They also allow companies to anticipate issues and then respond without much preplanning. Here are some of the other advantages to a digital supply chain model:

Digital Supply Chains Are Faster

New approaches to product distribution in the digital supply chain can reduce the delivery time for many products to just a few hours. Using advanced forecasting approaches such as predictive analysis, digital supply chains provide much more precise forecasts of customer demand. As opposed to monthly forecasting, digital supply chains carry out weekly and sometimes daily forecasting for fast-moving products. One example of this advantage is Amazon's "predictive shipping" model, which will ship products before a customer even places an order. After the order is placed, it will be matched with a shipment that is already in transit, which is then rerouted to the exact customer destination.

Digital Supply Chains Are More Flexible

Real-time supply chain planning means that businesses can react more flexibly to changing demands or supply situations. By minimizing planning cycles, digital supply chains enable the planning process to become more continuous and more responsive to changing requirements or constraints.

Digital Supply Chains Are More Granular

As the demand for more individualized products rise, there is a strong push toward micro-segmentation and mass customization. Digital supply chains allow businesses to manage customers in much more granular clusters, and also allow customers to select offerings that fit their needs exactly. For example, consider drone delivery, and the potential for individualizing the customer experience at all stages of the supply chain.

Digital Supply Chains Are More Accurate

Digital supply chains provide real-time, end-to-end transparency throughout the supply chain. The information produced ranges from top-level KPIs to granular process data, and this range provides a joining information basis for all levels of seniority and stakeholders along each function in the supply chain.

Digital Supply Chains Are More Efficient

Automating both physical tasks and planning means a boost in efficiency along the supply chain. For example, in a digital supply chain, robots handle the material along the warehouse process, from receiving and unloading, to putting away materials, to picking, packing, and shipping. All that said, because a digital supply chain leverages new technologies and connects systems that were never meant to be connected to the Internet, it can also introduce new risk to your business. (Yukselturk, E.,2018)

DISCUSSION

The Risks of Digital Supply Chains

When determining the potential risks associated with digital supply chains, one immediate concern are the potential security issues associated with the Internet of Things (IoT). In general, supply chain security is something that should be at the forefront of your supply chain risk management program. IoT sensors can monitor factors such as the temperature of a machine, its physical location, or its energy consumption. An increase in any of these factors could lead to a malfunction or failure, and accurate monitoring lets maintenance teams fix any potential issues before they become critical. The increased connectivity necessitated by this level of monitoring means that risk can propagate throughout the supply chain network all the way through to (or from) your customers. A digital supply chain gives malicious actors more opportunities to corrupt or disrupt machine processes along each step of the supply chain. At the same time, upgrading your supply chain will inevitably expose your business to a degree of financial risk, as it will require a hefty capital investment. Deciding whether the benefits of a digital supply chain are worth the financial risk will be up to you. Ultimately, for most organizations, the benefits will outweigh the risks.

Figure 2. Supply chain management applications

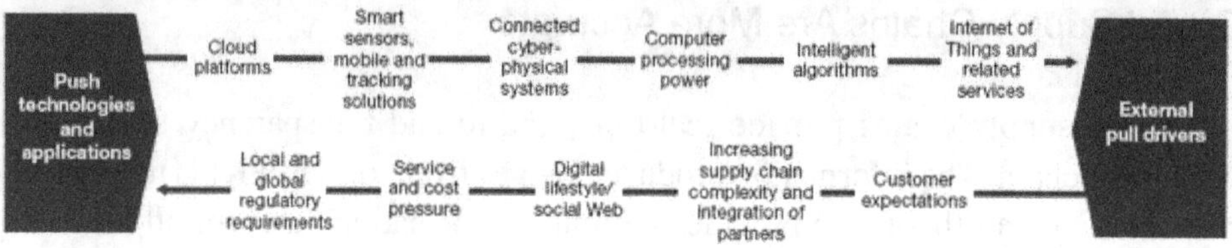

Increasing operational efficiency leveraging Supply Chain 4.0: Supply Chain 4.0 will impact all areas in supply chain management. We have developed the McKinsey Digital Supply Chain Compass (see figure on next page) to structure the main Supply Chain 4.0 improvement levers and to map them to six main value drivers. In the end, the improvements enable a step change in service, cost, capital, and agility. (Zeng, J.,2020)

Physical Flow

Logistics will take a huge step change through better connectivity, advanced analytics, additive manufacturing, and advanced automation. For example, as warehouses are being automated, we will see a significantly increasing amount of autonomous and smart vehicles, and 3-D printing changes warehousing and inventory management strategies completely. The next generation of touch, voice, and graphical user interfaces and their quick proliferation via consumer devices facilitates a much better integration of machines in almost any process in warehousing operations. For example, the breakthrough of optical head mounted displays, such as Google Glass, enables location-based instructions to workers, giving guidance for the picking process. Advanced robotics solutions have emerged for the improved picking of cases and single pieces, and the use of exoskeletons (that emulate the human physiology and can support straining manual movements) will have a major impact on warehouse productivity. In total, warehouse automations become much more holistic, with some warehouses being fully linked to production loading points, so that the entire process is carried out without manual intervention.

Autonomous and smart vehicles will lead to significant operating cost reduction in transportation and product handling and at the same time provide benefits regarding lead times and lower environmental costs. The use of self-guided vehicles in controlled environments (e.g., mines) or on-premises solutions (e.g., trains) as well as AGVs in warehouse environments are already operational and will further grow significantly in the near future. Autonomous trucks for use on public streets, however, are just being piloted in Europe and North America with promising results so far. Besides the automation of warehouse processes, additive manufacturing will also have a significant impact on physical flows in the supply chain. For example, 3-D printing has become much more relevant for a broad range of business applications, such as local production of slowly moving spare parts or tools. This development is driven by an expanding range of printing materials, rapidly declining prices for the printers, and increased precision and quality. By now, the first production facilities that operate exclusively with 3-D printers have been established.(Alan Long; 2009)

Performance Management

Performance management is indeed changing tremendously. Whereas in the past, the generation of KPI dashboards was a major task and KPIs were only available at aggregated levels, now granular data is available in real time from internal and external sources. This moves the performance management process from a regular, often monthly process to an operational process aimed at exception handling and continuous improvement. For example, planners can be pointed to critical supply chain disruptions and further supported by an automatic handling of minor exceptions or potential solutions for the larger ones. Automated root cause analyses are one approach for exception handling. The performance management system is able to identify the root causes of an exception by either comparing it to a predefined set of underlying indicators or by conducting big data analyses, leveraging data mining and machine learning techniques. Based on the identified root cause, the system will automatically trigger countermeasures, such as activating a replenishment order or changing parameter settings in the planning systems, such as safety stocks.

Order Management

Two examples of how order management is improved are no-touch order processing and real-time replanning, which lead to lower costs through automation of efforts, higher reliability due to granular feedback, and superior customer experience through immediate and reliable responses. No-touch order processing is the logical next step after implementing a reliable available to- promise (ATP) process. Through an integration of the ordering systems, linking to ATP, and through an enrichment with order rules, the system can be used to fully automate the ordering process. The goal is to have a complete "no-touch" process, where no manual intervention is required between order intake and order confirmation. Very stringent order rules that have to be followed, and continuously updated master data are prerequisites. Real-time replanning enables order date confirmations through instantaneous, in-memory replanning of the production schedule and the replenishment in consideration of all constraints. Therefore, the supply chain setup is always up to date, leading to a very reliable planning base. On top, additional services can be offered to the customers, e.g., a faster lead time for a certain premium fee, so the customer can see the feasibility and the updated dates at a glance.

Collaboration

The supply chain cloud forms the next level of collaboration in the supply chain. Supply chain clouds are joint supply chain platforms between customers, the company, and suppliers, providing either a shared logistics infrastructure or even joint planning solutions. Especially in noncompetitive relationships, partners can decide to tackle supply chain tasks together to save admin costs, and also to leverage best practices and learn from each other. Another major field within collaboration is the end-to-end/multitier connectivity. Where some automotive companies have already started collaborating throughout the entire value chain (e.g., from the cow farmer to the finished leather seat in the car), other companies still need to close this gap. The collaboration along the value chain allows for overall much lower inventories through an exchange of reliable planning data, a step change in lead time reduction through instantaneous information provision throughout the entire chain, and an early-warning system and the ability to react fast to disruptions anywhere.

Supply Chain Strategy

Following the need for further individualization and customization of the supply chain, supply chain setups adopt many more segments. To excel in this setting, supply chains need to master "microsegmentation." The granularization of the supply chain into hundreds of individual supply chain segments based on customer requirements and own capabilities designed in a dynamic, big data approach allows to mass-customize supply chain offerings. Tailored products provide optimal value for the customer and help minimize costs and inventory in the supply chain. (J.F.Moore.; 1993)

IMPLICATIONS STRATEGY AND INTEGRATION CHALLENGES

Digital Waste and Supply Chain Management

Digital waste prevents supply chains from leveraging the potential of Supply Chain 4.0 In today's supply chains many sources of digital waste can be found (in addition to the existing waste) that prevent the potential of Supply Chain 4.0. It is crucial to understand the sources of waste and develop solutions to reduce/avoid it in the future state. The sources of digital waste can be classified in three types:

Data Capturing and Management

Often, available data is handled manually (data collection in a system, paper-based data handling, etc.) and not updated regularly, e.g., master data on supplier lead time that is entered once (sometimes even only dummy numbers) and then remains unchanged for years. Another example in warehousing is advanced shipping notifications, which are received but not used to optimize the inbound process. On top of these examples, it is typically not clear which additional data could be leveraged to improve processes, e.g., sensing of supply disruptions – if the lead time of a supplier is continuously increasing, a warning should be sent out to make planners aware of the situation and enable them to mitigate supply disruptions at an early stage. In current systems, this signal will not be recognized and will lead to a lower supplier service level reported at the end of the month. If the worst comes to the worst, the issue will cause trouble in the assembly line replenishment and operational problems.

Integrated Process Optimization

Many companies have started to implement an integrated planning process, but very often this is still done in silos and not all information is leveraged to achieve the best planning result possible. In addition, it can frequently be observed that automatically determined planning or statistical forecast data is manually overwritten by planners. Especially for parts moving at medium or high speed, the manual overwrites usually have a negative impact on the forecasting accuracy. Beside the intracompany optimization, the process optimization between companies has not been fully leveraged yet and improvement potentials created by increased transparency are not realized. To get to the advanced level of integrated process optimization, the organizational setup, governance, processes, and incentives need to be aligned within and between partners in the supply chain.

Physical Process Execution of Humans and Machines

Nowadays, warehousing, assembly line replenishment, transport management, etc. is often done based on gut feeling, but not leveraging available data, e.g., to improve pick paths in the warehouse. Warehouse operations are still managed in batches of one to two hours, not allowing the real-time allocation of new orders and dynamic routing. Also, opportunities arising from new devices, such as wearables (e.g., Google Glass) or exoskeletons, are not leveraged. Planning The future supply chain planning will largely benefit from big data and advanced analytics as well as from the automation of knowledge work. Two example levers with significant impact are "predictive analytics in demand planning" and "closed-loop planning." Predictive analytics in demand planning analyses hundreds to thousands of internal as well as external demand influencing variables (e.g., weather, trends from social networks, sensor data) with Bayesian network and machine learning approaches to uncover and model the complex relationships and derive an accurate and granular demand plan. These new technologies enable a significant improvement of demand forecast accuracy, often reducing the forecasting error by 30 to 50 percent. Also, the days of a "single truth" regarding the forecasting numbers are over – these advanced algorithms provide probability distributions of the expected demand volume rather than a single forecast number.

This allows for targeted discussions, including upside potential and downside risks in the S&OPs, and advanced inventory management approaches. Widely automated and fully integrated closed-loop demand and supply planning breaks the traditional boundaries between the different planning steps and transforms planning into a flexible, continuous process. Instead of using fixed safety stocks, each replenishment planning considers the expected demand probability distribution and replenishes to fulfil a certain service level – the resulting implicit safety stocks are therefore different with every single reorder. Another powerful feature of closed-loop planning is the integration of pricing decisions with the demand and supply planning; depending on the stock levels, expected demand, and capability to replenish, prices can be dynamically adapted to optimize the overall profit made and minimize inventories at the same time. (Tijan, E.,2019)

Significance of Creating a Digital Supply Chain

When it is time for your business to make the transition to a digital supply chain, always remember this question: how can we use the data we generate to solve problems? Before you begin creating your own digital supply chain, there are some factors you'll want to consider:

Business drivers. Before you begin to digitize your supply chain, recognize the drivers behind this decision. What are your main goals that you would like to accomplish, and how can a digital supply chain help you reach those goals?

Fear of technology. Traditional supply chains typically employ an "if it ain't broke, don't fix it" mindset. Digitizing your supply chain will inevitably introduce new digital technology to your day-to-day business operations, which might make some decision-makers wary. The alternative, however, is to be left behind by your competitors, who are likely already investigating how to take their own supply chain online.

Metrics for success. Determine what tangible goals you'd like to achieve. For instance, maybe you'd like to cut time-to-market cycles, or add the ability to continually monitor suppliers for incidents that could increase risk.

Team members. Appoint team members who will be responsible for digitizing your supply chain based on their strengths. You'll need to include employees or consultants with experience in IoT, big data, blockchain, automation, security, and integration. You should also find an executive sponsor and a develop cross-departmental group so that you have insight into every link in your supply chain to guide your technology specialists. (Mitroff, I.I. 2019)

Application and Vision of the Future State

The digitization of the supply chain enables companies to address the new requirements of the customers, the challenges on the supply side as well as the remaining expectations in efficiency improvement. **Digitization brings about a Supply Chain 4.0, which will be…**

Faster: New approaches of product distribution reduce the delivery time of high runners to few hours. The basis for these services is built by advanced forecasting approaches, e.g., predictive analytics of internal (e.g., demand) and external (e.g., market trends, weather, school vacation, construction indices) data as well as machine status data for spare-parts demand and provides a much more precise forecast of customer demand. Forecasts are not carried out on a monthly basis, but weekly, and for the very fast-moving products even every day. In the future we will see "predictive shipping," for which Amazon holds a patent – products are shipped before the customer places an order. The customer order is later on matched with a shipment that is already in the logistics network (being transported towards the customer region) and the shipment is rerouted to the exact customer destination.

Flexible: Ad hoc and real-time planning allows a flexible reaction to changing demand or supply situations. Planning cycles and frozen periods are minimized and planning becomes a continuous process that is able to react dynamically to changing requirements or constraints (e.g., real-time production capacity feedback from machines). Once the products are sent, increased flexibility in the delivery processes allows customers to reroute shipments to the most convenient destination. New business models, such as Supply Chain as a Service for supply chain planning functions or transport management, increase the flexibility in the supply chain organization. Supply chain can be bought as a service and paid for on a by-usage basis instead of having the resources and capabilities in-house. The specialization and focus of service providers allow them to create economies of scale as well as economies of scope and also attractive outsourcing opportunities. For example, we will see an "Uberization" of transport: crowd-sourced, flexible transport capacity, which will lead to a significant increase in agility in distribution networks.

Granular: The demand of customers for more and more individualized products is continuously increasing. That gives a strong push towards microsegmentation, and mass customization ideas will finally be implemented. Customers are managed in much more granular clusters and a broad spectrum of suited products will be offered. This enables customers to select one of multiple "logistics menus" that exactly fits their need. New transport concepts, such as drone delivery, allow companies to manage the last mile efficiently for single and high-value dense packages.

Accurate: The next generation of performance management systems provides real-time, end-to-end transparency throughout the supply chain. The span of information reaches from synthesized top-level KPIs, such as overall service level, to very granular process data, such as the exact position of trucks in the network. This range of data provides a joint information basis for all levels of seniority and functions in the supply chain. The integration of data of suppliers, service providers, etc. in a "supply chain cloud" ensures that all stakeholders steer and decide based on the same facts. In digital performance management systems, clean-sheet models for warehousing, transport, or inventory are used to set targets automatically. To keep the aspiration of targets also in case of supply chain disruptions, systems will automatically adjust targets that cannot be achieved anymore to a realistic aspiration level. We will see performance management systems that "learn" to automatically identify risks or exceptions and will change supply chain parameters in a closed-loop learning approach to mitigate them. That enables the automatic performance management control tower to handle a broad spectrum of exceptions without human involvement and to only leverage the human planner for the disruptive events/new events – with this, a supply chain is continuously developing towards its efficient frontier. **Efficient:** Efficiency in the supply chain is boosted by the automation of both physical tasks and planning. Robots handle the material (pallets/boxes as well as single pieces) completely automatically along the warehouse process – from receiving/unloading to putting away to pick, pack, and ship. Autonomous trucks transport the products within the network. To optimize truck utilization and increase transport flexibility, cross-company transport optimization is applied to share capacities between companies. The network setup itself is continuously optimized to ensure an optimal fit to business requirements. To create an ideal workload in the supply chain, various transparency and dynamic planning approaches are leveraged to drive advanced demand shaping activities (e.g., special offers for delivery time slots with low truck utilization). (Oliver, M., 2000 and Partala, J. 2018)

CONCLUSION AND FUTURE PROSPECTS

Now let's take a look at the steps you should take when creating a digital supply chain that's secure, and successful, for your business.

Start with the Basics: First, identify existing problems with your current supply chain setup. It's important that you figure out whether you need to make any process improvements before you add new technology. Think about what links in your supply chain will be the easiest to digitize and start there. Remember, your existing supply chain will still need to function while you're transitioning to a digital model, so it's important that you create a plan that assures you can continue business operations during the shift.
Assimilate Disparate Functions: Rather than viewing discrete functions such as procurement and manufacturing as disparate elements, focus on how you will achieve desired business outcomes with various stakeholders. During this step, you might want to consider deploying a survey to collect information about needs and assess awareness. A more holistic approach to digitizing your supply chain will assure that there are no weak links. Think about how you can bring everything together to accomplish the business goals that you'll set out in the next step.

REFERENCES

Farahani P, (2015b) A vision on a digital supply chain management. 360 Bus Transform J.

Gimpel, H., & Röglinger, M. (2015). Digital transformation: changes and chances–insights based on an empirical study.

Hoberg, P. (2015). *Research Report: skills for digital transformation.* SAP SE and Technical University of Munich.

Long, A. (2009). Port Community systems. *World Customs Journal*, 3(1). Advance online publication. DOI: 10.55596/001c.91356

Mitroff, I. I. (2019). Pushing back on pervasive technology. *MIT Sloan Management Review*.

Moore, J. F. (1993, May-June). Predators and Prey. *Harvard Business Review*, 71(3), 75–86. PMID: 10126156

Oliver, M. (2000). An introduction to the evaluation of learning technology. *Journal of Educational Technology & Society*, 3(4), 20–30.

Partala, J. (2018). Provably Secure Covert Communication on Blockchain. *Cryptography*, 2(2), 18. DOI: 10.3390/cryptography2030018

Rutkowsky, S., I. Peteresen, and F. Klötzke. "Digital Supply Chains: Increasingly Critical for Competitive Edge." European AT Kearney/WHU Logistics Study (2015): 18.

Tijan, E., Aksentijević, S., Ivanić, K., & Jardas, M. (2019). Blockchain Technology Implementation in Logistics. *Sustainability (Basel)*, 11(11), 1185. DOI: 10.3390/su11041185

Yang, M., Fu, M., & Zhang, Z. (2021). The adoption of digital technologies in supply chains: Drivers, process and impact. *Technological Forecasting and Social Change*, 169, 120795. DOI: 10.1016/j.techfore.2021.120795

Yukselturk, E., Altıok, S., & Başer, Z. (2018). Using game-based learning with kinect technology in foreign language education course. *Journal of Educational Technology & Society*, 21(3), 159–173.

Zeng, J., Parks, S., & Shang, J. (2020). To learn scientifically, effectively, and enjoyably: A review of educational games. *Human Behavior and Emerging Technologies*, 2(2), 186–195. DOI: 10.1002/hbe2.188

ADDITIONAL READING

Ali, M. (2021). *Remote Work and Sustainable Changes for the Future of Global Business.* IGI Global. https://www.igi-global.com/book/remote-work-sustainable-changes-future/264375

Ali, M. (2022). *Future Role of Sustainable Innovative Technologies in Crisis Management.* IGI Global. https://www.igi-global.com/book/future-role-sustainable-innovative-technologies/281281

Ali, M. (2023). *Shifting Paradigms in the Rapidly Developing Global Digital Ecosystem: A GCC Perspective.* In Digital Entrepreneurship and Co-Creating Value Through Digital Encounters (pp. 145-166). IGI Global. https://www.igi-global.com/chapter/shifting-paradigms-in-the-rapidly-developing-global-digital-ecosystem/323525

Ali, M. (2023). T*axonomy of Industry 4.0 Technologies in Digital Entrepreneurship and Co-Creating Value.* In *Digital Entrepreneurship and Co-Creating Value Through Digital Encounters* (pp. 24–55). IGI Global., https://www.igi-global.com/chapter/taxonomy-of-industry-40-technologies-in-digital-entrepreneurship-and-co-creating-value/323520 DOI: 10.4018/978-1-6684-7416-7.ch002

Ali, M., & Wood-Harper, T. (2021). *Fostering Communication and Learning with Underutilized Technologies in Higher Education.* IGI Global. https://www.igi-global.com/book/fostering-communication-learning-underutilized-technologies/244593

Ali, M., Wood-Harper, T., & Kutar, M. (2023). Multi-Perspectives of Contemporary Digital Transformation Models of Complex Innovation Management. In *Digital Entrepreneurship and Co-Creating Value Through Digital Encounters* (pp. 79–96). IGI Global., https://www.igi-global.com/chapter/multi-perspectives-of-contemporary-digital-transformation-models-of-complex-innovation-management/323522 DOI: 10.4018/978-1-6684-7416-7.ch004

Ali, M. B. (2021). Internet of Things (IoT) to Foster Communication and Information Sharing: A Case of UK Higher Education. In Ali, M. B., & Wood-Harper, T. (Eds.), *Fostering Communication and Learning With Underutilized Technologies in Higher Education* (pp. 1–20). IGI Global., https://www.igi-global.com/chapter/internet-of-things-iot-to-foster-communication-and-information-sharing/262718/ DOI: 10.4018/978-1-7998-4846-2.ch001

Ali, M. B., & Wood-Harper, T. (2022). Artificial Intelligence (AI) as a Decision-Making Tool to Control Crisis Situations. In *Future Role of Sustainable Innovative Technologies in Crisis Management*. IGI Global., https://www.igi-global.com/chapter/artificial-intelligence-ai-as-a-decision-making-tool-to-control-crisis-situations/298931 DOI: 10.4018/978-1-7998-9815-3.ch006

Ali, M. B., Wood-Harper, T., & Ramlogan, R. (2020). A Framework Strategy to Overcome Trust Issues on Cloud Computing Adoption in Higher Education. In Modern Principles, Practices, and Algorithms for Cloud Security (pp. 162-183). IGI Global. https://www.igi-global.com/chapter/a-framework-strategy-to-overcome-trust-issues-on-cloud-computing-adoption-in-higher-education/238907/

KEY TERMS AND DEFINITIONS

Business Objectives: Try to think beyond operational efficiency here. Consider all the goals you want your business to meet and think about how your digital supply chain can help you reach those goals. Make sure you keep track of these goals so that you can use the data your digital supply chain produces to confirm whether or not you're meeting them.

Supply chain strategy: Following the need for further individualization and customization of the supply chain, supply chain setups adopt many more segments. To excel in this setting, supply chains need to master "microsegmentation." The granularization of the supply chain into hundreds of individual supply chain segments based on customer requirements and own capabilities designed in a dynamic, big data approach allows to mass-customize supply chain offerings. Tailored products provide optimal value for the customer and help minimize costs and inventory in the supply chain.

The Global Digitalization Trend: These has led to an emergence of closed loop supply chains and the development of a fundamentally new model of circular economy based on the 'take-make-reuse' principle. Today, the circular economy is the ground for achieving the sustainable development goals of SDG9 (sustainable industrialization) and SDG12 (sustainable production and consumption). Thus, the digital circular economy is characterized by non-waste production and consumption, minimal materials used per produced unit and transforming commercial and personal waste into a useful resource for further utilization.

Manage Supply Chain Risks: One of the most efficient ways to make risk identification and mitigation easier for your business is to employ tools that are designed to help. A single, real-time view of risk and business context allows you to communicate to the board and key stakeholders in a way that's framed around their priorities, keeping your risk posture in sync with the direction your business is moving.

Manage Supply Chain Reciprocity: One Reciprocity is an integrated cybersecurity risk management solution, designed to provide you with actionable insights to gain the visibility you need to stay ahead of threats and communicate the impact of risk on high-priority business initiatives. Turn the unknown into quantifiable and actionable risk insights with built-in expertise that identifies and maps risks, threats and controls for you, so you can spend less time setting up the application and more time using it. Reciprocity will even notify you automatically of any changes or required actions, so you can be on top of your risk posture like never before. Eliminate time-consuming, manual work and streamline collaboration by automating workflows and integrating with your most critical systems.

Chapter 12
A Prospective Analysis for Robotic Mobile Fulfillment Systems:
Assessing the Benefits of Automated Logistics

Badr Bentalha
https://orcid.org/0000-0003-1339-542X
Sidi Mohammed Ben Abdellah University, Morocco

ABSTRACT

In the current epoch, robotics offers numerous practical and commercial occasions. Warehouse order picking is a key task, especially for large-scale distribution companies. The Robotic Mobile Fulfillment System (RMFS) is an robotic order-picking arrangement constructed on robotic handling, currently designed for e-commerce warehouses. This article aims to understand the current realities of RMFS, how customers perceive this new technology, and the prospective challenges of integrating robots into Amazon's warehousing areas. The aim is to identify opportunities and threats in the use of Robotic Mobile Fulfillment Systems. This research paper will explore the potential benefits and risks of implementing RMFS in the future. The potential advantages of RMFS include increased operational efficiency, cost savings, and improved customer satisfaction. However, there can be risks involved such as cyber security, data privacy, and cost overruns. The paper will use a combination of prospective studies and existing research to assess the potential gains of RMFS and the associated risks.

DOI: 10.4018/979-8-3373-0086-3.ch012

Copyright © 2025, IGI Global. Copying or distributing in print or electronic forms without written permission of IGI Global is prohibited.

INTRODUCTION

In today's business landscape, many companies are embracing robotic and automated systems to drive productivity gains and enhance the quality of their goods and services. Service-oriented businesses, particularly retail, have been quick to adopt these high-tech developments to modernize their corporate operations and logistics processes.

Order picking in warehouses plays a pivotal role across various supply chain and distribution contexts, a role that has become even more pronounced with the recent surge in e-commerce. Traditionally, order picking has been a labor-intensive task. However, the booming e-commerce sector has necessitated the development of new warehousing solutions. Automating order-picking processes presents a viable opportunity to streamline operations (De Koster et al., 2007). Unlike manual order-picking systems, automated systems eliminate the need for pickers to travel, thereby accelerating delivery times.

One such automated order-picking system is the Robotic Mobile Fulfillment System (RMFS). This innovative robotic handling system is specifically designed for e-commerce warehouses (Merschformann et al., 2019). It employs robots that transport mobile shelves to workstations, where inventory is picked. By eliminating the need for pickers to travel, these robots enable high and reliable picking rates. Major e-commerce giants like Amazon, one of the largest online retailers in the USA, have adopted RMFS to enhance their local and international shipping capabilities. The implementation of such robotic systems addresses several challenges, including product delivery, labor shortages, and potential supply-demand imbalances.

Robotic Mobile Fulfillment Systems are highly sophisticated automated handling systems used in distribution warehouses and fulfillment centers. They integrate several advanced technologies to optimize the order-picking process. Mobile robotics play a central role in RMFS. Autonomous robots move freely around the warehouse, retrieving goods from shelves and transporting them to picking stations. These robots are equipped with advanced navigation systems, sensors, and computer vision systems to steer precisely and avoid obstacles. Warehouse management systems (WMS) and order management software control and optimize the flow of operations in the warehouse. They coordinate robot movements, assign picking tasks and efficiently route items to shipping zones.

The Internet of Things (IoT) and real-time tracking technologies, such as barcodes and RFID tags, are used to identify and track items throughout the picking process. This enables precise traceability and prevents errors. Automated storage systems, such as stacker cranes or mobile shelving systems, optimize the use of warehouse space and facilitate robot access to stored items. Finally, optimization algorithms and artificial intelligence are used to plan the most efficient routes for robots, forecast demand, and manage order priorities, to maximize productivity and minimize waiting times.

Future RMFS could involve closer collaboration between robots and human operators (Bentalha, 2024). Instead of working in separate areas, mobile robots would interact safely near humans. Thanks to advanced sensors and artificial intelligence, they would be able to anticipate and adapt to workers' movements. This collaboration would leverage the respective strengths of robots and humans for complex tasks. Machine learning algorithms will be increasingly used to continually optimize RMFS performance. By analyzing data from thousands of orders, these systems will be able to identify bottlenecks, adjust robot routes, forecast demand more accurately, and even suggest improvements to warehouse layout. This continuous optimization will increase efficiency and reduce operating costs. Augmented and virtual reality could be integrated into RMFS for a variety of purposes. For example, operators could visualize real-time product information and picking instructions. Maintenance technicians would use Augmented Reality to obtain diagnostic data and repair guides superimposed on robots. Virtual reality would also enable new processes to be simulated and tested before their physical implementation. To keep pace with constantly evolving needs and technologies, future RMFSs will adopt an even more modular and scalable design. The various hardware and software components can be easily upgraded or replaced, extending the system's lifespan. This "plug-and-play" approach will also enable new functionalities to be added, such as specialized robots for specific tasks. These potential developments aim to make RMFS even more intelligent, flexible, and efficient, to meet the challenges of modern logistics and omnichannel distribution.

So, what are the potential benefits and risks of introducing robotic mobile fulfillment systems in the future, and how can organizations best manage these risks in the future to ensure successful implementation?

To tackle the proposed issue, we will initially explore the interconnection and potential synergies between the Internet of Things (IoT), the Internet of Robotic Things (IoRT), and RMFS. Subsequently, we will outline our envisioned methodological strategy and the opportunities it presents. Lastly, we will reinforce our reasoning by drawing upon the findings from our empirical investigation, highlighting the diverse existing relationships and prospects.

1. ROBOTIC MOBILE DISTRIBUTION SYSTEMS: THEORETICAL AND CONCEPTUAL APPROACHES

1.1. Intelligent Supply Chains and Internet of Robotic Things

A supply chain is a group of companies that transmit materials, financial flows, and information to each other. Several independent players work together to manufacture a product and deliver it to the end user. Supply chains seek to meet the requirements of competitiveness and responsiveness, to develop the competitive advantages of the various players in these chains. The new chains are therefore interconnected, resilient, and intelligent (Hmioui & Bentalha, 2021). First and foremost, interconnection refers to the close integration of the different links in the chain, rather than operating in compartmentalized silos. Thanks to digital technologies such as IoT, traceability, and shared data platforms, information, products, and services flow seamlessly across the entire interconnected network. Secondly, resilience refers to the ability of these supply chains to withstand and rapidly adapt to external shocks and disruptions, be they natural disasters, supply disruptions, or major fluctuations in demand. This resilience is enhanced by redundancy, real-time visibility, process agility, and dynamic adjustment capabilities. Finally, intelligence refers to the integration of advanced technologies such as AI, machine learning, and predictive analytics (Bentalha & Boukare, 2024). These capabilities enable optimized decision-making, autonomous flow orchestration, continuous route optimization, and anticipation of future needs. Chains thus become more responsive, self-learning, and predictive. By becoming interconnected, resilient, and intelligent, the new supply chains considerably increase their agility, efficiency, and ability to cope with volatile and complex environments. This is a crucial transformation for adapting to the growing logistics challenges of the 21st century in a rapidly changing world.

Intelligent logistics involves the global application of integrated digital technology to automate logistics and warehousing. The aim is to improve resource utilization rates, and productivity levels and reduce logistics costs (Dou Xin-Xin et al., 2016). Intelligent logistics is a type of logistics system that uses AI and/or machine learning algorithms to automate and optimize the process of collecting, storing, and delivering items (Shamim & Bentalha, 2023). It integrates data from various sources such as sensors, inventory systems, and customer profiles to improve efficiency and accuracy. Intelligent logistics reduces costs, increases customer satisfaction, and improves safety. Examples of smart logistics include Amazon's use of robots and automated storage systems, UPS's use of analytics to optimize deliveries, and Walmart's use of AI to forecast demand. In addition, some companies are using machine learning algorithms to perform predictive maintenance and anticipate customer needs (Bouhtati et al., 2023). All these examples show how intelligent logistics can help companies become more efficient and reduce costs. The benefits of intelligent logistics include improved operational efficiency, increased customer satisfaction, reduced costs, and improved safety. Intelligent logistics can provide real-time updates on orders, optimize delivery routes, and improve inventory management. In addition, automated systems can help reduce human error, increase accuracy, and reduce the time and resources required for certain tasks.

Intelligent logistics is an implementation of the improvement and use of IoT (Internet of Things). It enables the emergence of real-time communication between products, machines, services, and people (Barreto et al., 2017). Consequently, it relies on the use of technological applications to enable effective planning as well as efficient management of warehousing and transportation systems. The underlying concept is the omnipresence around the human being of a variety of intelligent objects (Giusto et al., 2010). This global integration of the IoT with human beings in terms of communication and technical collaboration enables real-time decision-making. This partly explains the current craze for these various digital technologies. Indeed, according to (IDC, 2022), the total number of connected IoT devices will reach 55.9 billion worldwide by 2025.

IoT plays a crucial role in the implementation of an intelligent logistics initiative. It enables connected devices to remotely monitor data in real-time, draw conclusions, and provide solutions (Liu et al., 2020). The Internet of Things (IoT) is a network of physical objects - such as sensors, devices, and other items equipped with electronics, software, and other technologies - that can connect to an online network to exchange and collect data. Thanks to this connection, these objects can be monitored and controlled remotely, making them useful for a wide range of applications. What's more, IoT makes it possible to automate tasks such as energy efficiency, inventory management, and predictive maintenance.

The IoT, along with various fields such as artificial intelligence, machine learning, deep learning, and augmented reality, offers a new-generation class of intelligent robotics, called the "Internet of Robotic Things (IoRT)".

The IoRT is a network of robots and other physical devices connected to an online network to exchange and collect data. The IoRT connects robots, vehicles, and other physical objects to sensors, AI, and other technologies, enabling them to be monitored and controlled remotely. This connection enables increased automation, improved safety, energy efficiency, and predictive maintenance. In addition, the IoRT provides a platform for better collaboration between robots, humans, and machines.

Cutting-edge robotics and artificial intelligence technologies are revolutionizing business operations, leading to substantial reductions in labor costs and significantly streamlining production processes. A primary objective driving the integration of the Internet of Things (IoT) with robotics is to enhance robot mobility, object detection, tracking, and monitoring capabilities, as well as enable autonomous behavior (Batth et al., 2018). This convergence enables robots to perform a wide range of tasks within logistics operations, including loading, unloading, production activities, and quality control (Bentalha et al., 2019). The rapid growth in the adoption of robotics and IoT can be attributed to several key factors, such as the rise of e-commerce platforms, evolving consumer markets, advancements in research and development efforts, and, perhaps most significantly, the advent of Industry 4.0. The introduction of these robotic systems into warehousing environments has given rise to a new paradigm of mobile and robotized distribution systems (Bentalha et al., 2023).

1.2. Robotic Mobile Distribution Systems

The Robotic Mobile Fulfillment System (RMFS) is an innovative automated order-picking solution designed to boost productivity while minimizing the need for manual labor. These systems offer the flexibility to accommodate fluctuations in high-volume operations. An RMFS leverages mobile shelving units to store inventory items, with robots responsible for transporting these shelves to designated picking stations (Yudiansyah et al., 2020). As described by Lamballais et al. (2017), the system comprises a storage area, numerous mobile inventory shelves, robotic units, and multiple picking stations. Each mobile shelving unit houses various stock-keeping units (SKUs). When an order requires fulfillment, it is assigned to an available picking station. The robots then navigate beneath the inventory shelves containing the required SKUs and transport them to the designated picking station, where a human operator retrieves and processes the necessary items.

Robotic Mobile Fulfillment Systems are revolutionizing warehouse logistics by enhancing efficiency and reducing operational costs. These systems utilize advanced technologies such as Deep Reinforcement Learning (DRL) for optimizing order processing, navigation, and scheduling tasks. RMFS enhances storage efficiency and flexibility using AGVs.

This RMFS theme is still in the early stages of being understood by researchers. Indeed, few theoretical works have covered this theme.

Cheng et al. (2021) analyze RMFS with fixed shelves, considering AGV congestion, and optimize system parameters for improved performance. A mixed-robotic fulfillment system combines traditional automated storage with robotic mobile systems for efficient order picking, addressing challenges faced by e-commerce retailers for time-critical orders (Cheng et al., 2022). Keung et al. (2022) discuss an industrial Internet of Things-driven robotic mobile fulfillment system for storage location assignment and order picking, emphasizing resource synchronization and sharing in the process. Wang et al. (2022) evaluate a robotic mobile fulfillment system with multiple picking stations, focusing on performance under zoning policy. The paper explores the efficiency of this system in warehouse operations. The Mobile Robot for Automated Storage & Retrieval System is a robotic fulfillment system used in automated factories, distribution centers, and e-commerce operations for efficient material handling and continuous operation (Zagade et Patle, 2022).

Lamballais et al. (2022) discuss dynamic resource reallocation in a robotic mobile fulfillment system to optimize operations in response to changing demand, enhancing efficiency and adaptability in fulfillment processes. The RMFS optimizes pod storage for efficient order picking, enhancing system throughput and adaptability to real-time order demands in modern intelligent warehousing (Wu, 2022). Øvsthus et al. (2023) present a mobile robotic manipulator for autonomous warehouse operations, combining unmanned ground vehicle, manipulator, and vision sensors for object detection, pose estimation, and pick-and-place actions. Lee et al. (2023) introduce a Robotic Mobile Fulfillment System-based Automated Kitting System to optimize parts supply in Samsung Electronics' production line, enhancing operational performance and stability. The RMF system enhances order-picking efficiency through strategic storage location assignment, optimizing human-robot collaboration, and sustainable warehousing management in logistics operations (Chen et Li, 2024).

RMFS optimizes batch order scheduling in warehouses, reducing costs and enhancing efficiency through deep reinforcement learning algorithms like EDRL-OBOS (Cheng et al., 2024). Robotic Mobile Fulfillment Systems optimize order picking using Deep Reinforcement Learning, enhancing efficiency in order allocation, shelf selection, and robot scheduling, and handling large-scale orders effectively (Zhu et al., 2024). While RMFS technology shows great promise, challenges remain in scaling these systems for larger operations and ensuring seamless integration with existing logistics frameworks. The development of a mobile robot platform for a smart warehouse management system enhances operational efficiency, reduces costs, and integrates with existing industrial control frameworks for modernizing warehouse operations (Samigulin et al., 2024). Further research is needed to address these complexities and enhance system capabilities.

The e-commerce sector, a service industry centered around piece-picking operations, is experiencing a surge in customer demand for rapid and efficient service delivery (Bogue, 2016; Bentalha, 2022). Traditional manual picking systems are optimized for processing large batch orders. However, e-commerce orders tend to be smaller in size, while the warehouses are often vast, resulting in lengthy travel distances for human pickers. The RMFS was conceived as a solution to enhance picking productivity and reduce labor expenses by leveraging mobile robotic technologies (Boysen et al., 2017). The synergistic collaboration between robots and mobile shelving units aims to eliminate unproductive movements by human pickers.

One of the most prominent examples of embracing this form of warehouse management is demonstrated by Amazon, which has placed a strong emphasis on robotizing various logistics functions, both internally and externally. Amazon's Robotic Mobile Fulfillment Systems utilize robots to move shelves, enhancing speed and efficiency in product delivery, yet raising concerns among employees regarding workload, safety, and job security (Bentalha, 2024).

Amazon's facilities now feature more than 520,000 robots of diverse and complementary types, deployed across their global operations (Table 1).

Table 1. Various robots in Amazon centers

Robots	Description
Kiva	Load-carrying robots with a payload capacity of 450 kg and an approximate speed of 5 km/h.
Hercules	Robots similar to Kiva but with an enhanced lifting capacity of 1500 kg.
Pegasus	An updated version of the original Kiva robot, 19 cm thinner with a 560 kg payload.
Pegasus X-Sort Drive	A modular robotic platform called Pegasus can be outfitted with various accessories on top of its base unit.
Xanthus	A versatile training unit capable of transporting pods as well as other types of accessories.
Bert	A mobile robot using cameras and sensors to autonomously navigate, can be programmed by workers to transport packages.
Ernie	They are designed to operate within vertical storage stacks, using a robotic arm to retrieve and present bins to human workers.
Scooter	An automated tractor specialized in returning empty bins within the facility.
Kermit	An automated guided cart using magnetic navigation and ground beacons to control direction and speed.
Scout	A six-wheeled autonomous delivery robot for last-mile deliveries to customer doorsteps.
Drones	Prime Air drones are capable of aerially delivering packages weighing up to 2.26 kg directly to customers.

Source: Personal elaboration

The Kiva robots are engineered to cater to consumer demands through a computerized system that delivers order fulfillment solutions. By connecting to a WiFi network, the robots can adhere to and execute the orders that have been assigned, following the parameters set by the software control system. Additionally, Kiva robots possess object recognition capabilities facilitated by integrated automated navigation and surveillance systems. Each robot is equipped with two cameras that can scan and interpret QR codes on pathways and items. Furthermore, every mobile shelf unit has a barcode affixed to its underside, ensuring accurate identification and retrieval of the desired shelf in advance.

The accuracy of the Amazon Kiva robot's work can be as high as 99.99%, which can significantly reduce the likelihood of human error. The adoption of robots can significantly increase employee productivity as well as reduce operating costs by approximately 20% (Yudiansyah et al., 2020; Bogue, 2016). In fact, with the introduction of the Kiba robot in Amazon's logistics center, the existing 60-75-minute circulation speed was accelerated to around 15 minutes, and the space available for inventory utilization increased by 50% (Lee, 2019). This speed of delivery is crucial for the mass retail business and also for Amazon's new "Just Walk Out" store system (Bentalha & Hmioui, 2022). According to Amazon's estimates, the use of mobile robots in its warehouses has increased storage capacity by 50% and shipping speeds by 20% or more. The robots make it possible to process millions of orders every day quickly and reliably.

Despite the scale of its robotic deployment, Amazon continues to employ hundreds of thousands of human workers in its logistics facilities. Robots focus on repetitive, physically demanding tasks, while humans supervise operations, perform complex tasks, and ensure quality control. According to a study by the MWPVL Research Center (2022), an employee working alongside Amazon's mobile robots can process up to 4 times more orders than an employee in a non-automated warehouse. This increase in productivity enables Amazon to ship faster (Boudri et al., 2024). Analysts agree that Amazon's robotic capabilities give it a major long-term competitive advantage over other e-commerce giants. Few companies have the resources to invest so heavily in this disruptive technology.

The adoption of this robotization in RMFS has mixed stakes. Broadly speaking, there are two points of view on the effects of adopting these robots. The first favors the job-suppression effect, suggesting that the increased use of robots may affect employment and wages (Yang et al., 2021). In contrast, the second view defends the productivity effect, according to which there may be an increase in labor demand in industries or tasks associated with robot adoption (Fu et al., 2021).

2. METHODOLOGICAL FRAMEWORK

The central focus of this research revolves around the integration of robotic technologies within the warehousing operations of e-commerce enterprises. The adoption of robots appears to offer potential advantages in terms of reducing lead times, minimizing costs, and enhancing operational flexibility. However, there exists a paucity of scientific investigations delving into the ramifications of these technological advancements and their prospective future evolution within this domain.

So, how do the new robotized mobile distribution systems manage to increase Amazon's current productivity? To what extent can these systems evolve in the future to reinforce digital transformation and informational integration within the framework of new digital and connected business models?

We selected Cyberspace users' comments by reading and analyzing online discussions posted on YouTube and related to the theme. The aim is to understand how web users currently perceive this new technology and also to identify prospective elements that may explain the future evolution of this form of digital and connected enterprise.

We chose the users of YouTube channels. This channel offers the advantage of international notoriety, the presence of long videos, and strong interaction between participants via comments. To gain insights into customer perspectives, a random sampling approach was employed to select comments from various virtual communities. The selection criteria focused on the content, themes, and relevance of the comments. The goal was to utilize random sampling to segment the study population into different customer types.

The focal point revolves around Amazon's deployment of robotic systems to manage order fulfillment operations. From the customer's perspective, these robots remain concealed behind the scenes and out of direct sight (Bentalha, 2023). To analyze customers' perceptions, we opted to examine their reactions after viewing videos showcasing RMFS technology. Granting customers physical access to the warehouse facilities is not feasible, and online video viewings present an opportunity to engage with a virtual public accomplished of providing pertinent and effective feedback. The choice to delimit our study to the case of Amazon is justified by the company's pioneering role, innovative management approaches, and significant technological advancement compared to competitors. Amazon has introduced robotics at every stage of the logistics value chain, maintains an ambitious goal for complete supply chain robotization, and actively pursues acquisitions and develops robotic inventions. Amazon represents a unique case, combining a high-performance global supply chain with advanced robotization and a futuristic vision for service delivery logistics.

The initial step in the content analysis process involved gathering comments from the research subjects. Subsequently, the collected corpus underwent double-coding to categorize the messages into distinct themes. The analysis of 408 opinions and comments enabled the identification of significant viewpoints pertinent to the study's topic. The determination of the sample size was guided by the principle of theoretical saturation. The investigation was terminated when the results exhibited a high degree of similarity across the targeted profiles. The collated opinions were then subjected to statistical processing using the IRAMUTEQ software. Following the qualitative analysis, a complementary perspective methodological approach was adopted, justified by the specific nature of the research question (Bentalha & Alla, 2024). In this research, the ability to explore the future trajectory of RMFS as an ongoing modern trend was considered.

Foresight is an analytical and reflective approach that seeks to prepare for the future (Bentalha et al., 2020; Hmioui et al., 2020). Prospective studies involve the use of various qualitative and quantitative methodologies to analyze trends, identify drivers of change, and build medium- and long-term evolution scenarios. Beyond its anticipatory role, foresight also aims to stimulate discussion and dialogue between the stakeholders concerned, to co-construct desirable futures. This participatory approach aims to foster a shared understanding of the issues and challenges at stake. Futures studies represent a wide range of approaches and techniques aimed at exploring and anticipating possible medium- and long-term futures. Rather than a single discipline, foresight is an interdisciplinary field that draws on a variety of methodologies from the social sciences, operations research, engineering, strategic management, and more.

Foresight is a methodical and scientific approach that involves formulating a set of conditional and causal projections, encompassing the key attributes of a specific society or group of societies (Figure 1). It does not aim to predict the future with certainty, but rather to develop plausible scenarios based on current trends and data. The core principle of foresight is to systematically analyze the present state of affairs and identify potential future developments, challenges, and opportunities. Instead of attempting to foretell a single predetermined future, the foresight approach recognizes the inherent uncertainty and complexity of societal systems. By considering various factors, drivers, and interdependencies, it explores multiple possible futures that could unfold under different circumstances and conditions. This approach acknowledges that the future is not set in stone but is shaped by the decisions, actions, and interactions of various stakeholders, as well as broader societal, technological, economic, and environmental forces. Through rigorous analysis, consultation with experts, and the integration of diverse perspectives, foresight studies aim to provide valuable insights and recommendations to inform strategic decision-making and policy formulation.

Figure 1. The main stages in a prospective approach (Personal elaboration)

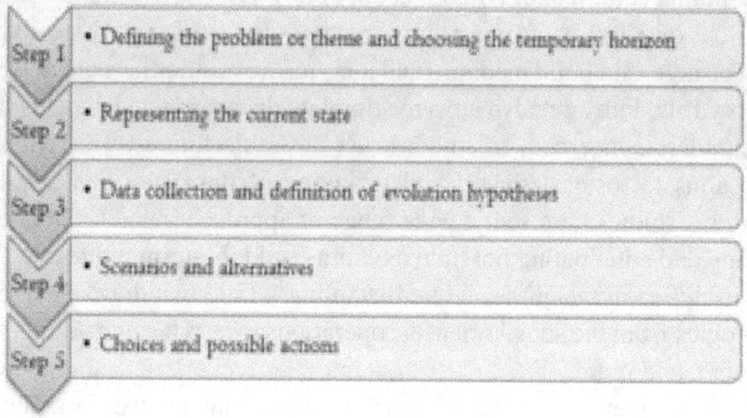

Prospective studies aim to formulate a systematic model to explain the nature of future problems and challenges, by mobilizing several reasonable alternatives. In this work, we propose possible alternatives and logistical perspectives for Amazon's modern, robotized supply chain and RMFS.

3. RESULTS AND DISCUSSION

Reading the various comments and analyzing the words and occurrences allows us to explore the relationship between the use of robotization in warehouses and web users' perceptions of the subject. Firstly, the choice of robotization appears to be a positioning choice for rivals. Indeed, several comments relate the use of robots and compare it with those of competitors or the market trend. Secondly, robotization enables better inventory management. Indeed, whether in comments or reviews, there is a broad consensus that the use of robots has saved space and sped up delivery. Thirdly, the distribution network and shipping service are improved. Previously, the online retailer's workers would walk miles to pick up items ordered by customers. This caused many problems, such as the inability to deliver products on time, overcapacity and material shortages, and lack of efficiency and productivity. Fourthly, robotization helps improve the customer experience and order delivery. Indeed, human-robot interaction is a topic of choice for many discussions.

Thus, we have synthesized the various benefits sought from the use of robots in Amazon's storage areas (Figure 2).

Figure 2. The virtual community's perception of the effectiveness of introducing robots into RMFS (Statistical study)

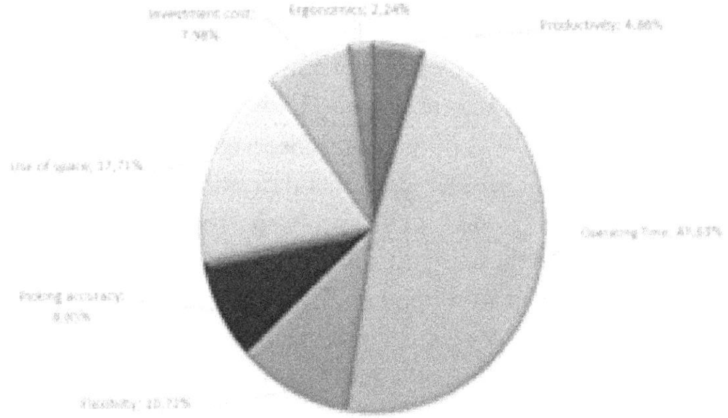

There are 7 main categories of motivation behind the use of robots discussed by the online community. Firstly, the factor perceived as most important for the effectiveness of this RFMS introduction is "Operating time" at 47.83%. This suggests that the community considers the gain in operating time to be the main benefit of using robots in these establishments.

Productivity" at 4.86% and 'Flexibility' at 10.72% are also perceived as relatively important factors, indicating that robots are seen as improving productivity and offering greater flexibility in operations. Indeed, compared with fully manual order-picking systems, an RMFS reduces the amount of manual work involved in order-picking operations. Flexibility is also sought and discussed as a primary objective in the use of robots. The gondolas used in an RMFS can be flexible so that the size of their compartments can be adapted. They can be adapted to handle goods of various natures and dimensions.

However, aspects such as "Investment" (7.98%), "Ergonomics" (2.24%), and "Picking accuracy" (8.85%) have lower percentages, which means that the community does not consider them to be major advantages of introducing robots. Picking accuracy can be reformed by the use of RMFS. This is because, compared with manual systems, robots move around the warehouse and pick up orders in different places at the same time. Finally, ergonomics, as robotization aims to improve working conditions and ergonomics for pickers. Instead of constantly moving around the warehouse, pickers carry out picking at fixed picking stations.

Our analysis similarly fixated on the worries, doubts, and problems surrounding the robotization of Amazon's storerooms, as discussed by Internet users. We identified 5 main categories discussed. Obstacles of a social nature are relatively more discussed in the various comments. Social risks such as employee redundancy, the risk of injury, or even the possibility of robotization taking over from humans, are some of the issues discussed by Internet users. These doubts are extensively existing and take up the lion's share (79%) of the risks observed in connection with the use of robots in Amazon's RMFS. This suggests that the online community believes that issues related to wage-earning and social aspects constitute the major challenge to the introduction of robots in these establishments. This probably reflects concerns that robots will replace human labor, potentially leading to job losses and negative social impacts. The community seems concerned about the implications of this automation on working conditions and employment.

The adoption of robotic and automation technologies faces skepticism from some internet users who struggle to comprehend the underlying mechanisms and lack the essential assistance to navigate this robotic world. Furthermore, concerns have been raised regarding the environmental impact of these technologies. Various discussions have highlighted the potential for robotization to contribute to pollution and depletion of natural resources. The production, operation, and eventual disposal of robots could lead to increased emissions, energy consumption, and waste management challenges, adversely affecting the environment. For some individuals, there exists a deep-seated apprehension towards novel digital technologies – a distrust of machines. They perceive these new technologies as threats to human labor, fearing that robotic systems will eventually replace human workers. Additionally, the integration of robotic technologies raises challenges related to coordination and collaboration between humans and machines. The crux of the matter lies in effectively managing the human-machine association and addressing potential struggles in terms of management, communication, and collaborative efforts.

In this way, we were able to identify the main verbatims for each challenge and obstacle (Table 2).

Table 2. Obstacles to the use of robots in Amazon's RFMS

Obstacles	Verbatims
Salaried and social (79%)	✓ *"But when Amazon introduces robots that would do this hard labor we all complain and worry that robots would take over our jobs"* ✓ *"So what happens to all those workers when everything goes robotic"* ✓ *"Work is becoming a scary thing With technology they are turning humans into robots"*
Pollution (5%)	✓ *"I'm not gonna waste the time explaining why one company with unlimited expansion is a bad thing Amazon does way too much pollution Their bags and boxes are way too big for most items shipped"*
Reluctance to use smart technology (3%)	✓ *"Rise of the machines is imminent"* ✓ *"With technology they are turning humans into robots"* ✓ *"I imagine being in that maze of pods is like trying to navigate the Hogwarts hall with the moving staircases Watching these things almost crash"*
Problems of coordination and collaboration (4%)	✓ *"Especially with favoritism and uppity managers"*
Poor understanding of smart technology implications (9%)	✓ *"We don't have laws that can control future technology like that"*

Source: Statistical study

We have also introduced a generic approach to measuring the trend of user reviews. The demonstration of generic models formed from user comments and reviews is based on a lexical analysis model. The result obtained with the sentiment analysis method is 46% positive opinions (Figure 3).

Figure 3. Trend analysis and sentiment of comments (Statistical study (https://text2data.com))

This graph represents a sentiment analysis performed on all comments. The horizontal scale shows a score, linked to the sentiment expressed, ranging from negative on the left to positive on the right. This visualization seems to provide a synthetic overview of the dominant feelings expressed, positive in this case. Trend analysis also shows a high degree of subjectivity in the comments. High subjectivity in the comments analyzed could indicate that the opinions expressed are highly personal, based on individual experiences and opinions rather than objective facts. A high level of subjectivity would mean that the positive or negative feelings identified are largely based on subjective perceptions, emotions, and points of view, rather than on factual or measurable elements. In the context of sentiment analysis, high levels of subjectivity can complicate the interpretation and generalization of results, as the opinions expressed are strongly colored by the individual experiences and perspectives of the commentators. This does not necessarily call into question the validity of the overall sentiment analysis but suggests that the results should be viewed with caution and placed in context. The trends identified reflect the subjective perceptions and opinions of a given set of people rather than objective truths.

On another level, we analyzed future investments to be made and found a predominance of investment effort in communication technologies, computers and digital workstations, drones, and floating delivery, high-tech video and camera, and an integrated approach to RMFS automation (Table 3).

Table 3. Future capital investment for RMFS

Variables	Items	Verbatims
Digital communication	Promotions, communication, telephones	✓ *"Most of Amazon's profits come from Amazon Web"* ✓ *"and available information That certainly helps"*
Computers & digital stations	Algorithms, computers, workstations, software	✓ *"Even if the software is wrong or Putting a small item in a large box"* ✓ *"The oppression Take control of marketing Bring in computers and robots"* ✓ *"When the computer knows exactly what size box an order needs"*
Drones	Drones, airports, airships, floating realization	✓ *"But industrial like drones Downside is blimp licensing"*
Video & cameras	Video, camera	✓ *"I still saw people doing work Hopefully in the future we can have something like a fully automated warehouse system Then we can progress"* ✓ *"That was the fuzzy pro-Amazon advertisement for them There are plenty of videos from Employees"*
Complete automation	Automated	✓ *"Would be cool if there was a fully automated warehouse"* ✓ *"I wonder if Amazon will become fully automated"*

Source: Statistical study

From an organizational point of view, storage area managers need to embrace modern technological development and value chain innovations. Indeed, this will drive new technological trends. Digital transformation is no longer an option in today's dynamic business environment. Put into perspective, these technologies will have beneficial implications for modern business communication and connectivity. The profit implications are significant, with great potential for cost reduction and movement optimization.

So, after analyzing the current situation of Amazon's RMFS robotization we can draw up some possible prospective scenarios. For years, Amazon has been trying to cope with wage protests linked to low wages and incessant pressure to unionize. Research conducted at Amazon sites predicted that the company could run out of workers to hire in the U.S. in the next few years if it didn't execute a series of radical changes, including increased automation of its warehouses. It seems that robot packers, robot movers, and robot deliverers could be an answer to these problems in the future. The company is the world's largest manufacturer of industrial robots. Its Boston facility already produces 330,000 robots a year. In the future, Amazon will complete this process of robotized industrialization and be able to generate fully robotized factories. In a more optimistic vision, the American company would be able to supply other branches of industry with robots adapted to their different needs. Amazon currently claims that robots and people will continue to work together in warehouses. One day, however, the company might be able to entrust robots with all the work it currently entrusts to human employees.

In this prospective vision, Amazon would continue its trajectory of large-scale automation by deploying fully robotized factories for its logistics operations. This ultimate stage of robotic industrialization would further push back the limits of what technology can achieve in order picking and shipping. With fully autonomous systems, from incoming goods to outgoing parcels, Amazon would achieve levels of productivity, efficiency, and quality control that are perhaps unrivaled. However, this scenario raises several major questions. From an economic point of view, the colossal investments required to design, implement, and maintain such complex robotic systems would be enormous, even for a giant like Amazon. This would require a rigorous analysis of long-term costs and benefits. In social terms, the complete replacement of human staff by robots would pose major challenges in terms of jobs and the need for a just transition. Amazon would need to take proactive measures to retrain and support its hundreds of thousands of potentially affected employees. From a technological point of view, although advances in robotics, computer vision, and artificial intelligence are remarkable, achieving a level of total reliability, flexibility, and autonomy to manage all the complex aspects of supply chains remains a huge challenge (Elhissoufi & Alla, 2024). The prospect of Amazon supplying complete robotic systems to other industries is interesting. This could accelerate the adoption of automation on an industrial scale. However, it would raise issues of security, liability, and dependence on a single dominant player. Ultimately, if technically feasible, such a scenario would push back the frontiers of what robotics can achieve. But it raises profound societal questions about the balance to be struck between efficiency gains, employment impacts, and the appropriate role of automation in our economic systems.

The second possible scenario is the integration of Amazon's various current robot models into a single digital form capable of performing a variety of tasks. This is a kind of single robot capable of handling the vast majority of products and operations. It's a new generation of warehouse robots capable of picking up goods, carrying them, transporting them, and delivering them to customers. A prototype called Cardinal lifts and sorts pre-packed orders. An extension of this kind of robot is possible, which will revolutionize the RMFS of the future. The idea of an "all-in-one" robot capable of performing multiple tasks such as picking, transporting, and potentially even the final delivery of goods would have many advantages. By extending this concept to other key materials handling tasks, we could design a new generation of agile, autonomous "universal robots". By integrating the functionalities currently distributed across different models of specialized robots, we would create a simpler, more flexible, and more efficient system. From an operational point of view, these high-performance robots would rationalize and streamline logistics flows by reducing transfers between different specialized systems. Their flexibility in adapting to different environments and product types would also be an asset in the face of frequently changing operational requirements. However, developing such a robust, intelligent robot combining so many advanced functions in a single system would represent a major technological challenge. Current limits in mechatronic design, decision-making systems, autonomous navigation, etc. would have to be pushed back. Significant breakthroughs in areas such as dexterous handling robotics would be required. What's more, these universal robots would have to meet stringent safety standards to interact safely near human operators during handling phases. Their development and production costs could also be higher than a fleet of specialized robots. Despite these challenges, the prospect of a highly integrated and flexible robotics platform for RMFS is attractive. If Amazon or other players meet these technical challenges, it could truly revolutionize logistics operations by offering a universal robotic solution that is both high-performance and scalable.

The third scenario relates to the abandonment of robotization or, at the very least, the reduction of the current trend marked by a strong introduction of robots. Indeed, we have noted fears and doubts in many comments about the human and social harms of this robotization. In addition, some current failures in terms of financing, innovation, or commercialization make the rapid robotization mechanisms of today's RMFS a subject of criticism. In 2019, Amazon revealed the failure of robotic deliveries via rolling drones named Scout. Amazon reportedly disbanded the 400-strong global team working on the project as part of its company-wide cost-cutting measures. Thus, the costs of innovation, energy, and future global prospects may cause Amazon's current progress in RMFS robotization to come to a halt or be scaled back. The breakneck pace of automation and robot deployment in Amazon's warehouses in recent years has indeed prompted its share of criticism and questioning. Concerns about the social and human impacts, with significant risks of job losses, are legitimate and should not be ignored, even if Amazon claims to want to maintain a balance with its human employees. So, one plausible scenario would be for Amazon to take a step back from its lavish robot deployment and adopt a more cautious, measured approach, at least in the short term. Several factors could motivate this choice in the future, such as the significant costs involved in developing, acquiring, and deploying hundreds of thousands of robots, the uncertainty regarding the actual return on investment of this massive automation, the growing concerns of employees and regulators about preserving jobs, and the need to also invest in other strategic areas beyond robotized logistics. However, it would probably be exaggerated to envisage a complete halt or abandonment of robotization at Amazon. The company has already achieved considerable efficiency gains and gained a key competitive advantage with this now-mature technology. A balanced, hybrid approach seems more realistic, combining highly robotized areas, others relying more on humans, and targeted investments in promising longer-term innovations once the technologies and business models have been validated. In short, while a slowdown in the pace of robotization is conceivable, Amazon should not abandon this strategic path altogether, at the risk of losing its technological lead in a sector that has become inescapable.

Table 4 summarizes the different scenarios identified by our prospective study.

Table 4. Summary of scenarios relating to the prospective development of Amazon RMFS

Scenario	Description	Benefits	Challenges/Risks
Scenario 1 - Fully robotized plants	Amazon deploys fully automated, unmanned logistics plants, pushing technological boundaries with complex end-to-end autonomous robotic systems.	- Maximum productivity and efficiency - Optimum quality control - Elimination of labor-related issues	- Colossal investments required - Major transition and social impacts - Enormous technical challenges for total autonomy
Scenario 2 - Intelligent universal robot	Development of a versatile "all-in-one" robot, combining multiple capabilities (pick, carry, deliver) in an integrated, flexible robotic platform.	- Streamlined logistics flows - Flexibility and adaptability to change - Scalable, centralized robotic solution	- Technological breakthroughs required - High security and development costs - Integration of multiple complex functionalities
Scenario 3 - Slowing down or stopping robotization	In the face of challenges and criticism, Amazon slows or halts its breakneck pace of robot automation in warehouses. Rebalancing with human staff.	- Responds to societal concerns - Reduces the need for massive investment - Maintains existing jobs	- Loss of operational efficiency - Stifling innovation - Risk of falling behind the competition

Source: Personal elaboration

So, these and other scenarios are likely. It seems that the topic of RMFS robotization is a rapidly developing one, both theoretically and empirically. The discussions analyzed and the prospective ideas conceived have confirmed and consolidated the multidimensional and primordial nature of the robotization of Amazon's RMFS. The various scenarios and analyses we discussed regarding the robotization of Amazon's order-picking systems - whether its acceleration, the emergence of multipurpose robots, or a possible slowdown - clearly illustrate the multidimensional and primordial nature of this theme.

One of the primary ethical concerns surrounding RMFS is the potential for widespread job displacement in the logistics sector. As robots take over tasks traditionally performed by humans, many workers may find themselves unemployed or forced to seek employment in other industries. The adoption of RMFS may exacerbate existing economic inequalities by concentrating wealth among those who own and develop the technology while displacing workers who rely on logistics jobs for their livelihoods. As human roles in logistics become increasingly automated, there are concerns about the quality of remaining jobs and the potential loss of human dignity in highly automated work environments. While RMFS may offer some environmental benefits through increased efficiency, the production and disposal of robotic systems also raise environmental concerns. The adoption of robotic mobile fulfillment systems in logistics presents both opportunities and challenges for society. While the potential benefits in terms of efficiency and productivity are significant, it is crucial to carefully consider and address the ethical implications and societal impacts of reducing human roles in this sector. By taking a proactive and thoughtful approach to the implementation of RMFS, we can work towards maximizing the benefits of automation while minimizing negative consequences for workers and society as a whole.

In technological terms, the robotization of RMFS represents a cutting-edge field of innovation, where complex technical challenges (robotic design, artificial intelligence, autonomous systems, etc.) and operational considerations for optimizing logistics flows are intertwined. The meteoric progress of recent years would not have been possible without the massive commitment to R&D of major players like Amazon. From an economic and strategic point of view, this large-scale automation has become a decisive competitive advantage for Amazon, enabling it to reach new levels of efficiency, productivity, and responsiveness in the face of growing demand. It represents a huge investment but with substantial operational gains in return. The impact on society and employment is an essential aspect where tensions and questions persist. While robots can lighten the burden of arduous tasks, their mass deployment raises understandable fears about job losses and the place we wish to give to automation in our economic systems. Finally, the ethical, environmental, and long-term sustainability issues raised by these high-tech systems will have to be taken into account in future developments, beyond mere efficiency considerations (Hmioui et al., 2024).

CONCLUSION

Robotics has unlocked numerous opportunities, particularly in the domain of warehouse order picking - an activity that previously necessitated substantial manual labor. Intelligent logistics aims to maximize profitability while delivering superior service by leveraging new digital technologies. The RMFS is an automated order-picking system that employs robots within e-commerce warehouses. The integration of robotic systems has transformed the operational dynamics within service companies, sparking methodological and managerial discussions. This article explored the perceptions of customers regarding the incorporation of robots in Amazon's warehousing facilities. Through a prospective study, we highlighted potential opportunities and compelling challenges associated with the utilization of digital RMFS.

The implementation of RMFS appears to impact several aspects of logistics performance. The study's findings revealed that robotization offers numerous advantages, primarily in terms of productivity enhancements, improved uptime, increased flexibility, higher picking accuracy, better space utilization, reduced investment costs, and improved ergonomics. Our objective is to address some of the research gaps identified in this scientific domain, as most work on digital technologies in logistics tends to be fragmented and partial. Additionally, few studies have analyzed RMFS from a managerial perspective.

Nevertheless, our work has certain limitations and future perspectives. Indeed, the data collection adopted by our qualitative study and their analysis might present a certain bias and a possible difficulty in generalizing the conclusions. The adoption of an analysis based on comments written in English and their analysis and explanation in French may also involve a linguistic bias. For future research, we would suggest complementing this work with a confirmatory quantitative study. Furthermore, we can link the results obtained by this work with the new perspectives of Amazon Go and examine how these different RMFS have modified the delivery approach for customers or last-mile logistics. Finally, it is conceivable to build future studies in diverse situations and technologies.

REFERENCES

Barreto, L., Amaral, A., & Pereira, T. (2017). Industry 4.0 implications in logistics: An overview. *Procedia Manufacturing*, 13(1), 1245–1252. DOI: 10.1016/j.promfg.2017.09.045

Batth, R. S., Nayyar, A., & Nagpal, A. (2018). Internet of robotic things: driving intelligent robotics of future-concept, architecture, applications and technologies. In 2018 4th International Conference on Computing Sciences (ICCS), 151-160. IEEE. DOI DOI: 10.1109/ICCS.2018.00033

Bayi, C. (2024, December). Tao, Xie., Lingjun, Wang., Daniel, Q., Tan., Xiongfei, Cao. (2024). Deep reinforcement learning driven cost minimization for batch order scheduling in robotic mobile fulfillment systems. *Expert Systems with Applications*, 255, 124589. Advance online publication. DOI: 10.1016/j.eswa.2024.124589

Bentalha, B. (2022). Smart Technologies for a Sustainable Service Supply Chain: A Prospective Perspective. *Journal of Environmental Issues and Climate Change*, 1(1), 77–89. DOI: 10.59110/jeicc.v1i1.81

Bentalha, B. (2023). Consumer Perception of Robotic Mobile Fulfillment Systems: A Netnographic Case Study of Amazon. In Innovation, Strategy, and Transformation Frameworks for the Modern Enterprise (pp. 243-264). IGI Global. DOI: 10.4018/979-8-3693-0458-7.ch010

Bentalha, B. (2024). Employees and Robots in Amazon's Robotic Mobile Fulfillment Systems: A Netnographic Analysis of a Supply Chain Transformation. In Blockchain Applications for Smart Contract Technologies (pp. 188-207). IGI Global. DOI: 10.4018/979-8-3693-1511-8.ch009

Bentalha, B., & Alla, L. (2024). Revealing the Subtleties: The Art of Qualitative Studies in Science and Management. In Applying Qualitative Research Methods to Management Science (pp. 1-21). IGI Global.

Bentalha, B., & Boukare, M. (2024). AI-Driven Territorial Intelligence: An Integrated Approach to Enhancing Digital Sovereignty. In Generative AI and Implications for Ethics, Security, and Data Management (pp. 231-261). IGI Global.

Bentalha, B., & Hmioui, A. (2022). Smart Service Supply Chain and Just Walk Out Technology: A Netnographic Approach. In: Ben Ahmed, M., Boudhir, A.A., Kara , İ.R., Jain, V., Mellouli, S. (eds). Innovations in Smart Cities Applications Volume 5. SCA 2021. Lecture Notes in Networks and Systems, vol 393. Springer, Cham. Pp. 223-236. https://doi.org/DOI: 10.1007/978-3-030-94191-8_18

Bentalha, B., Hmioui, A., & Alla, L. (2019). The digitalization of the supply chain management of service companies: a prospective approach. In *Proceedings of the 4th International Conference on Smart City Applications* (pp. 1-8). DOI: 10.1145/3368756.3369005

Bentalha, B., Hmioui, A., & Alla, L. (2020). Digital Service Supply Chain Management: Current Realities and Prospective Visions. In: Ben Ahmed M., Boudhir A., Santos D., El Aroussi M., Karas İ. (eds) Innovations in Smart Cities Applications Edition 3. SCA 2019. Lecture Notes in Intelligent Transportation and Infrastructure. Springer, Cham

Bentalha, B., Hmioui, A., & Alla, L. (2023). Green Transportation Balanced Scorecard: A VIKOR Fuzzy Method for Evaluating Green Logistics Initiatives. In International Conference on Digital Technologies and Applications (pp. 916-925). Cham: Springer Nature Switzerland. DOI: 10.1007/978-3-031-29857-8_91

Bogue, R. (2016). Growth in e-commerce boosts innovation in the warehouse robot market. Industrial Robot. *The Industrial Robot*, 43(6), 583–587. DOI: 10.1108/IR-07-2016-0194

Boudri, R., Bentalha, B., & Benjelloun, O. (2024). Phygital Marketing and the Pain of Paying: An Amazon Go Netnographic Case Study. In AI and Data Engineering Solutions for Effective Marketing (pp. 348-363). IGI Global.

Bouhtati, N., Alla, L., & Bentalha, B. (2023). Marketing Big Data Analytics and Customer Relationship Management: A Fuzzy Approach. In Integrating Intelligence and Sustainability in Supply Chains (pp. 75-86). IGI Global. DOI: 10.4018/979-8-3693-0225-5.ch004

Boysen, N., Briskorn, D., & Emde, S. (2017). Parts-to-picker based order processing in a rack-moving mobile robots environment. *European Journal of Operational Research*, 262(2), 550–562. DOI: 10.1016/j.ejor.2017.03.053

Cheng, C. (2021, December 30). Shasha, Wu., Luyao, Wang., Yaohua, Wu. (2022). Design and Performance Estimation of Mixed-Robotic Fulfillment System. *International Journal of Pattern Recognition and Artificial Intelligence*, 35(16), 2159057. Advance online publication. DOI: 10.1142/S0218001421590576

Cheng, C. (2021, November 07). Yanyan, Wang., Shasha, Wu., Jian, Zhang. (2021). Analysis and Optimization of the Robotic Mobile Fulfillment Systems Considering Congestion. *Applied Sciences (Basel, Switzerland)*, 11(21), 10446. Advance online publication. DOI: 10.3390/app112110446

De Koster, R., Le-Duc, T., & Roodbergen, K. J. (2007). Design and control of warehouse order picking: A literature review. *European Journal of Operational Research*, 182(2), 481–501. DOI: 10.1016/j.ejor.2006.07.009

Elhissoufi, M., & Alla, L. (2024). Artificial Intelligence in Costumer Acquisition: A Bibliometric Study. In AI and Data Engineering Solutions for Effective Marketing (pp. 1-22). IGI Global. DOI: 10.4018/979-8-3693-3172-9.ch001

Fu, X. M., Bao, Q., Xie, H., & Fu, X. (2021). Diffusion of industrial robotics and inclusive growth: Labour market evidence from cross country data. *Journal of Business Research*, 122(1), 670–684. DOI: 10.1016/j.jbusres.2020.05.051

Giusto, D., Iera, A., & Morabito, G., Atzori (Eds.), L., (2010). The Internet of Things, 20th Tyrrhenian Workshop on Digital Communications, Springer Science & Business Media. 441 p.

Hmioui, A., & Bentalha, B. (2021). Service supply chain management: A literature review. *International Journal of Logistics Systems and Management*, 40(3), 332–353. DOI: 10.1504/IJLSM.2021.120253

Hmioui, A., Bentalha, B., & Alla, L. (2020). Service supply chain: A prospective analysis of sustainable management for global performance. 2020 IEEE 13th International Colloquium of Logistics and Supply Chain Management (LOGISTIQUA). DOI: 10.1109/LOGISTIQUA49782.2020.9353940

Hmioui, A., Bentalha, B., & Beniaich, R. (2024). Green Supply Chain Management et développement territorial: Une revue de littérature. *Alternatives Managériales Economiques*, 6(2), 52–74.

International Data Corporation (IDC). (2022). IDC MarketScape: Worldwide Managed IoT Connectivity Services 2022 Vendor Assessment, IDC Media Center, [Online], https://www.idc.com/getdoc.jsp?containerId=US48061522 (Consulted 03 May 2024).

Jaeung, L. (2023). *Yooeui, Jin., Sungwook, Jang., Young, Jae, Jang., Il, Kyu, Lim., Seungmin, Jeong., Eoksu, Sim.* Sequential Decision-Making Framework for Robotic Mobile Fulfillment System-Based Automated Kitting System., DOI: 10.1109/WSC60868.2023.10407259

Keung, K. L., Lee, C. K. M., & Ji, P. (2022, April). Keung. K., L., C.K.H., Lee., Ping, Ji. (2022). Industrial internet of Things-driven storage location assignment and order picking in a resource synchronization and sharing-based robotic mobile fulfillment system. *Advanced Engineering Informatics*, 52, 101540. Advance online publication. DOI: 10.1016/j.aei.2022.101540

Kun, W. (2022, July). T., Hu., Zhi-Zue, Wang., Yunhai, Xiang., Jie, Shao., Xianwen, Xiang. (2022). Performance evaluation of a robotic mobile fulfillment system with multiple picking stations under zoning policy. *Computers & Industrial Engineering*, 169, 108229. Advance online publication. DOI: 10.1016/j.cie.2022.108229

Lamballais, T., Merschformann, M., Roy, D., de Koster, M. B. M., Azadeh, K., & Suhl, L. (2022). Dynamic policies for resource reallocation in a robotic mobile fulfillment system with time-varying demand. *European Journal of Operational Research*, 300(3), 937–952. DOI: 10.1016/j.ejor.2021.09.001

Lamballais, T., Roy, D., & De Koster, M. B. M. (2017). Estimating performance in a Robotic Mobile Fulfillment System. *European Journal of Operational Research*, 256(3), 976–990. DOI: 10.1016/j.ejor.2016.06.063

Lee, S. H. (2019). An analysis on the changes of logistics industry using internet of things. *Journal of Advanced Information Technology and Convergence*, 9(1), 57–66. DOI: 10.14801/JAITC.2019.9.1.57

Liu, Y., Zhang, W., Pan, S., Li, Y., & Chen, Y. (2020). Analyzing the robotic behavior in a smart city with deep enforcement and imitation learning using IoRT. *Computer Communications*, 150(1), 346–356. DOI: 10.1016/j.comcom.2019.11.031

Merschformann, M., Lamballais, T., De Koster, M. B. M., & Suhl, L. (2019). Decision rules for robotic mobile fulfillment systems. *Operations Research Perspectives*, 6(1), 100–128. DOI: 10.1016/j.orp.2019.100128

MWPVL International Inc. (2022). Amazon Global Supply Chain and Fulfillment Center Network. [On line] https://www.mwpvl.com/html/amazon_com.html (Consulted 20/05/2024)

Ørjan. (2023). *Øvsthus., Didrik, Nicolai, Robsrud., Lars, Muggerud., José, Amendola., Linga, Reddy, Cenkeramaddi., Ilya, Tyapin., Ajit, Jha*. Mobile Robotic Manipulator Based Autonomous Warehouse Operations., DOI: 10.1109/ICCMA59762.2023.10374743

Shamim, R., & Bentalha, B. (2023). Blockchain-Enabled Machine Learning Framework for Demand Forecasting in Supply Chain Management. In Integrating Intelligence and Sustainability in Supply Chains (pp. 28-48). IGI Global. DOI: 10.4018/979-8-3693-0225-5.ch002

Yang, X., Hua, G., Hu, L., Cheng, T. C. E., & Huang, A. (2021). Joint optimization of order sequencing and rack scheduling in the robotic mobile fulfilment system. *Computers & Operations Research*, 135(1), 105467. Advance online publication. DOI: 10.1016/j.cor.2021.105467

Yaohua, W. (2022). Dynamic Picking and Storage Optimization of Robotic Picking Systems. *Wireless Personal Communications*. Advance online publication. DOI: 10.1007/s11277-021-09190-9

Yudiansyah, A., Keke, Y., & Veronica, V. (2020). Can the mobile robot be a future order-picking solution?: A case study at Amazon fulfillment center. *Advances in Transportation and Logistics Research*, 3(1), 800–806.

Yue, C. Yisong, Li. (2024). Storage Location Assignment for Improving Human–Robot Collaborative Order-Picking Efficiency in Robotic Mobile Fulfillment Systems. *Sustainability*. Advance online publication. DOI: 10.3390/su16051742

Zhenyi, Z. (2024, July 20). Sai, Wang., Tuan-Tuan, Wang. (2024). Optimizing Robotic Mobile Fulfillment Systems for Order Picking Based on Deep Reinforcement Learning. *Sensors (Basel)*, 24(14), 4713. Advance online publication. DOI: 10.3390/s24144713

Chapter 13
Brand Characteristics, Perceived Quality of Freemium Users, and Premium Service Purchase Intention: The Case With Netflix Users

Sahika Dogan
https://orcid.org/0000-0001-6248-7289
Istanbul Bilgi University, Turkey

ABSTRACT

The rising popularity of online video streaming services challenge the dominancy of traditional television channels due to changing television viewing trends, as personalized individual services have also been integrated into online video streaming. This study aims to explore potential relationships between brand related characteristics, perceived quality and purchase intention among freemium online video streaming service users in the context of Netflix. Considering the changes in television viewing trends and the impressive amount of revenue drawn by the Netflix company from the Turkish audience, it is important to reveal which factors encourage free users to purchase paid membership. Findings revealed significant relationships between brand image, components of perceived quality (user friendliness, visual design, operation speed and safety) and purchase intention; while it was found that brand loyalty does not impact on users' purchasing decisions.

DOI: 10.4018/979-8-3373-0086-3.ch013

Copyright © 2025, IGI Global. Copying or distributing in print or electronic forms without written permission of IGI Global is prohibited.

1. INTRODUCTION

Personalized individual services have become an essential component of the Internet since the semantic web (web 3.0) era, which has been characterized by big data, personalization and creativity (Yengin, 2015). Semantic web enabled the development of technologies in terms of data finding, data sharing and integration of various datasets to create a personalized and meaningful Internet experience for users (Demirli & Kütük, 2010). The personalization of the Internet and its services has also continued its impact throughout web 4.0 and web 5.0 eras, which are marked for the rise of the Internet of Things (IoT) and emotional (symbiotic) web (Seyitoğlu, 2019, s. 56).

The increasing role of communication technology in society was foreseen by various theorists such as Harold Innis and Marshall McLuhan. For instance, Innis (2006) explained that the level of technology used by individuals determined the societal and economic structures individuals live in (s. 245). According to the theorist, technology is the key determinant of the contents produced, which are a reflection of power structures and relationships in a society (s. 247). Similarly, McLuhan (2001) argued that the power of communication technology did not stem from its content, but its structure (s. 43). In other words, contents are being formed in line with the structure and characteristics of the communication technology that is made available. This is also the case with online video streaming platforms, since the technological services offered come up with unique features that differ from conventional television channels. For example, individuals can choose the television shows that they wish to watch, within a collection of movies, documentaries and television series offered by online video streaming services. Viewers can decide the time they wish to view a television show and watch the same content more than once. Thanks to such features of online video streaming services, viewers are offered a unique and personalized media experience, whose limits are determined by the technology itself. For instance, content library of a particular online video streaming services can be perceived as a limitation, as the number of contents made available are determined by the service's online storage capacity, effectiveness and copyright agreements made between service providers and content producers.

Thus, the rising popularity of online video streaming services challenge the dominancy of traditional television channels due to changing television viewing trends. Netflix is one of the major actors among online video streaming platforms, with 192.95 million paid subscribers worldwide (Statista a, 2020). In the United States, Netflix ranked second after YouTube for being the most popular video streaming service by September 2019 (Statista b, 2020). In June 2020, Netflix announced that the company had more than 1.7 million paid subscribers from Turkey and the total revenue of the company received from Turkish subscribers was announced to be 53 million dollars (Digital Age, 2020). In line with these developments, the daily time spent with viewing conventional television channels are decreasing in Turkey. The research conducted by Turkish Radio and Television Council revealed the viewership among conventional television channels decreased by 30% in the last twelve years (Turkish Radio and Television Council, 2020).

The current study aims to analyze potential relationships between brand related characteristics, perceived quality and purchase intention among freemium online video streaming service users, by focusing on Netflix and its free members. The assessed brand related characteristics are brand loyalty and brand image; while the perceived quality characteristics are user friendliness, visual design, operation speed and safety.

Previous academic research explored the contents and usage of Netflix from various perspectives such as branding (Wayne, 2018), localization (Kokas, 2020), television viewing as a socialization activity (Stein et al., 2019), reception analysis of the first Turkish production on Netflix, "Hakan Muhafız" (Karaduman & Aciyan, 2019) and gender representations in Netflix shows (Bucciferro, 2019). Considering the changes in television viewing trends and the impressive amount of revenue drawn by the Netflix company from the Turkish audience, it is important to reveal which factors encourage free users to purchase paid membership. In line, the following sections will first present the literature review on designated the variables, methodological procedures, findings and the conclusions of the research study.

2. LITERATURE REVIEW

2.1. Brand Loyalty

Oliver (1999) defines brand loyalty as the consistent commitment to a particular product or service (p. 34). According to the theorist, such commitment would result with the repetition of the purchasing behavior from the same brand (Newman & Werbel, 1974; Oliver, 1999 p. 34; Tellis, 1988). Baalbaki (2012) state that brand loyalty is an essential indicator of how a brand is perceived by the consumer. In parallel, previous research revealed that customers who are loyal to a particular brand have positive feelings towards the brand and the company associated with it (Lobschat et al., 2013). Individuals, feeling engaged with a brand are more interested in producing and sharing information about it on social media (Yeh & Choi, 2011).

Similarly, Whitler and Farris (2017) explain that individuals who are loyal to a brand in the offline world are more likely to buy its products via online e-commerce sites.

Aaker (1991) places brand loyalty under the umbrella of brand equity besides with brand recognition, the perceived brand quality, brand image and brand value. In his further studies, Aaker (1996) explains that individuals are more likely to purchase a product or a service from a brand that they are familiar with. In this context, brand loyalty enables companies to hold high-price advantage, time advantage against innovations by competitors and price wars between companies (Aaker, 1996). According to Zaglia (2013), individuals loyal to particular brand are less sensitive about price increases in the favored brand's products and services.

Oliver (1999) also argues that brand loyalty can be considered under four categories, which are cognitive (perception of the brand's performance), affective (feeling of appreciation), conative (repurchasing intention) and action-based (loyal purchasing behavior). The theorist additionally explains that brand loyalty can be fostered during trial periods such as freemium membership, if companies allow a rational time period for potential consumers to discover their services (Oliver, 1999). Similarly, Lobschat et al. (2013) interpret the purchasing behavior after trial period as the first step taken towards the development of brand loyalty among new consumers.

2.2. Brand Image

Brand image is related with the structuralizing how companies aim their brands to be perceived by their consumers. Hung (2008) defines brand image as the idea created in the memory of the consumers about a particular brand. In a different explanation, Kotler and Barich (1991) state that brand image refers to a system of visuals and opinions that is presented for human awareness. Upshaw (1995) claims that brand image is not only limited with visuals and thoughts, but also related with words and associations.

Previous researchers explored brand image from different perspectives. For example, the study by Lien et al. (2015) assessed brand image in the context of online hotel reservation, who found out that brand image and price and value perceptions were essential elements that impact on consumers' purchasing intentions. Aghekyan-Simonian et al. (2012) explored the notion in the context of online shopping, who revealed that a particular product's brand image was highly influential over consumers' buying decisions. In another study, Martenson (2007) analyzed relationships between corporate brand image and customer satisfaction and found out that brand image significantly predicted consumer satisfaction and loyalty in the long run. Additionally, Gwinner & Eaton (2013) explored how a sporting event's image was transferred to a brand through sponsorship. Researchers argued when the sponsorship was made visible through placements of brand logo on event flyers and on-site visual installations, the sponsorship resulted with the enhancement of brand image among sports fans (Gwinner & Eaton, 2013, p. 49).

In light of the previous research findings, it can be stated that a positive brand image has the potential to increase purchasing motivations. Thus, it is essential for online video streaming services to create an appealing brand image, that portrays the catalogue, advantages and broadcasting features of the service.

2.3. Perception of Product and Service Quality

Product quality refers to the different features which enable products to have a capacity to respond to consumer demands and provides consumer satisfaction by upgrading products and making them free from any potential defects (Sethi, 2000, p. 12). Product quality is not only related with just the product itself, but the whole environment surrounding it, such as retail stores. For example, Dodds et al. (1991) explain that customers perceive store quality as a vital cue for the quality of the stores' products (p. 309). Thus, companies should prepare a well-rounded and satisfying customer journey that leads them to the purchasing decision.

There are various factors that impacts on the quality of a product. For example, Sethi (2000) found out that product quality was directly related with consumers' influence over the product development process, information integration in the production team and the quality orientation of the company (p. 13). The finding of Sethi (2000) indicates that product development is a two-way process; in which consumer feedback and demands play a key role. The findings of Küster et al. (2016) justifies this argument, which found out that both transactions related, and pre-purchase services were determinants of the customer navigation to purchasing experience (p. 111).

Online shopping experience differs from the retail store consumption behavior. Even though brand related characteristics are relevant for both retail stores and online store experiences, perception of quality in two realms may show differences. For example, while operation speed may not be an important component of customer retail experience, it may be essential for technological services provided online. In line, Hanson (2000) argues that a well-designed Internet website can provide a number of beneficial impacts such as building trust and confidence in the company, reinforcing an image of competence, functionality and usefulness which may motivate users to come back again (p. 44). Findings of Ghouri et al. (2017) provide evidence for this argument, which found out that prior online purchase experience had a positive impact on re-purchasing decision (p. 76).

Yoo and Donthu (2001) categorizes components of perceived quality by specifically taking online shopping experience into consideration. Theorists argue that perceived quality during online shopping is marked by user friendliness, visual design, operation speed and safety (p. 4). While user friendliness refers to the ease of use and ability to search, visual design is related with the service's web design and multimedia features (p. 5). Thirdly, operation speed is about the online processing and interactive responsiveness to consumer demands, while the fourth characteristic, safety, is related with the secure storage of customer personal and financial information (p.6). By taking Yoo and Donthu's (2001) approach into consideration, perceived quality is treated as one of the key variables that has the potential to impact on purchase intentions of free Netflix users to switch into premium membership.

3. METHODOLOGY

With the increasing usage of the Internet and its services worldwide, individuals started spending more time on the Internet in Turkey in the last five years (TÜİK, 2020). The television viewing habits of Turkish audience are evolving in parallel. The research conducted by Turkish Radio and Television Council (TRTC) on television viewing habits of Turkish individuals found out that the daily time spent with viewing traditional television channels decreased 30% in the last 12 years (Turkish Radio and Television Council, 2020). The research also indicated that there is a growth trend when it comes to online video streaming services, such as Netflix, which is the most popular online video streaming service with approximately 1,5 million members in the country. It is also expected that the online video streaming market will grow 30% until 2023 in Turkey (Turkish Radio and Television Council, 2020). In line with this situation, the current study aims to explore the relationship between perceived quality (as perceived by freemium users), brand related characteristics of online video streaming services and the premium service purchasing intentions of freemium users.

Figure 1. Research model of the study

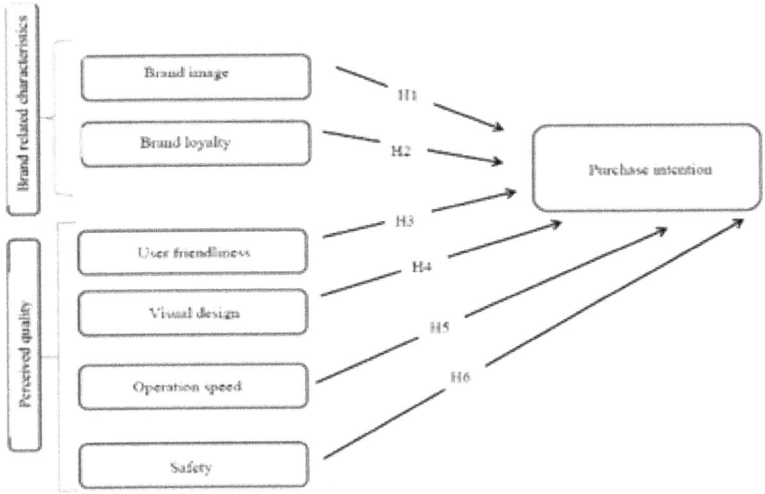

The research population is composed of individuals using online video streaming services in Turkey. Participants who started the survey encountered "Are you using Netflix?" as the first question, to eliminate non-Netflix users. The second question asked if participants were a freemium or a premium user for second step elimination.

The survey was conducted between 13 March – 13 May 2024 online via Survey Monkey application. 31 questions were directed towards respondents in total, including questions on demographics. 789 participants were reached. Participants were informed about the study on the introduction page, and their online permission were received for participation. With the removal of missing or non-user data, responses of 610 individual remained in the dataset. The data that support the findings of this study are available on request from the corresponding author. The data are not publicly available due to privacy or ethical restrictions.

The dependent variable of the study is purchasing intention, while brand related characteristics (brand loyalty, brand image) and perceived quality (user friendliness, visual design, operation speed, safety) are independent variables. The scale of the dependent variable (purchase intention) is adapted from the study of Chang and Chen (2008). The scale for brand related characteristics is developed by the researcher of the current study. Following the development of scale that included items on brand image and brand loyalty, the scale was pilot tested with 69 participants. As the reliability of the scale remained above 0,85, items were entered into a factor analysis to see whether the items of the scale were grouped under brand image and brand loyalty umbrellas. Groupings remained in line with the designated scale during the development process. The validated brand related characteristics scale is composed of 11 items. Items used in the scale are presented in Table 1.

Table 1. Items on brand related characteristics scale

I1: Netflix contents are always my first choice.
I2: Netflix would be my first choice to watch, even though I had membership to other online video streaming platforms at the same time.
I3: I don't feel loyal to Netflix (reverse coded).
I4: I am sure that contents provided by Netflix are the best among all online video streaming platforms.
I5: I think Netflix is an honest and a transparent company.
I6: I feel good when I watch shows on Netflix.
I7: I feel the urge to watch a show if it is a Netflix production.
I8: Netflix offers high quality productions.
I9: The services offered by Netflix are not functional (reverse coded).
I10: Netflix consistently offers satisfying services.
I11: Netflix productions are recognized at global level.

The perceived quality scale is adapted from the study of Yoo and Donthu (2001). which consisted of 9 items (2 items on user friendliness <i.e. Netflix is convenient to use>, 3 items on visual design <i.e. Netflix shows good scenes from TV shows during trailers>, 2 items on operation speed <i.e. Netflix services have quick processing> and 2 items on safety <i.e. I am confident of security with Netflix website>). All items are designed in line with Likert 5-point scale format (ranging from "1-I completely disagree to 5-I completely agree").

In line with the designated variables, 6 hypotheses are developed for exploration, which are as follows:

H1: There is a significant relationship between brand loyalty and purchase intention.

H2: There is a significant relationship between brand image and purchase intention.

H3: There is a significant relationship between user friendliness and purchase intention.

H4: There is a significant relationship between visual design and purchase intention.

H5: There is a significant relationship between operation speed and purchase intention.

H6: There is a significant relationship between safety and purchase intention.

The dataset was analyzed by using the latest version of SPSS software (SPSS 25). After the coding procedure, the data on demographics were obtained with frequency analysis. After computing independent and dependent variables, a reliability study was conducted to see whether the alpha value of each variable remain above 0.7. To assess potential relationships, independent and dependent variables were entered into multiple regression analyses, following correlation analysis.

4. FINDINGS

4.1. Demographics and Media Consumption

The 62% of respondents are female, while 38% are male. The average of participants' age is found to be 33, while the majority is composed of individuals aged 26-34 (39%), followed by 19-25 (34%), 35-44 (17%) and 45-59 (10%). The majority of respondents are university graduates (44%), followed by master's degree holders (28%), high school graduates (17%), PhD holders (6%) and primary school graduates (5%).

The majority of respondents state they are connected to the Internet for 2-3 hours (39,3%), followed by individuals spending 4-5 hours (36,7), 0-1-hour (17,3%) and 5 or more (6,7%) hours on the Internet.

All participants are freemium Netflix users. Participants are asked to order the online video streaming services they watch the most. The majority state they watch Netflix (69,3%) the most, which are followed by BeINConnect (13,7%), Blu TV (7,3%), Puhu TV (5,5%), Amazon Prime (3,9%) and other services (0,3%). beIN Connect is an online video streaming service, launched by Qatar-based sports and entertainment network company, beIN Media Group. Blu TV is a Turkish media provider launched in 2015 by Doğan Media Group in Turkey. Puhu TV was established by Turkish media company Doğuş Media Group in 2016. Amazon Prime was launched by Jeff Bezos, the CEO of Amazon.com Inc. in 2005. Even though Amazon Prime does not offer specific contents for Turkish audience, a marginal group of respondents state they follow the network's media contents. Netflix, beIN Connect, Blu TV and Puhu TV offer movies and television series produced in Turkey and in Turkish language, besides international television shows.

Participants are also asked to state the average time they spend on Netflix. The majority explain they watch Netflix for 2-3 hours on a daily basis (34,2%), followed by 4-5 hours (33,9%), 0-1 hour (26%) and 5 or more hours (5,9%).

4.2. Reliability and Factor Analyses

In order to test the reliability of independent and dependent variables, reliability analyses were conducted via SPSS.

Table 2. Reliability analyses results

Variable	Cronbach's alpha value	# of items
Brand related characteristics	0,91	11
Perceived quality	0,89	9
Purchase intention	0,94	3

The Cronbach's alpha values of each variable should be 0,7 or above to be reliable. Table 2 presents the findings of reliability analyses.

In order to test the consistencies of sub-variables two separate factor analyses were conducted for brand related characteristics and perceived quality variables. Table 3 reveals the results for factor analysis on brand related characteristics. The sub-variables, brand loyalty and brand image are grouped in line with the designated scale, except I8 (I8: Netflix offers high quality productions), which was primarily developed as a representative of the brand loyalty, however. However, the item loaded with the brand image items, thus included within the brand image scale.

Table 3. Factor analysis on brand related characteristics

Brand related characteristics	Components	
	1 (brand loyalty)	2 (brand image)
Brand related characteristic (BRC) 1	**0,896**	0,215
BRC 2	**0,824**	0,206
BRC 3	**0,811**	0,305
BRC 4	**0,810**	0,315
BRC 5	**0,808**	0,327
BRC 6	**0,796**	0,349
BRC 7	**0,587**	0,465
BRC 8	0,322	**0,565**
BRC 9	0,474	**0,648**
BRC 10	0,492	**0,786**
BRC 11	0,404	**0,805**

Table 4 reveals the results for factor analysis on perceived quality sub-variables. The groupings resulting from the factor analysis are in line with the groupings in the study of Yoo and Donthu (2000).

Table 4. Factor analysis on perceived quality

Perceived quality	**Components**			
	1 (user friendliness)	**2 (visual design)**	**3 (operation speed)**	**2 (safety)**
Perceived quality (PQ) 1	**0,913**	0,215	0,113	0,215
PQ 2	**0,899**	0,134	0,273	0,269
PQ 3	0,332	**0,734**	0,113	0,305
PQ 4	0,271	**0,696**	0,208	0,325
PQ 5	0,134	**0,638**	0,178	0,225
PQ 6	0,108	0,299	**0,736**	0,499
PQ 7	0,296	0,265	**0,647**	0,265
PQ 8	0,308	0,365	0,108	**0,912**
PQ 9	0,434	0,348	0,274	**0,866**

The final reliability analyses include seven variables in total, which include groupings obtained through factor analyses.

Table 5. Second reliability analyses results

Variable	**Cronbach's alpha value**	**# of items**
Brand loyalty	0,91	7
Brand image	0,75	4
User friendliness	0,82	2
Visual design	0,78	3
Operation speed	0,81	2
Safety	0,93	2
Purchase intention	0,94	3

Table 5 presents the results of final reliability analyses. All Cronbach's alpha values remain above 0.7.

4.3. Correlation Analysis

When correlations between the dependent variable and dependent variables are assessed, it can be observed that purchase intention (PI) has the highest correlation with visual design (VD) (r=0,628; p<0,01).

Table 6. Correlation analysis results

		BL	BI	UF	VD	OS	S	PI
Brand loyalty (BL)	r	1						
	p							
Brand image (BI)	r	.129**	1					
	p	.000						
User friendliness (UF)	r	.433**	.139**	1				
	p	.000	.003					
Visual design (VD)	r	.679**	.229**	.407**	1			
	p	.000	.000	.000				
Operation speed (OS)	r	.398**	.161**	.513*	.389**	1		
	p	.000	.000	.000	.000			
Safety (S)	r	.448**	.152**	.443**	.366**	.628**	1**	
	p	.000	.000	.000	.000	.000		
Purchase intention (PI)	r	.522**	.203**	.293**	.634**	.413**	.582**	1**
	p	.000	.000	.000	.000	.000	.000	

r: factor of correlation, **significant correlation at 0,01 level (two-way)

The lowest correlation in the analysis remains between brand loyalty and brand image (r=0,129; p<0,01), which is a significant finding, as both variables are deriving from the same umbrella variable (brand characteristics).

4.4. Multiple Regression Analyses

Regression analysis is a statistical method to assess potential relationships between two or more variables. Regression analysis is mainly utilized to test the hypotheses for a designated scientific study. By conducting a regression analysis, the researcher can obtain scientific evidence whether there is a significant relationship among the chosen variables. As the current study involves more than one independent variable, multiple regression analyses were conducted.

Table 7. Regression analyses results

Dependent variable: Purchase intention					
	B	**SD**	**Beta**	**t**	**p**
Brand loyalty	.086	.059	.088	1.309	.256
Brand image	.336	.018	.074	2.765	.000
User friendliness	.234	.043	.466	2.987	.000
Visual design	.145	.047	.351	4.932	.000
Operation speed	.192	.034	.234	4.323	.000
Safety	.076	.054	.432	1.923	.000

The findings of multiple regression analyses reveal highest significant relationships between user friendliness and purchase intention (Beta value=0,466; p=0,000), followed by safety and purchase intention (Beta value=0,432; p=0,000), visual design and purchase intention (Beta value=0,351; p=0,000), operation speed and purchase intention (Beta value=0,234; p=0,000) and brand image and purchase intention (Beta value=0,074; p=0,000). Thus, H2, H3, H4, H5 and H6 are accepted.

Table 8. Test results of hypotheses

Hypotheses	**p value**	**Result**
H1: There is a significant relationship between brand loyalty and purchase intention.	p>0,01	REJECTED
H2: There is a significant relationship between brand image and purchase intention.	p<0,01	ACCEPTED
H3: There is a significant relationship between user friendliness and purchase intention.	p<0,01	ACCEPTED
H4: There is a significant relationship between visual design and purchase intention.	p<0,01	ACCEPTED
H5: There is a significant relationship between operation speed and purchase intention.	p<0,01	ACCEPTED
H6: There is a significant relationship between safety and purchase intention.	p<0,01	ACCEPTED

Findings also indicate that brand loyalty does not predict purchase intention among free Netflix subscribers (Beta value=0,088; p=0,256). Thus, H1 is rejected.

5. DISCUSSION AND CONCLUSION

The current study aimed to explore potential relationships between brand related characteristics (brand loyalty; brand image), perceived quality (user friendliness; visual design; operation speed; safety) and free Netflix users' premium (paid) membership purchasing intention. A total of 610 participants responded the designed survey curated in line with the variables of the study. Analysis procedures utilized from reliability, factor, correlation and multiple regression analyses, which were conducted via SPSS 25 software, following the data coding procedures.

The results revealed that first hypothesis (H1: There is a significant relationship between brand loyalty and purchase intention) was rejected, which means brand loyalty does not predict consumers' purchase intentions. Even though Oliver (1999) claimed brand loyalty could be fostered during trial periods such as freemium membership, findings of the current study show that this situation is not the case in the context of online video streaming platforms. Brand loyalty is only sustained after premium members feel satisfied with the streaming platform, thus feel loyal towards the brand thereafter. Moreover, there is no clue whether trial period is the first step taken towards the development of brand loyalty among new consumers, as claimed by Lobschat et al. (2013).

The second hypothesis (H2: There is a significant relationship between brand image and purchase intention) measured the potential impact of another brand related characteristic, brand image on consumers' purchasing intention. The hypothesis is accepted as a consequence of the analysis. This situation indicates that brand image is an essential predictor of consumers' purchasing behavior. Therefore, online video streaming platforms should invest in their brand image and its components, which are categorized by Wijaya (2013) as brand identity, brand competence and benefit, brand personality, brand behavior and attitude and brand association (p. 62).

Findings also revealed that perceived quality predicted consumers' buying decision, as H3, H4, H5 and H6 hypotheses are accepted. Results indicated perceived quality characteristics (user friendliness, visual design, operating speed and safety) all have significant relationships between premium membership purchasing intensions of freemium Netflix users. Perceived quality is related with how individuals assess the quality of a particular brand, its products and its services according to its appearance, word-of-mouth (WOM) interactions, usability, visual presence and security. This finding indicates that freemium members should be provided services at premium level, so that they can explore each future offered by the Netflix, which would impact on their premium membership purchasing decisions.

Overall, this study provided important hints regarding marketing communication process of online video streaming services, by specifically focusing on Netflix freemium users. The effectiveness of marketing communication strategy is essential during the trial period, as potential consumers can easily be distracted by a more advantageous offer by a different company or may feel uncomfortable if trial-period company communication is extremely intense. According to the results, it can be stated that online video streaming services should invest in their brand image, visual design, user friendliness, operation speed and safety, which should be available for testing during freemium trial period.

The limitation of the current study is that it is solely limited with freemium Netflix users. Future research may explore whether the assessed variables are also relevant electronic media services other than video streaming. As it was revealed that brand loyalty does not predict purchase intention during trial period, future researches may also prefer examining during which stage of usage brand loyalty is achieved and sustained in the context of online video streaming services.

REFERENCES

Aaker, D. A. (1991). *Managing brand equity*. Free Press.

Aaker, D. A. (1996). *Measuring brand equity across products and markets*. Free Press. DOI: 10.2307/41165845

Aghekyan-Simonian, M., Forsythe, S., Kwon, W. S., & Chattaraman, V. (2012). The role of product brand image and online store image on perceived risks and online purchase intentions for apparel. *Journal of Retailing and Consumer Services*, 19(3), 325–331. DOI: 10.1016/j.jretconser.2012.03.006

Baalbaki, S. S. (2012). *Consumer perception of brand equity measurement: A new scale*. Dissertation prepared for the degree of Doctor of Philosophy. University of Texas.

Bucciferro, C. (2019). Women and Netflix: Disrupting traditional boundaries between television and film. *Feminist Media Studies*, 19(7), 1053–1056. DOI: 10.1080/14680777.2019.1667076

Chang, H. H., & Chen, S. W. (2008). The Impact of online store environment cues on purchase intention. *Online Information Review*, 32(6), 818–841. DOI: 10.1108/14684520810923953

Demirli, C., & Kütük, Ö. F. (2010). Anlamsal web (3.0) ve ontolojilerine genel bir bakış. *İstanbul Ticaret Üniversitesi. Fen Bilimleri Dergisi*, 9(18), 97–107.

Digital Age. (2020, June 17). Netflix Türkiye abone sayısı ve elde edilen gelir açıklandı. https://digitalage.com.tr/netflix-turkiye-abone-sayisi-ve-elde-edilen-gelir-aciklandi/ (Accessed 01 August 2020).

Dodds, W. B., Kent, B. M., & Grewal, D. (1991). Effects of price, brand and store information on buyers' product evaluation. *JMR, Journal of Marketing Research*, 28(August), 307–319.

Ghouri, A., Haq, M. A., & Khan, N. R. (2017). Customer perception on online purchase intention: The impact of online shopping orientations on online buying intention. *The Eurasia Proceedings of Science, Technology* [EPSTEM]. *Engineering & Mathematics*, 1, 76–82.

Gwinner, K. P., & Eaton, J. (2013). Building brand image through event sponsorship: The role of image transfer. *Journal of Advertising*, 28(4), 47–57. DOI: 10.1080/00913367.1999.10673595

Hanson, W. (2000). *Principles of Internet marketing*. South-Western College Publishing.

Hung, C. H. (2008). The effect of brand image on public relations perceptions and customer loyalty. *International Journal of Management*, 25(2), 237–246.

Innis, H. (2006). *İmparatorluk ve iletişim araçları*. Ütopya Yayınevi.

Karaduman, S., & Aciyan, E. P. (2019). Netflix'in ilk Türk dizisi "Hakan Muhafız" üzerine bir alımlama analizi. *Akdeniz Üniversitesi İletişim Fakültesi Dergisi. Aralık*, (32), 669–687.

Kokas, A. (2020). Chilling Netflix: Financialization and the influence of the Chinese market on the American entertainment industry. *Information Communication and Society*, 23(3), 407–419. DOI: 10.1080/1369118X.2018.1510534

Kotler, P., & Barich, H. (1991). A framework for marketing image management. *Sloan Management Review*, 2(32), 94–104. PMID: 10111301

Lien, C., Wen, M., Huang, L., & Wu, K. (2015). Online hotel booking: The effects of brand image, price, trust, and value on purchase intentions. *Asia Pacific Management Review*, 20(4), 210–218. DOI: 10.1016/j.apmrv.2015.03.005

Lobschat, L., Zinnbauer, M. A., Pallas, F., & Joachimsthaler, E. (2013). Why social currency becomes a key driver of a firm's brand equity: Insights from the automotive industry. *Long Range Planning*, 46(1–2), 125–148. DOI: 10.1016/j.lrp.2012.11.004

Martenson, R. (2007). Corporate brand image, satisfaction and store loyalty: A study of the store as a brand, store brands and manufacturer brands. *International Journal of Retail & Distribution Management*, 35(7), 544–555. DOI: 10.1108/09590550710755921

McLuhan, M. (2001). *Global köy*. Skala Yayıncılık.

Newman, J. W., & Werbel, R. A. (1973). Multivariate analysis of brand loyalty for major household appliances. *JMR, Journal of Marketing Research*, 10(4), 404–409.

Oliver, R. L. (1999). Whence consumer loyalty? *Journal of Marketing*, 63(4_suppl1), 33–44. DOI: 10.1177/00222429990634s105

Sethi, R. (2000). New product quality and production development teams. *Journal of Marketing*, 64(2), 1–14. DOI: 10.1509/jmkg.64.2.1.17999

Seyitoğlu, Z. (2019). *Türkiye'de dijital halkla ilişkilerde değişen müşteri deneyimi: Chatbot uygulamaları*. T.C. İstanbul Kültür Üniversitesi Lisansüstü Eğitim Enstitüsü Yayınlanmış Yüksek Lisans Tezi.

Statista. (2020a). Most popular video streaming services in the United States as of September 201, by monthly average users. https://www.statista.com/statistics/910875/us-most-popular-video-streaming-services-by-monthly-average-users/ (Accessed 13 July 2020).

Statista (2020b). Number of Netflix paying streaming subscribers worldwide from 3rd quarter 2011 to 2nd quarter 2020. https://www.statista.com/statistics/250934/quarterly-number-of-Netflix streaming-subscribers-worldwide/ (Accessed 13 July 2020).

Stein, J. B., Mongeau, P., Posteher, K., & Veluscek, A. (2019). Netflix and chill? Exploring and refining differing motivations in friends with benefits relationships. *The Canadian Journal of Human Sexuality*, 28(3), 317–327. DOI: 10.3138/cjhs.2018-0045

Tellis, G. J. (1988). Advertising Explore. Loyally and brand purchase: A two-stage model of choice. *JMR, Journal of Marketing Research*, 25(May), 134–144. DOI: 10.1177/002224378802500202

Turkish Radio and Television Council. (2020). http://www.rtuk.gov.tr (Accessed 03 March 2020).

Turkish Statistical Institute. (2020). http://www.tuik.gov.tr (Accessed 02 July 2020).

Upshaw, L. B. (1995). *Building brand identity: A strategy for success in a hostile marketplace*. John Wiley & Sons.

Wayne, M. L. (2009). Netflix, Amazon and branded television content in subscription video on demand portals. *Media Culture & Society*, 40(5), 725–741. DOI: 10.1177/0163443717736118

Whitler, K. A., & Farris, P. W. (2017, March). The impact of cyber-attacks on brand image: Why proactive marketing expertise is needed for managing data breaches. *International Journal of Advertising*, 3–9.

Wijaya, B. S. (2013). Dimensions of brand image: A conceptual review from the perspective of brand communication. *European Journal of Business and Management*, 5(31), 55–65.

Yeh, Y., & Choi, S. M. (2011). MINI-lovers, maxi-mouths: An investigation of antecedents to eWOM intention among brand community members. *Journal of Marketing Communications*, 11(3), 145–162. DOI: 10.1080/13527260903351119

Yengin, D. (2015). Yeni medyanın olanakları: Semantik web. *The Turkish Online Journal of Design. Art and Communication*, 5(1), 44–53.

Yoo, B., & Donthu, N. (2001). Developing a scale to measure the perceived quality of an internet shopping site (SITEQUAL). *Quarterly Journal of Electronic Commerce*, 2(1), 31–47.

Zaglia, M. E. (2013). Brand communities embedded in social networks. *Journal of Business Research*, 66(2), 216–223. DOI: 10.1016/j.jbusres.2012.07.015 PMID: 23564989

ADDITIONAL READING

Ali, M. (2021). *Remote Work and Sustainable Changes for the Future of Global Business.* IGI Global. https://www.igi-global.com/book/remote-work-sustainable-changes-future/264375

Ali, M. (2022). *Future Role of Sustainable Innovative Technologies in Crisis Management.* IGI Global. https://www.igi-global.com/book/future-role-sustainable-innovative-technologies/281281

Ali, M. (2023). *Shifting Paradigms in the Rapidly Developing Global Digital Ecosystem: A GCC Perspective.* In Digital Entrepreneurship and Co-Creating Value Through Digital Encounters (pp. 145-166). IGI Global. https://www.igi-global.com/chapter/shifting-paradigms-in-the-rapidly-developing-global-digital-ecosystem/323525

Ali, M. (2023). T*axonomy of Industry 4.0 Technologies in Digital Entrepreneurship and Co-Creating Value*. In *Digital Entrepreneurship and Co-Creating Value Through Digital Encounters* (pp. 24–55). IGI Global., https://www.igi-global.com/chapter/taxonomy-of-industry-40-technologies-in-digital-entrepreneurship-and-co-creating-value/323520 DOI: 10.4018/978-1-6684-7416-7.ch002

Ali, M., & Wood-Harper, T. (2021). *Fostering Communication and Learning with Underutilized Technologies in Higher Education*. IGI Global. https://www.igi-global.com/book/fostering-communication-learning-underutilized-technologies/244593

Ali, M., Wood-Harper, T., & Kutar, M. (2023). Multi-Perspectives of Contemporary Digital Transformation Models of Complex Innovation Management. In *Digital Entrepreneurship and Co-Creating Value Through Digital Encounters* (pp. 79–96). IGI Global., https://www.igi-global.com/chapter/multi-perspectives-of-contemporary-digital-transformation-models-of-complex-innovation-management/323522 DOI: 10.4018/978-1-6684-7416-7.ch004

Ali, M. B. (2021). Internet of Things (IoT) to Foster Communication and Information Sharing: A Case of UK Higher Education. In Ali, M. B., & Wood-Harper, T. (Eds.), *Fostering Communication and Learning With Underutilized Technologies in Higher Education* (pp. 1–20). IGI Global., https://www.igi-global.com/chapter/internet-of-things-iot-to-foster-communication-and-information-sharing/262718/ DOI: 10.4018/978-1-7998-4846-2.ch001

Ali, M. B., & Wood-Harper, T. (2022). Artificial Intelligence (AI) as a Decision-Making Tool to Control Crisis Situations. In *Future Role of Sustainable Innovative Technologies in Crisis Management*. IGI Global., https://www.igi-global.com/chapter/artificial-intelligence-ai-as-a-decision-making-tool-to-control-crisis-situations/298931 DOI: 10.4018/978-1-7998-9815-3.ch006

Ali, M. B., Wood-Harper, T., & Ramlogan, R. (2020). A Framework Strategy to Overcome Trust Issues on Cloud Computing Adoption in Higher Education. In Modern Principles, Practices, and Algorithms for Cloud Security (pp. 162-183). IGI Global. https://www.igi-global.com/chapter/a-framework-strategy-to-overcome-trust-issues-on-cloud-computing-adoption-in-higher-education/238907/

Chapter 14
OpenStreetMap and Digital Health: Enhancing Patient Care and Healthcare Delivery

Pujita Roy
https://orcid.org/0009-0007-7693-9232
North South University, Bangladesh

Ulfat Khan
Bankura Sammilani Medical College, India

Munir Ahmad
https://orcid.org/0000-0003-4836-6151
Survey of Pakistan, Pakistan

ABSTRACT

This chapter explored the applications of OpenStreetMap (OSM) in digital health, highlighting improvements in patient navigation, resource mapping, and epidemic response. Integrating OSM data into digital health platforms enhances patient journeys by providing real-time navigation and access to public transportation options. It can help in locating urgent care centers and mapping specialist providers, chronic condition support services, and mental health resources. During epidemics, OSM supports disease surveillance and vaccination site mapping. OSM can also help to identify underserved areas to promote telehealth and incorporate social determinants of health for a holistic approach. Challenges such as data accuracy, consistency, and completeness can be addressed through community moderation, partnerships, and supplementary data sources. Ensuring data currency through real-time updates

DOI: 10.4018/979-8-3373-0086-3.ch014

Copyright © 2025, IGI Global. Copying or distributing in print or electronic forms without written permission of IGI Global is prohibited.

and user feedback mechanisms can further enhance the reliability of OSM-based digital health applications.

INTRODUCTION

The healthcare sector is one of the most progressive sectors, which is always seeking to optimize the improvements of patient care and the healthcare system (Aceto et al., 2018; Al-Jaroodi et al., 2020; Awad et al., 2021; Karatas et al., 2022). At the core of this continual advancement is the technological element, which constantly presents novel approaches in identifying and handling diseases and enhancing patient care. The shift in the healthcare delivery system that emphasizes patient-centered care requires that research findings and patient details be correctly captured and easily retrievable by both caregivers and patients. Geographic data, including the locational position of healthcare points., is essential in this context (Cheng et al., 2020; Gul & Guneri, 2021; Wang, 2020). However, standard navigation applications often fail to meet these needs, either missing essential information or containing data inconsistencies. This is where OpenStreetMap (OSM) can play the role of an effective way out. OSM is a wiki-like project to build a free map of the world. As a source of fine-tuning location-based intelligence, OSM represents an opportunity to improve healthcare and everyday practice.

This is due to the high level of detail and the constant update of data in cooperation with the members, OSM provides healthcare providers and patients with access to updated geographical information. This can go a long way to boost the efficiency of managing health care delivery in general and the ability to plan, fund, and make health care accessible to the populace. It means that the importance of using OSM in digital health is manifold: First, due to the open sources, the data is well-updated and is inclusively large enough to encompass almost all types of healthcare facilities, pharmacies, and many other POIs (Grinberger et al., 2021; Minghini et al., 2022; Seto, 2022). Such dynamic updating also guarantees that healthcare providers and patients are capable of utilizing the most current information as a tool in implementing efficient decision-making processes in the provision of quality healthcare.

Secondly, OSM is based on an open-source model which means people can see what is going on and participate in the process. Ensuring that many people contribute to the project, not only improves the quality and reliability of the data collected but the contributors also feel a sense of ownership of the data collected (Herfort et al., 2021; Sarkar & Anderson, 2022; Schröder-Bergen et al., 2022). The other notable aspect of OSM is that it is an open-source tool and therefore changes and improvements of the tool and innovations can be made as and when required as they come from a global pool of users of the tool. Besides, this approach does not only enhance the definition and quality of the dataset but also enable it to be dynamic based on the current innovative healthcare issues encountered.

The objective of this chapter is to understand the potential of the OSM in digital health to know how this mapping tool can add value to the healthcare system. This paper also aims to demonstrate how the integration of OSM enables healthcare professionals to have geographical information that can be vital for several purposes, including health research and even delivery of healthcare services in areas with low provision. related to OSM integration and the possibilities for their resolution to facilitate its more efficient use in the context of digital health.

FUNCTIONALITIES OF OPENSTREETMAP

This section delves into the core functionalities of OSM that make it particularly valuable for digital health applications.

Collaborative Platform

OpenStreetMap distinguishes itself from traditional mapping services through its unique collaborative approach. Unlike conventional mapping systems that often limit user interaction to passive viewing, OSM operates as a dynamic, interactive platform. This allows anyone with an internet connection to actively contribute geographical data. Users can add new locations, edit existing entries, and provide detailed descriptions of various points of interest. This inclusive model harnesses the collective knowledge and efforts of a global community, resulting in a map that is continually updated and refined (Minghini et al., 2017; Poiani et al., 2016).

This collaborative nature ensures that OSM remains responsive to real-world changes. As new healthcare facilities are established, or existing ones are modified or closed, users can quickly update the map to reflect these changes. This makes OSM an incredibly accurate and reliable resource for up-to-date geographical information. Moreover, the ability to provide detailed descriptions enables contributors to include critical information that might be overlooked by traditional mapping services, such as the presence of specific medical departments, hours of operation, or accessibility features. This level of detail is invaluable in healthcare, where accurate and comprehensive information can significantly impact patient care and resource allocation (Herringer et al., 2023; Ihantamalala et al., 2020).

Points of Interest (POIs)

A crucial aspect of OSM for digital health is the concept of POIs. POIs are specific locations marked on the map that come with additional information, making them highly valuable for various applications. In the context of healthcare, POIs can represent a diverse array of vital locations, enhancing the utility of OSM for both healthcare providers and patients (Y. Li & Xu, 2021; Psyllidis et al., 2022).

POIs can mark essential healthcare facilities, including hospitals, clinics, urgent care centers, and specialized treatment centers such as oncology centers and ophthalmology clinics. By providing precise locations and detailed information about these facilities, OSM ensures that patients can easily find and access the care they need. Moreover, POIs can include both independent and chain pharmacies. This is particularly useful for patients needing to locate the nearest pharmacy to fill prescriptions, obtain over-the-counter medications, or seek pharmaceutical advice.

Furthermore, POIs can identify various allied health services such as physical therapy centers, mental health clinics, and dental offices. These services are integral to comprehensive healthcare, and having them clearly marked on a map helps patients access a full spectrum of care. Additionally, beyond direct medical care, POIs can denote support services crucial for patient well-being. This includes blood banks, ambulance services, senior citizen centers, and disability support centers. Marking these services ensures that patients and caregivers can easily find and utilize essential support resources.

Each POI on OSM can include detailed descriptions, contact information, operating hours, and other relevant data. This granularity of information makes OSM an invaluable tool for planning and navigating healthcare needs. Whether it's finding the nearest urgent care center in an emergency or locating a specialized clinic for ongoing treatment, the detailed and up-to-date POIs in OSM enhance healthcare delivery and patient outcomes.

Advantages of OSM over Traditional Mapping Services

When considering digital health applications, OSM offers several significant advantages over traditional mapping services.

- OSM data is freely accessible and editable, unlike traditional mapping services that may restrict access through paywalls or licensing agreements. This open access encourages developers to integrate OSM data into digital health platforms without financial barriers, promoting innovation and enhancing accessibility to geographic healthcare information.

- The open-source nature of OSM promotes transparency in data sourcing and updates. Users can view edits and contributions made by others, facilitating community-driven oversight and correction of any inaccuracies. This transparency ensures that healthcare providers and patients can rely on accurate, up-to-date geographic information critical for effective healthcare delivery.
- With a global community of contributors, OSM undergoes continuous improvement. New healthcare facilities, pharmacies, and allied health services are added regularly. Existing entries are updated with changes in operating hours, services offered, or contact details. Detailed descriptions are provided, enriching the map with comprehensive healthcare resource information. This dynamic updating process ensures that OSM remains a robust and evolving tool for healthcare navigation.
- Many applications utilizing OSM data allow users to download maps for offline use. This feature is particularly beneficial in areas with limited internet connectivity, ensuring healthcare providers and patients can access essential information about nearby facilities, pharmacies, and support services even without an internet connection. This offline capability enhances the reliability and usability of digital health tools based on OSM data, especially in emergencies or remote locations.
- The open nature of OSM data enables developers to customize map displays to meet specific digital health needs. For instance, a mental health services app can integrate OSM data to highlight details such as appointment booking options, insurance acceptance, and specific therapeutic specialties offered by mental health clinics. This customization capability enhances the relevance and usefulness of OSM-based digital health applications, catering directly to the diverse needs of healthcare providers and patients alike.

Thus, OSM's flexibility, transparency, continuous improvement, offline accessibility, and customization options make it a superior choice for digital health applications compared to traditional mapping services. By leveraging OSM's rich and freely editable data, developers can create innovative tools that enhance healthcare access, efficiency, and patient outcomes across diverse healthcare settings. By leveraging these core functionalities and advantages, OSM can empower the creation of robust and dynamic digital health solutions that can significantly enhance patient care and healthcare delivery. Table 1 shows the comparison of traditional mapping services vs. OpenStreetMap.

Table 1. Comparison of traditional mapping services vs. OpenStreetMap

Features	Traditional Mapping Services	OpenStreetMap
Data Editability	Limited or Restricted	Freely Editable
Data Transparency	Limited Visibility into Data Sources	Open-source, Edits Visible
Data Accuracy	Relies on Internal Processes	Community-driven Verification
Cost of Use	May Require Subscription Fees	Free and Open-source
Offline Accessibility	Limited or Requires Downloading Paid Apps	Downloadable Maps for Offline Use

APPLICATIONS OF OPENSTREETMAP IN DIGITAL HEALTH

This section showcases the practical applications of OSM in the realm of digital health. It explores how healthcare providers and patients can benefit from integrating OSM data into digital health platforms.

Improved Patient Navigation

In the context of digital health, leveraging OSM data significantly enhances patient navigation and accessibility to healthcare services through the following ways.

Digital health platforms can seamlessly integrate OSM data to streamline patient journeys to scheduled appointments. By providing turn-by-turn navigation features, complete with real-time traffic updates and estimated arrival times, patients can navigate efficiently to clinics, hospitals, or specialist offices. This integration minimizes the stress of navigating unfamiliar routes, ensuring patients arrive punctually and prepared for their appointments. Moreover, in moments of sudden illness or injury, OSM data within healthcare applications becomes invaluable. Patients can quickly locate the nearest urgent care centers, walk-in clinics, or emergency rooms. This capability not only facilitates prompt access to critical healthcare services but also optimizes healthcare resource utilization by directing patients to the most appropriate facilities based on their needs and geographic proximity (J. Li et al., 2022; Pagar et al., 2024; Rousell & Zipf, 2017).

In addition, recognizing the diverse transportation needs of patients, digital health apps utilizing OSM data can highlight public transportation options in proximity to healthcare facilities. This includes identifying nearby bus stops, train stations, or other transit hubs. For patients reliant on public transport, especially those with limited mobility or unfamiliarity with the area, this feature simplifies the journey to healthcare appointments. By displaying accessible public transportation routes, patients can confidently navigate their way to healthcare services, promoting independence and reducing logistical barriers. A typical workflow of utilizing OSM data in a digital health app for appointment scheduling is described in Figure 1.

Figure 1. A typical workflow of using OSM data in a digital health app for appointment scheduling

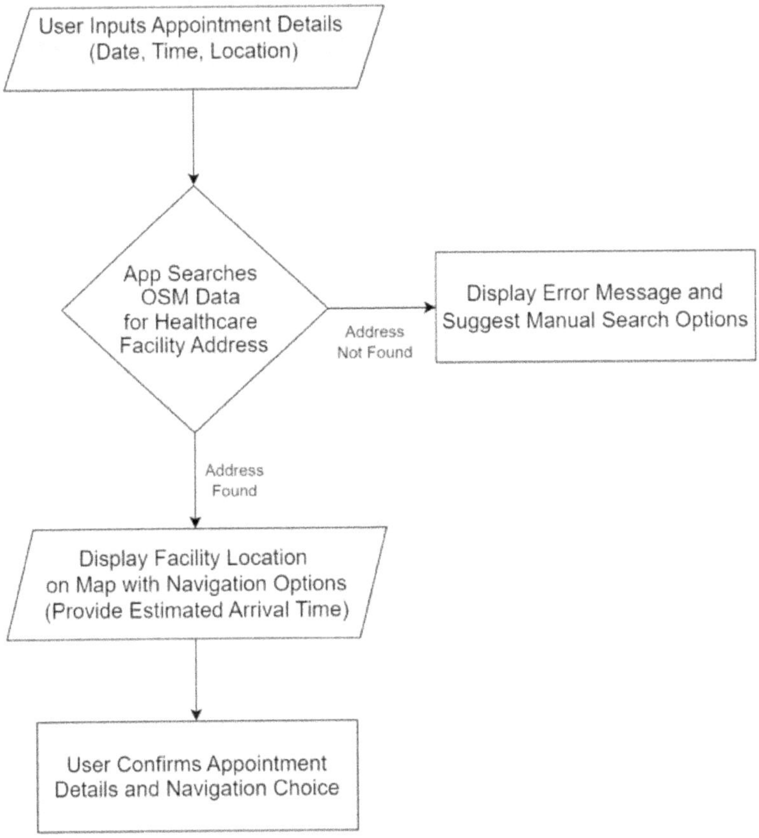

Enhanced Resource Mapping

Employing OSM data also enhances the mapping of essential resources for patients, facilitating easier access to specialized care and support services (Liu, 2021; Mooney et al., 2021; Vu et al., 2021).

Digital health platforms can harness OSM data to create detailed maps of specialist healthcare providers across various fields such as dermatology, cardiology, neurology, and more. By integrating comprehensive information about specialist practices and their locations, patients can efficiently locate and access care within their healthcare network or geographic area. This capability reduces the time and effort typically spent searching for appropriate specialists, ensuring timely access to specialized medical expertise and improving patient outcomes.

Moreover, for patients managing chronic conditions like diabetes, heart disease, or other long-term health issues, OSM data can map essential support services. This includes identifying diabetic clinics, nutritionists, specialized fitness centers, and other resources crucial for managing chronic conditions effectively. By visualizing these support services on a map, digital health platforms empower patients to proactively engage in their healthcare management, enhancing overall well-being and quality of life through easier access to necessary resources.

Furthermore, digital health applications focused on mental health can leverage OSM to map critical mental health support services. This includes identifying therapists, counseling centers, support groups, crisis hotlines, and other mental health resources within communities. By providing readily available information on mental health services, OSM-enabled apps enable individuals seeking mental health assistance to locate and connect with appropriate resources quickly and discreetly. This accessibility reduces barriers to mental health care, promotes early intervention, and supports holistic well-being for individuals navigating mental health challenges.

Epidemic and Outbreak Response

OSM data can play a pivotal role in facilitating rapid and effective responses to disease outbreaks (Minghini et al., 2022; Mooney et al., 2021) in certain ways as endorsed below.

Public health agencies can leverage real-time OSM data to map the geographical spread of infectious diseases. By visualizing disease hotspots and transmission patterns on a map, agencies can swiftly identify areas with high concentrations of cases and potential outbreak clusters. This spatial information is crucial for conducting targeted disease surveillance, implementing timely interventions, and allocating resources where they are most needed. OSM's dynamic and continuously updated dataset enables public health officials to monitor epidemic trends closely, supporting informed decision-making and proactive measures to contain and mitigate the spread of infectious diseases.

Furthermore, during vaccination campaigns, OSM data can be seamlessly integrated into public health applications to map vaccination sites across communities. By plotting vaccination centers, clinics, and other sites offering immunization services on a map, individuals can easily locate the nearest vaccination site. This accessibility empowers community members to schedule appointments conveniently, reducing logistical barriers and promoting widespread vaccine uptake. Additionally, OSM's capability to provide real-time updates on vaccination site availability and operational hours enhances the efficiency of vaccination campaigns, ensuring that vaccination efforts are well-coordinated and accessible to all segments of the population.

Advancements in Digital Health Using OSM Data

In addition to its current applications as summarized in Table 2, OSM data holds promise for advancing digital health in several innovative ways as illustrated below.

Table 2. Applications of OSM data in digital health platforms

Application Area	Description	Example
Improved Patient Navigation	• Appointment Scheduling & Navigation • Finding Urgent Care Facilities • Public Transportation Accessibility	• Turn-by-turn navigation to appointments • Locating the nearest urgent care centers • Displaying public transport options near healthcare facilities
Enhanced Resource Mapping	• Specialist Care Access • Support Services for Chronic Conditions • Mental Health Resource Discovery	• Mapping locations of specialists within a network • Identifying diabetic clinics or nutritionists • Locating therapists, support groups, or crisis hotlines
Epidemic and Outbreak Response	• Disease Surveillance and Tracking • Vaccination Site Location	• Mapping the geographical spread of infectious diseases • Identifying the nearest vaccination locations

Digital health platforms can utilize OSM data to identify regions with limited access to traditional healthcare facilities, such as rural or underserved areas. By mapping these areas, platforms can prioritize the implementation and promotion of telehealth services. Telehealth enables remote consultations and medical services via digital communication technologies, bridging geographic barriers and expanding healthcare access for populations in remote or isolated locations. OSM's detailed geographical data can help tailor telehealth initiatives to meet specific regional healthcare needs, enhancing healthcare equity and improving health outcomes for underserved communities.

Moreover, beyond physical healthcare infrastructure, OSM can incorporate data on social determinants of health (SDOH) to create a comprehensive understanding of community health needs. For instance, OSM can map factors such as food deserts (areas lacking access to fresh, healthy food), transportation deserts (areas with inadequate public transit options), socioeconomic factors, and environmental influences. By integrating SDOH data with OSM, digital health platforms can visualize and analyze these social determinants within communities. This holistic approach provides valuable insights into the underlying factors influencing health disparities and inequities. Such insights empower public health officials, policymakers, and healthcare providers to develop targeted interventions, allocate resources effectively, and address systemic barriers to health equity.

CHALLENGES AND LIMITATIONS OF OSM INTEGRATION

While OSM offers significant advantages for digital health, integrating its data presents certain challenges and limitations as elaborated in the following sub-sections.

Data Accuracy and Consistency

While OSM offers extensive benefits for digital health applications, concerns regarding data accuracy and consistency do arise due to its open and collaborative nature (Biljecki et al., 2023; Borkowska & Pokonieczny, 2022; Moradi et al., 2022). For example, a newly opened healthcare facility may not yet be mapped on OSM, leading to gaps in coverage for patients seeking up-to-date information. Similarly, existing listings such as pharmacy operating hours or service offerings may become outdated over time, potentially misleading users relying on OSM for current data.

OSM operates with a robust system of community moderation facilitated by dedicated volunteer moderators. These moderators actively review edits made to the map, flagging inconsistencies, and verifying the accuracy of contributed information. This community-driven approach helps maintain data integrity by ensuring that erroneous or outdated entries are corrected promptly through collaborative efforts. Moreover, automated algorithms can verify the consistency and accuracy of new data entries against existing information and geographic norms. This helps identify potential errors or discrepancies before they impact users. Users may be encouraged to provide feedback on map data accuracy directly through digital health applications. This feedback loop enables ongoing validation and correction of information based on real-time user experiences and observations in the field.

By combining community moderation with robust data validation processes, digital health platforms can mitigate the risks associated with potential inaccuracies in OSM data. These strategies not only uphold data quality standards but also enhance user trust and confidence in utilizing OSM for navigating healthcare resources effectively and reliably.

Limited Resource Representation

Despite its expansive geographical coverage, OSM may exhibit variations in data representation, particularly in underserved or rural areas where healthcare facilities and support services might be less comprehensively mapped (Herfort et al., 2023). For example, OSM may have limited representation of healthcare facilities and support services in underserved communities, impacting access to accurate and up-to-date healthcare resource information for residents. Further, similar challenges can arise in rural regions where sparse population density and geographic remoteness may result in fewer contributions and updates to OSM data compared to urban areas.

Organizations and community stakeholders can initiate targeted outreach efforts to engage residents in underserved areas. These outreach programs can educate and empower community members to contribute local healthcare resource information to OSM. By fostering local participation, OSM can gradually improve its coverage and accuracy in these areas, enhancing access to essential healthcare information for residents. Moreover, establishing partnerships with local healthcare providers is crucial for enhancing data representation in OSM. By collaborating closely with healthcare facilities in underserved or rural regions, organizations can ensure comprehensive data collection and regular updates for these facilities and surrounding support services. Local providers can contribute accurate information about their services, operating hours, and other relevant details directly to OSM, enriching the platform's utility as a reliable healthcare resource locator.

By implementing targeted outreach initiatives and fostering collaborations with local healthcare providers, stakeholders can mitigate the challenges of limited resource representation in OSM. These strategies not only promote community engagement and empowerment but also contribute to enhancing the overall inclusivity and usefulness of OSM as a valuable tool for navigating healthcare resources in diverse geographical settings.

Data Completeness

While OpenStreetMap OSM provides extensive geographic coverage, it may not always include all the detailed information necessary for specific healthcare needs, posing challenges for digital health applications (Herfort et al., 2023; Zhou, Wang, et al., 2022; Zhou, Zhang, et al., 2022). For instance, a digital health app focusing on mental health services might require detailed information about therapists' specialized treatment modalities, such as cognitive behavioral therapy (CBT). However, such specific details may not be consistently included in OSM data entries for mental health professionals.

Collaborating with healthcare professional communities can encourage the inclusion of relevant details within OSM entries for specific healthcare providers or facilities. Engaging therapists, clinics, and healthcare associations in contributing accurate and comprehensive information about their services, specialties, treatment modalities, and other relevant details to OSM enhances the platform's utility for digital health applications. This collaborative approach ensures that OSM reflects the diverse and specific needs of healthcare consumers seeking specialized services. Furthermore, digital health platforms can complement OSM data with information from other reliable sources, such as healthcare provider websites, professional directories, and industry databases. By integrating supplementary data sources, platforms can enrich their databases with comprehensive information on available services, treatment modalities, provider qualifications, patient reviews, and other pertinent details. This hybrid approach enhances the completeness and accuracy of information available to users, enabling more informed healthcare decision-making and improving the overall user experience of digital health applications.

By implementing strategies to enhance data collection standards and integrating supplementary data sources, stakeholders can address the challenge of data completeness in OSM for specific healthcare needs. These efforts not only support the accuracy and relevance of digital health platforms but also enhance accessibility to comprehensive healthcare information, ultimately improving patient outcomes and healthcare service delivery.

Data Currency

The dynamic nature of OSM presents challenges in maintaining up-to-date data, particularly for healthcare facilities that undergo frequent changes (Brauchler & Stoffels, 2020; Solís et al., 2021). For example, a clinic may relocate to a new address or change its operating hours, leading to discrepancies between the information in OSM and the current status of the facility.

Digital health platforms can implement integration methods that facilitate near real-time updates from the OSM community. By leveraging OSM's collaborative framework, platforms can receive timely notifications and updates regarding changes to healthcare facilities and services. This integration minimizes the lag between data changes in the real world and their reflection within the digital health platform, ensuring users have access to the most current and accurate information available. Moreover, to enhance data currency, digital health apps can incorporate user feedback mechanisms that allow patients and users to report discrepancies or outdated information directly within the platform. Users can flag inaccuracies or changes in healthcare facility details, such as relocation or revised operating hours, prompting verification and potential updates in OSM. This crowdsourced approach not only engages users in maintaining data accuracy but also facilitates continuous improvement and reliability of information within digital health applications.

By acknowledging these challenges and implementing appropriate mitigation strategies, healthcare providers and developers can leverage the strengths of OSM while minimizing the potential drawbacks. This collaborative approach ensures that digital health solutions built on OSM data remain accurate, reliable, and ultimately, beneficial for patients and healthcare delivery.

CONCLUSION

The practical applications of OpenStreetMap in digital health are extensive, enhancing patient navigation, resource mapping, and epidemic response. Integrating OSM data into digital health platforms improves patient navigation by providing turn-by-turn directions, real-time traffic updates, and public transportation options, ensuring patients arrive at appointments punctually and prepared. It also helps locate the nearest urgent care centers during emergencies, optimizing healthcare resource utilization. Additionally, OSM facilitates detailed mapping of specialist healthcare providers, chronic condition support services, and mental health resources, aiding patients in efficiently accessing necessary care. During epidemics, OSM data allows public health agencies to visualize disease spread and locate vaccination sites, supporting targeted interventions and vaccination campaigns. OSM's potential extends to identifying underserved regions, promoting telehealth services, and incorporating social determinants of health to address health disparities. Despite its benefits, OSM integration faces challenges like data accuracy, consistency, and completeness, especially in underserved or rural areas. To mitigate these, digital health platforms can leverage community moderation, targeted outreach, partnerships with local healthcare providers, and supplementary data sources. Ensuring data currency through real-time updates and user feedback mechanisms further enhances the reliability and effectiveness of digital health applications built on OSM data.

REFERENCES

Aceto, G., Persico, V., & Pescapé, A. (2018). The role of Information and Communication Technologies in healthcare: taxonomies, perspectives, and challenges. In *Journal of Network and Computer Applications* (Vol. 107). DOI: 10.1016/j.jnca.2018.02.008

Al-Jaroodi, J., Mohamed, N., & Abukhousa, E. (2020). Health 4.0: On the Way to Realizing the Healthcare of the Future. *IEEE Access : Practical Innovations, Open Solutions*, 8, 211189–211210. Advance online publication. DOI: 10.1109/ACCESS.2020.3038858 PMID: 34976565

Awad, A., Trenfield, S. J., Pollard, T. D., Ong, J. J., Elbadawi, M., McCoubrey, L. E., Goyanes, A., Gaisford, S., & Basit, A. W. (2021). Connected healthcare: Improving patient care using digital health technologies. In *Advanced Drug Delivery Reviews* (Vol. 178). DOI: 10.1016/j.addr.2021.113958

Biljecki, F., Chow, Y. S., & Lee, K. (2023). Quality of crowdsourced geospatial building information: A global assessment of OpenStreetMap attributes. *Building and Environment*, 237, 110295. Advance online publication. DOI: 10.1016/j.buildenv.2023.110295

Borkowska, S., & Pokonieczny, K. (2022). Analysis of OpenStreetMap Data Quality for Selected Counties in Poland in Terms of Sustainable Development. *Sustainability (Basel)*, 14(7), 3728. Advance online publication. DOI: 10.3390/su14073728

Brauchler, M., & Stoffels, J. (2020). Leveraging OSM and GEOBIA to create and update forest type maps. *ISPRS International Journal of Geo-Information*, 9(9), 499. Advance online publication. DOI: 10.3390/ijgi9090499

Cheng, L., Yang, M., De Vos, J., & Witlox, F. (2020). Examining geographical accessibility to multi-tier hospital care services for the elderly: A focus on spatial equity. *Journal of Transport & Health*, 19, 100926. Advance online publication. DOI: 10.1016/j.jth.2020.100926

Grinberger, A. Y., Schott, M., Raifer, M., & Zipf, A. (2021). An analysis of the spatial and temporal distribution of large-scale data production events in OpenStreetMap. *Transactions in GIS*, 25(2), 622–641. Advance online publication. DOI: 10.1111/tgis.12746

Gul, M., & Guneri, A. F. (2021). Hospital location selection: A systematic literature review on methodologies and applications. In *Mathematical Problems in Engineering* (Vol. 2021). DOI: 10.1155/2021/6682958

Herfort, B., Lautenbach, S., Porto de Albuquerque, J., Anderson, J., & Zipf, A. (2021). The evolution of humanitarian mapping within the OpenStreetMap community. *Scientific Reports*, 11(1), 3037. Advance online publication. DOI: 10.1038/s41598-021-82404-z PMID: 33542423

Herfort, B., Lautenbach, S., Porto de Albuquerque, J., Anderson, J., & Zipf, A. (2023). A spatio-temporal analysis investigating completeness and inequalities of global urban building data in OpenStreetMap. *Nature Communications*, 14(1), 3985. Advance online publication. DOI: 10.1038/s41467-023-39698-6 PMID: 37414776

Herringer, M., Ndiaye, L., & South, A. (2023). Developing a data validation method with OpenStreetMap Senegal and the Ministry of Health in support of accurate health facility data. *Proceedings of the OSM Science*, 42–44.

Ihantamalala, F. A., Herbreteau, V., Révillion, C., Randriamihaja, M., Commins, J., Andréambeloson, T., Rafenoarimalala, F. H., Randrianambinina, A., Cordier, L. F., Bonds, M. H., & Garchitorena, A. (2020). Improving geographical accessibility modeling for operational use by local health actors. *International Journal of Health Geographics*, 19(1), 27. Advance online publication. DOI: 10.1186/s12942-020-00220-6 PMID: 32631348

Karatas, M., Eriskin, L., Deveci, M., Pamucar, D., & Garg, H. (2022). Big Data for Healthcare Industry 4.0: Applications, challenges and future perspectives. In *Expert Systems with Applications* (Vol. 200). DOI: 10.1016/j.eswa.2022.116912

Li, J., Qin, H., Wang, J., & Li, J. (2022). OpenStreetMap-Based Autonomous Navigation for the Four Wheel-Legged Robot Via 3D-Lidar and CCD Camera. *IEEE Transactions on Industrial Electronics*, 69(3), 2708–2717. Advance online publication. DOI: 10.1109/TIE.2021.3070508

Li, Y., & Xu, L. (2021). The impact of covid-19 on pedestrian flow patterns in urban pois—An example from Beijing. *ISPRS International Journal of Geo-Information*, 10(7), 479. Advance online publication. DOI: 10.3390/ijgi10070479

Liu, Z. (2021). Identifying urban land use social functional units: A case study using OSM data. *International Journal of Digital Earth*, 14(12), 1798–1817. Advance online publication. DOI: 10.1080/17538947.2021.1988161

Minghini, M., Delucchi, L., Sarretta, A., Lupia, F., Napolitano, M., & Palmas, A. (2017). Collaborative mapping response to disasters through openstreetmap: The case of the 2016 Italian earthquake. In *Geoingegneria Ambientale e Mineraria* (Vol. 151, Issue 2).

Minghini, M., Sarretta, A., & Napolitano, M. (2022). OpenStreetMap Contribution to Local Data Ecosystems in COVID-19 Times: Experiences and Reflections from the Italian Case. *Data*, 7(4), 39. Advance online publication. DOI: 10.3390/data7040039

Mooney, P., Grinberger, A. Y., Minghini, M., Coetzee, S., Juhasz, L., & Yeboah, G. (2021). OpenStreetMap Data Use Cases During the Early Months of the COVID-19 Pandemic. In *COVID-19 Pandemic*. Geospatial Information, and Community Resilience., DOI: 10.1201/9781003181590-15

Moradi, M., Roche, S., & Mostafavi, M. A. (2022). Exploring five indicators for the quality of OpenStreetMap road networks: A case study of Québec, Canada. *Geomatica*, 75(4), 178–208. Advance online publication. DOI: 10.1139/geomat-2021-0012

Pagar, Mrs. N., Pardeshi, A., Mallick, N., Tejwani, A., & Ubale, T. (2024). Literature Survey on Indoor Navigation System Using QR Code and OSM. *IARJSET, 11*(2). DOI: 10.17148/IARJSET.2024.11204

Poiani, T. H., Rocha, R. dos S., Degrossi, L. C., & de Albuquerque, J. P. (2016). Potential of Collaborative Mapping for Disaster Relief : A Case Study of OpenStreetMap in the Nepal Earthquake 2015. *Hawaii International Conference on System Sciences, JANUARY*, 1–10. DOI: 10.1109/HICSS.2016.31

Psyllidis, A., Gao, S., Hu, Y., Kim, E. K., McKenzie, G., Purves, R., Yuan, M., & Andris, C. (2022). Points of Interest (POI): A commentary on the state of the art, challenges, and prospects for the future. *Computational Urban Science*, 2(1), 20. Advance online publication. DOI: 10.1007/s43762-022-00047-w PMID: 35789810

Rousell, A., & Zipf, A. (2017). Towards a landmark-based pedestrian navigation service using OSM data. *ISPRS International Journal of Geo-Information*, 6(3), 64. Advance online publication. DOI: 10.3390/ijgi6030064

Sarkar, D., & Anderson, J. T. (2022). Corporate editors in OpenStreetMap: Investigating co-editing patterns. *Transactions in GIS*, 26(4), 1879–1897. Advance online publication. DOI: 10.1111/tgis.12910

Schröder-Bergen, S., Glasze, G., Michel, B., & Dammann, F. (2022). De/colonizing OpenStreetMap? Local mappers, humanitarian and commercial actors and the changing modes of collaborative mapping. *GeoJournal*, 87(6), 5051–5066. Advance online publication. DOI: 10.1007/s10708-021-10547-7

Seto, T. (2022). *Development of OpenStreetMap Data in Japan*. DOI: 10.1007/978-981-19-1536-9_7

Solís, P., Anderson, J., & Rajagopalan, S. (2021). Open geospatial tools for humanitarian data creation, analysis, and learning through the global lens of YouthMappers. *Journal of Geographical Systems*, 23(4), 599–625. Advance online publication. DOI: 10.1007/s10109-020-00339-x

Vu, T. T., Vu, N. V. A., Phung, H. P., & Nguyen, L. D. (2021). Enhanced urban functional land use map with free and open-source data. *International Journal of Digital Earth*, 14(11), 1744–1757. Advance online publication. DOI: 10.1080/17538947.2021.1970262

Wang, F. (2020). Why public health needs GIS: a methodological overview. In *Annals of GIS* (Vol. 26, Issue 1). DOI: 10.1080/19475683.2019.1702099

Zhou, Q., Wang, S., & Liu, Y. (2022). Exploring the accuracy and completeness patterns of global land-cover/land-use data in OpenStreetMap. *Applied Geography (Sevenoaks, England)*, 145, 102742. Advance online publication. DOI: 10.1016/j.apgeog.2022.102742

Zhou, Q., Zhang, Y., Chang, K., & Brovelli, M. A. (2022). Assessing OSM building completeness for almost 13,000 cities globally. *International Journal of Digital Earth*, 15(1), 2400–2421. Advance online publication. DOI: 10.1080/17538947.2022.2159550

ADDITIONAL READING

Ali, M. (2021). *Remote Work and Sustainable Changes for the Future of Global Business*. IGI Global. https://www.igi-global.com/book/remote-work-sustainable-changes-future/264375

Ali, M. (2022). *Future Role of Sustainable Innovative Technologies in Crisis Management*. IGI Global. https://www.igi-global.com/book/future-role-sustainable-innovative-technologies/281281

Ali, M. (2023). *Shifting Paradigms in the Rapidly Developing Global Digital Ecosystem: A GCC Perspective*. In Digital Entrepreneurship and Co-Creating Value Through Digital Encounters (pp. 145-166). IGI Global. https://www.igi-global.com/chapter/shifting-paradigms-in-the-rapidly-developing-global-digital-ecosystem/323525

Ali, M. (2023). T*axonomy of Industry 4.0 Technologies in Digital Entrepreneurship and Co-Creating Value*. In *Digital Entrepreneurship and Co-Creating Value Through Digital Encounters* (pp. 24–55). IGI Global., https://www.igi-global.com/chapter/taxonomy-of-industry-40-technologies-in-digital-entrepreneurship-and-co-creating-value/323520 DOI: 10.4018/978-1-6684-7416-7.ch002

Ali, M., & Wood-Harper, T. (2021). *Fostering Communication and Learning with Underutilized Technologies in Higher Education*. IGI Global. https://www.igi-global.com/book/fostering-communication-learning-underutilized-technologies/244593

Ali, M., Wood-Harper, T., & Kutar, M. (2023). Multi-Perspectives of Contemporary Digital Transformation Models of Complex Innovation Management. In *Digital Entrepreneurship and Co-Creating Value Through Digital Encounters* (pp. 79–96). IGI Global., https://www.igi-global.com/chapter/multi-perspectives-of-contemporary-digital-transformation-models-of-complex-innovation-management/323522 DOI: 10.4018/978-1-6684-7416-7.ch004

Ali, M. B. (2021). Internet of Things (IoT) to Foster Communication and Information Sharing: A Case of UK Higher Education. In Ali, M. B., & Wood-Harper, T. (Eds.), *Fostering Communication and Learning With Underutilized Technologies in Higher Education* (pp. 1–20). IGI Global., https://www.igi-global.com/chapter/internet-of-things-iot-to-foster-communication-and-information-sharing/262718/ DOI: 10.4018/978-1-7998-4846-2.ch001

Ali, M. B., & Wood-Harper, T. (2022). Artificial Intelligence (AI) as a Decision-Making Tool to Control Crisis Situations. In *Future Role of Sustainable Innovative Technologies in Crisis Management*. IGI Global., https://www.igi-global.com/chapter/artificial-intelligence-ai-as-a-decision-making-tool-to-control-crisis-situations/298931 DOI: 10.4018/978-1-7998-9815-3.ch006

Ali, M. B., Wood-Harper, T., & Ramlogan, R. (2020). A Framework Strategy to Overcome Trust Issues on Cloud Computing Adoption in Higher Education. In Modern Principles, Practices, and Algorithms for Cloud Security (pp. 162-183). IGI Global. https://www.igi-global.com/chapter/a-framework-strategy-to-overcome-trust-issues-on-cloud-computing-adoption-in-higher-education/238907/

KEY TERMS AND DEFINITIONS

OpenStreetMap (OSM): is a collaborative project that creates a free, editable map of the world. It is built by a community of mappers who contribute and maintain data about roads, trails, cafés, railway stations, and much more. The data from OSM can be used in various applications, including geospatial analysis, navigation, and urban planning.

Spatial data: also known as geospatial data, refers to information that describes the physical location and shape of objects on Earth. This data can include coordinates (latitude and longitude), maps, satellite imagery, and any other data that can be associated with a specific location. Spatial data is essential for geographic information systems (GIS), remote sensing, and location-based services.

Volunteered Geographic Information (VGI): refers to geographic information created by volunteers, often through crowdsourcing. This can include contributions to platforms like OpenStreetMap, where individuals share local knowledge and updates about geographic features. VGI is a valuable source of data for mapping, disaster response, urban planning, and other geospatial applications.

Point of Interest (POI): is a specific location on a map that someone might find useful or interesting. Common examples include restaurants, hotels, gas stations, landmarks, and other notable locations. POIs are often used in navigation systems, location-based services, and travel planning applications.

Digital health: encompasses the use of digital technologies to improve health outcomes, healthcare delivery, and medical practices. It includes a wide range of tools and services, such as telemedicine, mobile health apps, electronic health records (EHRs), wearable devices, and AI-driven diagnostic tools. Digital health aims to make healthcare more efficient, accessible, and personalized.

Compilation of References

Aaker, D. A. (1991). *Managing brand equity*. Free Press.

Aaker, D. A. (1996). *Measuring brand equity across products and markets*. Free Press. DOI: 10.2307/41165845

Abbas, M. (2016). *Reliance Jio is world's largest startup with Rs 150,000 crore investment: Mukesh Ambani*. The Economic Times. https://economictimes.indiatimes.com/industry/telecom/reliance-jio-is-worlds-largest-startup-with-rs-150000-crore-investment-mukesh-ambani/articleshow/51613248.cms?from=mdr

Abidin, N. Z., & Tho, S. (2018). The development of an innovative resonance experiment using smartphones with free mobile software applications for tertiary education. *International Journal of Education and Development using ICT, 14*(1).

Abidin, C. (2016). Visibility labour: Engaging with influencers' fashion brands and #OOTD advertorial campaigns on Instagram. *Media International Australia, Incorporating Culture & Policy*, 161(1), 86–100. DOI: 10.1177/1329878X16665177

Abidin, C. (2020). Influencer marketing: A critical review and research agenda. *Journal of Marketing Management*, 36(7-8), 681–695. DOI: 10.1080/0267257X.2020.1773367

Aceto, G., Persico, V., & Pescapé, A. (2018). The role of Information and Communication Technologies in healthcare: taxonomies, perspectives, and challenges. In *Journal of Network and Computer Applications* (Vol. 107). DOI: 10.1016/j.jnca.2018.02.008

Advertising, L. (2023, September 26). The benefits of digital marketing. https://www.lucidadvertising.com/benefits-digital-marketing/

Agarwal, R., & Prasad, J. (1997). The role of innovation characteristics and perceived voluntariness in the acceptance of information technologies. *Decision Sciences*, 28(3), 557–582. DOI: 10.1111/j.1540-5915.1997.tb01322.x

Aghekyan-Simonian, M., Forsythe, S., Kwon, W. S., & Chattaraman, V. (2012). The role of product brand image and online store image on perceived risks and online purchase intentions for apparel. *Journal of Retailing and Consumer Services*, 19(3), 325–331. DOI: 10.1016/j.jretconser.2012.03.006

Agung, D. P., & Wijaya, A. (2019). Peran Paguyuban Duta Wisata "Sekargading" dalam Mengembangkan Pariwisata di Kabupaten Batang. *IJSED: Indonesian Jurnal of Sociology, Education, and Development*, 1(1), 60–70. DOI: 10.52483/ijsed.v1i1.6

Akbar, F. (2013). *What affects students' acceptance and use of technology*. Dietrich College of Humanities and Social Sciences.

Al Suwaidi, M. E. Y. M., Sidek, S. B., & Al-Shami, S. A. (2022). A Conceptual Framework of Fintech Laws and Regulations on the Risk Management of Financial Institutions in UAE. *Mathematical Statistician and Engineering Applications*, 71(3), 01-07.

Alanazi, M., Freeman, M., & Tootell, H. (2022). Exploring the factors that influence the cybersecurity behaviors of young adults. *Computers in Human Behavior, 136*(December 2021), 107376. DOI: 10.1016/j.chb.2022.107376

Al-Jaroodi, J., Mohamed, N., & Abukhousa, E. (2020). Health 4.0: On the Way to Realizing the Healthcare of the Future. *IEEE Access : Practical Innovations, Open Solutions*, 8, 211189–211210. Advance online publication. DOI: 10.1109/ACCESS.2020.3038858 PMID: 34976565

Allen, B., Bapst, B., & Hicks, T. A. (2023). Building a Cyber Risk Management Program. In *O'Reilly Media Inc*. https://learning.oreilly.com/library/view/building-a-cyber/9781098147785/

Allen, F., Gu, X., & Jagtiani, J. (2022). Fintech, Cryptocurrencies, and CBDC: Financial Structural Transformation in China. *Journal of International Money and Finance*, 124, 1–38. DOI: 10.1016/j.jimonfin.2022.102625

Almaiah, M. A., Almomani, O., Al-Khasawneh, A., & Althunibat, A. (2021). Predicting the acceptance of mobile learning applications during COVID-19 using machine learning prediction algorithms. *Emerging technologies during the era of COVID-19 pandemic*, 319-332.

Almakenzi, S., Bramantoro, A., & Rashideh, W. (2015). A Survivability Model for Saudi ICT Startups. *International Journal of Computer Science and Information Technologies*, 7(2), 145–157. DOI: 10.5121/ijcsit.2015.7213

Al-Mudimigh, A., & Anshari, M. (2020). Financial Technology and Innovative Financial Inclusion. *Financial Technology and Disruptive Innovation in ASEAN*, 119-129.

Alshurideh, M. T., Hassanien, A. E., & Masa'deh, R. (2021). *The Effect of Coronavirus Disease (COVID-19) on Business Intelligence* (1st ed. 2021, Vol. 334). Springer International Publishing AG. DOI: 10.1007/978-3-030-67151-8

Alzaza, N. S., & Yaakub, A. R. (2011). Students' awareness and requirements of mobile learning services in the higher education environment. *American Journal of Economics and Business Administration*, 3(1), 95–100. DOI: 10.3844/ajebasp.2011.95.100

Anaf, J., Freeman, T., & Baum, F. (2024). Privatisation of government services in Australia: What is known about health and equity impacts. *Globalization and Health*, 20(1), 32. DOI: 10.1186/s12992-024-01036-w PMID: 38627788

Anderson, E. (2010). *Social media marketing game theory and the emergence of collaboration*. Springer. DOI: 10.1007/978-3-642-13299-5

Andrews, K. R. (1971). *The concept of Corporate Strategy*. R.D. Irwin.

Ansoff, H. I. (1965). *Corporate Strategy: An Analytic Approach to Business Policy for Growth and Expansion*. McGraw-Hill.

Arner, D. W., Barberis, J. N., & Buckley, R. P. (2015). *The Evolution of Fintech: A New Post-Crisis Paradigm?* (SSRN Scholarly Paper 2676553). https://doi.org/ DOI: 10.2139/ssrn.2676553

Arora, A., Bansal, M., & Sharma, P. (2021). The impact of influencer credibility on brand loyalty: The role of social media marketing. *International Journal of Consumer Studies*, 45(5), 624–634. DOI: 10.1111/1470-6431.12651

Asamoah, D. A., Dinsmore, J. B., & Swani, K. (2024). Benefits, barriers, and facilitators of developing B2B mobile applications. *Journal of Business and Industrial Marketing*, 39(3), 537–552. DOI: 10.1108/JBIM-10-2022-0457

Aschemann, B. (2017). The Digital Readiness of Adult Education. The EBmooc for adult educators. *Magazin Erwachsenenbildung.at*: Vol. 11. *Issue, 30*. Springer Publications.

Attia, Z. I., Kapa, S., Lopez-Jimenez, F., McKie, P. M., Ladewig, D. J., Satam, G., Pellikka, P. A., Enriquez-Sarano, M., Noseworthy, P. A., Munger, T. M., Asirvatham, S. J., Scott, C. G., Carter, R. E., & Friedman, P. A. (2019). Screening for cardiac contractile dysfunction using an artificial intelligence-enabled electrocardiogram. *Nature Medicine*, 25(1), 70–74. DOI: 10.1038/s41591-018-0240-2 PMID: 30617318

Attia, Z. I., Noseworthy, P. A., Lopez-Jimenez, F., Asirvatham, S. J., Deshmukh, A. J., Gersh, B. J., Carter, R. E., Yao, X., Rabinstein, A. A., Erickson, B. J., Kapa, S., & Friedman, P. A. (2019). An artificial intelligence-enabled ECG algorithm for the identification of patients with atrial fibrillation during sinus rhythm: A retrospective analysis of outcome prediction. *Lancet*, 394(10201), 861–867. DOI: 10.1016/S0140-6736(19)31721-0 PMID: 31378392

Avci, U., & Askar, P. (2012). The comparison of the opinions of the university students on the usage of blog and wiki for their courses. *Journal of Educational Technology & Society*, 15(2), 194–205.

Awad, A., Trenfield, S. J., Pollard, T. D., Ong, J. J., Elbadawi, M., McCoubrey, L. E., Goyanes, A., Gaisford, S., & Basit, A. W. (2021). Connected healthcare: Improving patient care using digital health technologies. In *Advanced Drug Delivery Reviews* (Vol. 178). DOI: 10.1016/j.addr.2021.113958

Ayoub, R. M., Firth, C., & Nayaz, M. (2017). Cyber Resilience in the Digital Age. *EY & World Government Summit*. https://worldgovernmentsummit.org/api/publications/document?id=24717dc4-e97c-6578-b2f8-ff0000a7ddb6

Baalbaki, S. S. (2012). *Consumer perception of brand equity measurement: A new scale*. Dissertation prepared for the degree of Doctor of Philosophy. University of Texas.

Baer, J. (2022, May 31). *7 email marketing problems and 9 medicines to fix them*. Convince & Convert. https://www.convinceandconvert.com/digital-marketing/7-email-marketing-problems-9-medicines-fix/

Bagheri, S., Ridley, G., & Williams, B. (2023). Organisational Cyber Resilience: Management Perspectives. *AJIS. Australasian Journal of Information Systems*, 27, 1–28. DOI: 10.3127/ajis.v27i0.4183

Bajowala, S. S., Milosch, J., & Bansal, C. (2020, October). Telemedicine pays billing and coding update. *Current Allergy and Asthma Reports*, 20(10), 1–9. DOI: 10.1007/s11882-020-00956-y PMID: 32715353

Baker, W. E. (2009). Evaluation of Physician Competency and Clinical Performance in Emergency Medicine. *Emergency Medicine Clinics of North America*, 27(4), 615–626. DOI: 10.1016/j.emc.2009.07.010 PMID: 19932396

Balash, F., Yong, Z., & Bin Abu, B. (2011). Lecturers and educational technology: Factors affecting educational technology adoption in teaching. In *2nd International Conference on Education and Management Technology IPCSIT* (Vol. 13).

Balboni, B., Bortoluzzi, G., Tivan, M., Tracogna, A., & Venier, F. (2014). The Growth Drivers of Start-up Firms and Business Modelling: A First Step toward a Desirable Convergence. *Management*, 9(2), 131–154. https://ideas.repec.org//a/mgt/youmng/v9y2014i2p131-154.html

Bardin, L. (1998). *L'analyse de contenu*. Librairie Eyrolles.

Barlan, Z. A., & Kolopaking, L. (2014). Peran Paguyuban dalam Pembangunan Kawasan Desa. *Sodality: Jurnal Sosiologi Pedesaan*, 2(2), 115–123. DOI: 10.22500/sodality.v2i2.9419

Barreto, L., Amaral, A., & Pereira, T. (2017). Industry 4.0 implications in logistics: An overview. *Procedia Manufacturing*, 13(1), 1245–1252. DOI: 10.1016/j.promfg.2017.09.045

Batth, R. S., Nayyar, A., & Nagpal, A. (2018). Internet of robotic things: driving intelligent robotics of future-concept, architecture, applications and technologies. In 2018 4th International Conference on Computing Sciences (ICCS), 151-160. IEEE. DOI DOI: 10.1109/ICCS.2018.00033

Bayi, C. (2024, December). Tao, Xie., Lingjun, Wang., Daniel, Q., Tan., Xiongfei, Cao. (2024). Deep reinforcement learning driven cost minimization for batch order scheduling in robotic mobile fulfillment systems. *Expert Systems with Applications*, 255, 124589. Advance online publication. DOI: 10.1016/j.eswa.2024.124589

Bei, H. (2019). *Problems of Cybersecurity in the Context of Becoming and Development of the New Economy*. 454–464.

Bell, E., & Bryman, A. (2007). The ethics of management research: An exploratory content analysis. *British Journal of Management*, 18(1), 63–77. DOI: 10.1111/j.1467-8551.2006.00487.x

Bentalha, B. (2023). Consumer Perception of Robotic Mobile Fulfillment Systems: A Netnographic Case Study of Amazon. In Innovation, Strategy, and Transformation Frameworks for the Modern Enterprise (pp. 243-264). IGI Global. DOI: 10.4018/979-8-3693-0458-7.ch010

Bentalha, B. (2024). Employees and Robots in Amazon's Robotic Mobile Fulfillment Systems: A Netnographic Analysis of a Supply Chain Transformation. In Blockchain Applications for Smart Contract Technologies (pp. 188-207). IGI Global. DOI: 10.4018/979-8-3693-1511-8.ch009

Bentalha, B., & Alla, L. (2024). Revealing the Subtleties: The Art of Qualitative Studies in Science and Management. In Applying Qualitative Research Methods to Management Science (pp. 1-21). IGI Global.

Bentalha, B., & Boukare, M. (2024). AI-Driven Territorial Intelligence: An Integrated Approach to Enhancing Digital Sovereignty. In Generative AI and Implications for Ethics, Security, and Data Management (pp. 231-261). IGI Global.

Bentalha, B., & Hmioui, A. (2022). Smart Service Supply Chain and Just Walk Out Technology: A Netnographic Approach. In: Ben Ahmed, M., Boudhir, A.A., Kara , İ.R., Jain, V., Mellouli, S. (eds). Innovations in Smart Cities Applications Volume 5. SCA 2021. Lecture Notes in Networks and Systems, vol 393. Springer, Cham. Pp. 223-236. https://doi.org/DOI: 10.1007/978-3-030-94191-8_18

Bentalha, B., Hmioui, A., & Alla, L. (2020). Digital Service Supply Chain Management: Current Realities and Prospective Visions. In: Ben Ahmed M., Boudhir A., Santos D., El Aroussi M., Karas İ. (eds) Innovations in Smart Cities Applications Edition 3. SCA 2019. Lecture Notes in Intelligent Transportation and Infrastructure. Springer, Cham

Bentalha, B., Hmioui, A., & Alla, L. (2023). Green Transportation Balanced Scorecard: A VIKOR Fuzzy Method for Evaluating Green Logistics Initiatives. In International Conference on Digital Technologies and Applications (pp. 916-925). Cham: Springer Nature Switzerland. DOI: 10.1007/978-3-031-29857-8_91

Bentalha, B. (2022). Smart Technologies for a Sustainable Service Supply Chain: A Prospective Perspective. *Journal of Environmental Issues and Climate Change*, 1(1), 77–89. DOI: 10.59110/jeicc.v1i1.81

Bentalha, B., Hmioui, A., & Alla, L. (2019). The digitalization of the supply chain management of service companies: a prospective approach. In *Proceedings of the 4th International Conference on Smart City Applications* (pp. 1-8). DOI: 10.1145/3368756.3369005

Bertschy, K., Cattaneo, M. A., & Wolter, S. C. (2009). PISA and the Transition into the Labour Market. *Labour*, 23(s1), 111–137. DOI: 10.1111/j.1467-9914.2008.00432.x

Bhagat, R. S. (2002). Culture's consequences: Comparing values, behaviors, institutions, and organizations across nations.

Bhatia, A. (2010). *Approach Paper on Defining Public-Private Partnerships.* Ministry of Finance, Department of Economic Affairs, Government of India. Para 6.3. https://www.pppinindia.gov.in/assets/doc/20181/22330/33_pppacMinutes.pdf

Bhatia, J., & Palepu, A. R. (2016). Reliance Jio: Predatory Pricing or Predatory Behaviour? *Economic and Political Weekly*, 51(41), 33–39. https://www.jstor.org/stable/44165786

Biener, C., Eling, M., & Wirfs, J. H. (2015). Insurability of cyber risk: An empirical analysis. *The Geneva Papers on Risk and Insurance. Issues and Practice*, 40(1), 131–158. DOI: 10.1057/gpp.2014.19

Biernacki, M., Luśtyk, A., & Wisła, R. (2023). Differentiation of the digital economic development in Europe. Edited By Judyta Lubacha, Beata Mäihäniemi, Rafał Wisła. In *The European Digital Economy - Drivers of Digital Transition and Economic Recovery* (pp. 45–60). Routledge. DOI: 10.4324/9781003450160-5

Biljecki, F., Chow, Y. S., & Lee, K. (2023). Quality of crowdsourced geospatial building information: A global assessment of OpenStreetMap attributes. *Building and Environment*, 237, 110295. Advance online publication. DOI: 10.1016/j.buildenv.2023.110295

Bin-Nashwan, S. A., & Al-Daihani, M. (2021). Fundraising campaigns via social media platforms for mitigating the impacts of the COVID-19 epidemic. *Journal of Islamic Marketing*, 12(3), 576–597. DOI: 10.1108/JIMA-07-2020-0200

Biroli, A. (2022). Strategi Pengembangan Paguyuban Potre Madhura Melalui Pendidikan Jamu di Pulau Madura. *Resiprokal: Jurnal Riset Sosiologi Progresif Aktual*, 4(2), 250–261. DOI: 10.29303/resiprokal.v4i2.226

Björkdahl, J., Holgersson, M., & Teece, D. J. (2024). Digital Platform Grafting: Strategies for Entering Established Ecosystems. *California Management Review*, 66(3), 27–46. DOI: 10.1177/00081256241238453

Boerman, S. C., Willemsen, L. M., & Van Der Aa, E. (2017). Online influencers: A current state of research and future directions. *International Journal of Advertising*, 36(3), 261–284. DOI: 10.1080/02650487.2017.1329650

Bogue, R. (2016). Growth in e-commerce boosts innovation in the warehouse robot market. Industrial Robot. *The Industrial Robot*, 43(6), 583–587. DOI: 10.1108/IR-07-2016-0194

Boiral, O., Talbot, D., & Paillé, P. (2013). Leading by Example: A Model of Organizational Citizenship Behavior for the Environment. *Business Strategy and the Environment*, 24(6), 1–27. DOI: 10.1002/bse.1835

Boman, K., & Raijonkari, K. (2017). Online Video as a Marketing Tool: A quantitative survey on video marketing habits.

Borkowska, S., & Pokonieczny, K. (2022). Analysis of OpenStreetMap Data Quality for Selected Counties in Poland in Terms of Sustainable Development. *Sustainability (Basel)*, 14(7), 3728. Advance online publication. DOI: 10.3390/su14073728

Bouaziz, F., & Sghari, A. (2021). FinTech's Interpretations and Tunisian Ecosystem Analysis. In *Influence of FinTech on Management Transformation* (pp. 167–190). IGI Global., DOI: 10.4018/978-1-7998-7110-1.ch008

Boudri, R., Bentalha, B., & Benjelloun, O. (2024). Phygital Marketing and the Pain of Paying: An Amazon Go Netnographic Case Study. In AI and Data Engineering Solutions for Effective Marketing (pp. 348-363). IGI Global.

Bouhtati, N., Alla, L., & Bentalha, B. (2023). Marketing Big Data Analytics and Customer Relationship Management: A Fuzzy Approach. In Integrating Intelligence and Sustainability in Supply Chains (pp. 75-86). IGI Global. DOI: 10.4018/979-8-3693-0225-5.ch004

Boysen, N., Briskorn, D., & Emde, S. (2017). Parts-to-picker based order processing in a rack-moving mobile robots environment. *European Journal of Operational Research*, 262(2), 550–562. DOI: 10.1016/j.ejor.2017.03.053

Brauchler, M., & Stoffels, J. (2020). Leveraging OSM and GEOBIA to create and update forest type maps. *ISPRS International Journal of Geo-Information*, 9(9), 499. Advance online publication. DOI: 10.3390/ijgi9090499

Bucciferro, C. (2019). Women and Netflix: Disrupting traditional boundaries between television and film. *Feminist Media Studies*, 19(7), 1053–1056. DOI: 10.1080/14680777.2019.1667076

Buchmann, R. A., Polini, A., Johansson, B., & Karagiannis, D. (2020). Perspectives in Business Informatics Research. *19th International Conference on Business Informatics Research, BIR 2020, Vienna, Austria, September 21–23, 2020, Proceedings (Vol. 398):* Cadwalladr, C., & Graham-Harrison, E. (2018). *Revealed: 50 million Facebook profiles harvested for Cambridge Analytica in major data breach.* https://www.theguardian.com/news/2018/mar/17/cambridge-analytica-facebook-influence-us-election

Bureau, E. T. (2016, September). *Mukesh Ambani ushers in telecom revolution, Reliance Jio to launch services on September 5*. The Economic Times; Economic Times. https://economictimes.indiatimes.com/news/company/corporate-trends/mukesh-ambani-ushers-in-telecom-revolution-reliance-jio-to-launch-services-on-september5/articleshow/53970531.cms

Business Standard. (2016, July 17). *Airtel cuts pre-paid data tariffs giving up to 67% more data*. Business Standard; Business Standard. https://www.business-standard.com/article/companies/airtel-cuts-pre-paid-data-tariffs-giving-up-to-67-more-data-116071700348_1.html

Cahyana, U., Lestari, I., Irwanto, I., & Suroso, J. (2024). Development of a mobile learning network for science with augmented reality and its impact on students' literacy and numeracy. *International Journal of Innovative Research and Scientific Studies*, 7(2), 576–586. DOI: 10.53894/ijirss.v7i2.2685

Camillo, M. (2017). Cyber risk and the changing role of insurance. *Journal of Cyber Policy*, 2(1), 53–63. DOI: 10.1080/23738871.2017.1296878

Campbell, C., & Grimm, P. E. (2019). Social media influencers: A new way to reach the college student market. *Business Horizons*, 62(6), 787–796. DOI: 10.1016/j.bushor.2019.07.002

Cano, E. V. (2012). Mobile learning with Twitter to improve linguistic competence at secondary schools. *The New Educational Review*, 29(3), 134–147.

Carrigan, M., & Jordan, K. (2022). Platforms and Institutions in the Post-Pandemic University: A Case Study of Social Media and the Impact Agenda. *Postdigital Science and Education*, 4(2), 354–372. DOI: 10.1007/s42438-021-00269-x

Cebula, J. J., & Young, L. R. (2010). A Taxonomy of Operational Cyber Security Risks. *Carnegie-Mellon Univ Pittsburgh Pa Software Engineering Inst*, (December), 1–47.

Centre for Good Governance (2003). A Report.

Cervantes-Guzmán, J. N. (2021, April-June). [2021]. *Evolution of Entrepreneur Women from Traditional Companies to E-Business*. (In). *International Journal of Business Strategy and Automation*, 2(2), 32. DOI: 10.4018/IJBSA.20210401.oa3

Chand, K., Jangra, S., Singh, P. C., Tiwari, R. S., & Tiwari, R. (2023). Sustainability of Mobile Wallets in the Era of Low Cost Data Usage in India. In *Data-Driven Approaches for Effective Managerial Decision Making* (pp. 102–126). IGI Global. DOI: 10.4018/978-1-6684-7568-3.ch005

Chand, K., Tiwari, R., & Bhardwaj, K. (2021, December). Impact of Welfare Measures on Job Satisfaction of Employees in the Industrial Sector of Northern India1. In *Presented at IIF International Research Conference & Award Summit (November.* Claar, C., Portolese Dias, L., & Shields, R. (2014). Student acceptence of learning management systems: A study on demographics. *Issues in Information Systems*, 15(1).

Chang, H. H., & Chen, S. W. (2008). The Impact of online store environment cues on purchase intention. *Online Information Review*, 32(6), 818–841. DOI: 10.1108/14684520810923953

Cheng, C. (2021, December 30). Shasha, Wu., Luyao, Wang., Yaohua, Wu. (2022). Design and Performance Estimation of Mixed-Robotic Fulfillment System. *International Journal of Pattern Recognition and Artificial Intelligence*, 35(16), 2159057. Advance online publication. DOI: 10.1142/S0218001421590576

Cheng, C. (2021, November 07). Yanyan, Wang., Shasha, Wu., Jian, Zhang. (2021). Analysis and Optimization of the Robotic Mobile Fulfillment Systems Considering Congestion. *Applied Sciences (Basel, Switzerland)*, 11(21), 10446. Advance online publication. DOI: 10.3390/app112110446

Cheng, L., Yang, M., De Vos, J., & Witlox, F. (2020). Examining geographical accessibility to multi-tier hospital care services for the elderly: A focus on spatial equity. *Journal of Transport & Health*, 19, 100926. Advance online publication. DOI: 10.1016/j.jth.2020.100926

Cheng, Y., & Jiang, H. (2022). Customer–brand relationship in the era of artificial intelligence: Understanding the role of chatbot marketing efforts. *Journal of Product and Brand Management*, 31(2), 252–264. DOI: 10.1108/JPBM-05-2020-2907

Chen, Y., & Chiu, D. K. W. (2023). Digital Marketing and Service Strategies for Sustainable Development of Visual Culture: A Case Study of M+ Museum. In Gigauri, I., Palazzo, M., & Ferri, M. A. (Eds.), *Handbook of Research on Achieving Sustainable Development Goals With Sustainable Marketing* (pp. 68–91). IGI Global. DOI: 10.4018/978-1-6684-8681-8.ch004

Cheung, T. Y., Ye, Z., & Chiu, D. K. W. (2021). Value chain analysis of information services for the visually impaired: A case study of contemporary technological solutions. *Library Hi Tech*, 39(2), 625–642. DOI: 10.1108/LHT-08-2020-0185

Chiang, I. P., Wong, R., & Huang, C. H. (2019). Exploring the benefits of social media marketing for brands and communities. *International Journal of Electronic Commerce Studies*, 10(2), 113–140. DOI: 10.7903/ijecs.1547

Chin, G. Y. L., & Chiu, D. K. W. (2023). RFID-based Robotic Process Automation for Smart Museums with an Alert-driven Approach. In Tailor, R. (Ed.), *Application and Adoption of Robotic Process Automation for Smart Cities* (pp. 1–27). IGI Global. DOI: 10.4018/978-1-6684-7193-7.ch001

Christens, B. D., & Lin, C. S. (2014). Influences of Community and Organizational Participation, Social Support, and Sense of Community on Psychological Empowerment: Income as Moderator. *Family and Consumer Sciences Research Journal*, 42(3), 211–223. DOI: 10.1111/fcsr.12056

Christensen, C., Raynor, M. E., & McDonald, R. (2013). *Disruptive innovation*. Harvard Business Review.

Chu, S. T., Chiu, D. K. W., & Ho, K. K. W. (2024). Using infographics in disseminating healthy lifestyle information on social media is likely to increase uptake and sharing. *Health Information and Libraries Journal*, 41(3), 246–266. DOI: 10.1111/hir.12526 PMID: 38554025

Cloudflare. (2024). *What is Mirai?*https://www.cloudflare.com/learning/ddos/glossary/mirai-botnet/

Compeau, D. R., & Higgins, C. A. (1995). Computer self-efficacy: Development of a measure and initial test. *Management Information Systems Quarterly*, 19(2), 189–211. DOI: 10.2307/249688

Constantinides, E. (2014). Foundations of Social Media Marketing. *Procedia: Social and Behavioral Sciences*, 148, 40–57. DOI: 10.1016/j.sbspro.2014.07.016

Craigen, D., Diakun-Thibault, N., & Purse, R. (2014). Defining Cybersecurity. *Technology Innovation Management Review*, 4(10), 13–21. DOI: 10.22215/timreview/835

Crompton, H., & Burke, D. (2018). The use of mobile learning in higher education: A systematic review. *Computers & Education*, 123, 53–64. DOI: 10.1016/j.compedu.2018.04.007

Daer, A. R., Hoffman, R., & Goodman, S. (2014, September). Rhetorical functions of hashtag forms across social media applications. In *Proceedings of the 32nd ACM International Conference on the Design of Communication CD-ROM* (pp. 1-3). DOI: 10.1145/2666216.2666231

Dash, K. C. (2005). *Veto Players and the Deregulation of State-Owned Enterprises: The Case of Telecommunications in India*. Archive.org. https://web.archive.org/web/20080911040829/http://www.thunderbird.edu/wwwfiles/publications/magazine/fall2005/pdf-files/Telecom_RevJune27AS__1.pdf

Datta, A., & Majumdar, S. (2019). *Inside Reliance Jio's content factory*. Www.fortuneindia.com. https://www.fortuneindia.com/enterprise/inside-reliance-jios-content-factory/103723

De Koster, R., Le-Duc, T., & Roodbergen, K. J. (2007). Design and control of warehouse order picking: A literature review. *European Journal of Operational Research*, 182(2), 481–501. DOI: 10.1016/j.ejor.2006.07.009

de Vries, L. A., & Kühne, R. (2015). The influence of social media on consumer buying intention: A study among university students. *JMR, Journal of Marketing Research*, 2(4), 123–134. DOI: 10.11648/j.jmr.20150401.16

Demirli, C., & Kütük, Ö. F. (2010). Anlamsal web (3.0) ve ontolojilerine genel bir bakış. *İstanbul Ticaret Üniversitesi. Fen Bilimleri Dergisi*, 9(18), 97–107.

Denoo, L., & Yli-Renko, H. (2019). Entrepreneurship in a new digital industry: The emergence and growth of mobile health. In Baierl, R., Behrens, J., & Brem, A. (Eds.), *Digital Entrepreneurship* (pp. 79–98). Springer., DOI: 10.1007/978-3-030-20138-8_4

Digital Age. (2020, June 17). Netflix Türkiye abone sayısı ve elde edilen gelir açıklandı. https://digitalage.com.tr/netflix-turkiye-abone-sayisi-ve-elde-edilen-gelir-aciklandi/ (Accessed 01 August 2020).

Diwanji, V. S., Lee, J., & Cortese, J. (2022). Deconstructing the role of artificial intelligence in programmatic advertising: at the intersection of automation and transparency. *Journal of Strategic Marketing, ahead-of-print*(ahead-of-print), 1–18. DOI: 10.1080/0965254X.2022.2148269

Dodds, W. B., Kent, B. M., & Grewal, D. (1991). Effects of price, brand and store information on buyers' product evaluation. *JMR, Journal of Marketing Research*, 28(August), 307–319.

dos Reis, J. C. G., Amorim, M., Melao, N., & Matos, P. (2018). Digital Transformation: A Literatur Review and Guidelines for Future Research. *Trends and Advances in Information Systems and Technologies*, 1, 411–421. DOI: 10.1007/978-3-319-77703-0_41

Dublino, J. (2023, October 31). *The 6 biggest email marketing challenges and how to fix them*. business.com. https://www.business.com/articles/6-email-marketing-challenges-and-how-to-overcome-them/

Dwiningrum, N. R., Rahmawaty, P., & Ismawanto, T. (2018). Peran Paguyuban di Balikpapan dalam Mendukung Integrasi Sosial. *JSHP: Jurnal Sosial Humaniora Dan Pendidikan*, 2(1), 77–84. DOI: 10.32487/jshp.v2i1.295

Egnew, R. C., & Baler, S. G. (1998). Developing principles, goals, and models for public/private partnerships. *Administration and Policy in Mental Health*, 25(6), 571–580.

Eisenmann, T., Parker, G., & Van Alstyne, M. W. (2006). Strategies for two-sided markets. *Harvard Business Review*, 84(10), 92.

Elhissoufi, M., & Alla, L. (2024). Artificial Intelligence in Costumer Acquisition: A Bibliometric Study. In AI and Data Engineering Solutions for Effective Marketing (pp. 1-22). IGI Global. DOI: 10.4018/979-8-3693-3172-9.ch001

Elia, G., Margherita, A., & Passiante, G. (2020). Digital entrepreneurship ecosystem: How digital technologies and collective intelligence are reshaping the entrepreneurial process. *Technological Forecasting and Social Change*, 150, 119791. Advance online publication. DOI: 10.1016/j.techfore.2019.119791

Eling, M., & Schnell, W. (2016). What do we know about cyber risk and cyber risk insurance? *The Journal of Risk Finance*, 17(5), 474–491. DOI: 10.1108/JRF-09-2016-0122

Ellyta, E., Mustakim, U., & Rizieq, R. (2019). Pengembangan Adopsi Inovasi melalui Jaringan Komunikasi. *ZMIP: Zira'ah Majalah Ilmiah Pertanian*, 44(1), 83. Advance online publication. DOI: 10.31602/zmip.v44i1.1667

ENISA. (2022). *ENISA threat landscape report 2018 : 15 top cyber- threats and trends.*https://op.europa.eu/en/publication-detail/-/publication/6373c334-574d - 11e9-a8ed-01aa75ed71a1/language-en

Eriksson, J., Calling, S., Jakobsson, U., Wolff, M., Bolmsjö, B. B., & Nymberg, V. M. (2024). Inequity in access to digital public primary healthcare in Sweden: A cross-sectional study of the effects of urbanicity and socioeconomic status on utilization. *International Journal for Equity in Health*, 23(1), 72. DOI: 10.1186/s12939-024-02159-7 PMID: 38622678

Evans, D., & McKee, Jake. (2010). *Social media marketing the next generation of business engagement* (1st ed.). Wiley Technology Pub.

Ezat, A., Neumann, L., Sievert, S., Robra-Bissantz, S., Helmholz, P., & Perl, A. (2019). Herausforderungen im Datenschutz an der Hochschule. Generierung von Lösungsvorschlägen für Forschung und Lehre. In S Robra-Bissantz, O Bott, N Kleinefeld, K Neu, K Zickwolf: Teaching Trends 2018. Die Präsenzhochschule und die digitale Transformation (pp. 182-188). Waxmann.

Fan, M., Ndavi, J. W., Qalati, S. A., Huang, L., & Pu, Z. (2022). Applying the time continuum model of motivation to explain how major factors affect mobile learning motivation: A comparison of SEM and fsQCA. *Online Information Review*, 46(6), 1095–1114. DOI: 10.1108/OIR-04-2021-0226

Farahani P, (2015b) A vision on a digital supply chain management. 360 Bus Transform J.

Farris, P. W., Bendle, N., Pfeifer, P., & Reibstein, D. (2021). Marketing metrics: The manager's guide to measuring marketing performance. FT press.

Fernandes, C., Ferreira, J. J., Veiga, P. M., Kraus, S., & Dabić, M. (2022). Digital entrepreneurship platforms: Mapping the field and looking towards a holistic approach. *Technology in Society*, 70, 101979.

Fitriyani, R. (2012). Peranan Paguyuban Tionghoa Purbalingga dalam Pelestarian Tradisi Cap Go Meh. *Komunitas: International Journal of Indonesian Society and Culture*, 4(1), 73–81. DOI: 10.15294/komunitas.v4i1.2398

Flammini, F., Alcaraz, C., Bellini, E., Marrone, S., Lopez, J., & Bondavalli, A. (2024). Towards Trustworthy Autonomous Systems: Taxonomies and Future Perspectives. *IEEE Transactions on Emerging Topics in Computing, XX*(Xx), 1–13. DOI: 10.1109/TETC.2022.3227113

Fornell, C., & Larcker, D. F. (1981). Evaluating structural equation models with unobservable variables and measurement error. *JMR, Journal of Marketing Research*, 18(1), 39–50. DOI: 10.1177/002224378101800104

Frantti, T., & Korkiakoski, M. (2022). Security Controls for Smart Buildings with Shared Space. *2022 6th International Conference on Smart Grid and Smart Cities, ICSGSC 2022*, 156–165. DOI: 10.1109/ICSGSC56353.2022.9963114

Fruhlinger, J. (2022). *Stuxnet explained: The first known cyberweapon*. https://www.csoonline.com/article/562691/stuxnet-explained-the-first-known-cyberweapon.html

Fu, X. M., Bao, Q., Xie, H., & Fu, X. (2021). Diffusion of industrial robotics and inclusive growth: Labour market evidence from cross country data. *Journal of Business Research*, 122(1), 670–684. DOI: 10.1016/j.jbusres.2020.05.051

Gawelek, M. A., Spataro, M., & Komarny, P. (2011). Mobile perspectives: On iPads—why mobile? *EDUCAUSE Review*, 46(2), 28–30.

Ghouri, A., Haq, M. A., & Khan, N. R. (2017). Customer perception on online purchase intention: The impact of online shopping orientations on online buying intention. *The Eurasia Proceedings of Science, Technology* [EPSTEM]. *Engineering & Mathematics*, 1, 76–82.

Gimpel, H., & Röglinger, M. (2015). Digital transformation: changes and chances–insights based on an empirical study.

Giridharadas, A. (2018). *Winners take all : the elite charade of changing the world* (1st ed.). Alfred A. Knopf.

Girijan, K. P. (2024). Digital India Initiative: The Road Towards Sustainable Development. *Journal Commedies*, 1(1), 5–8.

Giusto, D., Iera, A., & Morabito, G., Atzori (Eds.), L., (2010). The Internet of Things, 20th Tyrrhenian Workshop on Digital Communications, Springer Science & Business Media. 441 p.

Gordon, L. A., Loeb, M. P., & Sohail, T. (2003). A framework for using insurance for cyber-risk management. *Communications of the ACM*, 46(3), 81–85. DOI: 10.1145/636772.636774

Grinberger, A. Y., Schott, M., Raifer, M., & Zipf, A. (2021). An analysis of the spatial and temporal distribution of large-scale data production events in OpenStreetMap. *Transactions in GIS*, 25(2), 622–641. Advance online publication. DOI: 10.1111/tgis.12746

Gul, M., & Guneri, A. F. (2021). Hospital location selection: A systematic literature review on methodologies and applications. In *Mathematical Problems in Engineering* (Vol. 2021). DOI: 10.1155/2021/6682958

Guzmán, J. B., & Lussier, R. (2015). *Success Factors for Small Businesses in Guanajuato, Mexico*. https://www.semanticscholar.org/paper/Success-Factors-for-Small-Businesses-in-Guanajuato%2C-Guzm%C3%A1n-Lussier/330a63d5d4069dde9b3f7ec5c70721733d922cb3

Gwinner, K. P., & Eaton, J. (2013). Building brand image through event sponsorship: The role of image transfer. *Journal of Advertising*, 28(4), 47–57. DOI: 10.1080/00913367.1999.10673595

Haim-Litevsky, D., Komemi, R., & Lipskaya-Velikovsky, L. (2023). Sense of Belonging, Meaningful Daily Life Participation, and Well-Being: Integrated Investigation. [IJERPH]. *International Journal of Environmental Research and Public Health*, 20(5), 1–16. DOI: 10.3390/ijerph20054121 PMID: 36901132

Hair, J. F.Jr, Matthews, L. M., Matthews, R. L., & Sarstedt, M. (2017). PLS-SEM or CB-SEM: Updated guidelines on which method to use. *International Journal of Multivariate Data Analysis*, 1(2), 107–123. DOI: 10.1504/IJMDA.2017.087624

Hakimi, M., Katebzadah, S., & Fazil, A. W. (2024). Comprehensive Insights into E-Learning in contemporary Education: Analyzing trends, challenges, and best practices. [JETL]. *Journal of Education and Teaching Learning*, 6(1), 86–105. DOI: 10.51178/jetl.v6i1.1720

Hameed, F., Qayyum, A., & Khan, F. A. (2024). A new trend of learning and teaching: Behavioral intention towards mobile learning. *Journal of Computers in Education*, 11(1), 149–180. DOI: 10.1007/s40692-022-00252-w

Hamidi, H., & Chavoshi, A. (2018). Analysis of the essential factors for the adoption of mobile learning in higher education: A case study of students of the University of Technology. *Telematics and Informatics*, 35(4), 1053–1070. DOI: 10.1016/j.tele.2017.09.016

Han, I., & Shin, W. S. (2016). The use of a mobile learning management system and academic achievement of online students. *Computers & Education*, 102, 79–89. DOI: 10.1016/j.compedu.2016.07.003

Hanlon, A. (2023, March 20). *The AIDA model*. Smart Insights. https://www.smartinsights.com/traffic-building-strategy/offer-and-message-development/aida-model/

Hanson, W. (2000). *Principles of Internet marketing*. South-Western College Publishing.

Hariharan, N. K. (2021). *Cyber-risk management: identification, prevention, and mitigation techniques. September 2020.*

Hartini, S. (2018). Peran Paguyuban dalam Peningkatan Motivasi Kewirausahaan Pengrajin Batik. *Jurnal Ilmiah UPT P2M STKIP Siliwangi, 5*(1), 21–26. DOI: 10.22460/p2m.v5i1p21-26.786

Hart, S., Margheri, A., Paci, F., & Sassone, V. (2020). Riskio: A Serious Game for Cyber Security Awareness and Education. *Computers & Security*, 95, 101827. Advance online publication. DOI: 10.1016/j.cose.2020.101827

Hattke, F., & Hattke, J. (2019). Lead by example? The dissemination of ethical values through authentic leader inspiration. *International Journal of Public Leadership*, 15(4), 224–237. DOI: 10.1108/IJPL-06-2019-0034

Heinzelmann, P. J., Lugn, N. E., & Kvedar, J. C. (2005, December). Telemedicine in the future. *Journal of Telemedicine and Telecare*, 11(8), 384–390. DOI: 10.1177/1357633X0501100802 PMID: 16356311

Herari, N. (2023). Customer Journey on Digital Omnichannel Local Culinary MSME "Dapur Buk Rien" (A PESO and REAN Model Approach with Qualitative Network Analysis) [Master's Thesis, LSPR Institute of Communication & Business]. https://doi.org/DOI: DOI: 10.13140/RG.2.2.20193.28001

Herfort, B., Lautenbach, S., Porto de Albuquerque, J., Anderson, J., & Zipf, A. (2021). The evolution of humanitarian mapping within the OpenStreetMap community. *Scientific Reports*, 11(1), 3037. Advance online publication. DOI: 10.1038/s41598-021-82404-z PMID: 33542423

Herfort, B., Lautenbach, S., Porto de Albuquerque, J., Anderson, J., & Zipf, A. (2023). A spatio-temporal analysis investigating completeness and inequalities of global urban building data in OpenStreetMap. *Nature Communications*, 14(1), 3985. Advance online publication. DOI: 10.1038/s41467-023-39698-6 PMID: 37414776

Herringer, M., Ndiaye, L., & South, A. (2023). Developing a data validation method with OpenStreetMap Senegal and the Ministry of Health in support of accurate health facility data. *Proceedings of the OSM Science*, 42–44.

Himanshi Lohchab. (2024, September 5). *Jio's disruptive entry revolutionised India's telecom market.* The Economic Times; Economic Times. https://economictimes.indiatimes.com/industry/telecom/telecom-news/et-graphics-jios-disruptive-entry-revolutionised-indias-telecom-market/articleshow/113104507.cms?from=mdr

Hmioui, A., Bentalha, B., & Alla, L. (2020). Service supply chain: A prospective analysis of sustainable management for global performance. 2020 IEEE 13th International Colloquium of Logistics and Supply Chain Management (LOGISTIQUA). DOI: 10.1109/LOGISTIQUA49782.2020.9353940

Hmioui, A., & Bentalha, B. (2021). Service supply chain management: A literature review. *International Journal of Logistics Systems and Management*, 40(3), 332–353. DOI: 10.1504/IJLSM.2021.120253

Hmioui, A., Bentalha, B., & Beniaich, R. (2024). Green Supply Chain Management et développement territorial: Une revue de littérature. *Alternatives Managériales Economiques*, 6(2), 52–74.

Hoberg, P. (2015). *Research Report: skills for digital transformation.* SAP SE and Technical University of Munich.

Hodijah, C. (2023). Optimalisasi Digital Marketing Sebagai Media Pemasaran Produk Dan Sekaligus Pelestarian Seni Budaya Sunda Paguyuban Ranggon Uyut Di Desa Cikeruh Jatinangor. *JPM: Jurnal Pengabdian Mandiri, 2*(1), 29–34. https://bajangjournal.com/index.php/JPM/article/view/4660

Holgersson, M., Baldwin, C. Y., Chesbrough, H., & Bogers, M. L. (2022). The forces of ecosystem evolution. *California Management Review*, 64(3), 5–23. DOI: 10.1177/00081256221086038

Honarbakhsh, S., Sporton, S., Monkhouse, C., Lowe, M., Earley, M. J., & Hunter, R. J. (2021). Remote clinics and investigations in arrhythmia services: What have we learnt during coronavirus disease 2019? *Arrhythmia & Electrophysiology Review*, 10(2), 120–124. DOI: 10.15420/aer.2020.37 PMID: 34401185

Howarth, F. (2014). The role of human error in successful security attacks. *IBM Security Intelligence Website*, 1–6. https://securityintelligence.com/the-role-of-human-error-in-successful-security-attacks/

Hsieh, Y.-J., & Wu, Y. J. (2019). Entrepreneurship through the platform strategy in the digital era: Insights and research opportunities, *Computers in Human Behavior*, Volume 95, Pages 315-323, ISSN 0747-5632, https://doi.org/DOI: 10.1016/j.chb.2018.03.033

Hsu, H. H. (2012). The acceptance of Moodle: An empirical study based on UTAUT. *Creative Education*, 3(8), 44–46. DOI: 10.4236/ce.2012.38B010

Huang, P. S., Paulino, Y., So, S., Chiu, D. K. W., & Ho, K. K. W. (2021). Editorial - COVID-19 Pandemic and Health Informatics (Part 1). *Library Hi Tech*, 39(3), 693–695. DOI: 10.1108/LHT-09-2021-324

Huang, P.-S., Paulino, Y. C., So, S., Chiu, D. K. W., & Ho, K. K. W. (2022). Guest editorial: COVID-19 Pandemic and Health Informatics Part 2. *Library Hi Tech*, 40(2), 281–285. DOI: 10.1108/LHT-04-2022-447

Huang, P.-S., Paulino, Y. C., So, S., Chiu, D. K. W., & Ho, K. K. W. (2023). Guest editorial: COVID-19 Pandemic and Health Informatics Part 3. *Library Hi Tech*, 41(1), 1–6. DOI: 10.1108/LHT-02-2023-585

Hulland, J. (1999). Use of partial least squares (PLS) in strategic management research: A review of four recent studies. *Strategic Management Journal*, 20(2), 195–204. DOI: 10.1002/(SICI)1097-0266(199902)20:2<195::AID-SMJ13>3.0.CO;2-7

Hung, C. H. (2008). The effect of brand image on public relations perceptions and customer loyalty. *International Journal of Management*, 25(2), 237–246.

Hwang, K., & Zhang, D. (2023). The impact of social media influencers on consumer behavior: A systematic review. *International Journal of Advertising*, 42(1), 4–22. DOI: 10.1080/02650487.2022.2100571

IBM. (2024). *What is cyber risk management?*https://www.ibm.com/topics/cyber-risk-management

Ihantamalala, F. A., Herbreteau, V., Révillion, C., Randriamihaja, M., Commins, J., Andréambeloson, T., Rafenoarimalala, F. H., Randrianambinina, A., Cordier, L. F., Bonds, M. H., & Garchitorena, A. (2020). Improving geographical accessibility modeling for operational use by local health actors. *International Journal of Health Geographics*, 19(1), 27. Advance online publication. DOI: 10.1186/s12942-020-00220-6 PMID: 32631348

İlçi, A. (2014). *Investigation of pre-service teachers' mobile learning readiness levels and mobile learning acceptance levels* (Master's thesis, Middle East Technical University).

INDEF. (2024). *Peran Platform Digital terhadap Pengembangan UMKM di Indonesia.*

Inge Panneels, Susan Lechelt, Alessandra Schmidt, Aykut Coşkun (2024). Data-driven innovation for sustainable practice in the creative economy - Ecological, social, and cultural aspects (In) Data-Driven Innovation in the Creative Industries. Edited By *Melissa Terras, Vikki Jones, Nicola Osborne, Chris Speed. pp.243-266. Routledge.* International Telecommunications Union (ITU). https://www.itu.int/en/ITU-D/Innovation/Pages/Digital-Transformation-Accelerators.aspx accessed on 26.9.2024.

Innis, H. (2006). *İmparatorluk ve iletişim araçları.* Ütopya Yayınevi.

International Data Corporation (IDC). (2022). IDC MarketScape: Worldwide Managed IoT Connectivity Services 2022 Vendor Assessment, IDC Media Center, [Online], https://www.idc.com/getdoc.jsp?containerId=US48061522 (Consulted 03 May 2024).

Jacobides, M. G. (2019). In the ecosystem economy, what's your strategy? *Harvard Business Review*, 97(5), 128–137.

Jacobides, M. G., Cennamo, C., & Gawer, A. (2018). Towards a theory of ecosystems. *Strategic Management Journal*, 39(8), 2255–2276. DOI: 10.1002/smj.2904

Jaeung, L. (2023). *Yooeui, Jin., Sungwook, Jang., Young, Jae, Jang., Il, Kyu, Lim., Seungmin, Jeong., Eoksu, Sim.* Sequential Decision-Making Framework for Robotic Mobile Fulfillment System-Based Automated Kitting System., DOI: 10.1109/WSC60868.2023.10407259

Jain, A. Bagga, R.K. and Vijaya Sekhar K.S., (2010) 'Capacity Building for eGovernance: Learning by Doing Methodology' in Gupta et al (Eds.) *Enablers of Change: Selected e-Governance Initiatives in India*, ICFAI University Press. pp 52-62.

James, M. (Interviewer), & Eric, Schmidt. (Interviewee). (2013). *Reimagining India: A Conversation with Eric Schmidt* [Interview transcript]. McKinsey & Company.

Jamwal, J. (2013). *Khidmat Center – An initiative of J&K Bank: Bridging the Digital Divide in Jammu and Kashmir.* 10 September, Locally Published. pp 11.

Jha, L. (2017, October 11). *Reliance Jio's expenditure on sponsorship deals pegged at Rs300 crore.* Mint. https://www.livemint.com/Companies/vD8XvmORUotYwuS69CksBM/Reliance-Jio-spend-on-sponsorship-deals-pegged-at-Rs300-cror.html

Jiang, X., Chiu, D. K. W., & Chan, C. T. (2023). Application of the AIDA model in social media promotion and community engagement for small cultural organizations: A case study of the Choi Chang Sau Qin Society. In Dennis, M., & Halbert, J. (Eds.), *Community Engagement in the Online Space* (pp. 48–70). IGI Global. DOI: 10.4018/978-1-6684-5190-8.ch004

Jockey Club Announces Institute of Philanthropy - bringing together local, regional and global thought leadership for the betterment of society - corporate news - about HKJC - The Hong Kong jockey club. (n.d.). https://corporate.hkjc.com/corporate/corporate-news/english/2023-09/news_2023091101328.aspx?b_cid=EWHPJSC_PACM_CORPNEWSsep-2023_

Johnson, A. M. (2009). Business and Security Executives Views of Information Security Investment Drivers: Results from a Delphi Study. *Journal of Information Privacy and Security*, 5(1), 3–27. DOI: 10.1080/15536548.2009.10855855

Joo, Y. J., Kim, N., & Kim, N. H. (2016). Factors predicting online university students' use of a mobile learning management system (m-LMS). *Educational Technology Research and Development*, 64(4), 611–630. DOI: 10.1007/s11423-016-9436-7

Jordan, K. (2017). Examining the UK Higher Education sector through the network of institutional accounts on Twitter. *First Monday*, 22(5), 5. DOI: 10.5210/fm.v22i5.7133

Joy, T., & Bahl, S. (2018). Disruption by Reliance Jio in Telecom Industry. *International Journal of Pure and Applied Mathematics*, 118(20), 43–49. https://www.acadpubl.eu/hub/2018-118-21/articles/21a/6.pdf

Kalyani, P. (2016). An Empirical Study on Reliance JIO Effect, Competitor's Reaction and Customer Perception on the JIO'S Pre- Launch Offer. *Journal of Management Engineering and Information Technology*, 3(5), 18–36. DOI: 10.5281/zenodo.183437

Kaplan, A. M., & Haenlein, M. (2010). Users of the world, unite! The challenges and opportunities of Social Media. *Business Horizons*, 53(1), 59–68. DOI: 10.1016/j.bushor.2009.09.003

Kapoor, R., & Lee, J. M. (2013). Coordinating and competing in ecosystems: How organizational forms shape new technology investments. *Strategic Management Journal*, 34(3), 274–296. DOI: 10.1002/smj.2010

Karaduman, S., & Aciyan, E. P. (2019). Netflix'in ilk Türk dizisi "Hakan Muhafız" üzerine bir alımlama analizi. *Akdeniz Üniversitesi İletişim Fakültesi Dergisi. Aralık*, (32), 669–687.

Karatas, M., Eriskin, L., Deveci, M., Pamucar, D., & Garg, H. (2022). Big Data for Healthcare Industry 4.0: Applications, challenges and future perspectives. In *Expert Systems with Applications* (Vol. 200). DOI: 10.1016/j.eswa.2022.116912

Karthick, M., Somesh, V., Gudadhe, N., Boopathi, B., Padmanabhan, S., Tiwari, R., & Sharma, A. (2023). Structural analysis of motorcycle spokes design using finite element analysis with alloy materials. *Materials Today: Proceedings*. Advance online publication. DOI: 10.1016/j.matpr.2023.04.380

Kaspersky. (2019). What is Cyber Security? | Definition, Types, and User Protection | Kaspersky. In *Www.Kaspersky.Co.Uk* (p. Home/Resource Centre/Definitions). https://www.kaspersky.com.au/resource-center/definitions/what-is-cyber-security

Kazi, B. U., Shaikh, M. S. I., & Munna, A. S. (Eds.). (2023). *Contemporary approaches of digital marketing and the role of machine intelligence*. IGI Global., DOI: 10.4018/978-1-6684-7735-9

KBBI. (2023). *Paguyuban (KBBI)*. Kbbi.Web.Id. https://www.kbbi.web.id/Paguyuban

Kehrbusch, B., & Engels, G. (2023). Digital Transformation-Towards Flexible Human-Centric Enterprises. In Vogel-Heuser, B., Wimmer, M., & Vieweg, S. (Eds.), *Digital Transformation: Core Technologies and Emerging Topics from a Computer Science Perspective* (pp. 497–526). DOI: 10.1007/978-3-662-65004-2_20

Kemlu, R. I. (2023). *5 Reasons Why You Should Invest in Indonesia Today!* https://kemlu.go.id/vancouver/en/news/25150/5-reasons-why-you-should-invest-in-indonesia-today

Kessler, A. (2007). Success factors for new businesses in Austria and the Czech Republic. *Entrepreneurship and Regional Development*, 19(5), 381–403. https://ideas.repec.org//a/taf/entreg/v19y2007i5p381-403.html. DOI: 10.1080/08985620701439959

Kessler, A., & Frank, H. (2009). Nascent Entrepreneurship in a Longitudinal Perspective: The Impact of Person, Environment, Resources and the Founding Process on the Decision to Start Business Activities. *International Small Business Journal*, 27(6), 720–742. DOI: 10.1177/0266242609344363

Keung, K. L., Lee, C. K. M., & Ji, P. (2022, April). Keung. K., L., C.K.H., Lee., Ping, Ji. (2022). Industrial internet of Things-driven storage location assignment and order picking in a resource synchronization and sharing-based robotic mobile fulfillment system. *Advanced Engineering Informatics*, 52, 101540. Advance online publication. DOI: 10.1016/j.aei.2022.101540

Khare, S. (2022, January 6). *Jio Rs. 499 Prepaid Recharge Plan With 1-Year Disney+ Hotstar Subscription Revived: All the Details*. Gadgets 360. https://gadgets360.com/telecom/news/jio-rs-499-prepaid-recharge-plan-revived-disney-plus-hotstar-28-days-validity-2gb-high-speed-data-benefits-2692228

Kiechel, W. (2010). *Lords of strategy: The secret intellectual history of the new corporate world*. Harvard Business Press.

Kim, B., Kim, H., & Jeon, Y. (2018). Critical Success Factors of a Design Startup Business. *Sustainability (Basel)*, 10(9), 9. Advance online publication. DOI: 10.3390/su10092981

Kim, J., Lee, Y., & Park, J. (2022). The role of social media influencers in shaping consumer behavior in the digital age: A comprehensive review. *Journal of Business Research*, 142, 524–538. DOI: 10.1016/j.jbusres.2021.12.035

Kimura, R., Reeves, M., & Whitaker, K. (2019). *The new logic of competition*. Boston Consulting Group Report.

Kim, W. C. (2005). Blue ocean strategy: From theory to practice. *California Management Review*, 47(3), 105–121. DOI: 10.1177/000812560504700301

Klimburg, A. (2012). *NATIONAL CYBER SECURITY FRAMEWORK MANUAL*.

Kohnke, A., Cole, M. L., & Bush, R. (2014, July). Incorporating UTAUT predictors for understanding home care patients' and clinician's acceptance of healthcare telemedicine equipment. *Journal of Technology Management & Innovation*, 9(2), 29–41. DOI: 10.4067/S0718-27242014000200003

Kokas, A. (2020). Chilling Netflix: Financialization and the influence of the Chinese market on the American entertainment industry. *Information Communication and Society*, 23(3), 407–419. DOI: 10.1080/1369118X.2018.1510534

Kotler, P., & Barich, H. (1991). A framework for marketing image management. *Sloan Management Review*, 2(32), 94–104. PMID: 10111301

Kumar, R. P. (2016, August 30). *Reliance Jio effect: Data charges slashed, here's a comparison for the best deal*. The Economic Times; Economic Times. https://economictimes.indiatimes.com/news/company/corporate-trends/reliance-jio-effect-data-charges-slashed-heres-a-comparison-for-the-best-deal/articleshow/53926255.cms?utm_source=contentofinterest&utm_medium=text&utm_campaign=cppst

Kun, W. (2022, July). T., Hu., Zhi-Zue, Wang., Yunhai, Xiang., Jie, Shao., Xianwen, Xiang. (2022). Performance evaluation of a robotic mobile fulfillment system with multiple picking stations under zoning policy. *Computers & Industrial Engineering*, 169, 108229. Advance online publication. DOI: 10.1016/j.cie.2022.108229

Kurup, R. (2019, July 29). *MTNL to be a BSNL subsidiary*. Business Line. https://www.thehindubusinessline.com/info-tech/mtnl-to-be-a-bsnl-subsidiary/article28749551.ece

Kuswanto, K., & Anderson, I. (2023). Structural Model of Community Participation in Rural Development in Jambi Province, Indonesia. *Population and Economics*, 7(2), 115–141. DOI: 10.3897/popecon.7.e97189

Lakshminarasimha, K., & Abraham, K. J. (2021). *Forbes India - Telecom In India–propelling Digital Growth*. Forbes India. https://www.forbesindia.com/blog/enterprise/does-indias-telecom-sector-still-need-restrictive-policies/

Lam, A. H. C., Ho, K. K. W., & Chiu, D. K. W. (2023). Instagram for student learning and library promotions? A quantitative study using the 5E Instructional Model. *Aslib Journal of Information Management*, 75(1), 112–130. DOI: 10.1108/AJIM-12-2021-0389

Lamballais, T., Merschformann, M., Roy, D., de Koster, M. B. M., Azadeh, K., & Suhl, L. (2022). Dynamic policies for resource reallocation in a robotic mobile fulfillment system with time-varying demand. *European Journal of Operational Research*, 300(3), 937–952. DOI: 10.1016/j.ejor.2021.09.001

Lamballais, T., Roy, D., & De Koster, M. B. M. (2017). Estimating performance in a Robotic Mobile Fulfillment System. *European Journal of Operational Research*, 256(3), 976–990. DOI: 10.1016/j.ejor.2016.06.063

Lam, E. T. H., Au, C. H., & Chiu, D. K. W. (2019). Analyzing the use of Facebook among university libraries in Hong Kong. *Journal of Academic Librarianship*, 45(3), 175–183. DOI: 10.1016/j.acalib.2019.02.007

Lampadarios, E., Kyriakidou, N., & Smith, G. (2017). Towards a new framework for SMEs success: A literature review. *International Journal of Business and Globalisation*, 18(2), 194. DOI: 10.1504/IJBG.2017.081954

Lan, Y. F., & Sie, Y. S. (2010). Using RSS to support mobile learning based on media richness theory. *computers & education, 55(2)*, 723-732.

Leavy, B. (2019). Value innovation and how to successfully incubate "blue ocean" initiatives. *Strategy and Leadership*, 46(3), 10–20. DOI: 10.1108/SL-02-2018-0020

Lee, S. S., & Osteryoung, J. S. (2001). A Comparison of Determinants for Business Start-Up in the U.S. and Korea. *Journal of Small Business Management*. https://www.tandfonline.com/doi/abs/10.1111/1540-627X.00018

Lee, I., & Shin, Y. J. (2018). Fintech: Ecosystem, business models, investment decisions, and challenges. *Business Horizons*, 61(1), 35–46. DOI: 10.1016/j.bushor.2017.09.003

Lee, J. K., & Lee, W. K. (2008). The relationship of e-Learner's self-regulatory efficacy and perception of e-Learning environmental quality. *Computers in Human Behavior*, 24(1), 32–47. DOI: 10.1016/j.chb.2006.12.001

Lee, S. H. (2019). An analysis on the changes of logistics industry using internet of things. *Journal of Advanced Information Technology and Convergence*, 9(1), 57–66. DOI: 10.14801/JAITC.2019.9.1.57

Leung, Y. L., Chan, R., Chiu, D. K. W., & Tian, R. (2023). (in press). Investigating the Consumption Behavior of Young Adults Using Online Food Delivery Platforms during the COVID-19 Pandemic. *Aslib Journal of Information Management*. Advance online publication. DOI: 10.1108/AJIM-05-2023-0177

Lewis, E. S. E. (1899). Side talks about advertising. *The Western Druggist*, 21(2), 65–66.

Lien, C., Wen, M., Huang, L., & Wu, K. (2015). Online hotel booking: The effects of brand image, price, trust, and value on purchase intentions. *Asia Pacific Management Review*, 20(4), 210–218. DOI: 10.1016/j.apmrv.2015.03.005

Ligo, A. K., Kott, A., & Linkov, I. (2021). How to Measure Cyber-Resilience of a System with Autonomous Agents: Approaches and Challenges. *IEEE Engineering Management Review*, 49(2), 89–97. DOI: 10.1109/EMR.2021.3074288

Li, H., Zhang, C., & Kettinger, W. J. (2022). Digital Platform Ecosystem Dynamics: The Roles of Product Scope, Innovation, and Collaborative Network Centrality. *Management Information Systems Quarterly*, 46(2), 739–770. DOI: 10.25300/MISQ/2022/15444

Li, J., Qin, H., Wang, J., & Li, J. (2022). OpenStreetMap-Based Autonomous Navigation for the Four Wheel-Legged Robot Via 3D-Lidar and CCD Camera. *IEEE Transactions on Industrial Electronics*, 69(3), 2708–2717. Advance online publication. DOI: 10.1109/TIE.2021.3070508

Lim, H., Tan, Y., & Yeo, L. (2022). The role of storytelling in influencer marketing: Engaging consumers through narrative. *Journal of Marketing Communications*, 28(5), 551–566. DOI: 10.1080/13527266.2020.1784542

Limna, P., & Kraiwanit, T. (2022). The Rise of Fintech: A Review Article. *STOU Academic Journal of Research and Innovation*, 2, 35–46.

Lin, C.-H., Chiu, D. K. W., & Lam, K. T. (2022). Hong Kong Academic Librarians' Attitudes Towards Robotic Process Automation. *Library Hi Tech*, 42(3), 991–1014. DOI: 10.1108/LHT-03-2022-0141

Lin, J. C., Kavousi, Y., Sullivan, B., & Stevens, C. (2020, May 1). Analysis of outpatient telemedicine reimbursement in an integrated healthcare system. *Annals of Vascular Surgery*, 65, 100–106. DOI: 10.1016/j.avsg.2019.10.069 PMID: 31678131

Linkov, I., & Alexander Kott. (2018). Fundamental Concepts of Cyber Resilience: Introduction and Overview Motivation: Why Cyber Resilience? *Cyber Resilience of Systems and Networks*.

Li, S. M., Lam, A. H. C., & Chiu, D. K. W. (2023). Digital transformation of ticketing services: A value chain analysis of POPTICKET in Hong Kong. In Santos, J. D., & Pereira, I. V. (Eds.), *Management and Marketing for Improved Retail Competitiveness and Performance* (pp. 156–179). IGI. Global.

Li, S., Bu, Y., Zhang, Z., & Huang, Y. (2024). Digital entrepreneurship intention and digital entrepreneurship behavior: The mediating role of managing learning and entrepreneurship education. *Education + Training*.

Li, S., Xie, Z., Chiu, D. K. W., & Ho, K. K. W. (2023). Sentiment Analysis and Topic Modeling Regarding Online Classes on the Reddit Platform: Educators versus Learners. *Applied Sciences (Basel, Switzerland)*, 13(4), 2250. DOI: 10.3390/app13042250 PMID: 39354955

Liu, Y., Chiu, D. K. W., & Ho, K. K. W. (2023). Short-Form Videos for Public Library Marketing: Performance Analytics of Douyin in China. *Applied Sciences (Basel, Switzerland)*, 13(6), 3386. DOI: 10.3390/app13063386

Liu, Y., Li, H., & Carlsson, C. (2010). Factors driving the adoption of m-learning: An empirical study. *Computers & Education*, 55(3), 1211–1219. DOI: 10.1016/j.compedu.2010.05.018

Liu, Y., Zhang, W., Pan, S., Li, Y., & Chen, Y. (2020). Analyzing the robotic behavior in a smart city with deep enforcement and imitation learning using IoRT. *Computer Communications*, 150(1), 346–356. DOI: 10.1016/j.comcom.2019.11.031

Liu, Z. (2021). Identifying urban land use social functional units: A case study using OSM data. *International Journal of Digital Earth*, 14(12), 1798–1817. Advance online publication. DOI: 10.1080/17538947.2021.1988161

Li, Y., & Xu, L. (2021). The impact of covid-19 on pedestrian flow patterns in urban pois—An example from Beijing. *ISPRS International Journal of Geo-Information*, 10(7), 479. Advance online publication. DOI: 10.3390/ijgi10070479

Lloyd, G. (2020). The business benefits of cyber security for SMEs. *Computer Fraud & Security*, 2020(2), 14–17. DOI: 10.1016/S1361-3723(20)30019-1

Lobschat, L., Zinnbauer, M. A., Pallas, F., & Joachimsthaler, E. (2013). Why social currency becomes a key driver of a firm's brand equity: Insights from the automotive industry. *Long Range Planning*, 46(1–2), 125–148. DOI: 10.1016/j.lrp.2012.11.004

Long, A. (2009). Port Community systems. *World Customs Journal*, 3(1). Advance online publication. DOI: 10.55596/001c.91356

Loonam, J. (2021). Towards Digital Transformation: Implications for Strategic Change. In Reviving Businesses With New Organizational Change Management Strategies (pp. 56-70). IGI Global.

Loonam, J., & O'Regan, N. (2022). Global value chains and digital platforms: Implications for strategy. *Strategic Change*, 31(1), 161–177. DOI: 10.1002/jsc.2485

Loonam, J., Zwiegelaar, J., Kumar, V., & Booth, C. (2022). Cyber-Resiliency for Digital Enterprises: A Strategic Leadership Perspective. *IEEE Transactions on Engineering Management*, 69(6), 3757–3770. DOI: 10.1109/TEM.2020.2996175

Loukianov, A., Burningham, K., & Jackson, T. (2023). The patterning of the discursive space in search for the# goodlife: A network analysis of the co-occurrence of Instagram hashtags. *The Information Society*, 39(1), 62–78. DOI: 10.1080/01972243.2022.2125604

Lu, S. S., Tian, R., & Chiu, D. K. W. (2023). Why do people not attend public library programs in the current digital age? *Library Hi Tech*, 42(4), 1237–1265. DOI: 10.1108/LHT-04-2022-0217

Lv, B., Deng, Y., Meng, W., Wang, Z., & Tang, T. (2024). Research on digital intelligence business model based on artificial intelligence in post-epidemic era. *Management Decision*, 62(9), 2937–2957. DOI: 10.1108/MD-11-2022-1548

Lynch, P. J., Horton, S., & Marcotte, E. (2016). *Web style guide: foundations of user experience design* (4th ed.). Yale University Press.

Madhavan, P. M., & Chirputkar, A. (2020). ANALYSIS OF THE IMPACT OF RELIANCE JIO INFOCOMM LTD ON INDIAN ECONOMY: A CASE STUDY. *PalArch's Journal of Archaeology of Egypt / Egyptology, 17*(6), 4452–4461. https://archives.palarch.nl/index.php/jae/article/view/1695

Magretta, J., 2012. Understanding Michael Porter: The essential guide to competition and strategy. Harvard business press.

ManageEngine. (2024). *PayPal users targeted in a phishing scam.*https://www.manageengine.com/log-management/phishing-attacks/paypal-phishing-email-scam.html

Marotta, A., Martinelli, F., Nanni, S., Orlando, A., & Yautsiukhin, A. (2017). Cyber-insurance survey. *Computer Science Review*, 24(December), 35–61. DOI: 10.1016/j.cosrev.2017.01.001

Martenson, R. (2007). Corporate brand image, satisfaction and store loyalty: A study of the store as a brand, store brands and manufacturer brands. *International Journal of Retail & Distribution Management*, 35(7), 544–555. DOI: 10.1108/09590550710755921

Matimbwa, R., & Anney, V. N. (2016). Teachers' and students' perceptions of self-driven acceptance of mobile phone use as an ICT teaching tool. *Journal of Emerging Trends in Educational Research and Policy Studies*, 7(2), 91–106.

Mazzucato, M. (2015). *The Entrepreneurial State Debunking Public vs. Private Sector myths*. Public Affairs.

McBain, L., & Morgan, D. (2005). Telehealth, geography, and jurisdiction: Issues of health care delivery in Northern Saskatchewan. *Canadian Women's Studies*, 24, 123–129.

McKeon, G., Steel, Z., Wells, R., Newby, J., Hadzi-Pavlovic, D., Vancampfort, D., & Rosenbaum, S. (2021). A mental health-informed physical activity intervention for first responders and their partners delivered using Facebook: Mixed methods pilot study. *JMIR Formative Research*, 5(4), e23432. DOI: 10.2196/23432 PMID: 33885376

McLuhan, M. (2001). *Global köy*. Skala Yayıncılık.

Mehrotra, S. (2021). *Vodafone Idea loses over 4 million subscribers, Jio and Airtel dominate market share: TRAI*. Republic World. https://www.republicworld.com/technology-news/mobile/vodafone-idea-loses-over-4-million-subscribers-jio-and-airtel-dominate-market-share-trai.html

Mehta, I. (2017, June 1). *Reliance Jio Is Driving Indian Internet Growth, Says The Mary Meeker Report*. HuffPost. https://www.huffpost.com/archive/in/entry/reliance-jio-is-driving-indian-internet-growth-says-the-mary-me_a_22120777

Menard, A. (2017). *How can we recognize the real power of the Internet of Things?* McKinsey Consulting.

Menz, M., Kunisch, S., Birkinshaw, J., Collis, D. J., Foss, N. J., Hoskisson, R. E., & Prescott, J. E. (2021). Corporate Strategy and the Theory of the Firm in the Digital Age. *Journal of Management Studies*, 58(7), 1695–1720. DOI: 10.1111/joms.12760

Merschformann, M., Lamballais, T., De Koster, M. B. M., & Suhl, L. (2019). Decision rules for robotic mobile fulfillment systems. *Operations Research Perspectives*, 6(1), 100–128. DOI: 10.1016/j.orp.2019.100128

Miles, M. B., Huberman, A. M., & Saldana, J. (2013). *Qualitative Data Analysis: A Methods Sourcebook*. SAGE Publications.

Milian, E. Z., Spinola, M. M., & Carvalho, M. M. (2019). Fintechs: A literature review and research agenda. *Electronic Commerce Research and Applications*, 34, 100833. DOI: 10.1016/j.elerap.2019.100833

Miller, S., & Bossomaier, T. (2024). *Cybersecurity, Ethics, and Collective Responsibility*. Oxford University Press. DOI: 10.1093/oso/9780190058135.001.0001

Minghini, M., Delucchi, L., Sarretta, A., Lupia, F., Napolitano, M., & Palmas, A. (2017). Collaborative mapping response to disasters through openstreetmap: The case of the 2016 Italian earthquake. In *Geoingegneria Ambientale e Mineraria* (Vol. 151, Issue 2).

Minghini, M., Sarretta, A., & Napolitano, M. (2022). OpenStreetMap Contribution to Local Data Ecosystems in COVID-19 Times: Experiences and Reflections from the Italian Case. *Data*, 7(4), 39. Advance online publication. DOI: 10.3390/data7040039

Mitroff, I. I. (2019). Pushing back on pervasive technology. *MIT Sloan Management Review*.

Moerdijat, L. (2023, August 4). *Segera Atasi Kendala dalam Transformasi Digital di Sektor UMKM*. MPR RI. https://www.mpr.go.id/berita/Segera-Atasi-Kendala-dalam-Transformasi-Digital-di-Sektor-UMKM

Mooney, P., Grinberger, A. Y., Minghini, M., Coetzee, S., Juhasz, L., & Yeboah, G. (2021). OpenStreetMap Data Use Cases During the Early Months of the COVID-19 Pandemic. In *COVID-19 Pandemic*. Geospatial Information, and Community Resilience., DOI: 10.1201/9781003181590-15

Moore, J. F. (1993, May-June). Predators and Prey. *Harvard Business Review*, 71(3), 75–86. PMID: 10126156

Moradi, M., Roche, S., & Mostafavi, M. A. (2022). Exploring five indicators for the quality of OpenStreetMap road networks: A case study of Québec, Canada. *Geomatica*, 75(4), 178–208. Advance online publication. DOI: 10.1139/geomat-2021-0012

Mulier, L., Slabbinck, H., & Vermeir, I. (2021). This Way Up: The Effectiveness of Mobile Vertical Video Marketing. *Journal of Interactive Marketing*, 55(1), 1–15. DOI: 10.1016/j.intmar.2020.12.002

Murphy, G. (2011). Post-PC devices: A summary of early iPad technology adoption in tertiary environments. *E-Journal of Business Education & Scholarship of Teaching*, 5(1), 18–32.

MWPVL International Inc. (2022). Amazon Global Supply Chain and Fulfillment Center Network. [On line] https://www.mwpvl.com/html/amazon_com.html (Consulted 20/05/2024)

Nabila, F., Huda, S., & Utami, A. F. (2023). Pembentukan Paguyuban sebagai Wadah Interaksi antar Pelaku UMKM di Desa Kedungpari. *Jurnal Pengabdian Masyarakat Nusantara (Pengabmas Nusantara), 5*(3).

Nalintippayawong, S., Waiyawatpattarakul, N., & Chotipant, S. (2018). Examining the Critical Success Factors of Startup in Thailand Using Structural Equation Model. *10th International Conference on Information Technology and Electrical Engineering (ICITEE)*, Bali, Indonesia, 2018, pp. 388-393, DOI: 10.1109/ICITEED.2018.8534854

Nelson, A., Herron, D., Rees, G., & Nachev, P. (2019). Predicting scheduled hospital attendance with artificial intelligence. *NPJ Digital Medicine*, 2(1), 26. DOI: 10.1038/s41746-019-0103-3 PMID: 31304373

Newman, J. W., & Werbel, R. A. (1973). Multivariate analysis of brand loyalty for major household appliances. *JMR, Journal of Marketing Research*, 10(4), 404–409.

Nugraha, A. Z. (2014). Peran Kapital Sosial dalam Meningkatkan Kesejahteraan Anggota Paguyuban: Studi Kasus pada Ikatan Silaturahmi Keluarga Putra Bengawan (IKPB). *Empati: Jurnal Ilmu Kesejahteraan Sosial*, 3(1), 8–21. DOI: 10.15408/empati.v3i1.9759

Obare, S. O. (2020). Successful STEM Women of Color Must Network Differently. In Leggett-Robinson, P., & Villa, B. (Eds.), *Overcoming Barriers for Women of Color in STEM Fields: Emerging Research and Opportunities* (pp. 1–18). IGI Global., DOI: 10.4018/978-1-7998-4858-5.ch004

Oliver, M. (2000). An introduction to the evaluation of learning technology. *Journal of Educational Technology & Society*, 3(4), 20–30.

Oliver, R. L. (1999). Whence consumer loyalty? *Journal of Marketing*, 63(4_suppl1), 33–44. DOI: 10.1177/00222429990634s105

Ørjan. (2023). *Øvsthus., Didrik, Nicolai, Robsrud., Lars, Muggerud., José, Amendola., Linga, Reddy, Cenkeramaddi., Ilya, Tyapin., Ajit, Jha*. Mobile Robotic Manipulator Based Autonomous Warehouse Operations., DOI: 10.1109/ICCMA59762.2023.10374743

Orlando, A. (2021). Cyber risk quantification: Investigating the role of cyber value at risk. *Risks*, 9(10), 184. Advance online publication. DOI: 10.3390/risks9100184

Orozco, J., Tarhini, A., Masa'deh, R., & Tarhini, T. (2015). A Framework of IS/Business Alignment Management Practices to Improve the Design of IT Governance Architectures. *International Journal of Business and Management*, 10(4), 1–12. DOI: 10.5539/ijbm.v10n4p1

Padmalosan, P., Vanitha, S., Kumar, V. S., Anish, M., Tiwari, R., Dhapekar, N. K., & Yadav, A. S. (2023). An investigation on the use of waste materials from industrial processes in clay brick production. *Materials Today: Proceedings*. Advance online publication. DOI: 10.1016/j.matpr.2023.01.238

Pagar, Mrs. N., Pardeshi, A., Mallick, N., Tejwani, A., & Ubale, T. (2024). Literature Survey on Indoor Navigation System Using QR Code and OSM. *IARJSET, 11*(2). DOI: 10.17148/IARJSET.2024.11204

Pal, M. (2021). A Literature Review to Assess The Importance of Community Participation and Health Promotion in Community Development. *IJRSFP: International Journal of Recent Scientific Research*, 12(6), 42043–42048. DOI: 10.24327/ijrsr.2021.1206.6015

Pandagle, V. (2023). *Airbus Cyber Attack: Work of USDoD Hacker, Linked to Turkish Airlines Employee Account Hack.* CyberExpress. https://thecyberexpress.com/airbus-cyber-attack-usdod-turkish-airlines/

Parker, G. G., Van Alstyne, M. W., & Choudary, S. P. (2016). *Platform revolution: How networked markets are transforming the economy and how to make them work for you.* WW Norton & Company.

Partala, J. (2018). Provably Secure Covert Communication on Blockchain. *Cryptography*, 2(2), 18. DOI: 10.3390/cryptography2030018

Parveen, F., Jaafar, N. I., & Ainin, S. (2015). Social media usage and organizational performance: Reflections of Malaysian social media managers. *Telematics and Informatics*, 32(1), 67–78. DOI: 10.1016/j.tele.2014.03.001

Perez, M. V., Mahaffey, K. W., Hedlin, H., Rumsfeld, J. S., Garcia, A., Ferris, T., Balasubramanian, V., Russo, A. M., Rajmane, A., Cheung, L., Hung, G., Lee, J., Kowey, P., Talati, N., Nag, D., Gummidipundi, S. E., Beatty, A., Hills, M. T., Desai, S., & Turakhia, M. P. (2019). Large-scale assessment of a smartwatch to identify atrial fibrillation. *The New England Journal of Medicine*, 381(20), 1909–1917. DOI: 10.1056/NEJMoa1901183 PMID: 31722151

Permana, I., Asral, A., Kodratila, E. Y., & Putra, M. (2023). Literasi Digital Marketing Sebagai Upaya Peningkatan Penjualan Pada Paguyuban UMKM Kecamatan Serang Baru Kabupaten Bekasi. *Joong-Ki: Jurnal Pengabdian Masyarakat*, 2(1), 117–123. DOI: 10.56799/joongki.v2i1.1295

Perri-Moore, S., Routen, T., Shao, A. F., Rambaud-Althaus, C., Swai, N., Kahama-Maro, J., D'Acremont, V., Blaise, G., & Mitchell, M. (2015). Using an eIMCI-Derived Decision Support Protocol to Improve Provider– Caretaker Communication for Treatment of Children Under 5 in Tanzania. *Global Health Communication*, 1(1), 41–47. DOI: 10.1080/23762004.2016.1181486 PMID: 27525308

Petrosyan, A. (2024). *Worldwide Digital Population 2024.*

Pituch, K. A., & Lee, Y. K. (2006). The influence of system characteristics on e-learning use. *Computers & Education*, 47(2), 222–244. DOI: 10.1016/j.compedu.2004.10.007

Poiani, T. H., Rocha, R. dos S., Degrossi, L. C., & de Albuquerque, J. P. (2016). Potential of Collaborative Mapping for Disaster Relief : A Case Study of OpenStreetMap in the Nepal Earthquake 2015. *Hawaii International Conference on System Sciences, JANUARY*, 1–10. DOI: 10.1109/HICSS.2016.31

Pollock, T. (2017). *Reducing human error in cyber security using the Human Factors Analysis Classification System (HFACS)*. https://digitalcommons.kennesaw.edu/ccerp%0Ahttp://digitalcommons.kennesaw.edu/ccerp/2017/research/2

Porter, M. E. (1980). *Competitive Strategy*. The Free Press.

Porter, M. E. (2001). Strategy and the Internet. *Harvard Business Review*, 79, 62–78. PMID: 11246925

Porter, M. E., & Heppelmann, J. E. (2014). How smart, connected products are transforming competition. *Harvard Business Review*, 92(11), 64–88.

Portman, R., & Carper, T. (2019). *How Equifax Neglected Cybersecurity and Suffered a Devastating Data Breach*.

Prahalad, C. K., & Ramaswamy, V. (2004). Co-creating unique value with customers. *Strategy and Leadership*, 32(3), 4–9. DOI: 10.1108/10878570410699249

Press Trust of India. (2017, December 25). *Reliance Jio subscriber base touches 160 million*. ETTelecom.com; PTI. https://telecom.economictimes.indiatimes.com/news/reliance-jio-subscriber-base-touches-160-million/62237555

Przybylski, A. K., Murayama, K., & DeHaan, C. R. (2013). When boredom strikes: Affective, cognitive, and behavioral consequences of boredom. *Journal of Experimental Psychology. General*, 142(4), 1154–1163. DOI: 10.1037/a0033736

Psyllidis, A., Gao, S., Hu, Y., Kim, E. K., McKenzie, G., Purves, R., Yuan, M., & Andris, C. (2022). Points of Interest (POI): A commentary on the state of the art, challenges, and prospects for the future. *Computational Urban Science*, 2(1), 20. Advance online publication. DOI: 10.1007/s43762-022-00047-w PMID: 35789810

Putnam, R. D. (2001). *Bowling Alone: The Collapse and Revival of American Community* (1st ed., Vol. 1). Simon & Schuster.

Quan, Z., & Zhang, Y. (2025). A Historical Review on Learning with Technology: From Computers to Smartphones. In *Encyclopedia of Information Science and Technology*, Sixth Edition. DOI: DOI: 10.4018/978-1-6684-7366-5.ch004

Quesenbery, W. (2001). *What Does Usability Mean: Looking Beyond 'Ease of Use.'* WQ Usability. https://www.wqusability.com/articles/more-than-ease-of-use.html

Quraishi, N. T., Bayani, B. M., Yashar, N. S., Daudzai, N. M., Salamzada, N. R., Amini, N. M., & Hakimi, N. M. (2024). Integration of Mobile Learning Technologies in Afghanistan Universities: Opportunities and Challenges. *Education Specialist*, 2(1), 1–14. DOI: 10.59535/es.v2i1.227

Raatikainen, M. J., Uusimaa, P., van Ginneken, M. M., Janssen, J. P., & Linnaluoto, M. (2008). Remote monitoring of implantable cardioverter defibrillator patients: A safe, time-saving, and cost-effective means for follow-up. *Europace*, 10(10), 1145–1151. DOI: 10.1093/europace/eun203 PMID: 18703585

Rahman, W. N. A., Mutum, D. S., & Ghazali, E. (2022). Consumer Engagement With Visual Content on Instagram: Impact of Different Features of Posts by Prominent Brands. *International Journal of E-Services and Mobile Applications*, 14(1), 1–21. DOI: 10.4018/IJESMA.295960

Ray, S., Jain, K., Birru, P., & Mohata, R. (2024). A case study of BYJU'S failure. *World Journal of Advanced Research and Reviews*, 21(3), 674–689. DOI: 10.30574/wjarr.2024.21.3.0765

Reis, L., Carvalho, L. C., Silveira, C., & Brasil, D. X. (2022). *Digitalization As a Driver for Smart Economy in the Post-COVID-19 Era* (1st ed.). IGI Global. DOI: 10.4018/978-1-7998-9227-4

Ricci, R. P., Morichelli, L., Quarta, L., Sassi, A., Porfili, A., Laudadio, M. T., Gargaro, A., & Santini, M. (2010). Long-term patient acceptance of and satisfaction with implanted device remote monitoring. *Europace*, 12(5), 674–679. DOI: 10.1093/europace/euq046 PMID: 20200019

Roege, P., Collier, Z., Chevardin, V., & Chouinard, P. (2017). Bridging the Gap from Cyber Security to Resilience. In *Resilience and Risk* (pp. 383–414). DOI: 10.1007/978-94-024-1123-2_14

Role of Artificial Intelligence in Social Media Marketing. (2019). *International Journal of Recent Technology and Engineering, 8*(4S3), 66–69. https://doi.org/DOI: 10.35940/ijrte.D1001.1284S319

Rousell, A., & Zipf, A. (2017). Towards a landmark-based pedestrian navigation service using OSM data. *ISPRS International Journal of Geo-Information*, 6(3), 64. Advance online publication. DOI: 10.3390/ijgi6030064

Rutkowsky, S., I. Peteresen, and F. Klötzke. "Digital Supply Chains: Increasingly Critical for Competitive Edge." European AT Kearney/WHU Logistics Study (2015): 18.

Sachdeva, S. (2006). *'Twenty-Five Steps to Successful e-Governance', I-WAYS, Digest of Electronic Government Policy and Regulation 29*. IOS Press.

Saha, S. (2017). *Airtel and Jio offer Rs 149, Rs 349 and Rs 399 plans: What all you get and which one is better*. India Today. https://www.indiatoday.in/technology/news/story/airtel-reliance-jio-offer-rs-149-rs-349-and-rs-399-tariff-plans-which-one-is-better-1037312-2017-09-04

Saikat, S., Dhillon, J. S., Ahmad, W. F. W., & Jamaluddin, R. A. (2021). A Systematic Review of the Benefits and Challenges of Mobile Learning during the COVID-19 Pandemic. *Education Sciences*, 11(9), 459. DOI: 10.3390/educsci11090459

Salamzadeh, A., & Kawamorita Kesim, H. (2017). The enterprising communities and startup ecosystem in Iran. *Journal of Enterprising Communities: People and Places in the Global Economy*, 11(4), 456–479. DOI: 10.1108/JEC-07-2015-0036

Sammut, S. (2001). Processus de démarrage en petite entreprise : Système de gestion et scénarios. *Revue de l'Entrepreneuriat / Review of Entrepreneurship, 1*(1), 61-76. https://doi.org/DOI: 10.3917/entre.011.0061

Sánchez, R. A., & Hueros, A. D. (2010). Motivational factors that influence the acceptance of Moodle using TAM. *Computers in Human Behavior*, 26(6), 1632–1640. DOI: 10.1016/j.chb.2010.06.011

Sanchez, R., Carvajal, A. L. P., Fransisco, C., Pagtalunan, E. C., Alon-Rabbon, K., Llego, J., Sanchez, A. M. P., Pangilinan, A. M., & Sanchez, J. J. D. (2024). *The Power of Influence: Leading by Example for Greater Role and Productivity* (1st ed., Vol. 1). ETCOR Educational Research Center Research., https://etcor.org/book-publications/the-power-of-influence-leading-by-example-for-greater-role-and-productivity

Sands, S., Campbell, C. L., Plangger, K., & Ferraro, C. (2022). Unreal influence: Leveraging AI in influencer marketing. *European Journal of Marketing*, 56(6), 1721–1747. DOI: 10.1108/EJM-12-2019-0949

Sanga, C., Mlozi, M., Haug, R., & Tumbo, S. (2016). Mobile learning bridging the gap in agricultural extension service delivery: Experiences from Sokoine University of Agriculture, Tanzania. *International Journal of Education and Development using ICT*, 12(3).

Santisteban, J., & Mauricio, D. (2017). Systematic Literature Review of Critical Success Factors of Information Technology Startups. *Academy of Entrepreneurship Journal, 23*(2), 0-0. https://www.abacademies.org/articles/systematic-literature-review-of-critical-success-factors-of-information-technology-startups-6638.html

Sarkar, D., & Anderson, J. T. (2022). Corporate editors in OpenStreetMap: Investigating co-editing patterns. *Transactions in GIS*, 26(4), 1879–1897. Advance online publication. DOI: 10.1111/tgis.12910

Saroia, A. I., & Gao, S. (2019). Investigating university students' intention to use mobile learning management systems in Sweden. *Innovations in Education and Teaching International*, 56(5), 569–580. DOI: 10.1080/14703297.2018.1557068

Sarrab, M., Al-Shihi, H., Al-Manthari, B., & Bourdoucen, H. (2018). Toward educational requirements model for mobile learning development and adoption in higher education. *TechTrends*, 62(6), 635–646. DOI: 10.1007/s11528-018-0331-4

Schreieck, M., Huang, Y., Kupfer, A., & Krcmar, H. (2024). The Effect of Digital Platform Strategies on Firm Value in the Banking Industry. *Journal of Management Information Systems*, 41(2), 394–421. DOI: 10.1080/07421222.2024.2340825 PMID: 38974483

Schröder-Bergen, S., Glasze, G., Michel, B., & Dammann, F. (2022). De/colonizing OpenStreetMap? Local mappers, humanitarian and commercial actors and the changing modes of collaborative mapping. *GeoJournal*, 87(6), 5051–5066. Advance online publication. DOI: 10.1007/s10708-021-10547-7

Scott Kruse, C., Karem, P., Shifflett, K., Vegi, L., Ravi, K., & Brooks, M. (2018). Evaluating barriers to adopting telemedicine worldwide: A systematic review. *Journal of Telemedicine and Telecare*, 24(1), 4–12. DOI: 10.1177/1357633X16674087 PMID: 29320966

Sengupta, D. (2017, October 25). *RCom may shut its wireless business in next 30 days, employees put on notice period.* The Economic Times; Economic Times. https://economictimes.indiatimes.com/news/company/corporate-trends/first-on-et-rcom-may-shut-its-wireless-business-in-next-30-days-employees-put-on-notice-period/articleshow/61213636.cms

Sesic, M. D. DeruSimić, L., & Deru, J.-P. (2010). Cultural diversity-based projects and their effects on sustainable development. In *The Sustainability of Cultural Diversity. Nations, Cities and Organizations* (pp. 1–26). Edvard Elgar Publishers.

Sethi, R. (2000). New product quality and production development teams. *Journal of Marketing*, 64(2), 1–14. DOI: 10.1509/jmkg.64.2.1.17999

Seto, T. (2022). *Development of OpenStreetMap Data in Japan*. DOI: 10.1007/978-981-19-1536-9_7

Seyitoğlu, Z. (2019). *Türkiye'de dijital halkla ilişkilerde değişen müşteri deneyimi: Chatbot uygulamaları*. T.C. İstanbul Kültür Üniversitesi Lisansüstü Eğitim Enstitüsü Yayınlanmış Yüksek Lisans Tezi.

Shamim, R., & Bentalha, B. (2023). Blockchain-Enabled Machine Learning Framework for Demand Forecasting in Supply Chain Management. In Integrating Intelligence and Sustainability in Supply Chains (pp. 28-48). IGI Global. DOI: 10.4018/979-8-3693-0225-5.ch002

Sharma, R., Kamble, S., Gupta, S., Belhadi, A., Rana, N. P., & Kumar, K. (2023). Interlinkages Between Digital-Social Entrepreneurship and Technological Capabilities for Sustainable Value Creation. [JGIM]. *Journal of Global Information Management*, 31(1), 1–26. DOI: 10.4018/JGIM.328515

Sharma, S., Srivastav, S., Gupta, A., & Manglick, A. (2022). Application of Technology and Innovation in Fintech and Its Adaptability in India. *2nd International Conference on Innovative Practices in Technology and Management*, 2, 305-311. IEEE.

Shaw, A., Moodley, M., & McSporran, K.. (2021). Safety and effectiveness of an integrated telehelth-led supported discahrges service for COVID-19. *Thorax*, 76, A1–A205.

Shiddiqah, R., & Adi, K. R. (2023). Peran Paguyuban terhadap Pertumbuhan UMKM di Kawasan Sentral Industri Tahu Takwa Desa Tinalan Kota Kediri. *Jurnal Integrasi Dan Harmoni Inovatif Ilmu-Ilmu Sosial (JIHI3S), 3*(12), 1346–1355. DOI: 10.17977/um063v3i12p1346-1355

Shi, X., Liang, X., & Ansari, S. (2024). Bricks without straw: Overcoming resource limitations to architect ecosystem leadership. *Academy of Management Journal*, 67(4), 1084–1123. DOI: 10.5465/amj.2021.1440

Shrivastava, B., John, S., Kalesh, B., & Bhaskar, U. (2010, May 24). *Ambanis scrap non-compete agreements*. Livemint. https://www.livemint.com/Home-Page/fKCkWOUMUIEW8v78AJfL2M/Ambanis-scrap-noncompete-agreements.html

Singh, H. (2019, November 27). *Vodafone Idea: Everything to know about India's ailing private telco*. ETTelecom.com; ETTelecom. https://telecom.economictimes.indiatimes.com/news/vodafone-idea-everything-to-know-about-indias-ailing-private-telco/72258027

Singh, J., Patel, C., & Chaudhary, N. K. (2024). Resilient Risk-Based Adaptive Authentication and Authorization (RAD-AA) Framework. *Lecture Notes in Electrical Engineering, 1075 LNEE*, 371–385. DOI: 10.1007/978-981-99-5091-1_27

Singh, G., & Garg, S. K. (2020, April 1). *Consumer Retention Policies Followed by Telecom Companies- A Post Jio Scenario*. Papers.*ssrn*.com. https://papers.ssrn.com/sol3/papers.cfm?abstract_id=3565769

Smith, L. (2012). Biographical method. *J. Goodwin. Biographical research Volume one: Biographical research: starting points, debates and approaches*, 1-36..

Sokolova, K., & Kefi, H. (2020). The role of micro-influencers in social media marketing: The effectiveness of influencer marketing on brand awareness and purchase intention. *Journal of Marketing Communications*, 26(3), 276–295. DOI: 10.1080/13527266.2018.1536860

Solís, P., Anderson, J., & Rajagopalan, S. (2021). Open geospatial tools for humanitarian data creation, analysis, and learning through the global lens of YouthMappers. *Journal of Geographical Systems*, 23(4), 599–625. Advance online publication. DOI: 10.1007/s10109-020-00339-x

Song, M., Podoynitsyna, K., Van Der Bij, H., & Halman, J. I. M. (2008). Success factors in new ventures: A meta-analysis. *Journal of Product Innovation Management*, 25(1), 7–27. DOI: 10.1111/j.1540-5885.2007.00280.x

Sriram, K. V., Poojary, A. A., Jawa, V., & Kamath, G. B. (2022). Return on investment and return on ad spend at the action level of AIDA using last touch attribution method on digital advertising platforms. *International Journal of Internet Marketing and Advertising*, 17(1-2), 111–132. DOI: 10.1504/IJIMA.2022.125145

Statista (2020b). Number of Netflix paying streaming subscribers worldwide from 3rd quarter 2011 to 2nd quarter 2020. https://www.statista.com/statistics/250934/quarterly-number-of-Netflix streaming-subscribers-worldwide/ (Accessed 13 July 2020).

Statista. (2020a). Most popular video streaming services in the United States as of September 201, by monthly average users. https://www.statista.com/statistics/910875/us-most-popular-video-streaming-services-by-monthly-average-users/ (Accessed 13 July 2020).

Stein, J. B., Mongeau, P., Posteher, K., & Veluscek, A. (2019). Netflix and chill? Exploring and refining differing motivations in friends with benefits relationships. *The Canadian Journal of Human Sexuality*, 28(3), 317–327. DOI: 10.3138/cjhs.2018-0045

Stuart, E., Thelwall, M., & Stuart, D. (2019). Which image types do universities tweet? *First Monday*, 24(3). Advance online publication. DOI: 10.5210/fm.v24i3.9225

Šumak, B., Polancic, G., & Hericko, M. (2010, February). An empirical study of virtual learning environment adoption using UTAUT. In *2010 Second international conference on mobile, hybrid, and on-line learning* (pp. 17-22). IEEE.

Sun, Y. (2024). A Qualitative Study of the Psychological Effects of Motivational Quotes. *Proceeding of the 3rd International Conference on Literature, Language, and Culture Development*, 27–33. DOI: 10.54254/2753-7064/33/20240042

Swacha-Lech, M. (2017). The main challenges facing the retail banking industry in the era of digitalization. Journal of Insurance. *Financial Markets and Consumer Protection*, 26(4), 94–116.

Swamy, M. (2007). *Exploring New Horizons through ICTs: A Handbook for Women's organizations in Karnataka*. IT for Change.

Tam, T., Rao, A., & Hall, J. (2021). The good, the bad and the missing: A Narrative review of cyber-security implications for australian small businesses. In *Computers and Security* (Vol. 109, p. 102385). DOI: 10.1016/j.cose.2021.102385

Tan, F. B., & Chou, J. P. (2008). The relationship between mobile service quality, perceived technology compatibility, and users' perceived playfulness in the context of mobile information and entertainment services. *International Journal of Human-Computer Interaction*, 24(7), 649–671. DOI: 10.1080/10447310802335581

Tellis, G. J. (1988). Advertising Explore. Loyally and brand purchase: A two-stage model of choice. *JMR, Journal of Marketing Research*, 25(May), 134–144. DOI: 10.1177/002224378802500202

Teo, T., Zhou, M., Fan, A. C. W., & Huang, F. (2019). Factors that influence university students' intention to use Moodle: A study in Macau. *Educational Technology Research and Development*, 67(3), 749–766. DOI: 10.1007/s11423-019-09650-x

Thakor, A. V. (2020). Fintech and banking: What do we know? *Journal of Financial Intermediation*, 41, 100833. DOI: 10.1016/j.jfi.2019.100833

Thekeepitsimple. (2021, April 8). *Vodafone Case Study Of Vodafone & Idea Merger-Reasons, Analyses*. t K Itsim . https://www.thekeepitsimple.com/vodafone-case-study/

Tijan, E., Aksentijević, S., Ivanić, K., & Jardas, M. (2019). Blockchain Technology Implementation in Logistics. *Sustainability (Basel)*, 11(11), 1185. DOI: 10.3390/su11041185

Tiwari, R., Chand, K., Bhatt, A., Anjum, B., & Thirunavukkarasu, K. (2021). Agriculture 5.0 in India: Opportunities and Challenges of Technology Adoption. *A Step Towards Society 5.0*, 179-198..

Tiwari, R. (2022). *Effect of Perception and Satisfaction on Preference for Mobile Wallet. Chand K, Tiwari R., & Sapna (2022). Effect of Perception and Satisfaction on Preference for Mobile Wallet*. FIIB Business Review.

Tiwari, R., Agrawal, P., Singh, P., Bajaj, S., Verma, V., & Chauhan, A. S. (2023). Technology Enabled Integrated Fusion Teaching for Enhancing Learning Outcomes in Higher Education. *International Journal of Emerging Technologies in Learning*, 18(7), 243–249. DOI: 10.3991/ijet.v18i07.36799

Tiwari, R., Chand, K., & Anjum, B. (2000). Crop insurance in India: A review of pradhan mantri fasal bima yojana (PMFBY). *FIIB Business Review*, 9(4), 249–255. DOI: 10.1177/2319714520966084

Tossell, C. C., Kortum, P., Shepard, C., Rahmati, A., & Zhong, L. (2015). You can lead a horse to water but you cannot make him learn: Smartphone use in higher education. *British Journal of Educational Technology*, 46(4), 713–724. DOI: 10.1111/bjet.12176

Traxler, J. (2007). Defining, discussing, and evaluating mobile learning: The moving finger writes and having writ. *International Review of Research in Open and Distance Learning*, 8(2), 1–12. DOI: 10.19173/irrodl.v8i2.346

Trebon, K. (2005) *Citizen Service Levels Interagency Committee (CSLIC)*, USA Services e-Gov Program. 202-501-1802.

Tressler, C. (2018). *Netflix phishing scam: Don't take the bait.* https://consumer.ftc.gov/consumer-alerts/2018/12/netflix-phishing-scam-dont-take-bait

Tunggal, A. T. (2024). *What is the WannaCry Ransomware Attack?*https://www.upguard.com/blog/wannacry#:~:text=WannaCry exploited a known vulnerability,months prior to the attack.

Turkish Radio and Television Council. (2020). http://www.rtuk.gov.tr (Accessed 03 March 2020).

Turkish Statistical Institute. (2020). http://www.tuik.gov.tr (Accessed 02 July 2020).

United Nations Development Programme. (2005). *Trends and Challenges in Public Administration Reform in Asia and the Pacific*. Keen Publishing.

United Nations Educational, Scientific and Cultural Organization. (2009). EFA global monitoring report 2009: Overcoming inequality: Why governance matters. UNESCO. https://unesdoc.unesco.org/ark:/48223/pf0000192144

Upshaw, L. B. (1995). *Building brand identity: A strategy for success in a hostile marketplace*. John Wiley & Sons.

Usman, M. A., & Sun, X. (2023). The impact of digital platforms on new startup performance: Strategy as moderator. *Heliyon*, 9(12).

Van Alstyne, M. W., Parker, G. G., & Choudary, S. P. (2016). Pipelines, platforms, and the new rules of strategy. *Harvard Business Review*, 94(4), 54–62.

Van Gelderen, M., Thurik, R., & Bosma, N. (2006). Success and Risk Factors in the Pre-Startup Phase. *Small Business Economics*, 24(4), 365–380. DOI: 10.1007/s11187-004-6994-6

Venkatesh, V., & Davis, F. D. (2000). A theoretical extension of the technology acceptance model: Four longitudinal field studies. *Management Science*, 46(2), 186–204. DOI: 10.1287/mnsc.46.2.186.11926

Venkatesh, V., & Morris, M. G. (2000). Why don't men ever stop to ask for directions? Gender, social influence, and their role in technology acceptance and usage behavior. *Management Information Systems Quarterly*, 24(1), 115–139. DOI: 10.2307/3250981

Venkatesh, V., Morris, M. G., Davis, G. B., & Davis, F. D. (2003). User acceptance of information technology: Toward a unified view. *Management Information Systems Quarterly*, 27(3), 425–478. DOI: 10.2307/30036540

Verizon Business. (2024). 2024 Data Breach Investigations Report. *Verizon Business Journal*, 1–60. file:///C:/Users/Edward S. Forde/Downloads/rp_Verizon-DBIR-2014_en_xg.pdf

Versland, T., & Erickson, J. L. (2017). Leading by example: A case study of the influence of principal self-efficacy on collective efficacy. *Cogent Education*, 4(1), 1286765. https://www.tandfonline.com/doi/full/10.1080/2331186X.2017.1286765. DOI: 10.1080/2331186X.2017.1286765

Vestil, M. (2023, May 19). *Developing a consistent brand voice across social media channels*. Agility PR Solutions. https://www.agilitypr.com/pr-news/public-relations/developing-a-consistent-brand-voice-across-social-media-channels/

Vijaya Sekhar, K. S., & Bagga, R. K. (2012). Citizen's experiences of eGovernance with Technology as Focus: A case study on eSeva in Andhra Pradesh. Proceedings of International Conference on Public Policy and Governance (PPG-2012), IISc, Bangalore. Excel India Publishers. Vol. II, Pp. 521-528.

Vijaya Sekhar, K. S., & Pallavi, K. (2014) 'ICT based Opportunities for women entrepreneurs in Andhra Pradesh' In *Building Bridges: Contemporary Research in Gender Studies*, University of Hyderabad, March 24-26, 2014.

Vishwanath, A. (2022). *The weakest link How to Diagnose, Detect, and Defend Users from Phishing*. MIT Press., DOI: 10.7551/mitpress/14653.001.0001

Vithal, D. V. R., Bagga, R. K., & Vijaya Sekhar, K. S. (2013). Thirty Years of eGovernance in CSI. In Kapoor, S., Gollamudi, P., Bhatt, N., & Iyer, H. P. (Eds.), *Inclusive Growth through eGovernance* (pp. 39–50). Universities Press.

von Kameke, L. (2024). *Share of Micro, Small, and Medium-sized Enterprises (MSMEs) in Total Number of Enterprises in Southeast Asia in 2022, by Country.* https://www.statista.com/statistics/1317161/asean-share-of-micro-small-medium-sized-businesses-by-country/#:~:text=At%20the%20end%20of%202019,of%20MSMEs%2C%20over%2065%20million

Vu, T. T., Vu, N. V. A., Phung, H. P., & Nguyen, L. D. (2021). Enhanced urban functional land use map with free and open-source data. *International Journal of Digital Earth*, 14(11), 1744–1757. Advance online publication. DOI: 10.1080/17538947.2021.1970262

Wang, F. (2020). Why public health needs GIS: a methodological overview. In *Annals of GIS* (Vol. 26, Issue 1). DOI: 10.1080/19475683.2019.1702099

Wangqu, J., & Neto, L. P. (2023). Verification of Two-Step Flow Model in the Process of City International Image Communication Based on Data Mining and Empirical Analysis. *MDPI: Journalism and Media*, 4(4), 1039–1047. DOI: 10.3390/journalmedia4040066

Wang, Y., Yue, L. Q., Rajagopalan, N., & Wu, B. (2024). The entry-deterring effects of synergies in complementor acquisitions: Evidence from Apple's digital platform market, the iOS app store. *Strategic Management Journal*, smj.3639. DOI: 10.1002/smj.3639

Wayne, M. L. (2009). Netflix, Amazon and branded television content in subscription video on demand portals. *Media Culture & Society*, 40(5), 725–741. DOI: 10.1177/0163443717736118

Werth, O., Cardona, D. R., Nowatschin, J., Werner, M., Guhr, N., & Breitner, M. H. (2019). Challenges of the Financial Industry—An Analysis of Critical Success Factors for FinTechs. *AMCIS 2019 Proceedings*. https://aisel.aisnet.org/amcis2019/ebusiness/ebusiness/4

Whitler, K. A., & Farris, P. W. (2017, March). The impact of cyber-attacks on brand image: Why proactive marketing expertise is needed for managing data breaches. *International Journal of Advertising*, 3–9.

Wijaya, B. S. (2013). Dimensions of brand image: A conceptual review from the perspective of brand communication. *European Journal of Business and Management*, 5(31), 55–65.

Witman, P. D., & Mackelprang, S. (2022). The 2020 Twitter Hack – So Many Lessons to Be Learned. *Journal of Cybersecurity Education. Research and Practice*, 2021(2). Advance online publication. DOI: 10.62915/2472-2707.1089

Wong, I. H. S., Fan, E. C. H., Chiu, D. K. W., & Ho, K. K. W. (2024). Internet Celebrities' Influence on Youths' Diet Behaviors: A Gender Study on Social Media. *Aslib Journal of Information Management*, 76(5), 778–799. DOI: 10.1108/AJIM-11-2022-0495

Wormald, A., Shah, S. K., Braguinsky, S., & Agarwal, R. (2023). Pioneering digital platform ecosystems: The role of aligned capabilities and motives in shaping key choices and performance outcomes. *Strategic Management Journal*, 44(7), 1653–1697. DOI: 10.1002/smj.3475

Xu, B., & Li, D. (2014). An Empirical Study of the Motivations for Content Contribution and Community Participation in Wikipedia. *Information & Management*, 52(3), 275–286. Advance online publication. DOI: 10.1016/j.im.2014.12.003

Xue, B., Yao, R., Ye, Z., Chan, C.-T., Chiu, D. K. W., & Zhong, Z. (2024). Social Media Analytics for Academic Music Library: A Case Study of CUHK Center for Chinese Music Studies. *Library Hi Tech*. Advance online publication. DOI: 10.1108/LHT-12-2023-0616

Xu, L., Yang, S., Liu, Y., Newbert, S. L., & Boal, K. (2023). Seeing the forest and the trees: Exploring the impact of inter-and intra-entrepreneurial ecosystem embeddedness on new venture creation. *Academy of Management Journal*, 66(6), 1954–1982. DOI: 10.5465/amj.2021.0791

Yang, Y., & Zhai, P. (2022). Click-through rate prediction in online advertising: A literature review. *Information Processing & Management, 59*(2), 102853-. https://doi.org/DOI: 10.1016/j.ipm.2021.102853

Yang, Z. (2020). Development of Online Marketing During Coronavirus Epidemic. *E3S Web of Conferences, 218*, 1020-. DOI: 10.1051/e3sconf/202021801020

Yang, M., Fu, M., & Zhang, Z. (2021). The adoption of digital technologies in supply chains: Drivers, process and impact. *Technological Forecasting and Social Change*, 169, 120795. DOI: 10.1016/j.techfore.2021.120795

Yang, X., Hua, G., Hu, L., Cheng, T. C. E., & Huang, A. (2021). Joint optimization of order sequencing and rack scheduling in the robotic mobile fulfilment system. *Computers & Operations Research*, 135(1), 105467. Advance online publication. DOI: 10.1016/j.cor.2021.105467

Yaohua, W. (2022). Dynamic Picking and Storage Optimization of Robotic Picking Systems. *Wireless Personal Communications*. Advance online publication. DOI: 10.1007/s11277-021-09190-9

Yeh, Y., & Choi, S. M. (2011). MINI-lovers, maxi-mouths: An investigation of antecedents to eWOM intention among brand community members. *Journal of Marketing Communications*, 11(3), 145–162. DOI: 10.1080/13527260903351119

Yengin, D. (2015). Yeni medyanın olanakları: Semantik web. *The Turkish Online Journal of Design. Art and Communication*, 5(1), 44–53.

Ye, Z., Shang, X., Shafait, Z., & Xu, Y. (2022). Impact of Leading by Example on Employees' Organizational and Job Psychological Ownership: A Moderated Mediation Study. *Frontiers in Psychology*, 13, 888653. Advance online publication. DOI: 10.3389/fpsyg.2022.888653 PMID: 35874387

Yip, K. H. T., Lo, P., Ho, K. K., & Chiu, D. K. (2021). Adoption of mobile library apps as learning tools in higher education: A tale between Hong Kong and Japan. *Online Information Review*, 45(2), 389–405. DOI: 10.1108/OIR-07-2020-0287

Yoo, B., & Donthu, N. (2001). Developing a scale to measure the perceived quality of an internet shopping site (SITEQUAL). *Quarterly Journal of Electronic Commerce*, 2(1), 31–47.

Yudiansyah, A., Keke, Y., & Veronica, V. (2020). Can the mobile robot be a future order-picking solution?: A case study at Amazon fulfillment center. *Advances in Transportation and Logistics Research*, 3(1), 800–806.

Yue, C. Yisong, Li. (2024). Storage Location Assignment for Improving Human–Robot Collaborative Order-Picking Efficiency in Robotic Mobile Fulfillment Systems. *Sustainability*. Advance online publication. DOI: 10.3390/su16051742

Yu, H. H. K., Chiu, D. K. W., & Chan, C. T. (2023). Resilience of symphony orchestras to challenges in the COVID-19 era: Analyzing the Hong Kong Philharmonic Orchestra with Porter's five force model. In Aloulou, W. (Ed.), *Handbook of Research on Entrepreneurship and Organizational Resilience During Unprecedented Times* (pp. 586–601). IGI Global.

Yu, H. Y., Tsoi, Y. Y., Rhim, A. H. R., Chiu, D. K. W., & Lung, M. M. W. (2022). Changes in habits of electronic news usage on mobile devices in university students: A comparative survey. *Library Hi Tech*, 40(5), 1322–1336. DOI: 10.1108/LHT-03-2021-0085

Yukselturk, E., Altıok, S., & Başer, Z. (2018). Using game-based learning with kinect technology in foreign language education course. *Journal of Educational Technology & Society*, 21(3), 159–173.

Zaglia, M. E. (2013). Brand communities embedded in social networks. *Journal of Business Research*, 66(2), 216–223. DOI: 10.1016/j.jbusres.2012.07.015 PMID: 23564989

Zeng, J., Parks, S., & Shang, J. (2020). To learn scientifically, effectively, and enjoyably: A review of educational games. *Human Behavior and Emerging Technologies*, 2(2), 186–195. DOI: 10.1002/hbe2.188

Zheng, J., Lam, A. H. C., & Chiu, D. K. (2023). Evaluating the effectiveness of learning commons as third spaces with the 5es usability model: The case of Hong Kong University of Science and Technology Library. In *Third-Space Exploration in Education* (pp. 123–143). IGI Global.

Zhenyi, Z. (2024, July 20). Sai, Wang., Tuan-Tuan, Wang. (2024). Optimizing Robotic Mobile Fulfillment Systems for Order Picking Based on Deep Reinforcement Learning. *Sensors (Basel)*, 24(14), 4713. Advance online publication. DOI: 10.3390/s24144713

Zhou, Q., Wang, S., & Liu, Y. (2022). Exploring the accuracy and completeness patterns of global land-cover/land-use data in OpenStreetMap. *Applied Geography (Sevenoaks, England)*, 145, 102742. Advance online publication. DOI: 10.1016/j.apgeog.2022.102742

Zhou, Q., Zhang, Y., Chang, K., & Brovelli, M. A. (2022). Assessing OSM building completeness for almost 13,000 cities globally. *International Journal of Digital Earth*, 15(1), 2400–2421. Advance online publication. DOI: 10.1080/17538947.2022.2159550

Zhu, F., & Iansiti, M. (2012). Entry into platform-based markets. *Strategic Management Journal*, 33(1), 88–106. DOI: 10.1002/smj.941

About the Contributors

Mohammed Albakri is a distinguished academic and tech industry leader with over a decade of experience. Currently, he serves as the Programme Director of Business Management with Innovation and Technology at the University of Salford. Holding a Ph.D. in Information Systems from the University of Manchester, his leadership in digital transformation has significantly impacted both academia and industry. Recognised by the UK Teaching Excellence Framework (TEF) and the Research Excellence Framework (REF), Dr. Albakri's multidisciplinary research spans artificial intelligence, cloud computing, cybersecurity, and critical systems thinking. His consulting work with government agencies focuses on improving community infrastructure and closing the digital divide. As a Senior Fellow of Higher Education (SFHEA), he excels in leading and developing innovative academic programs, refining his teaching skills in digital transformation and information systems technology.

***

Neha Agarwal is a research scholar at HRDC Economics, University of North Bengal, Siliguri, West Bengal, India. Before joining PhD, she worked as an Assistant Professor of Economics at the Indian Institute of Legal Studies, Siliguri, West Bengal, India.

Munir Ahmad is a seasoned professional in the realm of Spatial Data Infrastructure (SDI), Geo-Information Productions, Information Systems, and Information Governance, boasting over 25 years of dedicated experience in the field. With a PhD in Computer Science, Dr. Ahmad's expertise spans Spatial Data Production, Management, Processing, Analysis, Visualization, and Quality Control. Throughout his career, Dr. Ahmad has been deeply involved in the development and deployment of SDI systems specially in the context of Pakistan, leveraging his proficiency in Spatial Database Design, Web, Mobile & Desktop GIS, and Geo Web Services Architecture. His contributions to Volunteered Geographic Information (VGI) and Open Source Geoportal & Metadata Portal have significantly enriched the geospatial community. As a trainer and researcher, Dr. Ahmad has authored over 50 publications, advancing the industry's knowledge base and fostering innovation in Geo-Tech, Data Governance, and Information Infrastructure, and Emerging Technologies. His commitment to Research and Development (R&D) is evident in his role as a dedicated educator and mentor in the field.

Adem Akbıyık is an Associate Professor at Sakarya Business School, Department of Management Information Systems at Sakarya University. He has been involved in international projects in distance education and information systems as a visiting student at the École Supérieure de Commerce Chambery in France, a researcher at Athabasca University's Center for Distance Education Research in Edmonton, Canada, a postdoctoral researcher at Canada's McMaster University. He conducts training and seminars in Project Management, IT Project Management, Requirements Management, Qualitative Analysis, Mixed-Methods Research, and Text Mining.

Badr Bentalha teaches Supply Chain and Operations Management at National School of Business and Management – Fez, Sidi Mohamed Ben Abdellah University – Morocco. Dr. Bentalha investigates the structural dynamics and control of complex networks, applying his findings to supply chain management, Industry 4.0, risk analysis, and digital supply chains. His work emphasizes the intersection of supply chain management, operations research, industrial engineering, and digital technology. As a professor, he teaches undergraduate, graduate, and doctoral courses in operations management, supply chain management, logistics, management information systems, and strategic management. Through guest lectures, webinars, and scholarly presentations, he engages students and fosters an active learning environment. Professor Bentalha specializes in supply chain and operations management, operations research, and service management. He is passionate about integrating knowledge across disciplines to solve real-world problems. He has delivered numerous invited plenary talks, keynotes, and panel discussions at conferences and global webinars.

Dickson K.W. Chiu received the B.Sc. (Hons.) degree in Computer Studies from the University of Hong Kong in 1987. He received the M.Sc. (1994) and Ph.D. (2000) degrees in Computer Science from the Hong Kong University of Science and Technology (HKUST). He started his own computer consultant company while studying part-time. He has also taught at several universities in Hong Kong. His teaching and research interest is in Library & Information Management, Service Computing, and E-learning with a cross-disciplinary approach involving library and information management, e-learning, e-business, service sciences, and databases. The results have been widely published in nearly 400 international publications (most of them have been indexed by SCI/-E, SSCI, and EI, such as top journals MIS Quarterly, Computer & Education, Government Information Quarterly, Decision Support Systems, Information Sciences, Knowledge-Based Systems, Expert Systems with Application, Information Systems Frontiers, IEEE Transactions, including many taught master and undergraduate project results and around 20 edited books. He received a best paper award at the 37th Hawaii International Conference on System Sciences in 2004. He is an Editor (-in-chief) of Library Hi Tech, a prestigious journal (SSCI IF=3.4), and a Senior Editor of the Journal of Organizational Computing and Electronic Commerce (SCIE IF=2.9). He is the Editor-in-chief Emeritus of the International Journal on Systems and Service-Oriented Engineering (founding) and the International Journal of Organizational and Collective Intelligence, and serves on the editorial boards of several international journals. He co-founded several international workshops and co-edited many journal special issues. He also served as a program committee member for over 300 international conferences and workshops. Dr. Chiu is a Senior Member of both the ACM and the IEEE and a life member of the Hong Kong Computer Society. According to Google Scholar, he has about 10,000 citations, h-index=51, i-10 index=205, and ranked worldwide 1st in "LIS," "m-learning," and "e-services." He received nearly 1,000 citations in 2022 and 2,600 in 2023.

Sahika Dogan is an associate professor at Faculty of Communication, Istanbul Bilgi University, where she also serves as the Director of the Public Relations and Corporate Communication MA Program. Her recent research interests include the emerging business models in digital media and social inclusion patterns in human resources practices.

Anjali Gupta is a dedicated and passionate research scholar at the Institute of Management Studies and Research, Maharshi Dayanand University, Rohtak. With a profound interest in research, Anjali has actively participated in numerous workshops, faculty development programs, and conferences organized by renowned institutes. Recognized for her scholarly contributions, Anjali has successfully presented and published several research papers in prestigious conferences. Her relentless pursuit of knowledge and commitment to academic excellence make her a valued contributor to the field of research. Anjali Gupta continues to inspire and make significant contributions to the scholarly community through her exceptional work.

Noprita Herari is an academician specializing in digital communication and the Managing Director of the Journal of Communication and Public Relations (JCPR). Appointed in 2024 by the Ministry of Cooperatives and Small and Medium Enterprises of Indonesia, she serves as a Non-Physical DAK PK2UMK Mentor for Bekasi City, focusing on digital business development. With over a decade of experience in e-commerce and digital media, Noprita has successfully launched culinary and branding businesses using digital platforms, as well as a fashion business that integrates conventional and digital marketing strategies. Her expertise in digital marketing for MSMEs is academically recognized; she was the Best Graduate in Business and Communication Management at the LSPR Institute of Communication and Business, and her thesis on digital omnichannel strategies for local culinary MSMEs was honored as one of the best. Noprita actively coaches MSMEs in digitalization, conducts research, and publishes extensively. Her notable works include the internationally published "Advertising: Methods, Research, and Practices" and the nationally acclaimed "Digitalisasi UMKM dan Koperasi (Transformasi Digital)."

John Loonam is a Lecturer in Management and Director of Executive MBA Programmes at Dublin City University Business School. He holds a Bachelor of Arts in European Studies and a Masters of Business Studies from the University of Limerick. He received his PhD in Business Studies at Trinity College, Dublin. John teaches in the fields of management and strategic management at both Undergraduate and Postgraduate level. John has worked with the grounded theory methodology in exploring his research focus on the role of Top Managers & Executive Teams in leading Enterprise-wide Information System initiatives.

Marlina S.E, M.M was born on March 18, 1982, in Jakarta, is a community development practitioner and a permanent lecturer at the LSPR Institute of Communication and Business in Jakarta and Bekasi, Indonesia. With decades of experience at the managerial level, Marlina also serves as the founder and CEO of a company. She holds the National Lecturer Identification Number 0318038206 and the Unique Number of Indonesian Educators and Education Personnel (NUPTK) 6650760661230192. Marlina's notable contributions include her role as Administrator of the Bekasi Keren Women's Community from 2020 to 2022, where she supported hundreds of women entrepreneurs in developing their businesses. In 2023, she furthered her impact by mentoring micro, small, and medium enterprises in the West Java Champion MSME Program. Additionally, Marlina holds certifications from Indonesia's National Professional Certification Agency (BNSP) in Digital Marketing and Mentor Qualification Three, underscoring her expertise and dedication to community and business development.

Pujita Roy is a highly accomplished professional with a Bachelor in Dental Surgery from the University of Dhaka, Bangladesh. She completed her internship at the prestigious Holy Family Red Crescent Hospital in Dhaka, where she honed her clinical skills. With a deep passion for research, Pujita pursued a Master's in Public Health at North South University, where she also engaged in a research internship, further fueling her drive to contribute to global health. Pujita is known for her innovative thinking and her commitment to pushing the boundaries of traditional practice. She is not content to serve only one community but is determined to make a difference on a global scale. Pujita's dedication to her work is matched only by her kindness and empathy, making her a compassionate and thoughtful individual who genuinely cares about the well-being of others. Her passion for research and her desire to serve the world make her a truly inspiring figure.

Karun Sanjaya is an Assistant Professor at Symbiosis Law School, Nagpur and a Research Scholar at VIT School of Law, Vellore Institute of Technology, Chennai, India. He specializes in the area of Intellectual Property Laws. He is a recipient of many awards including the prestigious Justice V.R. Krishna Iyer Memorial Merit Awards in the year 2019 and 2022. He has published over sixty research items and is a keen researcher in diverse areas of law including Intellectual Property Laws.

Kasturi Srinivasa Sekhar holds PhD in Public Administration with a focus on electronic Governance. His interest areas include Public Service Delivery, Citizen Satisfaction towards ICT based services and eParticipation. He is recipient of Best Paper Award for his paper Measuring Sustainability in eGovernance Projects. He is currently with Research Center for eGovernance (RCeG) at IIIT, Hyderabad and has over 23 years of work experience. He is Life member of Computer Society of India [CSI] and recipient of the coveted 'CSI Service Award' for the year 2012 for his significant contribution to e-Governance at National Level.

Amira Sghari is Assistant Professor in Management studies at the Higher School of Economic and Commercial Sciences of Tunis in Tunisia. She received a Ph.D. degree in management science, in 2013, from the Aix-Marseille University, France. Dr. Sghari is member of a Research Unit on Management Studies. Her research interests include strategy and organizational structure, organizational change and information management.

Mohana Sundari, with over eleven years of academic experience in Business Management, strongly believes in the democratic and proactive system of teaching and management, where each student is encouraged to participate and contribute to the learning process. With an impressive research portfolio, she has published several papers in well-reputed journals indexed in SCOPUS, showcasing a deep understanding of the subject matter and a passion for research. She also demonstrates a commitment to lifelong learning, having continuously upgraded her skills and knowledge through various certifications from NPTEL, ATAL, and other FDPs, workshops, and trainings. She has served as a resource person for numerous events and conferences and has also been a member of the Board of Studies for other institutions.

Rajesh Tiwari is working as Professor, Academic Coordinator and Chair Head-Finance in Graphic Era (Deemed to be University), Dehradun. He has over twenty years of rich experience in academics and industry. He is MBA (Finance), Chartered Financial Analyst (CFA), UGC-NET, PhD in Management. He has previously worked as Director in Indus University, Ahmedabad, United Group-Greater Noida (Affiliated to Guru Gobind Singh Indraprastha University, New Delhi), Sai Balaji Group-Pune. He has been academic coordinator for Management Programmes of Staffordshire University, UK and other reputed B Schools. He has won best paper award two times. He has published research papers in reputed journals indexed in Scopus and presented papers in national and international journals. He is actively involved in Faculty Development Programme and Management Development Programme. He has been engaged in social initiatives through plantation, blood donation, cleanliness drive and functional literacy programmes. He has been associated with Ministry of MSME, Government of India for Management Development Programmes and Entrepreneurship Development Programmes. He has 5 patents under his credit. He can be reached at ambitioncfarajesh@gmail.com.

Index

Symbols

A

B

C

D

E

www.ingramcontent.com/pod-product-compliance
Lightning Source LLC
LaVergne TN
LVHW080604300926
849162LV00005B/1042